PSYCHOLOGY AND PHILOSOPHY
THE WORLD OF THOUGHT

General Editors
J. M. PARRISH, M.A. (Oxon.)
JOHN R. CROSSLAND, F.R.G.S.

PSYCHOLOGY AND PHILOSOPHY
THE WORLD OF THOUGHT

PSYCHOLOGY : PHILOSOPHY
ETHICS : EDUCATION
POLITICAL SCIENCE

Advisory Editor
C. E. M. JOAD, M.A., *Head of the
Department of Philosophy and Psychology
Birkbeck College, University of London*

Edited by
T. K. BARRETT, M.A. (Cantab.), *Lecturer
in Education, University College, London*

ODHAMS PRESS LIMITED
LONG ACRE, LONDON, W.C.2

CONTENTS

6 CONTENTS

CONTENTS

INTRODUCTION

by PAUL CHADBURN, B.A., B.Litt.(Oxon)

THE subjects this book is written about appear, at a first glance, academic and abstract—Psychology, Ethics, Education, Political Science, Philosophy. Roughly, we may say that the titles cover these fields : how the mind works ; man's search for a standard of conduct ; how the mind is trained and equipped for life, and how character is formed ; man's responsibilities as a citizen ; the mind's quest for knowledge about the universe.

All these subjects would, fifty years ago, have been considered to lie exclusively in the provinces of the experts. The fact that they are presented in the pages that follow in a simple, non-technical form is evidence of the widening outlook of the world during the last half-century. Though we are at the present time not a little bewildered by the economic and political aspect of international affairs, still we may take hope for the future in this—that the general body of opinion, represented by the non-expert, is becoming aware as never before that the key to the problems confronting us to-day lies in the cultivation of an inquiring mind that can see behind the appearances of things into their causes.

The subjects that are treated in this book are not ones that can be applied to immediate material ends ; it cannot be said that a knowledge of Philosophy or educational theory would advance anyone in business; nor would Political Science. But, as people are coming to realise more and more, there are other matters to be attended to to-day lying outside the immediate sphere of business or profession. Our awareness of the world—the world inside each one of us, as well as society around and the universe beyond—has enormously extended during the present century. We are less unwilling to face facts than were our ancestors—the men who made Galileo recant his theory that the earth moved round the sun, and those who heaped abuse on Darwin for declaring man's remote affinity with the ape. We can bear to be told more facts about ourselves—the way our minds work, the hidden contents of our memories, the desires lurking beneath consciousness ; we can follow the scientist and the philosopher with interest, instead of shutting our eyes in dread, when they invite us to accompany them into the realms of speculation about the origins of our knowledge and the nature of the universe.

We see now that subjects like Psychology, Political Science, Physics, Philosophy have ultimately a great deal to do with our own lives ; they teach knowledge of ourselves and of our fellows, point out the way of advance, clear away superstitions and age-old fallacies, cultivate cool-headed reasoning. Philosophy and Psychology are the enemies of cant, they blow back the dust that propagandists and self-interested reactionaries would throw into our eyes. They teach us to look at life logically and constructively. It is only when enough minds in an educated democracy can so look at life that we may expect a right understanding of citizen by citizen, nation by nation.

As our awareness grows, we see the relation between the various branches of knowledge, a relation the experts are themselves beginning to realise more fully than ever before. So, for instance, Psychology has come out of the study and the laboratory. It has entered the schoolroom. Many schools now have trained psychologists attached to the staff ; examinations for measuring the *quantity* of knowledge possessed, are giving way here and there to psychological tests of the *quality* of intelligence. Psycho-Therapy, a branch of Psychology that deals with nervous diseases, is coming under the consideration of the medical profession. Doctors now consider the possibility that a physical symptom of disease may be caused by mental disorder.

Philosophy and Science afford another example of this co-operation. Philosophy has always built its systems largely on the findings of the physicists, and also, as in the contemporary instance of Einstein, on mathematical research. The question of the relation between Philosophy, which asks *why* a thing (or *phenomenon* to employ the technical term) comes about and Science, which asks *how*, is one that much needs settling to-day.

It is an interesting fact that this inter-relation between some of the great intellectual branches of human activity is being accompanied to-day by increasing specialisation in the daily activities of a large number of civilised people. Machinery has had much to do with this. But machinery.

which has come in for so much abuse from those who habitually look backwards and not forwards, should itself, under
an enlightened administration, make it possible for each
worker to enjoy considerably more leisure than formerly.

This, the problem of leisure, is one of the great tasks that
education has before it. There will in the future be more
and more leisure. Not, it is to be hoped, the leisure of the
unemployed man, not that leisure that is the hardest work
of all, but time for a well-equipped mind to keep abreast of
all that is best in art and literature, all that is most significant
in thought, all that is most cogent in citizenship. It cannot,
unfortunately, be said yet that education in general prepares
the mind to get the most from leisure. The problem of the
rival claims of a vocational and a cultural training has not
yet been solved.

WHY THE PSYCHOLOGIST IS IN DEMAND TO-DAY

THE inter-relation between subjects of study, the dependence of one upon another, is shown in this book. Psychology, which includes the comparatively recent subject,
Psycho-Analysis, is a good starting-off ground for such cultural
studies as are collected here. Psychology was at one time
subordinate to Philosophy, for it deals with how we receive
our knowledge; and this is one of the outstanding problems
of philosophy too. But in the nineteenth century, with the
discoveries of men like William James in America, Ebbinghaus
in Germany, and McDougall in England, all of whom we
shall read about in the sections that follow, Psychology
widened its scope considerably. It quickly split into a
number of schools, each one examining a new field of experience, or making its investigations from another angle, until
to-day there is scarcely any aspect of life to which the findings
of Psychology do not extend. Its great importance in the
sphere of Education we have already mentioned ; and it is
indispensable to parenthood, for it shows how easily the
child's mind may become warped by wrong treatment in
early infancy.

Psycho-Analysis has itself split into three chief schools.
Freud covers the sexual field, and he has obtained important
results in the cures of cases of neuroses, or nervous diseases
of a sexual origin due to repression in infancy. Jung's
most important contribution has been to classify human
beings into two main divisions, the *extravert*, or person whose

life is bound up in the exterior world, and the *introvert*, the person who is turned inwards, the dreamer. Jung has established many subdivisions that are most useful for the treatment of unbalanced patients. Adler's theory, known as *Individual Psychology*, is concerned chiefly with the adjustment of the individual to society and with the well-known inferiority complex. Adler's theories (especially in America) have perhaps been used more than those of any other psychologist in the service of society—to eradicate, for example, such menaces as the gangster.

Then there is the school of Psychology known as *Behaviourism*, associated with the names of Watson in America, and Pavlov in Russia. It is allied to a school of thought in Philosophy, of which we shall read later on, called *Materialism*. Animals and persons, according to Behaviourism, can be conditioned to react in a defined manner, rather like puppets responding to the finger-movements of the showman. As might be expected, this school of thought has found favour in the Soviet Union, where the underlying conception of social organisation is materialism, or the denial that ideas have any influence on social history, and the assertion that material conditions alone mould the political forms and intellectual systems of Society.

Another method of psychological approach, called the *Gestalt* school, starts from the assumption that our impressions do not come to us singly, but in wholes—that when we perceive a bicycle wheel in motion, for example, our impression is not made up of a number of spokes in motion, but is something more than the sum of individual units, something that comes of the unity of the whole. It is not difficult to perceive in this theory a relation to views put forward by present-day political theorists who believe in the totalitarian State. The State, according to the Nazis and the Fascists, is something more than the sum total of the individual wills that it contains.

So it must be clear that Psychology to-day is related to all kinds of subjects outside its immediate sphere, to Education, Philosophy, Political Science, Mothercraft. Nor is its offspring, Psycho-Analysis, as was thought up to a short time ago, a kind of *enfant terrible*, butting in where it is not wanted and has no business, or a quack prescribing unscientifically for the patient. It has weathered the storm of criticism, and is accepted as a science of invaluable use in many human fields.

THE FORWARD MARCH OF EDUCATION

EDUCATION is something we all know about, for all of us have experienced it in one form or another. Yet probably most of us, both when we are at school and when we have left school, are unaware of the road that stretches far back into history, the road that has been hewn out slowly and with difficulty by the great educational reformers. Still more of us neglect to look to the future—where this road will lead ; and to connect education with citizenship. Yet Education is inseparable from the State, and consequently from our responsibilities at election time. As in its particulars, the methods to be employed, Education is identified with Psychology, so in its general lines Education is inseparable from politics, for Education has always been organised in the interest of those holding political power. In the old days in England Education was for the prince ; then it was for the gentleman ; later, with the rise of the bourgeoisie in the eighteenth and nineteenth centuries, the middle class created facilities for itself, and founded its great public schools, such as Uppingham, Cheltenham, Wellington.

But all the time a fight has been going on for the education of the worker. Step by step advance has been made : the Society for Promoting Christian Knowledge ; Robert Raikes with his Sunday schools ; the social reformer, Robert Owen, who sought to better the lot of the children of his employees ; Lancaster, who discovered the monitorial system, boys teaching boys. Slowly the fight has gone on to win more years of the child's life from the claws of industry, until the present time, when the raising of the school age is one of the chief issues before the Government.

The greatest thinkers in the educational field, men whose teaching is discussed in this book, Plato, John Locke, Rousseau, have been thinkers in other fields as well, philosophers and social reformers, because, as we have said, Education is a part of the study of Society. Our view on Education is dependent on the view we take about Society. We must have opinions about the State and the individual's relation to the State, who shall rule, and in whose interests, before we can begin to hold valuable views about the preparation of the citizen for his place in Society. This brings us to Political Science, a subject which is rapidly becoming popular as people begin to see the perplexities and complexities involved

in being a member of a modern State, particularly of a democratic State. If the people are not to be dictated to, but are
themselves to govern, then they must have a clear view of
the issues involved in their responsibilities. They must know
what is meant by representative government, they must
understand the methods of election, the possible alternatives
to the present electoral system. They should understand
how the State functions, and how the administration might
be reformed. Everything relating to the constitution of
society is fit matter for Political Science. It is a controversial
subject, and one that covers much ground. It is essential,
therefore, to approach it with a clear mind, for theories of
government abound with fallacies.

THE SEARCH FOR REALITY

THIS, the necessity of clear-thinking, brings us to Philosophy. Below all philosophical theory there is logic,
and if the study of Philosophy brought no more to the reader
than this—the faculty of the logical connection of ideas, it
would still be one of the most valuable of all subjects. A
good many people still fight shy of Philosophy because they
say to themselves, " After all, each philosopher holds a different
system, one theory contradicts another, and nobody gets
any further on—besides, of what conceivable use is
it ? "

Such people would probably not be inclined to turn to
Philosophy because of its quality already mentioned, that of
clearing away mental cobwebs. Nothing could induce them
to read what the greatest minds of all time have thought
about the universe in which we live. They would not be
interested in such purely " academic " subjects as the origin
of our ideas, appearance and reality, the problem of causes
and effects, mind and matter, the question of the moral
qualities, Goodness, Truth, Beauty. They would trust to
" common sense." But such people are becoming rarer.
More and more are we becoming conscious of the need of
seeing life, in the words of Matthew Arnold, " steadily and
as a whole." More people than ever want to know, and
philosophy has been defined as the " knowledge of all time
and existence." The philosopher seeks reality beneath the
appearance. This, if anything, is what we need to find
to-day, if we are to overcome the difficulties that beset
our path.

HOW THIS BOOK IS ARRANGED

WE have shown how the various subjects dealt with in this book are inter-connected. Accordingly, the articles that follow have been arranged so as to facilitate progressive study : starting from what may be called the world inside us, the human mind and its mechanism, we proceed to the training of the mind in school and university, thence to man in relation to Society, and finally to man and the Universe. Thus the articles work outwards, expanding, like ripples on the surface of a pebble-struck pond, from the brain itself to the outermost bounds of the brain's knowledge.

Besides the divisions constituted by the articles separately, the book falls into three main parts : (1) The Individual ; (2) The Individual in Society ; (3) The External World.

(1) *The Individual.* Under this heading are grouped (*a*) the articles on Psychology and Psycho-Analysis, and (*b*) that on Ethics. It has been thought advisable to introduce this last article in the first part, although it is really a subject in Philosophy, firstly, because the standards of conduct, the values of good or evil a man attaches to his actions and those of other people, are essentially an individual matter ; secondly, because the article fittingly rounds off the study of psychology which, as a science, is not concerned with moral judgments on human actions, but with the causes and mechanism of behaviour.

(2) *The Individual in Society.* This part contains (*a*) the history of the theory and practice of Education and a review of modern reforms in many lands ; (*b*) an exposition of existing educational facilities in England ; (*c*) a discussion of man as a citizen, containing theories of government and a review of the British constitution in action.

(3) *The External World.* Three articles on Philosophy make up this part. The first gives a review of the main problems of Philosophy ; the second is a retrospective history of Philosophy ; and in the last, the subject is brought into the spotlight of the present with a study of one of the most vital problems of to-day—that concerned with the relation between Philosophy and Science.

At the end of each article will be found information for those who wish to continue their studies ; some of the best books are described, and hints are given about opportunities for attending lectures and study circles.

PSYCHOLOGY : THE SCIENCE OF MIND

by W. STEPHENSON, M.Sc., Ph.D., Lecturer in Psychology,
University College, London

PSYCHOLOGY deals with many and various matters ; it is difficult to know where to begin, but if I lie back in my chair for a moment and try to leave my mind a " blank," then sooner or later something will occur to me and I shall write about that. Here in my very first thought there arise many problems of great concern to a psychologist. I should like to know, for instance, what happens when my mind is a " blank," and how things " occur to me." And the word " write " brings the thought to my mind that there are psychologists who spend the greater part of their energies in studying the psychology of handwriting. They are concerned with questions of the kind : how should children be taught to write ? Do men usually write boldly and women in small and timid characters ? Can one's temperament be " read " from one's handwriting ? Can handwriting scales be made, to measure excellence of handwriting ?

But when I do allow my mind to relax, to be a " blank," the very next thought that comes to my mind is that the Derby is to be run at Epsom to-morrow. There will be so much excitement there that I shall be able to look up into the grandstands and see the tint of its sea of faces turn pinker and pinker as the horses near the winning-post. I wonder how on earth I remembered such a detail, and then recall having read it in Sir Francis Galton's *Memories of My Life*. How, then, do I remember the thousands of things I do, and why cannot I recall them all just when I like ? I wonder why my face should turn pink when I am excited, and blanch a deathlike white when I am terribly afraid. As for the racing itself, I should like to know what it is that makes people congregate in such vast numbers to see horses run, whether some people are " born " gamblers, or whether gambling is merely a social habit.

QUESTIONS WE WOULD ALL LIKE ANSWERED

I LIE back in my chair again, and once more allow myself to relax. This time, within a few seconds, I find myself

16

listening to my wireless set. It has been playing all the time, but I have not noticed it until now. A violinist is playing sweet music, and, as I continue to listen, strange feelings well up into my heart (or so I feel), and tender emotions seem to flood my whole body. I am, as we say, in emotional rapport with the music. I then begin to ask my psychological questions. I should like to know what makes some music sweet and pleasant to listen to, whilst there is music of another kind for which no words are strong enough to express my dislike. I begin to wonder about feelings and emotions, and at least a thousand questions surge into my mind, all requiring the attention of psychologists of the future. I begin to think of music, and wonder why it is so devoid of humour. And what is the nature of musical genius, the ability above all others in the world that I envy ? Is it something that cannot receive an explanation, an eternal mystery of mankind, or can it be understood in terms of some very simple abilities that we all have in some degree, every man and woman of us ?

I can ask questions of this kind about every single thought I have, every feeling I experience, every action I perform or desire I have. Questions about insanity on the one hand and genius on the other, about the humdrum things of life like seeing and hearing, our petty pleasures and pains, questions about odd things like trances, hypnotism, telepathy, and dreams, and questions about religious feelings and scientific beliefs, about love and hate, marriage and murder—all these things and a thousand more supply questions of concern to the psychologist. We should remember, too, that there are millions of men and women in the world about whom we can ask these questions for every thought they have, every feeling, desire, emotion, or striving, for every moment of their lives, asleep or awake.

These questions are the raw material of psychology. It is out of these that we have to fashion our science. With these mental processes, and living behaviour as its ground-work, it is readily appreciated that psychology has no easy task to face, but this complexity of its material is no excuse for the belief of so many people that psychology can never become scientific. The psychologist, like a chemist or physicist, simply seeks to set down the facts and to search for new facts. He has to classify them, like a geologist his soils and rocks. He has to investigate them in his own way, to try to find out the laws of psychology, and to give the facts an explanation. By which we mean that he does not hope to give his facts any ultimate explanation, but is satisfied if he can get somewhere near the truth. For truth, indeed, ever recedes further from the scientist's grasp the nearer he gets to it.

Psychology, however, is not concerned only with adults. It has much to say and do about children. Should this seem a fatuous remark, then it is well to be reminded that psychology has not always been interested in children. It is true that Plato, the great Greek philosopher, recognised that children differed one from another—one being more intelligent than another—but all down the medieval centuries and until the close of the nineteenth century very few questions of a psychological kind were asked about children. They were considered to be similar lumps of clay, as it were, to be moulded at will for goodness or evil, for learning or for ignorance, at the hands of their parents, teachers, or tutors. But matters are very different now, and child psychology is at present perhaps the most vital of all the many branches of psychology.

HOW PSYCHOLOGY HELPS THE PARENT AND THE TEACHER

IT should be of interest to look for a moment or two at some of the methods that are used by psychologists in their studies on children. There is usually nothing very remarkable about these methods, and yet the facts they bring forward are often of a kind that would have occasioned no little surprise to psychologists of only twenty or thirty years ago. Take, for example, the kinds of incidental observations that a modern psychologist makes when he sees a baby at play. When it is a few months old a baby will stretch its hand out for a rattle that is held suitably before it, and, having grasped it, will use the rattle as it was intended to be used. But now suppose that *two* rattles happen to be held out, one for the one hand, and one for the other. Baby will take one, hold it, and then grasp the other ; only when it has both will it begin to rattle them.

There seems to be nothing very remarkable in this until we observe that somehow the baby *cannot* use only the one rattle when the two are held out for it. The two are just like *one* so far as baby is concerned. This seemingly innocuous observation is of no little consequence to a modern psychologist of at least one school of psychology.

But the difficulty about incidental observations is to know just what they *mean*. Thus, there comes a time in the life of almost every boy when he plays at make-believe " motors " in an all-absorbing way. You may observe that he plays the same game over and over again. For scores of times a day, for perhaps many months, he drives his car at leisure with a pan-lid for a steering-wheel and a walking-stick or poker for a brake. But, having observed this, it would be as well to know what is behind this monotonous repetition of the same game. Is it just harmless make-believe, a habit, or something that the boy likes very much, and therefore is prepared to play over and over again ? Or is it something of a very different nature, a minor compulsion or obsession, something the boy cannot help himself doing ? I shall refer later to a boy who played games that his mother thought were just the harmless pleasures of a boy, whereas, in point of fact, they were quite otherwise.

From observations, often overlooked by others, but to a psychologist sometimes pregnant with meaning, let us turn to some of the experiments made by psychologists. Let us take a girl—we shall call her Molly. She is seated at a low table, and is looking at a perfectly plain grey board. A minute ago I had shown her a sheet of cardboard on which were pasted twenty small coloured patches of paper, four each of red, and blue, green, yellow, and black, placed in rows of four, the colours being in irregular order. That is, the first row contained the colours, red, blue, yellow, green, and the second row, black, green, red, blue, and so on.

Molly only saw this sheet of colours for a few moments, and certainly had no time to remember very much about them. Yet now she is looking at the grey board, and can see the colour chart quite clearly, when, of course, it is really not there at all. I ask her to read off the colours one by one, and she does so. I say, " How many reds are there ? " She counts, moves her fingers to help her to count them, and gives the correct answer. She is looking at an image of the chart all the time ! There are many children like Molly, with this unsuspected facility, to which the name *eidetic imagery* is given. It is on record that a small child, having seen a picture of a crocodile for a moment or so, thereafter counted the number of its teeth quite accurately from her eidetic image.

A CURIOUS TRICK OF MEMORY

AN experiment of a very different kind, and of much greater significance for psychology, is as follows : Let us take Molly again, and having seated her comfortably, let us give her the following twenty-one tasks to perform one after the other :

1. Count backwards from 55 to 17.
2. Make a monogram of your initials.
3. Multiply 5457 by 6337 (in writing).
4. Print in block capitals your name and address.
5. Name 10 Christmas presents you would like to have.
6. Write out a verse of poetry.
7. Write 15 two-letter words.
8. Name any 10 liquids.
9. Draw a vase holding flowers.
10. Draw a rough map of England, and put in the approximate situation of London, Liverpool, Newcastle, Southampton, Hull, Bristol.
11. Name 8 things that are coloured yellow.
12. Write down the names of an author, a town, and a county, with names beginning with the same letter.
13. Name 12 animals.
14. Write down 15 words beginning with S.
15. Name any 10 foreign capitals.
16. Draw 5 objects in the room.
17. Describe any picture you have seen.
18. Write out the 12 times table.
19. Give the names of 10 flowers.
20. Write down 6 words to rhyme with *sing*.
21. Shut your eyes and write down the names of as many objects as you can remember seeing on the table before you. A time limit of 2 minutes will be allowed you.

In the first task Molly is asked to count backwards from 55 to 17. Having completed this she begins task 2, making a monogram of her initials. In task 3 she is asked to multiply 5457 by 6337, but before she has time to finish her task I stop her, without saying anything about why I have done so. Whereas tasks Nos. 1 and 2 were allowed to be completed, task No. 3 is *not* completed. So we go down the list, allowing some tasks to be completed (these we call C tasks), whilst others are stopped before they can be completed (and these we call U tasks). When all twenty-one are finished in the above way, Molly is required to recall the tasks upon which she had just been engaged. She did not know beforehand that her " memory " was to be tested, and now she merely has to recall any of the tasks she can, just as they come to her mind.

It is found that, no matter what the tasks may be, or in what order they may be given, children recall on the average about *twice* as many of the U tasks as they do the C tasks. They recall the tasks which were interrupted before they could be completed, and tend to forget the tasks that were completed. At first sight this might not seem to be a very remarkable fact. But the mental processes behind it are profoundly significant, for just the same processes can be found to lie at the back of dreams on the one hand, and some forms of insanity on the other. The man who strives unceasingly for unattainable ends, and the mental conflicts that ravage the souls of so many men and women and children, have their prototype in these simple interrupted tasks (U tasks).

PROBING THE CHILD MIND

AND so we might continue to give illustrations of the methods used for obtaining facts about children. At the one extreme we might keep a complete record of everything that a single child does from the moment of its birth, taking many thousands of feet of films of its more interesting moments. We might have seven cameras focused on the one little mite as it kicks and plays in its play-pen, each photographing from its own angle, as was done in some lengthy experiments by a famous American child psychologist. Or, at the other extreme, we might test thousands of children with the same test, as was done a year ago when more than 30,000 school children in Scotland were tested for their intelligence.

From the facts gathered, by whatever means, attempts have to be made to draw general conclusions about the child and its psychology. Nor must we make the mistake of thinking that the child and the adult are the poles apart. There cannot be one complete psychology for adults and another different one for children. In almost every detail of a psychological kind there is something of the child in every adult, more perhaps than they are aware of, and something of the adult in every child.

Professor Pavlov, the famous Russian psychologist, has spent close on forty years doing psychological work with dogs as his subjects of experiment. And not one but scores more are researching on mice, rats, apes, and even on the humble farmyard hen. That psychologists should work with apes is understandable. Apes are so human that it seems impossible nowadays that anyone could have doubted their dumb abilities to think and feel and behave as we do. But what shall we say about the rats that are trained to run through complicated labyrinths, miniature Hampton Court mazes, without making a mistake ? And what, to be sure, shall we say about performing fleas ? And hens—who would think that they have a psychology, and are studied most assiduously by some psychologists ?

Of course we have known for a long time, ever since hens were hens in a farmyard, that some are " bad-tempered," and cry a lie to all theories of equality in the hen-pen. The psychologist, however, goes much farther than this, and shows that the processes that govern the thinking of adults and children seem to be operating also in the case of the lowly hen. We eat much more when we sit down to a table laden with good things than we eat when the table is niggardly served. It is the same with the hen. If a small pile of corn is put down in front of the hen when it is hungry, it will eat so much of it and then be replete. If the pile had been twice as big, it would have eaten much more before being appeased. It estimates its appetite by the size of the pile of corn in front of it.

But how do these experiments and observations on animals serve psychology ? Is animal psychology the same in essentials as human ? There does indeed seem to be a difference, but only one of degree. The ape thinks like a young baby, and we can learn lessons for human psychology of the very greatest importance from some of the experiments that have been made with rats and mice. This is particularly the case for some of the very fine experimental work of Professor Lashley in Chicago.

I mentioned the performing flea, but insects are always a topic of absorbing interest to a psychologist. So highly and socially organised are the ants that it has been said of them that if only they had been the size of rabbits they might have been masters of the world. There is a solitary wasp which, born alone, with no contact with any other wasp during its development from pupa to maturity, enters into the world and proceeds to kill just *one* particular variety of fly as prey. All solitary wasps of the same variety seek out and kill one and the same kind of fly as prey. It is common parlance that instinct explains the way in which the wasp performs its miracle of pre-ordained activity. But we should like to know exactly what instinct means, and whether human beings have any instincts of the same kind as those of insects, birds, and animals.

HEALING THE WOUNDED MIND

I HAVE introduced, very briefly, the three main divisions of psychology—adult, child, and animal. But each is capable of very much subdivision. There are pure and applied aspects of adult psychology, for normal and abnormal persons ; and pure psychology is worked at by many different schools, each in its own particular way. But that there are all these different branches and schools of psychology should not lead us to conclude, as many do, that there is no general body of psychology about which many psychologists agree.

Abnormal psychology is, of course, a fascinating subject. There are hundreds of psychiatrists in England alone, medical psychologists whose work is in mental hospitals, caring for the insane and anti-social individuals that make up the most unhappy sections of the community. Other branches of psychology owe very much indeed to the work of some of these psychiatrists, and names like Dr. Kraepelin, the greatest of German psychiatrists, and Drs. Charcot and Janet of France, should be as well known to every well-educated person as is the name of their illustrious descendant, Professor S. Freud.

Perhaps the first lesson that abnormal psychology teaches us is that there is no clear line of demarcation between insanity and sanity. We are all a bit insane at times, if not usually, and even the most abnormal have glimpses of under-standing and feeling. There must be thousands of men and women outside the walls of a mental hospital who see " visions " and hear " voices." There is only a difference in degree between the inane anger and rage of an abusive woman and the raving madness of the mania patient in hospital. Both might tear up their own and other people's clothes, break everything within their reach, and generally behave in a thoroughly terrible way.

PSYCHOLOGY'S PLACE IN PRACTICAL AFFAIRS

FINALLY there are many applied psychologies, still in their infancy, but developing strongly nevertheless, such as industrial psychology, and the psychologies of salesmanship, law, art, and, indeed, of every branch of human endeavour. What has been learnt in the pure psychologies of the adult and the child is applied to the practical affairs of man. Thus, in industrial psychology, young men and women can be advised as to what careers they are best fitted for. They are measured for some of the abilities and characteristics determined in the first place in pure psychology, and then, knowing that a high intelligence is certainly required for success in the study of law, the individual with a desire to become a lawyer can be advised according to the standard of his intellectual endowments, and similarly for all the many walks and rôles of life.

One other psychological field is of increasingly great importance. It is social psychology. There are psychologists who believe that psychology should begin by studying the social forces first, and that only afterwards shall we be able to understand the full psychology of the single adult or child. There can be no doubt about the strength of these social forces : we have only to witness the happenings at a general election in England, or in the many countries in Europe at the moment who have adopted dictatorships, to realise their significance. How is it possible, we wonder, that a whole nation can suffer a dictatorship, when a nation like ourselves, for the main part, would, at the moment, face it bewildered and unbelieving ? Social psychology should be able to tell us something about these national matters. At the other extreme it has also to concern itself with the problems of children who are " social " whilst others are not, and with the flocking of birds. It should tell us why hens group themselves into a " family," with one hen " bossing " the others. It should tell us, too, how this hen differs from the budding dictator of to-day.

It has been worth while, I hope, to look over the main fields of psychology in the above very brief and rapid way. It will be agreed that we have touched upon topics of complexity at least as great as those that physics or chemistry has to face. There is, perhaps, more of interest in a single thought than in everything that physics or chemistry has to concern itself with in what Professor Julian Huxley has called this very lop-sided scientific age. Psychology is in great need of some of the money and brains at present expended on researches in physics and the other sciences. It is a subject fraught with the greatest of consequences for mankind, and yet more money has been spent to fight the blighting progress of the Colorado beetle than is spent on all the psychological laboratories in the British Isles.

It is all the more to be marvelled at, then, that psychology has reached the position in which it can give a tolerable picture of these complexities along scientific lines. In the following pages I am to sketch out these scientific lines, these general findings and conclusions and explanations that make up the main body of modern psychology.

THE LINK BETWEEN EXPERIENCES : ASSOCIATIONISM

How, then, shall we begin this systematic Study of Psychology ? The best method, perhaps, is by way of a little history. The story of Psychology begins with two laws of association, formulated by Plato and Aristotle over two thousand years ago. The first is called the *law of association by contiguity* (meaning " near together "). An example will readily show what is meant by this law. When I was twelve or thirteen years old, news was brought to me that a certain old friend of the family had committed suicide. I was playing Mendelssohn's " Spring Song " at that moment. And even to-day if I should think of this friend, or see his son, the " Spring Song " floats hauntingly into my mind. If I hear the song, I recall this man and the events attending that fateful Sunday morning. The song and the news are ineffaceably linked together. In the same way the word " black " is linked to " white," and " king " to " queen."

The law of association by contiguity concerns all such pairs of linked ideas. The " Spring Song " and the news of the suicide were experienced by me together, and, according to the law, I always tend to remember experiences if they occur together. If the two ideas or events occurring together, or shortly after one another, are A and B, then thereafter if I experience A alone, I shall immediately tend to recall also

B, and *vice versa*. If the two experiences are very striking ones, the tendency to associate them will be the stronger. Otherwise, the more often I experience two things together, the more shall I tend to remember them as linked together—a law that our teachers used to rely upon when they made us learn poetry " by heart " by repeating the verses over and over again.

This law at once appealed to the psychologists who, with the rise of modern science, were searching for purely mechanical explanations of psychological events. Thus, Dr. Hartley (1705–57) supposed that, to take the example of the " Spring Song " and the suicide, when I played the song, certain minute vibrations were set up in a particular spot in my brain, which in their turn gave rise to " vibratiuncles," movements which were responsible for the conscious state represented by my *knowing* or experiencing the tune. The news of the suicide set up corresponding vibrations and vibratiuncles. And since the two sets of vibrations occurred almost together (in point of *time*, but it was an easy slip to make it also the same point in the brain itself) they automatically became linked or fused together. Thereafter I had merely to cause vibrations corresponding to the idea of the " Spring Song," and these set going the vibrations which give rise to the ideas about the suicide.

The association of the two ideas had a counterpart, it was supposed, in the structure of the brain, a linkage between physiological impressions, each representing one of the associated ideas. It is not difficult to see, too, that not only separate and simple " ideas," but complicated and very tangled ones, could be supposed to be associated by virtue of this law. Thus, if I see the name of my native village or town, a vast complex of " memories " may come to my mind, these being like a network of associations interwoven about that name.

The second law of association is called association by *similarity*. Plato gave an example of the operation of this law—a picture of Simmias, he said, made him recall Simmias himself. It is widely held, however, that this law of association by similarity is just a variety of the law of association by contiguity. The picture of Simmias and Simmias himself are similar, so that the ideas I have associated about Simmias, and which would normally arise to my mind if he were before me in flesh and blood, are just as freely aroused by the picture.

UNWINDING THOUGHTS LIKE THREAD FROM A BALL

ASSOCIATIONISM was a broad movement in psychology, just as Marxism, for example, is a political movement. It had an imposing array of adherents, from Hobbes (1588–1679) and Hume (1711–76), the English philosophers, to William James (1842–1910), the American psychologist. It not unnaturally developed as a consequence of such a long history, but one of its greatest tenets was the above law of association by contiguity. It was fascinating to think, as this law beguiled one into thinking, that everything that one had ever experienced was linked together in a long chain, like a ball of the finest silk wound up in the brain, with one end in infancy, and the other winding on and on at the present moment, and that beginning at any part of the chain one could recall the associated items. All this linkage would be in virtue of the law of contiguity, since what I experience at this moment would be associated with what I experience in the next, and so on throughout one's lifetime.

This notion is far from dead and old-fashioned. Psycho-analysts still make use of it. When the analyst makes you recline on his couch, and asks you to " associate," he is making use of this principle. By unwinding the silken threads, so to speak, that represent one's mass of associations, the psycho-analyst helps one to remember the events of childhood, to recall, by association, events that have become buried under the weight of more recent associations.

But if association by contiguity explained the way two ideas became linked together, and again linked to others in the above long chain, how did associationists explain the knowing or consciousness that I have of any item ? It is one thing to associate the " Spring Song " and suicide together, but how did the mental content of the song itself, and the ideas I have of my friend, arise in my mind ? The solution was found in *sensations*.

SORTING OUT OUR SENSATIONS

THE associationists held that certain very rudimentary sensations, ideas, or feelings, are produced natively in the mind by stimulation of it through one's senses—the eyes, ears, nose, taste-buds, hot, cold, pain, and pressure spots on the skin. These sensations were considered to be elements of consciousness, just as electrons are considered to be elements of matter. The thoroughgoing associationist believed that these sensations were themselves produced by purely mechanical and physical means.

Sensations were classified into those of sight, sound, taste, smell, pressure, warmth, cold, pain, movement, and others. Sight sensations were of two kinds, colours, and black and white. Red, yellow, green, blue were primary colours, and these with black and white could be compounded into the three hundred or so different colours that we experience. It was found that if a white disc is looked at for less than one-tenth of a second, it is not seen as pure white, but as grey instead. Likewise a coloured disc shown in the same way appears colourless. Again, some people are colour-blind—they have more or less no red or green sensations ; some are yellow-blue, and others again totally colour-blind. In the same way, after eliminating smell sensations (for it is well known that if we hold our noses we cannot distinguish the taste of a piece of onion from that of a slice of apple), there were supposed to be four elementary taste sensations or feelings—sweet, sour, salty, and bitter. About five hundred different tastes could be supposed to be built up from these four elementary taste sensations. Turning to other sensations, we know that some persons are insensible to pain, just as there are those who are colour-blind or deaf. A Londoner recently had all his teeth extracted without feeling any pain. Another had his finger decimated, and could not feel even a twinge of pain.

Again, the tongue can serve as a tactual or " feeling " organ, giving rise to sensations that tell us something about the texture of the food we eat. Sloppy food has its own " feel," and there is a peculiar slipperiness about jellies, egg custards, etc. This tactual function of the tongue is apt to be over-looked when children's food is being prepared. We think too much of the hotness and coldness and flavour, and not at all about the " feel " of food—a neglect of no little signifi-cance, perhaps, in the dietary of children.

In all the above cases the sensations are connected with their appropriate sense organs, and the sensations are first aroused when these sense organs are stimulated. Sight sensa-tions arise after certain waves of light have impinged on the eye. But we can also call up *images*, visual and auditory, and perhaps of other sensory kinds, without the need for this external stimulation of the sense organs. And there are still other sensations for which we can find no sense organs or specific nerves, called the elementary *affections*, sensations such as pleasure and " unpleasure," excitement and tranquillisation, tension and relaxation.

We can now understand what is meant by Associationism, the great movement to which we have referred. Sensations were supposed to be the bricks, so to speak, of psychological activity ; and association-by-contiguity was the mortar by which these bricks were held together. All mental activity was supposed to derive ultimately from these two, sensations and association. Not only were new colours compounded from the elementary colour sensations, but thinking, imagination, judgment, and the deepest intricacies of the human mind were supposed to be built up from sensations by the process of association-by-contiguity.

Associationists believed that all mental activity could be explained by mechanics, by physical processes in time and space. They believed that the fundamental principles of psychology were those involved in the notions of " sensation " and of association-by-contiguity. These seemed to explain everything in psychology—a fitting conclusion, it was thought, to the progress of psychology down the twenty centuries of its development. This associationism is to-day far from dead. The psycho-analysts still continue to make use of its notions, and, with the added trappings that recent discoveries in physiology afford them, the modern behaviourists are also thoroughgoing associationists.

PROFESSOR PAVLOV'S PUPPET SHOW : BEHAVIOURISM

BEHAVIOURISM is the typical American's notion of what the science of psychology should be. It begins by throwing overboard the study of mental or psychical activities. Consciousness, sensations, ideas, and emotions, the behaviourist believes, cannot be studied scientifically. Instead, the scientific psychologist must follow in the footsteps of the physicists and physiologists ; he must be a detached observer of behaviour, measuring it with yard-stick and stop-watch. Thus an emotion, which you or I think of as a peculiar mental state, is thought of by the behaviourist in terms of the panting heart, which can be recorded on a cardiagraph, a blushing cheek, recorded by a selenium-cell attachment, quivering lips, blood changes, muscular paralysis—all of which are *measurable*.

All these, and still more subtle bodily activities, the hormones and internal secretions, are all that a scientific psychologist can concern himself with when he studies " emotions." Similarly for " thinking "—this has to be studied in the mouth ; measurements have to be taken of the movements of muscles and changes in the larynx. The behaviourist does not deny that each individual has experiences that he calls " thinking " or " emotional." But he holds that whereas any number of physicists can study one and the same bar of metal, only one psychologist at a time can study an act of thinking, and that act must be his own, because by no means can he observe the thinking in another person's mind.

Just as the physicist has his electrons, and the associationist his " sensations," so, too, the behaviourist has his small units out of which he believes human behaviour is formed. His units are called reflexes.

If a threatening gesture is made near my eyes, my eyelids rapidly and automatically blink. The gesture is a *stimulus* that sets going a predetermined *response*, the blinking ; and the chain of cause and its effect is called a *reflex*. Again, if I cross one leg over the other as I sit in a chair, and someone gives my knee a sharp tap below the knee-cap, my leg gives a jerk. Or, to give another example of hundreds having their ramifications in the human body, if I am hungry and I see an apple, my salivary glands will begin to function quite automatically, *i.e.* my mouth will water.

Now physiologists have traced out what happens in such reflexes. In the case of the knee-jerk—and it is typical of all others—the skin is stimulated (the sharp tap below the knee-cap), as shown diagrammatically in Fig. 1. Thereupon a nerve current passes along a nerve track, called the afferent nerve, to the spinal cord (or to the brain, as the case may be), where, after passing through a network of other connector nerves and extremely fascinating junctions (called synaptic junctions), the nerve current flows into a nerve track leading from the spinal cord to the muscle (the efferent nerve) which, so activated, makes the necessary response or reaction (the knee-jerk). The whole circuit, from stimulus to response, is called a *reflex arc*, and it is with units of this kind that reflexology builds up its explanation of all psychological behaviour. These units serve the same purpose in reflexology as sensations served in associationism. They are the bricks out of which all *behaviour* is built.

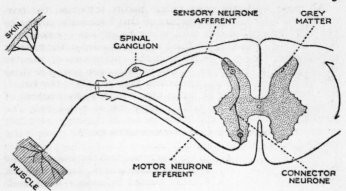

1. THE PATH OF A REFLEX ACTION

Let us see how the reflexologist or behaviourist manages this feat of explanation. It begins with Professor Pavlov's work on dogs, so that we might look for a moment at the brain of a dog, shown in Fig. 2. The top part of the brain —the cerebral cortex—is larger in proportion to the rest (the thalamus and medulla) the higher we mount up the scale of evolved animals. A fish, reptile, or mouse has relatively little cerebral cortex, whereas in man it is by far the biggest part of the brain (see Fig. 2). The spinal cord is just a prolongation of the medulla, and just as there are connector nerves and synapses in the spinal cord, so the medulla and the thalamus, and the whole brain, are centres of still more reflex arcs and systems of arcs.

The medulla is, in this way, a kind of telephone exchange for nerves coming from all the visceral organs of the body— the heart, stomach, lungs, arteries, sex organs, and so forth. All the essential functions of life are under its immediate control, and they could not function without its control any more than the knee can jerk if the spinal cord is destroyed. The thalamus, in the same way, is intimately connected with one's emotions. The cerebellum, or lesser cortex, is specially concerned with all the muscles of the body. The cerebral cortex, the glory of mankind, is the seat of the associations about which we have said so much in the previous pages. It is the seat of learning and the arch-comptroller of all other parts and functions of the nervous system and body.

The reflex systems centred at the medulla, as we have mentioned, are specially concerned with the visceral organs upon which sheer living depends. Stimuli, coming from the visceral organs or sense organs, set going complex systems of reflex arcs, the end of which are specific reactions, notably related to food and to sex activity. These systems of reflexes are innate, part and parcel of the animal or human being, inborn and developing along with it. Each system functions mechanically, or can do so, just like the knee-jerk reflex.

PAVLOV'S EXPERIMENTS WITH DOGS

PAVLOV holds that there are only a few of these complex reflex systems, namely, complex reflexes relating to food and food-seeking, to pugnacity, to active and passive defence, to freedom, to curiosity, to play, and to species reflexes such as sex and parental care. A matter of great interest is that if, to take the case of a dog, the cerebral cortex is destroyed and the dog still lives, it lives mechanically by way of these unconditioned reflexes. When it is hungry it will search unceasingly for food. It may not recognise food when it sees it, but as soon as it is fed the searching will cease and the dog may lie down and go quietly to sleep. It may then awaken and be strangely pugnacious, or it may romp about and play. If it now should be restrained in any way it will struggle until it is released, and if it is not released it may collapse in a paroxysm of fear. It may be dumbly curious, and perhaps sexually interested in another dog. Finally, hunger will call once more, and the whole process will repeat itself.

The dog will never learn anything. It will never learn to come for food when the food-basin is rattled, to answer to a name, to go to a bed, to know the biscuit-tin when it sees it, nor to learn the thousand and one things that a dog acquires in its lifetime. It will live instead at the mercy of its *unconditioned* reflexes. It will be like a machine, working undeviatingly and inexorably towards mere living and propagation. These unconditioned complex reflexes are known to most psychologists by another name—the *instincts*, about which we shall have more to say later.

HOW DOGS CAN BE MADE TO RESPOND TO THE DINNER-BELL

UNCONDITIONED reflexes, their innate or inborn development, and their integration into complex systems, represent

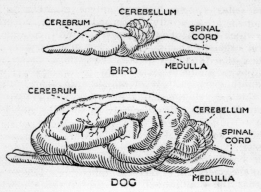

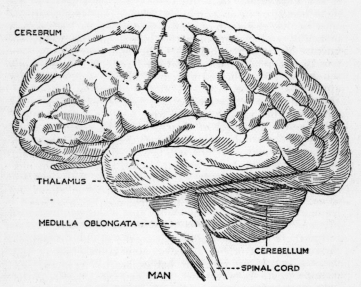

2. THE BRAIN OF MAN, DOG, AND BIRD

The drawing shows how much the cerebrum, the seat of intelligence, predominated in the human brain over that part in the brain of bird and dog. The cerebellum, which is connected with the movements of the muscles, however, shows similar development in all three.

2

the first principle of reflexology. The second great principle is called *conditioning*. The favourite example of conditioning is that first described by Pavlov, in his experiments on the salivary reflex of the dog. As is well known, if a dog is hungry and it is shown a bone, its salivary glands begin to function—its mouth waters. But if, instead of displaying the bone alone, first a bell is rung, and *then* the bone is shown, and if this order is repeated a few times when the dog is fed, the salivary glands will ultimately be set going when the dog hears the sound of the bell alone. The bell now serves as a stimulus to set the salivary glands working, instead of the food itself.

This conditioning cannot take place, it would seem, without the operation of the cerebral cortex. It is here, some-how, that the conditioned reflexes (as these newly learnt responses are called) seem to be stored up. According to the reflexologists, or behaviourists, all higher intellectual activity is just a complex system of conditioned reflexes. Reflexes are the bricks, and conditioning the mortar in the behaviour structure of the human being. To be intelligent is to be able to make and retain these conditioned reflexes. Intelligence itself is but a complicated system of habits, acquired in the individual's lifetime.

For this reason Professor Watson, founder of behaviourism in America, has said that if he were given a dozen healthy babies, and full control of their growth, he could make of them what he would, one a genius, the other a low-grade defect, and so forth. Moreover, behaviourists are not afraid to try out their theories. Tender babies, fifteen months old, have been taught to emulate the man on the flying trapeze (so far as physical tricks are concerned) ; they climb up inclined planes, and go about the nursery on roller-skates.

LEARNING BY ROTE AND LEARNING BY REASON

Now there can be no doubt that on the physical side there is much of truth in the work and contentions of the behaviourist. If we give our babies greater freedom, and put appropriate opportunities in their way, they can be taught a surprising range of tricks. But it may well be wondered whether these are built up in the purely mechanical fashion of conditioning. There can be, for the behaviourist, no mediation of a mental kind in the process of learning these tricks, just as, for the old associationist, there was no mediation of thought-like processes when two ideas were associated. Perhaps we can appreciate some of the shortcomings of behaviourism if we first look at a few obvious facts that meant the death-knell to associationism.

Ebbinghaus (1850–1909), a famous German psychologist, used sets of nonsense syllables of the following kind to perform experiments on the law of association by contiguity :

mif	. . .	zon
toz	. . .	nig
fem	. . .	bak
paf	. . .	yub

One was supposed to have no ideas when one read " mif " or " zon," and if they were repeated in this order a sufficient number of times it was supposed that by sheer association the pair were learnt together, so that if some one said " mif," one would respond at once with the word " zon." Thousands of experiments were made with these nonsense syllables, and one of the greatest of experimental psychologists (Professor Titchener (1867–1927) said that they were the most important contribution to psychology since the days of Aristotle.

The trouble began when a student in a well-known laboratory read a list of nonsense syllables several hundred times without making a single association, without remembering a single pair of the syllables he had been reading ! He hadn't been told that he had to learn the list ! The associations were made with ease as soon as he knew that he was expected to make them. In the same way I might walk along a street every day of my life and yet I should be hard put to say how many shops there are and in what order they occur. I have perceived them hundreds of times together or in sequence, but they are not therefore associated.

Obviously, then, association by contiguity is not exactly the mechanical process it was supposed to be. Not only must we often make an *intention* to learn, we often cannot " learn " without performing other *acts* of a purely mental kind. Thus it would take me some time to learn the following list of numbers by heart by merely hoping that consecutive numbers would be associated one to the other if I repeated the numbers time and time again :

$$7348593572535 8$$

But if the same numbers are organised, if they are thought of as follows, it is much easier to learn the list :

$$7348 \qquad 5935 \qquad 725 \qquad 358$$

The question then arises as to whether mental processes like thinking, judgment, and intention are not essential, and whether associations would ever be formed without such *acts* first being made. Perhaps even the dog cannot be conditioned to a bell unless it thinks in some way about it ; and who knows what thoughts have passed in the mind of the performing flea before it learns its repertoire of tricks ? On the other hand, there does seem to be something purely automatic and mechanical about the way some people are able to learn things by rote.

But having admitted this much that is very valuable in behaviourism, it still remains true that by far the greater part of what we learn " by heart " is dependent upon prior mental acts. If I make a firm intention to learn a piece of poetry, and if I think about and organise the material, if also I frequently try to recall what I have learnt, then it is certain that the learning will be greatly facilitated. But there are further difficulties about this matter which we leave for the moment. Meanwhile, since we have so far been told nothing about the processes that enter into the mental activities themselves, the *intentions*, the *judgments*, the *organisation*, and so forth, we have now to search for principles other than those of associationism and of behaviourism upon which to build up an orderly science of psychology.

THE CONSCIOUS MIND : BEING AWARE OF THINGS

WE begin this search by defining psychology as the science of the mind, and we shall consider the mind from two aspects : one, its activity at any particular moment, and the other the state that it has been in—its development from birth to old age, its structure and capacities. The first is the study of consciousness, or states of awareness. The other is the study of the structure of the mind. We shall begin with the former, with the experiences of which we are aware (and some we are not aware of) at any particular moment, with the teeming thoughts, desires, feelings, wishes, states of sleep, hypnotic conditions, that constitute the state of a person's mind from moment to moment. Some of these states last only a fraction of a second—thought, we say, has the speed of lightning, although, to be sure, a state of sleep seems to be constant for many hours. Again, only the individual himself can examine these states in any direct way. We can all *introspect*, some better than others—that is, look at our own conscious states much as a biologist looks at a section of a worm in a microscope. Admitting this, we can begin by classifying these various states of awareness. Three kinds of states have been known since the dawn of psychology— Cognitions, Feelings, and Volitions or Conations (what we know, what we feel, and what we will). We shall examine each class in turn, beginning with the cognitions.

Are there any straightforward laws, we have to ask, for cognition ? Cognition includes our sensory perceptions, what we see, hear, taste ; our images, whether visual, as in dreams, or auditory, as in the reverie of a music-lover ; and our thoughts, the deductions we draw, the acts of reason we perform. Is there anything common to this wide range of experience ? Are there laws of cognition that cover every-thing from the very simplest perception to the most intricate act of reasoning or the highest flight of the imagination ? We shall see now that just as Newton put order into Nature by his laws of motion, so the modern psychologist has made order out of the teeming masses of our cognitions.

The senses, as we all know, are the eyes, ears, nose, taste-buds of the tongue, cold and heat spots on the skin, and subtle organs such as those concerned with resistance to pressure. It is through these organs, we believe, that we learn about the external world. The eyes tell us that the grass is green, a fire red, a cathedral large ; the ears inform us that a band is playing outside, the church bell ringing, a baby crying in the street ; and the nose is breathing in for us the honeyed smell of violets. Through the senses we learn that grass is green, a fire is hot, and ice is cold.

But if we think about it twice we might convince ourselves that grass is not green, a fire is not hot, and ice is not cold. Physics tells us that the greenness of grass depends on the ether waves that reach the eyes. These stimulate the nerves leading from the eyes to the brain, and only somewhere in ourselves is the notion of greenness evolved. The human being is first and foremost a set of physical instruments, the senses receiving some of the myriads of ether waves and particle movements that surround him. Waves of air particles im-pinge upon the ear, minute particles reach and touch my organs of taste, smell, and pressure. Ether waves from the fire pass to the heat spots on my body.

Moreover, only a small fraction of all the existing ether waves affect my eyes or other organs. I cannot perceive wireless waves, X-rays, ultra-violet, or infra-red rays. We may well wonder what the outside world would appear to be if our eyes could make use of all the ether wave-lengths, from 10–24 mm. of X-rays to the 10,000 metre wave-lengths of wireless, instead of being restricted as they are to a range lying between 0·0015 and 0·0008 mm.

WHEN WE MIGHT SEE WITH OUR EARS

EQUALLY surprising is the fact that the self-same ether waves, say those coming from a red-hot fire, lead me to perceive redness if they enter my eye, and warmth if they fall on the heat spots on my body. The selfsame pressure can hurt me at one part of my body, and tickle me at another. What is perceived is decided by the particular nerves that are stimulated, and not by the ether waves themselves. If we could perform an operation, and interchange the nerves leading from the eyes and the ears, then we would hear with our eyes and see with our ears. Soft music, perhaps, would be heard as we looked at the fire, and a dream-like image perceived as we listened to a concert ! We can well say, with Professor Spearman :

> " Could, by some surgical operation, the sensory nerves be detached from their present receptors and interchanged with one another, then a voice might be seen or a face heard, a toothache might be converted into a taste of chocolate, or a blow of a fist into the fragrance of jasmine."

Again, once stimulated, all the various nerves leading from the sense-organs act alike. Each afferent nerve merely carries a nerve impulse along its path, and the experimental work of Dr. Adrian at University College, London, has shown that all these nerve impulses are alike, whether they pass to or from the eye, ear, nose, or any other organ. Thus, somewhere outside the nerves themselves, perhaps in the synapses between the nerves in the brain, the great work is done that leads to the mental experiences I have. Ether waves from an outside source, chemical processes in the eye, nerve impulses in the nerves leading to synapses, chemical processes in the synapses, all these intervene between the outside world and the mental state that is aroused within me.

From this discussion of the senses we meet at once the

problem of reality. We believe that the apple tree we see is a photographic image of a real tree outside, that the fire is itself hot, and that the brass band we are listening to is itself making the noises we hear. We believe that the mental states we experience are exact representations of real objects in the world outside, that the brass band is not merely something emitting sound waves which, reaching my ear, give rise to mental states of noise. But by the same token we shall have to believe that the surgeon's scalpel is itself suffering pain, which it passes on to us when it cuts. And the feather will be enjoying tickling sensations, which it hands on to us in an appropriate way. The truth seems to be that the outside world merely emits waves and particle motions or pressures, and all the colours, pleasures, pains, tunes, and perfumes are creations of our own mental states. The world is apparently an attenuated mixture of electrons, protons, neutrons, positrons, deutrons, and ether waves, but we believe it is a world of sunshine, green hills, warm winds, and gently swaying trees.

CAN WE BELIEVE THE TESTIMONY OF OUR SENSES?

NEVERTHELESS, we cannot but believe that the world outside is real, and that it contributes largely to our cognition. Dreams and visions, we feel sure, are certainly creations of the individual concerned, but the trees outside are not. The hallucinatory voices that so many saints and the mentally afflicted have heard are equally insubstantial things. How, then, do we distinguish between these and reality? The real object passes the test of many senses, for we not only see a tree but we can touch it, smell it, press against it, put our teeth into and even taste it and feel its warmth. Visions and hallucinations are not quite so accommodating. We seem to experience those mental states as real which pass the test of all the senses, and which we find that other people also experience apparently just as we do.

But here we shall leave the riddle of reality for the present, except to offer a reminder that although we seem to have drawn our deductions from physics and physiology rather than from pure psychology, we shall find that we arrive at the same conclusions from purely psychological considerations. We shall find that we ourselves contribute very largely to the experiences we naïvely believe come to us by way of our senses.

It seems easy to believe that the new-born baby experiences

certain very rudimentary and poorly differentiated mental states. We cannot prove what they are. The young fawn runs unerringly at birth, and its perception seems to be well developed from the first day of its life. But the baby is certainly not so well endowed. Nevertheless, its sensory organs soon begin to function, in however dull and dim a fashion ; and we have to infer that these give rise to lowly mental states, and that the baby tends to become aware of them, conscious of them. Moreover, it soon becomes aware that it is itself the liver or experiencer of these mental states. My daughter, at twenty-one months, was often heard to say with evident satisfaction, " Baby eats," " Baby shouts, " Baby crying," fitting the actions to the words. *She is not only aware of eating, shouting, and crying, but knows that it is herself who is the experiencer*.

It is a mistake, however, to suppose that the young child perceives the outside world through its senses just as we do. My daughter had apparently never perceived shadows until she was twenty-one months old. There are many mentally defective children who have never yet perceived that various coins are different in size and colour. It seems well, however, to formulate a general law that we tend to be aware of sensory experiences, and that at the same time we are aware that *we* are the experiencers.

The obvious law of awareness also applies for adults. We tend to become aware of mental states produced by way of the senses, and we are also aware that *we* are the experiencers. We are also aware at once of many of the *characters* or characteristics of the experiences : we see a tree at once as tall, a stone as hard and solid. Thus, I may awake in a strange bedroom and see a white-robed woman in the room. After rubbing my eyes, and taking stock of the situation, I find that I am merely looking at the window curtains lit up by the moon. The long white curtain has its *characters*, its flowing form, its whiteness, its solidity, and I am aware of some of these immediately in the white-gowned woman I think I see, with her flowing dress, her solid shape, her tall stately figure bent slightly towards me and swaying gently.

OUR MEAGRE "MENTAL SPAN"

But it would be unfortunate if we became aware at one and the same moment of all the various mental states that the senses could lead us to experience. We read our newspaper without noticing the raucous wireless or the chatter of others in the room. We listen to a friend without hearing the tear and rush and noise of the train. That is, we select what we want to attend to. But selection is a matter of volition and not essentially of cognition.

It is, however, a law of cognition that we cannot attend to very many separate things at once. Even taking the case of music-hall performers, who have spent years in learning to do things simultaneously, if more than five or six dots are printed on a card and exposed to their regard for only a fraction of a second, and if they rely purely upon their eyes,

3. DOTS THAT FORM FOURS

and do not *think* about the dots, then they will be unable to say how many dots there were on the card.

Our *mental span*, as it is called, is limited to about six different items, and this span is nearly the same for all in-dividuals, stupid and intelligent alike, and cannot be improved upon by practice. We are limited in span for touch, hearing, and smell, as well as for sight.

On the other hand, if we perform a little thinking, we can " span " many more than six separate dots at a time. Thus, if the dots in Fig. 3 are exposed for a fraction of a second to a person who has not seen them before, he will probably perceive them all at once as three sets of four dots. When we organise the dots we offset the restrictions imposed upon us by our meagre span. The long and arduous training we have had in reading has resulted in groups of letters that we recognise at a glance, and we " take in " the meaning of paragraphs and phrases without having to read all the words contained.

Similarly with hearing. All this shows a vast organisation built up from the mere simple physical waves and the sentient states that they might give rise to in the minds of a naïve or untutored individual.

PERCEPTION OF WHOLES

4. THE CUP THAT JEERS

WE can best begin to discuss the laws of organisation by looking at the drawing of a cup (Fig. 4). At first it looks like a white cup or goblet on a dark background. But if we look at it again, it is a drawing of two dark profiles facing each other on a white background. The physics of the drawing does not alter, but we see it in two different ways.

When we see the cup it appears to be standing slightly away from the paper and background. The cup is technically called the *figure*, and the rest of the drawing is its *ground*, and, alternatively, when I see the two profiles jeering at each other, they are the figure, and the rest is the ground. In the same way, Fig. 5 can be seen as a row of pyramids, or the top of a black fence, or as a white tooth-edged canopy hanging downwards. The set of dots, organised into groups of

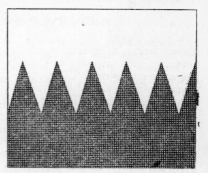

5. PYRAMID OR CANOPY ?

four (Fig. 3), make a figure on a white ground, and as in all these cases, if we look at the dots carefully we shall see that the

figure appears to stand out from the ground with a solidity
of its own.

Fig. 6. below is the same all the time, but it can be seen as
a figure now in one and now in another perspective. We
could give any number of these figures-and-grounds (or
" wholes," " configurations," *Gestalten*, as they are variously
called). According to the present-day Berlin *Gestalt* psychologists, our perceptions, visual or otherwise, are organised on
this plan of a figure and a ground, and this is the native,
instinctive way the mind organises its sensory data. The

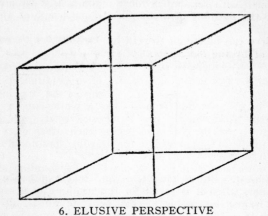

6. ELUSIVE PERSPECTIVE

human being, according to this view, has an invincible and
untaught and unanalysable ability to perceive only *wholes*,
figures, on a *ground*. These wholes are not built up from
elements like sensations by processes such as association, but
simply pop into the mind intuitively, like bolts from the blue.

THE PART INTUITION PLAYS IN OUR PERCEPTIONS

BUT this does not mean that every *whole* or *Gestalt* is independent of past experiences. It is true that we often
know what a paragraph means at a glance, and that the
meaning is a figure on the ground of sentences and letters.
But this meaning is the consequence of a long, slow process
of training and teaching. The following experiment shows
how new *Gestalten* are built up in the course of only a few

minutes' practice. A sheet of paper is taken, containing mixed capital letters, row after row, of the following kind :

AXTKILOPXTGOKIJNOXPOT

We then proceed to train ourselves to cancel out all the letters X, O, and I as we come to them. At first we perceive most of the other letters besides X's, O's, and I's. But with practice we see only the letters we wish to cancel, standing out in groups of three or four at a time, each group a *Gestalt* on a background of the other undifferentiated letters. So it is, although with very much more practice, that we are able to grasp the meaning of a complicated paragraph at a single glance.

Children can be taught to read by " wholes," by sentences instead of by the old method of separated letters like c-a-t,

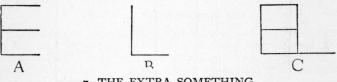

A   B   C

7. THE EXTRA SOMETHING

or f-a-t-h-e-r. But so taught, a child may experience diffi-culty, later, when it is asked for the meaning of a separate word. It may be unable to spell separate words, although it can write sentences. I have recently heard of cases of this kind where parents have complained that their children cannot play the game *Lexicon*, even though they have been taught to read. They had been taught to read by the " whole " method and now cannot recognise that f-a- could be the beginning of the word " father." In short, these children have yet to learn how to spell, and have yet to know the meaning of separate words—words which enter into sentences that they can read, and the meaning of which they grasp.

The *Gestalt* psychologists, then, teach that much in our perceptual life seems to be experienced to some extent intuitively in an instinctive way. They remind us, too, that a perception is no mere sum of parts. Thus, the third figure above need not be merely the additive sum of the first two figures. They would say that there is something intuitive about the composite figure, something put there by the individual. No explanation is offered for this intuitive something ; for the *Gestalt* psychologist, it falls out of the blue and is inexplicable. But we have already seen that " wholes " can be built up by practice, and we suspect that most instances mentioned by *Gestalt* psychologists have been so determined. We could not perceive the *cup that jeers* if we had not already built up notions about cups so drawn on paper, and similarly for faces drawn in profile. As in the case of reading, vast experiences lie at the back of these perceptions. We have still to ask, of course, just *how* experience has functioned in this way. But in whatever direction we may proceed, from the particular to the more general, or *vice versa*, the *Gestalt* psychologist would say that the processes are interwoven through and through with *Gestalt* formations, with new wholes, each involving inexplicable features.

THE ENGLISH POINT OF VIEW

THE *Gestalt* psychologist cannot say, except physiologically, how the new *whole* is constructed—that is, why he calls it " intuitive." Certain British psychologists, however, have discovered a little more about the *modus operandi* of these *wholes*. The associationists believed that perceiving and thinking were explained in terms of association by similarity and by contiguity at bottom ; the *Gestalt* psychologists point out that psychologically this is far from what really takes place, and they replace associationism by intuitionism. But Englishmen, at least, can rarely believe in intuition for very long without wanting to explain it. Let us see, then, what this English point of view is.

If a child sees two aunts, and notices for itself that one is very much stouter than the other, or richer than the other, or a better sport than the other, what is the nature of this noticing ? Does it just see a very stout aunt near a very thin one, and does a *Gestalt* arise intuitively in mind, in which the one aunt is a figure and the other a ground ? Or, if I perceive the two drawings A and B (Fig. 8), and then I conclude that A is upside-down with respect to B, how have I drawn the conclusion ?

Or, again, if I look at the drawings opposite C, and then at those opposite D, and if I observe that all those opposite C are alike because they are drawn with full lines, whilst those at D are also alike, in a different way, because they are all drawn with dotted lines, what are the processes entering into this thinking ?

The English psychologist, Professor C. Spearman, has suggested that when a person is aware of any two items

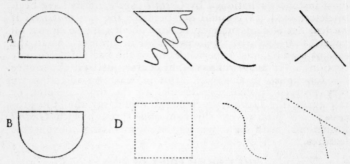

8. UPSIDE-DOWN TEST AND TEST OF LIKENESS

(two perceptions, two sets of ideas or thoughts, two feelings or two conclusions, etc.), he tends immediately to *educe* (or draw out) a *relation* between them. This relation is intuitive in nature : so far as we can understand, it can receive no prior explanation in terms of other psychological processes acting at the moment, just as the *Gestalt* is supposed to be intuitive. But whereas the *Gestalt* or *whole* arises intuitively without prior awareness of parts about which the eduction takes place, in the case of *eduction* of a relation, there is usually

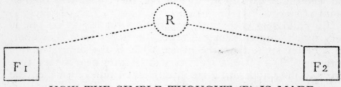

9. HOW THE SIMPLE THOUGHT (R) IS MADE

a perception or awareness of parts, about which the eduction takes place. This, according to the Spearman psychologists, is the prototype of all cognitive organisation. It is one of the ways in which *new* cognitive experiences are produced. It can be represented as in Fig. 9.

F_1 and F_2, technically called the fundaments, represent

the two items first in awareness, and R is the relation educed
between them. The various relations that can be educed
have been discovered. When a child educes that one shape
is upside-down compared with another,[1] an eduction that
some mentally defective children never seem able to make,
the eduction is called *spatial*. Although it has the same
nature, this spatial relation is not the same experience as a
likeness relation such as we educe between full-lined or dotted
drawings.[1]

HOW A BABY MAKES COMPARISONS

SOME of the early eductions of a child are of great interest.
At 1 year 4 months old my daughter always turned pictures
of horses, people, engines, etc., up the right way, as though

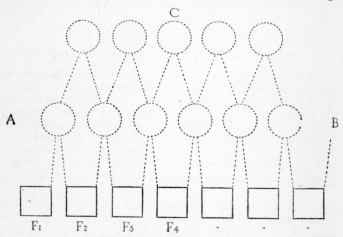

10. HOW COMPLEX THINKING IS DONE

she could clearly educe the difference between the right way
up and the wrong way up of a person, or horse, or tree.
At 1 year 10 months she first began to educe big-little
relations : of two grapes, one large and the other *very* small,
she would call the latter " tiny " ; the same response was
given for two baths, two animals (cat and kitten), and two
baskets, etc. But only things that were *alike* in the first place,
both grapes, or baths, or the same animals, were compared

[1] See Fig. 8, page 46.

in this way. She could not say which was smaller, a large orange or a very small apple. And, similarly, the two items compared had to be strikingly different in size for the eductions to be made. One grape had to be extremely small, and the one bath was six feet long, whilst the other was a baby's.

The diagram (Fig. 9) is the simplest way in which eduction of relations takes place. As they occur in adults they are complicated in at least three different ways. Two of these ways are shown in Fig. 10.

The same system of relations might be educed in a strata

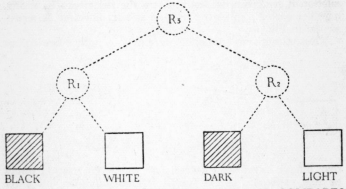

BLACK   WHITE   DARK   LIGHT

11. HOW THE MIND DISTINGUISHES AND COMPARES

form, one fundament being compared with another, and then with another, and so on as from A to B in diagram 10. This may occur in the case of comparing the three full-lined or three dotted-lined drawings in Fig. 8. Or, having educed relations *along* one strata, further relations can be educed between the relations already educed, and so on in an increasing hierarchy, strata *above* strata as at A upwards towards C. Thus, let us look at the following analogy :

Black : White : : Dark : Light

We may educe that Black is the opposite of White, and also that Dark is the opposite of Light, and then at another strata we may educe that these two relations are themselves alike. It could be represented as in Fig. 11 above.

HOW THE MINDS OF THE INVENTOR AND NOVELIST WORK

Two important laws of cognition have now been described, that of *awareness*, and that of eduction of relations. We have hinted, too, that the *Gestalt* viewpoint about cognition might be resolved into the above two laws, together with another somehow dependent upon visual or auditory or verbal, or any other imagery. But there is a third most important law of cognition that is also due to Professor Spearman, called the law of *correlate eduction*. It states that if I am aware of a fundament (or tend to be) and a relation, I shall tend to educe a correlate fundament. That is, if one F_1 and the relation R are given, we tend to educe a fundament F_2 which, together with F_1, gives the relation already in mind, as represented in Fig. 12.

Thus, the given fundament might be a light beige colour

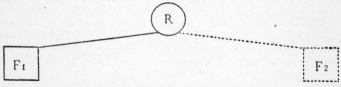

12. THE MISSING FUNDAMENT

that I have never seen before, and the given relation might be that expressed as " a similar colour and tone, but twice as dark," and it is possible for me to *imagine* (as we say) a colour twice as dark as the original one. The newly imagined colour is not culled from my memory, for I may not have seen the colour before. It is my own invention, so to speak. The inventions of a man like Edison, the music of a Delius, the novels of a Mary Webb, all the creative and imaginative activities in the arts and sciences and in everyday life, seem to be woven through and through with this process of correlate eduction.

Organisation, then, seems to depend on these processes of eduction. Instinctively we educe relations between things, and correlate eductions too. Our perceptions, visual or otherwise, our deepest thoughts and happiest flights of the imagination depend on these processes at bottom. They will depend, undoubtedly, on other things besides, on training, on mental imagery and habits, but eduction seems to be the essential process. The only doubt is that some of our perceptions are already organised in a generalised way that we cannot yet clearly specify instinctively. The perception of space seems to be of this nature. But organised perceptions of this kind must have been developed in the course of man's long history, just as new *Gestalten* are developed in his lifetime (as we saw in the case of the Cancellation experiment).

HOW IMAGINATION "EDITS" OUR PERCEPTIONS

TURNING from the processes to their products, we have found convincing evidence that what we perceive need bear little relation to the physical things outside us. The *Gestalt* groups of letters in the Cancellation experiment are very different from those printed on the paper. In the same way, at the cinema we really look at series of stationary pictures. The same still picture is thrown several times on the screen, with dark intervals between each ; but we see movement in every subtle shade and degree. There is certainly no physical movement there, so that it must be the product of our imagination (as we say). It is not, as is popularly believed, due to the fusion of one picture with the next—the dark intervals, and other features of the projection are actually intended to prevent this fusion, which normally leads to " blurring."

Again, if we look out of one eye only it is physically impossible to see things in three dimensions. Instead, everything should appear to be flat, as though printed on a sheet of paper. But we certainly imagine we see things in three dimensions. If we look out of a window we can see that a building outside is only as big as the window-pane near us, yet if the window-pane is not there to remind us of this fact, we see the building as the large structure we know it to be when we are near it.

In this way we seem to judge all our sizes by the sizes normally perceived when we can touch them, or when we are near them. A person at the other side of the street still appears to be six feet tall, yet we need only hold up a finger-tip, and we can see that the finger-tip is taller than this six-footer. The camera never makes mistakes of this kind. It is interesting to think that if a person could live all his life and never be nearer than fifty yards to other human beings, the first time he came within touching distance of a group of people he might still think that he was a giant and the other people pigmies.

WHAT IS MEMORY ?

THE old belief was that our memories are somehow stamped in the brain, and the modern behaviourist can only amplify this by saying that what is stored in the cerebral cortex and its bodily connections is a vastly complicated system of conditioned reflexes, all ready for discharging under appropriate stimulation. According to this view, my " seven times " arithmetic table is represented by certain reflexes and their muscular endings : when the button is pressed, so to speak, my muscles gabble off " seven times one are seven," and so forth. There is something akin to truth about this, perhaps, for much that is learnt by rote.

The view that " memory " is represented in the brain by *engrams*, or *dispositions*, is of this same physiological nature. Once an idea is conscious, it is psychical in nature : but when it is no longer conscious it ceases to be psychical, and leaves only a physiological impression, engram, or disposition. But it might also be held that after ceasing to be conscious an idea becomes *subconscious*. By this we mean that it is still of a psychical nature, but too faint for us to be aware of it. It might even be held that every cognitive activity we have experienced continues throughout our lifetime to persist subconsciously, although with infinitesimal intensity. In point of fact, however, we can only say that *cognitive experiences, by occurring at all, tend to occur later with greater ease. This is the first law of " memory."* To some extent, therefore, we " remember " all our cognitive experiences, just because they have occurred.

But common sense tells us that we really remember, in fact, very little of what we have cognised throughout our lifetime. Think of the myriads of cognitions we have on any one day ! How few we remember ! But this is because of the operation of a second law : *cognitive experiences which are the more clearly (consciously or unconsciously) motivated, or volitionally determined, have an additional " memory " value.* Thus, the interrupted tasks (p. 20), we found, were remembered more readily than the completed tasks. The *wish* (a volitional matter) to complete the tasks had not been fulfilled, and this apparently gives additional memory value to these interrupted tasks. Likewise, we remember those things most which we *will* to remember, as was seen in the case of the experiments with nonsense syllables (p. 35). It is those cognitions that matter most to us that are retained especially well—all those that are especially important to our volitional life, including our desires, motives, wishes, urges, and instincts, as well as to our deliberate will. Thus, when Professor Freud says that we remember everything we have experienced, from the moment of our birth, and that psycho-analysis can bring these " memories " back, he is referring to only those " memories " which are governed by this second law of memory.

Again, the psycho-analyst holds that all our culture is a *sublimation* of instinctive impulses. Our sublimations, that is, the interests we have acquired, the knowledge we have gained, have behind them the content of our " memory " : and this, in so far as it is enduring, could only have been built up on a foundation of volition-like processes. As we shall see, the dynamic instincts are of this volition-like nature, at bottom the very kind of psychological construction which our sublimations could only be built upon.

There are at least three stages to distinguish between in what is popularly called " memory." First, there is the *impression* stage, when we cognise either consciously or sub-consciously (as when we perceive a friend in a street and only afterwards realise that we have passed him without con-sciously recognising him), or perhaps when we merely repeatedly move certain muscles over and over again and so impress certain behaviour upon ourselves represented by the poetry we are learning by heart. Next, the retention stage ; either a state persists subconsciously, or a static pattern has been embossed into the body as a system of reflexes. The subconscious persistence, of course, may have its nervous counterpart, as electronic or other electrical conditions.

The next stage is that in which these persisting states can be reactivated under certain conditions, and we are said to " recall," " reproduce," or " remember." The possibilities present themselves that we probably cognise without much truly being retained, and much might be retained without our ever being able to recall it, and we can never determine how much we " remember " without actual reproduction. The behaviourist's reflexes can only fade away with time, as memory seems to do. But our notion of a subconscious mind is far from that of a static set of stamped-in patterns representing our memory. Subconscious activities are obviously, if we believe in them at all, like conscious ones in respect of dynamic flux—we think over things subconsciously as well as consciously. Thus, the memories of my youth may be very different now compared with my actual experiences at that time, because they have been worked over subconsciously since my youth (which is just what we mean by saying they have been worked over in my subconscious mind).

Yet that some things are " remembered " seems obviously true. There is still one other process that might explain very much of what we *believe* we remember, as well as much that we believe we had forgotten. It is the process of correlate eduction. Often we can be misled into thinking that we are recalling something previously experienced, when really we are educing a new experience by way of correlate eduction. If I try to recall what I did last year on holiday some vestiges of persisting states may be aroused, and notably those volitionally determined, about which something has to be said later, but more often than not I may fill up these vestiges by means of correlate eductions, and confuse these with true " memories." This, in any case, is a nice way out of the difficulty of a mind stored with an infinite number of ready-to-hand " memories." We need only remember a little, and we invent the rest.

TWO EARLY PSYCHOLOGISTS PROPOUND A STRANGE PARADOX

WE have said a great deal about the nature of cognition, and it is now time to describe the nature of " feelings " and of volition. By " feelings " we mean experiences such as pleasure, anxiety, anguish, joy, sorrow, apprehension, and fear. These are mental experiences, like cognitions, but with a different quality. It is a matter of great interest to ask whether they fit the same laws as do the cognitive experiences. It was said that cognition begins by way of the senses. Have our feelings any organs, then, comparable with the eyes, ears, nose, etc. ? Feelings seem to be intimately connected with physical behaviour : we feel sorrow and sob at the same time, we feel shy and blush, we feel afraid and our hair stands on end, we feel excited and our whole body seems to quiver. It is not surprising, therefore, that psychologists have sought for a causal connection between these physical activities and feelings.

James, in 1884, and Lange, in 1885, put forward the theory that feeling is merely the conscious state of which these physical activities are the sense organs. Just as the sensation of redness requires the eye, in the first place, before it is experienced, so a feeling of fear would depend in the first place upon nervous currents reaching the brain from the hair that stands on end, or from the cheeks that blanch, or from similar bodily behaviour. According to this view, when we feel sorry for ourselves this is because we are weeping : the tear glands send their little messages, drop by drop, to the brain, and these, somehow, are transformed into the mental experience, the feeling of sorrow. In the same way, when we are running away from danger, the fear we experience is produced by the running. Which, most of my readers will agree, seems very silly.

WHY WE FEEL DEPRESSED

IT is true that feelings of fatigue, hunger, and visceral feelings generally, seem to depend on physical changes. But what we have learnt from the study of cognition should warn us that the mental experiences of a " feeling " kind can bear no relation to the crude bodily actions : somewhere the feelings arise, but they are mental acts *sui generis*. We might be sure that they will not be tied like slaves to any such crude bodily activities. Just as we can imagine we see things, and just as we put far more into our perceptions than exists in the universe outside us, so we might expect that our feelings will be free from any rigid domination of activities like that of hair that stands on end or a cheek that blanches. More often than not, we first *feel*, and then the bodily actions follow. We feel shy, and then the blush floods our face and neck. We feel afraid, and then the hair stands on end.

There are many unhappy people in the world who feel continually depressed, or who suffer from an indescribable anguish and anxiety all day long. The physiologist looks for hormones in their blood-streams, and believes that he has found in them the cause of the depression or anxiety. The psychologist, however, whilst admitting a correlation between these hormones and the mental states, would rather look for purely psychological causes, and sees as much or more reason to believe that the feelings have caused the greater secretion of hormones. The feelings of depression and anxiety are so devastating, take up so much of the sufferer's personality, that the psychologist wants to know about them and not be put off by vague theories that they are caused by hormones and the like. The psychologist's viewpoint is that if such processes can be shown to enter into feelings, they are only links in the causes that have led up to the way we feel, and we may be sure that man has liberated himself from them by now.

Are there any known laws, then, about feelings ? Can they be organised, as perceptions and knowledge are ? Are there any processes for feeling, like those of eduction for cognition ? We shall have to answer these questions later, when they are discussed again in the light of the facts that have to be described about emotions and instincts. For the present, therefore, we leave feelings, and turn to volition.

Volition is a word that most psychologists are nowadays careful to avoid. By volition we mean acts of at least apparent free will, like choosing, deciding, and " willing."

THE GRIM PERSISTENCE OF THE WILL

WHAT are the laws of volition ? The first is that *volition is the more truly free, the more it is made on the basis of cognition, of knowledge and reason.* The more truly conscious the event, the more essential is volition to action. The next law is that *having decided, or " willed " an act, the action contemplated tends to be put into operation.* The retort to this will be that we often decide to get up in the morning, and yet the intention is rarely immediately successful. Often, too, the more strongly we *will* to do something, the less do we succeed. Nevertheless, we do ultimately get out of bed, and when we have done so, it must have been prefaced by an effective volition. (Which, admittedly, seems like being wise after the event.) And what we all know as " will-power " is not the same as the volition under present consideration.

The third law of volition seems to be that, *once begun, the willed act will tend to continue until it has been fulfilled or completed.* This is true of the impulses and motives that are deep down in our minds, the instincts about which we are to hear something later. But it seems also as true of any of the actions we have begun, any of the activities we have chosen to begin, any act of volition. An example of this was mentioned in an early section in connection with the experiment with the twenty-one different tasks. The child resolves to do task No. 1, and proceeds with its performance. If the task is completed, the volition ceases to have its *determining tendency.* But if the task is interrupted before completion, then the tendency still remains to complete it.

This law is fraught with the greatest consequences for man. A wish is but half-way to a willed act ; and, as the psycho-analyst has shown, deeply unconscious " wishes " function as though they were willed acts. The wish-fulfilment theory of dreams put forward by Professor Freud and many of the strange obsessions and disturbances of life, have behind them the working of this law of volition.

I can now raise the topic of *conation.* Conation means, according to dictionaries, action by or through volition, and this is precisely what I have expressed above as the third law of volition. But very few psychologists ask themselves for laws of volition. The struggles we make to succeed in life, the purposes we pursue, these we call conative, and we can see some degrees of volition behind all such actions. But for the behaviourist these are merely a matter of organised reflexes, all highly and rigidly determined physiologically, bodily and muscularly, without any possibility of volition entering to upset this nicely balanced machine. He points out that when we *strive*, the muscles move, the legs strain, the heart pants, and these are essential features of conative activity. The associationists would add that since these bodily activities give rise automatically to *feelings*, lo ! feelings are the backbone of conation.

These associationists, and many psychologists to-day, hold that conative activity can be reduced to cognition and feelings, and that there is no such thing as a volitional act. When I decide to post a letter, according to this view, I bring to my mind an image of the post-box and of myself posting the letter—all purely a cognitive matter. I then remember to post the letter, just as I remember and recall anything else. Or suppose that it is the close of a three miles' race, and that the runner is striving with every ounce of energy to maintain his lead. He wills, strives, desires to win. This intense striving is undoubtedly accompanied by many profound bodily changes—the hands are clasped, the jaw is set, breathing is laboured, muscles tortured ; he suffers, feels pain, as well as grim elation and satisfaction at the thoughts of success. He clearly holds in mind, too, the tape towards which he is striving. From the beginning of the race, and long before it, he has imagined himself breaking the tape, has pictured the cheering crowd and anticipated the pleasures of success.

All these together, the image of the goal ahead, the physical activity and the accompanying feelings, constitute conation—so the behaviourist and the associationist believe. In addition I would add the still small voice of volition, which decided in the first place to run the race, and which still sets its seal on tactical matters in the course of the race—that is, as a result of cognition, decisions have to be made during the course of the race (as when the runner has to make a " spurt,' or " take it easy "), and the decisions put into operation are volitional acts.

THE WORKSHOP OF THE HUMAN MIND

Now that we have discussed the main divisions of the mind, we can go on to consider particular abilities and show how they may be measured and tested. Cognitions, as we saw, are a broad group of activities seemingly different in quality from feelings and from volitions. But it is possible to classify cognitions further into several types. Plato, for instance, considered that there were two kinds of cognitive activities—the *Sensory* and the *Intellectual*. The perception of a picture would be largely a sensory cognition, whilst arguing out a proposition would be an intellectual one. Intellectual activities were later subdivided into those of a *conceptual*, *judging*, and of a *reasoning* nature, and there were added others, the *memories* and the *imagined* activities, as well as those specially involving *attention* and *speech*. The word reasoning thus stood for all the activities of a similar kind, namely, those involving syllogism, inference, deduction, and the like. Others also subdivided it into scientific, as distinct from logical, and again as distinct from theological reasoning.

There can be but little harm done by so classifying activities, so long as we remember the limitations of this method. The classifications, in the first place, are not in the least necessarily for the *psychological* characteristics of the cognitions—rather as in the case of reasoning, the activities were classified on logical or on philosophical grounds. Whatever else we want psychology to be, we want it to be free from the very narrow confines of logic and the ever doubtful ones of philosophy. Further, there is small point in classifying activities indefinitely. Rather, we want to know to what end such classification is pursued.

In a thoroughly practical way, the modern experimental

psychologist has developed a scientific method for investigating the psychology of the various cognitions : he tentatively accepts a classification, and then tries it out, or tests it, to see whether it is really psychological, and not a mere exercise in classification.

This is the method of individual psychology. The individual psychologists, of whom I am one, make their psychology depend on the measurement of abilities ; from these they find hints of the most essential and important psychological processes entering the various abilities. In due time, too, they will subject these processes to still further experiment and measurement. This process, we believe, cannot but be the backbone of a truly scientific psychology. In any case, let us see how it works, beginning with activities that we might reasonably classify under the heading " memory."

HAVE YOU A GOOD MEMORY?

WHAT kinds of memory activities are there ? There is all the body of our disposable knowledge—the arithmetic we have learnt, and so forth. There is the massive body of information that we can give retrospectively—the memories, as we call them, of our day-to-day experiences. We might ask individuals to learn pieces of poetry, etc., and then test their *immediate* memory—how much they have learnt in ten minutes, say. Or we might measure their more solid *remote* memory—how much they remember a week or so after they first learnt the poetry.

Further, we saw that retention might be a persisting subconscious state ;[1] or that we might retain very little, but supplement that little by correlate eduction and so beguile ourselves into thinking that we have retained far more than we really have ; and we saw, too, that volitional activities tend to have a *determining tendency*,[2] tend to continue until resolved by the completion of the willed act.

We should try to determine how far these theories " hold water." Is the ability to make determining tendencies, for instance, the same as the ability to memorise poetry ? Is the ability to memorise poetry the same as the ability to educe correlates ? Finally, there is *recollection* and *recognition*. Can abilities be measured for these, and are they the same as the other memory abilities ? Here, then, is room for much thought and experimental work.

[1] See page 62.   [2] See page 55.

In point of fact we can now measure at least three or four different memory abilities, for verbal, numerical, visual perceptual, and for auditory material. Probably there are many more, but less general, abilities of this kind. Thus, we all know the man who can remember all the names of the horses running during the current weeks of the flat-racing season : his is too specific an ability for us to trouble very much about. The verbal memory ability, however, seems to cover the ability to learn poetry readily, to learn lists of isolated words, to remember information of a literary kind. Similarly the numerical memory shows itself in special facility with the learning of mathematical formulæ, information about numbers, learning of long lists of numbers, etc.

It seems that these are different abilities : if one person is gifted in verbal memory, this is no indication at all of how gifted he is in the other memory abilities. Moreover, it does not follow that the person with the greatest memory ability for numbers *knows* most about numbers or mathematics. What he knows is the result of training and opportunity. What his ability is may depend on this training, but it also may be quite independent of it : it may be an *innate* ability, an inborn factor. More often than not, of course, we might find that these memory abilities depend on how much the individuals are interested in numbers, words, and the like. But the interest may in the first place have been due to a special inborn ability, since, to be sure, nothing succeeds like success, and if an individual finds that he can readily learn poetry by heart he is likely to grow up with an interest in such matters.

MEMORY NOT A SIGN OF INTELLIGENCE

THERE would seem to be no all-round ability for memory. A person usually has a good memory for some things and a bad one for others. We can see how these special memories enter into other abilities : Mozart, for instance, must have had a phenomenal auditory memory, since he only needed to play a long piece of music once in order to remember it. It has been found, too, that memory abilities have very little to do with intelligence. The most intelligent person has not necessarily got the best memory abilities, and there are mentally defective children with astonishingly efficient memories.

Generally speaking, we psychologists are very careful not to judge a person's intelligence on his or her memory abilities :

we are a little suspicious of people with only excellent memories to commend them. But, to some extent, the more intelligent the person the more he is able to memorise, and the better his memory : this might be evidence for the theory that has already been mentioned, that often we use correlate eduction, and believe that we have remembered what in fact we have newly educed. As we shall see, eduction seems to be the hall-mark of intelligence, and this might partly explain the connection between memory abilities and intelligence ability.

But what of the theory of persisting subconscious states ? We see the significance of some such theory if we ask whether we can improve our memories. We certainly seem to be able to improve them in the following narrow way. We may be quite unable to remember the order of appearance of shops in a street well known to us, even though we have walked down that street all the days of our life. But this is because we have never really cognised sufficient about these shops, even though we have seen them every day. If next time we walk down this street we carefully notice all the shops, their names, where their windows are, etc., then we shall be very much more likely to remember all these matters later, purely because we have now cognised them, whereas before we have never clearly done so.

Once we have noticed, or observed, or attended to these various details as a whole (all cognitive activities), then we tend to remember them all as a whole, apparently without any intention on our part. But if in addition we make a firm *intention* to remember these various details (a volitional activity, although it may be that the intention is often merely a way of saying that we have attended with great clearness to the matter), then we shall be still more likely to succeed. And if, as we walk down the street, we close our eyes and test our recall of the order of appearance of the shops, then there is still more likelihood that we shall better remember the order.

To improve our memory in the above respects, we have merely to be sure that we have really cognised, make a firm intention to remember, and make frequent tests of how much we have retained by testing it. This is true also of learning lists of words or poetry.

TESTS THAT GIVE A CLUE TO TEMPERAMENT

THERE remains for consideration another memory ability, called *fluency of ideas*, about which a considerable amount of research work is being done to-day. The ability is quite easy to measure with tests of the following kind :

1. *Say as many words as you can, all different, in 1 minute.*
2. *Say all the words you can in 1 minute that begin with the letter L.*
3. *Say as many two-syllable words as you can, like " often," " given," in 1 minute.*

People who succeed well at any one of these tests, tend to do so at others, and the person who gives the longest lists of words per minute has, of course, apparently the greatest ability of this kind. At present we do not know how this ability is related to other memory abilities ; but we know that it is in no way related to intelligence. Some highly intelligent people find peculiar difficulty in the tests. The tests involve the ready recall of simple words that should be, one would think, quite free to rise to consciousness with ready fluency. It has been found that the person who does best at these tests is often of a cheerful disposition, happy, original-minded, temperamental. They are, indeed, perhaps the only tests of temperament known to psychology. But what do they indicate from the point of view of memory, especially of the recall stage of memory ? The best thing to be said, for the present, is that perhaps the most fluent person carries a mass of subconscious states in a condition ready for fluent recall.

OLD LAMPS AND NEW

OUR memories, certainly, are in some way concerned with experiences we have once had. But it is a mistake to suppose that the mind holds perfect copies of these past experiences, like small lamps tucked away somewhere in the brain that are ever ready to light up and become conscious. There is always something new about what we recall. We have to bring what is being recalled clearly into consciousness, and this involves everything that enters into any other cognition.

It is easy to appreciate, therefore, that the act of recalling allows for many changes to be made, many new features to be emphasised, and many details to be added to what we believe is recalled in a pure and untouched state from the storehouse of the mind. Nevertheless, it is important to draw a clear distinction between what is recalled, and the essentially new cognitions of which we are capable from

minute to minute. I can never recall experiences that I had
at Scarborough last year if I was never there ; but I can
certainly think about Scarborough, and have new thoughts
about it.

We have now, then, to examine the essentially new cognitions we make. These, we have hinted, are all subserved
by the processes of *eduction*—the eduction of relations when
we are actively analysing or synthesising our ideas, or when
we are organising them in one way or another, and the eduction of correlates when we are producing either the least or
the greatest flights of the imagination. We have already
seen that, besides the memory activities, there are many
other classes of cognitions.

As before, the individual psychologist sets out patiently to
measure all these different *acts*, to see whether different
abilities can be measured for them. Is there a special ability
for each of these classes of cognitions, or are they all one and
the same ability in disguise ? These are all ways in which
new cognitions arise to mind, and it is of great interest that
there does seem to be one ability running through all these
different classes. Research shows that one ability is necessary and essential for them all, although there are, in the
case of some of the above types of cognition, lesser abilities
added to this common one.

The common or general ability we call eductive ability,
although most psychologists have another name for it, " intelligence." For my own part, when I talk of intelligence I
mean eductive ability.

HOW A BABY'S INTELLIGENCE IS MEASURED

EVEN the young baby educes relations. But how are we to
measure this ability to educe relations for such young
children ? It has to be remembered that the measurement is
effected, whenever we measure an ability, in terms of the
individual differences shown by a group of people. In this
way we might decide to compare (which is really what we
do) the abilities of as many children as we can between the
ages 6 months and, say, 2 years of age. Suppose that we
begin with 50 babies, all physically sound, each just 6 months
old, and follow their careers until they are 2 years old. We
shall suppose that all have similar homes, and all are happy
and well looked after. We shall suppose, too, that the
parents know nothing at all about what is to be done to their

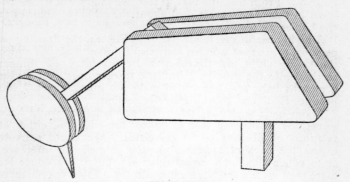

13. TOY TEST

babies. We would give each baby some toys of a special
kind, and a psychologist would observe the babies, separately
in their own nurseries, playing with them. One such toy
might be a tray of brass weights, of different diameters and
lengths, each fitting into its own recess in the tray.

The psychologist would note at what age the baby began
to lift these weights out of their recesses, and when it first
tried to replace weights so lifted. At a year we would notice,
perhaps, that it tries to replace weights by a trial-and-error
method, trying first one recess and then another before
finding one large enough to hold the weight. Next we would
observe at what age the child is satisfied only when the
weights fit nicely into their correct recesses—it feels and sees
that a small weight does not properly fit a large recess, and
thereupon proceeds to find a recess fitting the weight. At
$1\frac{1}{2}$ years of age a baby under my observation was able to
replace 15 such weights correctly in their recesses (all the
recesses being empty to begin with), the weights differing
in diameter one from another by only 2 mm.

Next, we observe at what age the child begins to depart
from the crude trial-and-error method, and instead picks up
a large weight, and now without trying it in the first recess
it may happen upon, proceeds instead to try it only in large
recesses. At 2 years of age the baby may see (educe) that
the large weight and the large recess are alike in some way,
and trial and error is no longer the method it uses to attain

its ends. From this one toy (or test, we might call it) we can learn in this way a great deal about the eductive abilities of the babies we test.

A highly useful toy, made use of in Fig. 13, the drawing on page 63, consists of wooden sections of different shapes which the young child can fit together by inserting the thinner sections into the grooves round the thicker ones. At 1 year 9 months baby may set out to make a " quack-quack," and produce the figure shown from five sections.

About each such toy, then, the psychologist would have something to observe that is *critical* for eduction, either of relations of likeness or of correlates. We could scarcely expect the baby of 1 year 9 months to make an inference, or to educe a difficult causal relation ; but it can educe far more than we are apt to give it credit for. From the observations of the child's free activity with such toys the psychologist can estimate the number of instances of eduction of a clearly recognisable kind made by the child. The baby who educes most quickly and most frequently, and who gives the most brilliant flashes of correlate eduction, who makes all the eductions at an early age that most babies make at a later age, that baby will have the highest eductive ability of those compared in the study I have been describing.

It is important to note that we would not confuse eductions of the above kind with the child's language ability. But, properly examined, even the baby's vocabulary could help us to determine the nature of its eductions and their frequency.

Now, although no one has yet made a very comprehensive study of the kind outlined above, many psychologists have really made use of the same notions in constructing tests for measuring, or scaling, the intelligence of young pre-school children. It has been found that, *on the average*, children at 9 months of age will look for a spoon that has fallen out of their hands, or will look at themselves knowingly in a mirror. On the average, an 8 months' baby can perform neither of these perceptual feats. At 2 years of age the average baby can draw vertical or horizontal lines on paper.

We require only a large number of such tests, as they are called, and intelligence is at once made measurable. If your baby can solve all the tests of an average 9 months' old baby, but not any tests involving greater maturity than this, its *mental age* is said to be 9 months. If its chronological age is

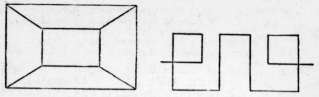

14. A MENTAL SNAPSHOT

A Binet Test for children of 9. The child is allowed to look at the figures for ten seconds and then asked to draw them from memory.

also 9 months, baby is up to the average for these tests. If it is only 6 months old, then it is considerably brighter than the average baby of 6 months : it is indeed as bright as the average 9 months' baby. The fact can be expressed as a mental ratio, as we shall see later.

BINET TACKLES A TWO-THOUSAND YEARS' OLD PROBLEM

A BINET, a Parisian psychologist, was the first to realise, in 1903, that intelligence could be measured relative to a scale in the way described above. Binet is indeed a notable figure in psychology : apart from his work on intelligence he was perhaps the first to do purely psychological work on reasoning, a topic that had engaged the minds of men from philosophical and logical viewpoints for over two thousand years. A sample of Binet's tests (as revised for use in London by Professor Burt) will give some idea of the essential simplicity of the world-famous Binet-Simon test :

The average three-year-old child is able to—
    (a) point to its nose, mouth, and eyes upon request ;
    (b) give its sex—" Are you a boy or a girl ? "
    (c) name a penny, pocket-knife, and a key.
The average four-year-old child is able to—
    (a) count four pennies ;
    (b) compare two lines and say which is the longer.
The average five-year-old performs the following :
    (a) draws a square from a copy ;
    (b) says how old he is ;
    (c) names the colours red, yellow, green, blue ;
    (d) says which is the heavier of two weights.
The average six-year-old can—
    (a) count 13 pennies ;
    (b) draw a diamond from a copy.

3

The average seven-year-old is able to—
(a) recognise missing features in a drawing of a
face (*e.g.* nose, eye, mouth missing) ;
(b) say what is the difference between a fly and a
butterfly, wood and glass, paper and cardboard.

There are tasks of this kind for all ages from 3 to 16.
It might be thought that children have to be *taught* most of
the tasks, and that they therefore cannot be very satisfactory
tests of eductive ability or of intelligence. The point about
the tasks is this, however, that no amount of teaching at,
say, 2 years of age will make it possible for the child to name
the colours red, green, etc. (a five-year-old task). A certain
maturity is needed that no amount of training can offset,
and that which matures (amongst other things) is the child's
ability to educe more and more difficult relations, and more
and more complex correlates. If a boy can solve all the tasks
up to and including those for the average eight-year-old his
mental age is said to be 8 years, irrespective of his chronological
age. The Binet test is used for measuring a child's *intelligence
quotient*, or mental ratio, which is simply the ratio of the
child's mental age to its chronological age, expressed as a
percentage. That is—

$$\text{I.Q.} = 100 \times \frac{\text{Mental Age}}{\text{Chronological Age}}.$$

Thus, if the boy with a mental age of 8 years is only 6 years
old chronologically, his I.Q. is 133. The baby who solved
all the tasks up to and including those of an 8 months' baby,
and whose chronological age was only 6 months, would also
have an I.Q. of 133. It seems that, within limits, a child's
I.Q. remains constant throughout its life. Most individuals,
children and adults, have an I.Q. between 85 and 115. A
child is likely to be brilliant if its I.Q. is 140 or more, and the
highest I.Q. ever recorded is in the neighbourhood of 190.
It has been estimated that, of all the geniuses down the pages
of history—Newton, Descartes, Bacon, Aquinas, Shakespeare,
Milton, and so on in glorious array—John Stuart Mill had
perhaps the highest I.Q., a figure round about 200. Which
means that at 5 years of age, Mill could do all the tasks of
the average ten-year-old. On the other side of the picture,
mental deficiency is suspected if an individual's I.Q. is less
than 70, and mental idiots have much less than this. There
are men and women with mental ages of only 2 years or less.

Although a person's I.Q. remains approximately constant, his mental age of course increases gradually from year to year, the increase becoming less and less marked after the age of 14 to 16 years. The higher the original I.Q., the higher, so it seems, the individual's mental age grows. The idiot stops growing, mentally, at 8 years of age, whereas the

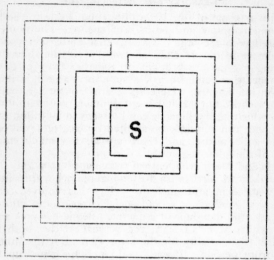

15. MAZE GUIDE TO MENTAL AGE

A Porteus Test for children of 14½. The child is asked to find a way out from the centre of the maze. If a mistake is made, he is started again from the centre. The number of trials required is a guide to his " mental age."

highly intelligent individual can continue growing in eductive ability until he is 30 years old or more.

The constancy of the I.Q. raises the question, Is intelligence innate, or acquired ? Is it handed down by heredity, or does each child begin, like a clean slate, to be made intelligent or stupid by the training it gets ? Is it better to be born with a silver spoon in one's mouth, with all the advantages that wealth and a happy environment can afford, or is one's intelligence independent of environment ? Measurements by means of the Binet test show that identical twins tend to have very similar intelligence quotients, and that children of highly intelligent parents tend also to be highly intelligent. The children of professional men have an average I.Q. of 115, whilst those of labouring-class parents have only 95 on the average.

HEREDITY AND INTELLIGENCE

WHILST some of this large difference is due to the better opportunities and culture of the one set of children compared with the other, it seems that perhaps not all of it is so determined. If children from professional and from labouring parents are brought up together from birth in an orphanage, the child from the superior parents is itself of superior intelligence. Heredity seems to set its mark for ever on a child, but a suitable environment is certainly necessary in which its intelligence can blossom to its fullest extent. Intelligence can certainly be stunted by lack of social opportunities and culture, and there are all too many cases on record of the following kind :

Bessie and Mary are identical twins, aged 16 years. Bessie has lived from birth with foster-parents who are illiterate, poverty-stricken, and unclean. Mary has enjoyed all that music, art, good schools, and social contacts can afford her as the adopted daughter of a doctor. Bessie has now an I.Q. of 98, whilst Mary's is 115, yet we suspect that both began life with a potentiality for the same I.Q. But the Binet test is far from perfect. Bessie would perhaps show up better in a more satisfactory test of I.Q., whilst Mary might not, after all, be really as intelligent as the 115 I.Q. would have us suppose.

The Binet test, which supplies the I.Q. measurement, is itself to some extent dependent on culture. It is interesting that it is more subject to social influences than to physical ones. A child can have enlarged tonsils or adenoids, be under-nourished, and be subject to severe colds without its I.Q. being materially influenced. But a chronic emotional disturbance, and a poor environment, may affect the I.Q. very much indeed. Certain canal-boat children, and the children of wandering gipsies, had an I.Q. of only 65 on the average when measured by the Binet test ; yet no one would say that these children are anything like so low in intelligence as this. More about backward children will be found in the section, *Education in a Changing World.*

SOME TESTS INSPIRED BY BINET'S SCALE

THERE are, of course, many other tests of intelligence besides the Binet-Simon. Many have been devised to try to obviate some of the faults of the Binet, and almost everyone has heard of the intelligence tests that many educational committees apply nowadays in their annual scholarship examinations. It is interesting to look for a moment at some of the better-known types of tests that can be applied to children in the same way as one applies written papers on arithmetic or English.

The following are samples of verbal tests of intelligence :

1. SYNONYM-ANTONYMS.

If the two words have the same meaning, put an " S " between them ; if they are opposites in meaning, put an " O " between them :

good	.	.	.	bad
conquer	.	.	.	subdue
gather	.	.	.	scatter
administer	.	.	.	superintend
endless	.	.	.	perpetual

2. CLASSIFICATION.

In each set of four words three mean things that are alike in some way. Cross out the remaining word :

comb	hammer	scissors	brush
table	stool	wood	box
there	here	when	down
message	book	write	know
anxiety	trepidation	flurry	excitement

3. DISARRANGED SENTENCES.

In each of the following sentences cross out the two words that have been interchanged :
(*a*) The furiously was barking dog all night.
(*b*) The flowers began to sprout up with dreary growth, making for the vigorous months of barrenness.
(*c*) A kind man may have cause for his feelings, but you cannot count on their being gloomy.
(*d*) The queen in her royal haste had forgotten to take off her crown and her great robes.

4. ANALOGIES.

Pick out that word of the four on the right which best
completes the sentence on the left :

Good is to *Bad* as *White* is to . horse black toy evil
Drum is to *Beat* as *Whistle* is to . play tune blow fingers
Dirt is to *Soap* as *Ink* is to . paper black eraser pen
Money is to *Cheap* as *War* is to . g l o r i o u s successful
                                           easy bloodless

5. INFERENCES.

Answer the following questions :

(a) Mary has a pink dress and red hair ; Joan has a
blue dress but has not got red hair ; Molly
has black hair and a green dress ; Ann has
red hair and a blue dress. One of these four
has black hair and a blue dress, which is it ?

(b) A runs faster than B, but slower than C ; B runs
faster than D : who runs fastest—A, B, C,
or D ?

Recent experiments have shown, however, that tests of the
above verbal nature measure not only eductive ability, but
also something in the nature of verbal facility. Thus, the
arts students in a university succeed very much better, on
the average, than the science students in tests like Numbers
1, 2, and 3 above. On the other hand, the science students
are superior in the analogies test (No. 4). The tests 1, 2,
and 3 are just what we might expect arts students to do well
at, since it is their daily work to be interested in words. But
the analogies test can involve eduction more critically than
it does mere words and their meanings, and hence the science
student proves his superior eductive ability when the test
is a fair one of eduction. But perhaps the difference is not
that the average science student is really more intelligent
than the average arts student (although I believe that there
is some evidence in that direction) ; it may be merely that
the science student is trained more than the arts student to
think logically and systematically, which would certainly help
him in the analogies test.

Nowadays a great deal of attention is being given to non-
verbal tests of eductive ability. Tests of the following kind
measure eductive ability very well under many circumstances.
In the left-hand test in Fig. 16 find the line in each row that
slopes away most from the vertical *direction*. In the right-hand
drawing pair together the figures in top and bottom rows
whose lines have identical *proportions*.

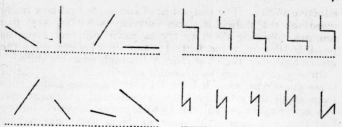

16. TESTS WITHOUT WORDS

In tests of the above kind care is taken to ensure that all the testees know precisely what has to be done : thereafter it is only the speed with which they can solve the tasks that determines their score. The psychologist thus tries to measure eductive ability without use of words or past experiences.

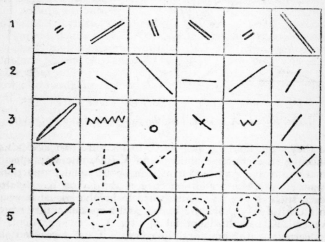

17. THE SERIES TEST

Find the two drawings in each set that must be interchanged to make a progressive series of lines increasing regularly in length.

There are very many different tests of the non-verbal kind, and by use of them we seem best able to measure eductive ability. The method is, of course, to find how many questions the individuals can correctly solve in, say, five minutes, allowing them to try as many different types as possible (the more the better) ; and he who can solve the greatest number the most quickly has high eductive ability.

In any case, when we measure eductive ability by use of these non-verbal tests it is found that the same ability runs through all the activities, such as reasoning, judgment, etc. We can measure the abilities to solve reasoning tests, and we find that it is largely the same ability as that measured by these non-verbal tests. But, like a planet with its moons and satellites, this eductive ability is often overlaid with other abilities. Thus, the verbal intelligence tests are now known,

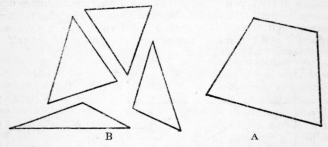

B   A

18. A TEST THAT MEASURES TWO ABILITIES

Draw lines in A to show how the figures at B can fit into it.

as they were for long suspected, to measure two abilities at once—g (the eductive ability) and V (in some way specific to tests involving verbal forms)—in about equal proportions. Another interesting addition to g is the factor K. *Spatial* tests, such as Fig. 18 (which seem to involve visual imagery in a critical way), measure both g and a special ability which we call K. A third special ability, A, seems particularly concerned with auditory imagery: it is measured by musical ability tests, but again g enters into them as well as A.

The list of special abilities can be greatly extended, even though these four are the most general (after the eductive ability). In the following family tree I have listed some of the particular abilities that can be measured :

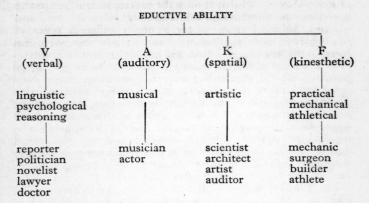

EDUCTIVE ABILITY

V (verbal)	A (auditory)	K (spatial)	F (kinesthetic)
linguistic psychological reasoning	musical	artistic	practical mechanical athletical
reporter politician novelist lawyer doctor	musician actor	scientist architect artist auditor	mechanic surgeon builder athlete

At the top of the tree the abilities are probably innate, but as we proceed downwards they become more and more dependent upon training and experience. Nor are the final abilities at the bottom of the tree supposed to be dependent on only those directly above it : to some extent something of all will enter into every final ability of which man is capable. If it seems surprising that I should call " doctoring " an ability, it has only to be remembered that if need be we certainly could measure doctors for their ability to look after the patients they serve, and that the doctor has ability that the auditor hasn't. The ability, of course, is largely a result of training ; but it may still depend on some of the other abilities, themselves less open to training. There can be no doubt, for instance, that the most successful doctor requires high g ability and high psychological ability, as well as a reasonable practical ability and kinesthetic ability, if he is to be a successful surgeon.

EVERY MAN A GENIUS AT SOMETHING

THE above family tree is concerned only with cognitive activities ; but the end-products, whether a man becomes a lawyer or an artist, etc., will depend upon other activities, upon his character and temperament, as well as upon what opportunity has come his way. There is no end to the number of highly special abilities that we might add to this table. It is probably true that everyone is a bit of a genius at something—even if it is only the extraordinary facility that one man has in fastening up his waistcoat.

Before I describe a few of these special abilities it is as well to note that I always talk about *abilities* : in every case something is measured, and that something is undoubtedly *behaviour* in the widest sense of the word. The people tested have to respond in specific ways to certain situations, and upon the kind of responses made we measure their abilities. I can never hope to measure their *capacities*, but only the actual manifestation of them as abilities. Thus, although I began from a purely idealistic and mental point of view in psychology, by talking about consciousness and the like, I end as much a behaviourist as any psychologist—psychology is made to depend upon the abilities measured, and the abilities can only be measured in terms of the person's behaviour.

But it is time to look a little further into some of the special abilities. The V ability, popularly called verbal intelligence, is still the subject of researches, and we know very little about its nature. It is obviously connected, however, with the ability to form *gestalt* with verbal material. Closely connected with V are the linguistic, psychological, and reasoning abilities. Linguistic ability is best seen in a secondary school, where girls are often superior to boys in the mechanical learning of modern languages. But language abilities become very specialised as we grow, so that men are usually more inventive than women with respect to verbal material, making them the better essayists and novelists.

Reasoning ability is usually regarded as the highest level of all in the scale of intelligence, or of intellect, and the highest flights of intellect, presumably, are needed in syllogistic deductions of the following kind :

> " *All men are mortal.*
> *Socrates is a man.*
> *Therefore Socrates is mortal.*"

For many of the older philosophers reasoning was an infallible process, the method by which eternal truths were made known to man. Great philosophers like St. Augustine, St. Thomas Aquinas, Locke, Kant, Spinoza, Plato, and Aristotle, wrote about reasoning without ever finding out anything truly psychological about it. The early psychologists like Wundt, William James, and Pillsbury were equally lost in the logical and philosophical aspects of reasoning.

19. WHICH OF THE FOLLOWING STATEMENTS APPLIES TO THIS PICTURE?

(*a*) *The old man says:* " *Will you tell me or not?* " *and the man with the black moustache answers:* " *Why should I?* "

(*b*) *The old man says:* " *So that's it, is it?* " *and the other man says:* " *My heavens! What have I done!* "

(*c*) *The old man says:* " *I think I've seen you before,*" *and the other answers:* " *Oh, I don't think so, sir.*"

It was only in 1874 with Brentano and Binet that reasoning began to be regarded from the psychological viewpoint. Binet, after a series of experiments, could find no difference between mere perception and reasoning in respect of the processes entering into the experiments. Reasoning merely involved shifts of attention and mental imagery, otherwise there was nothing mysterious about it. Recent experiments bear out Binet's conclusion that there is no essential difference between perception and reasoning: both involve eduction in a critical way. Moreover, a simple non-verbal test like that illustrated on page 71, in which the directions of different lines have to be compared, can measure eductive ability every bit as well as almost any reasoning test. Some very interesting work has been done, too, with syllogisms of the above kind, in which it has been shown that one cannot improve one's ability to educe the conclusion to the syllogism. No amount of practice can increase the speed at which the eduction is made.

Many verbal tests of intelligence include reasoning tests of the following kind :

> " *Tom runs faster than Jim :*
> *Jack runs slower than Jim :*
> *Which is the slowest of the three ?* "

Dr. Murdoch tried out some twenty types of reasoning tests of the above kind in an experiment performed at University College, London, to see whether a special ability was needed to solve them other than eductive ability. He found that all the tests involved eduction (g) as well as the verbal ability (V), and that only four involved something in addition that might be called the " reasoning " ability.

Another special ability, which at first sight cannot seem to involve anything other than the fruits of experience, is called " psychological " because it concerns the facility with which some individuals are able to judge the character and conduct, the moods, idiosyncrasies, and sentiments of their neighbours. They somehow know what a twitching lip portends, what wide-open eyes and the seemingly aimless movement of an arm may mean, and somehow perceive these when others would never do so. In the same way there are special tests for measuring musical abilities, mechanical abilities, and so forth. None of them can be measured, it would seem, free from eductive ability, although they would be if we concerned ourselves only with individuals of the same intelligence or eductive ability.

The *Gestalt* psychologists have had much to say about wholes and configurations, and the rôle these play in cognitive organisation. Tests of the following kind have been used to discover whether some people are better able than others to perceive visual " wholes."

How quickly have you been able to grasp what the drawing opposite represents ? With many items of this kind we can measure how well individuals are able to grasp them. But so measured, it is found that the ability has very little to do with intelligence as measured by all other tests : as we might suspect, tests of this kind depend critically on past experience (if we had never seen a cow, or a drawing of one, we might have

20. PICTURE PUZZLE

perceived the above as a chair, or something else), perhaps on *fluency of ideas*, perhaps on visual imagery, or perhaps it is a narrow and special ability to perceive visual perceptual *wholes*. In any case, it does not seem to be the essential and crucial kind of process that we look for as the basis of cognitive organisation.

The measurement of abilities over the wide range described in previous pages thus supplements the conclusions we drew from our study of conscious activity : when we measure eductive ability in any one class of cognition, it is found that the same ability stretches into all other classes, from the mere estimating of length on the one hand to the most recondite acts of reasoning on the other, and this is what might be expected if there is such an important process as eduction underlying all mental organisation. The *Gestalt* processes do not seem to serve in this all-comprehensive way.

THE MENTAL PROCESSES OF GENIUS

THERE are still other cognitive abilities that can be measured, especially interesting ones being imagination and suggestibility. Two different abilities lie confused in the word " imagination." Tests of correlate eduction [1] measure the constructive, intelligent features of an imaginative kind, whilst less controlled imagination, with its random flights of ideas and lack of control, is much the same thing as *fluency* of ideas, the tests for which were described.[2] The person with the ready fluency is likely to be regarded as highly imaginative ; but the world's constructive thinkers, artists, actors, inventors, scientists, and teachers make use of a very different ability, that of eduction of relations and correlates. Most tests of intelligence involve the eduction of relations only, and very few measurements have ever been made of the more inventive correlate eduction—it is difficult to ensure that past experiences play no part in the tests devised for measuring correlate eduction.

Finally, a paragraph on *suggestion* and *suggestibility*. Are some people more suggestible than others, and how does such an ability fit into our cognitive scheme ? The young child, from 1 year to 1 year 6 months in the case of my daughter, is very highly suggestible. That is, we have only to say, " Go get your teddy," and baby immediately obeys, wherever she is and whatever she is doing. Of course she has to know what and where her teddy is. But soon it takes all one's persuasion to get baby to obey quite so unhesitatingly. Soon it is as likely to do the opposite as it is to do what one so badly wants it to do. But what the baby grows out of as an individual it retains when it is a member of a crowd. A cry of : " Lynch him ! " is accepted absolutely unhesitatingly by the howling mob, just as : " Go get your teddy " is accepted by baby.

WHY WE SUCCUMB TO THE ADVERTISEMENT SLOGAN

SUGGESTION, then, is best regarded from the viewpoint of " memory." We first acquire beliefs without adequate grounds to support them : we retain what is so learnt, and afterwards we are *suggestible* about these beliefs—that is, they are recalled and are still accepted uncritically. Having had suggested to us from countless hoardings that " Fivexe's Beer is best of all," it is more than likely that next time we want a drink, the word " Fivexe " will occur immediately to mind. A person is not suggestible to ideas that are not already held in his mind. All the suggestion in the world will never make me drink " Fivexe's beer " if I am a staunch

[1] See page 69.   [2] See page 61.

teetotaller. And how extraordinary a thing is suggestion ! If a comedian makes a " broad " joke on the wireless, a minor storm is raised in the wireless world. But he can be highly suggestive on the same matter, and all is well !

Again, if men and women run amok, lynching and butchering a fellow human being, there must be something retained in their minds, something of which they are capable, deeply down perhaps and normally repressed, that lends itself to this inhuman behaviour. We have strange hints of memory contents in the mind, strange behaviour of which we are still capable on occasion, archbishop and thief, philanthropist and gambler alike.

All these various abilities, then, can be regarded as evidences of " structures of the mind." By which we mean that people have these various abilities, and by which we infer that either there are actual structures corresponding to them, or, more precisely, underlying *processes* accounting for them. By measuring abilities we begin from psychological facts, and we hope to find out something about the processes.

LIGHTS AND SHADES OF PERSONALITY : THE SENTIMENTS AND THE EMOTIONS

HAVING examined the cognitive, it is now time to look more closely at the affective (" feeling ") structures of the mind, whilst, later, volitional structures will need our attention. I have already introduced the topic of " feelings " (pages 53–55), but did not attempt to specify any laws for these features of our conscious experiences. As usual, let us begin by asking whether the " affects," as they are called, have been classified into apparently different groups or classes.

There is in the first place a broad group of simple feelings of pleasure, and of " unpleasure " : the first time I see a glowing colour, or hear a sweet tone, I experience them as pleasant, whilst a harsh tone or colour I experience at once as disagreeable. Wundt (1832–1920), the great experimentalist, founder of psychological laboratories, considered that there are three different kinds of affects of this elementary kind— pleasure and disagreeableness, excitement and calm, and strain and relaxation. But the classical associationists held that there are as many different feelings as there are ideas, whilst perhaps most psychologists to-day believe that there is only one elementary type of feeling—pleasure and " un-pleasure " or disagreeableness. We have a hint, at least, that it is apparently very difficult to classify such feelings.

There are, again, our *higher* feelings, the feelings some of us have of gratitude, trust, and joy, feelings of a religious, æsthetical, or political kind. These undoubtedly seem to be as numerous as ideas themselves, for we can feel the awkward-ness resulting from a *faux pas*, no less than the solemnity of a funeral. Again, many " feelings " seem to be most intim-ately connected with bodily activities—the " appetites " of hunger and sexual pleasure, together with feelings of fatigue and lassitude. Very similar, too, are our *emotions*, crude and elemental feelings of anger, rage, fear, and sensual love, the various *passions* of man.

But appetites and emotions, as we shall see later, are nowadays regarded as experiences apart from the affects : they are more intimately connected with bodily activities, whereas there is nothing directly bodily in the pleasure and " unpleasure " feelings. But our *moods* seem to be affective. Moods of ill-humour may persist all day, colouring all our experiences, from the office-boy we curse for a minor mistake to the churlish thanks we give for a favour done us. There are patients in mental hospitals, and many more outside the walls of these great and much misunderstood institutions, whose moods may last for weeks on end, dreary weeks of despondency, depression, excitement, or anxiety. Mental hospitals, indeed, have a great deal to teach us about feelings : many patients have no higher feelings, no experiences of joy, happiness, and the like.

WHAT A "FEELING" REALLY IS

LET us draw a distinction between the elementary affects and moods on the one hand, and the appetites and emo-tions on the other. What, then, can we say about the former —the affects ? We are ready to believe that a brass band is making a noise, and that a fire is hot (whereas these are our own mental states), but we make no such mistakes about our feelings. These we know are *ours* with nothing corre-sponding to them in the world outside. We project our mental experience of noise upon the innocent band, but we do not say that the door-mat is feeling annoyed when we trip up over it and feel annoyed as a consequence. It is true, of course, that we say the " sea rages," and that there are " happy hunting-grounds." But in such cases we know quite well that we are merely projecting our experiences on the feeling-less world outside, a process graced in psychology by the special name " empathy."

In the first place, then, feelings are essentially conscious experiences, and we know that *we* experience them, and that *we* cognise them. Secondly, feelings do not seem to have a *memory* value : a feeling is never recognised as something we have " remembered," but merely as something newly produced in the mind at the time. Thirdly, we know that some kinds of feelings can be combined within narrow limits, although more often than not they retain their independence. If we lose a pound note and find a shilling at the same time, the unpleasure of the one does not mix well with the lesser satisfaction of the other. If we learn that our greatest friend is dead, and at the same time that we have been unusually lucky at business, the sorrow and the pleasure come alter-nately to mind, although, to be sure, the sorrow is not so deep and sincere, and the pleasure not so unrestrained, as would have been the case had they been occasioned separately. But had the business news been gloomy, the sorrow for our friend's death would have been extremely deep.

Again, one feeling often offsets another : just as colours contrast with one another, so feelings are affected by a similar law. The danger felt at sea in a storm of drenching rain and driving wind is all the more unpleasant if we are in view of port. The grave-diggers' comedy serves to heighten the feelings we have of the impending tragedy awaiting Hamlet when, in a moment, Ophelia's bier is to be carried in.

HOW SENTIMENTS CRYSTALLISE INTO "CHARACTER"

BUT so far I have discussed the affections purely ; it will be as well to look at them in their more usual cognitive settings. Feelings become attached, so to speak, to particular cognitions or systems of ideas.

Parental love, feelings of friendship, admiration, contempt ; sentiments connected with honesty, courage, manliness, cruelty, and the like ; the masses of sentiments about our-selves, our self-esteem, pride, ambition, conceit ; all these and many more are built up as we grow, and in all of them the feelings have become attached to systems of ideas, know-ledge, and cognitions generally. According to Professor William McDougall, a person's *character* can only be understood in terms of his sentiments. These, organised into more or less harmonious wholes, with a certain continuity in their action, constitute character.

Sentiments are thus indications of more or less enduring structures of the mind, in which both cognitive and affective experiences are concerned. Again, there are those subtle and sometimes snobbish experiences, our *tastes*. One man acquires a taste for golf, another for expensive and exclusive suits, another for goldfish.

Is there a difference, then, between a taste and a sentiment ? We can have a taste for cigars, but masses of sentiment (and no taste) about our old pipes. Perhaps, as Professor McDougall suggests, there is a difference in that tastes are rather like tools, things we make use of, whereas sentiments are driving forces to action. If I am tired and feel lonely, the sentiments connected with smoking may send me in search of matches and a cosy chair, but whether I smoke cigars, cigarettes, or a pipe will depend upon my taste.

EVERYTHING MUST EITHER PLEASE OR ANNOY

WHAT, then, of the nature of all these various feelings, sentiments, and tastes ? What laws can we propose for them ? The modern theory (though it must be recalled that advances are being made continually) is that there is one and only one kind of elementary feeling experienced as degrees of either pleasure or " unpleasure." And the first law of affect might be stated as follows : *every cognitive experience tends to be experienced together with feelings of pleasure or unpleasure.* Such feelings have little or nothing to do with the great hedonistic principle of pleasure and " pain," the pleasure-pain principle that is the basis of psycho-analytical theory, and asserts that individuals strive unconsciously towards pleasurable ends, and away from painful ones. The hedonistic principle is a law of conation, not of affection. The first law of affection, if we may return to it, is true of all cognitions : we recognise tastes, noises, smells, colours, and textures or surfaces that we touch or " feel," as either pleasant or unpleasant in some degree. If it is asked why we have these feelings, then no answer can be given. They are ultimate and irreducible items for psychology.

For any other laws of affect we have to turn to more complicated matters, and here I shall give only a general indication of the background out of which such laws have to be forged. Already I have mentioned laws concerned with contrast, and combination of higher feelings, but our immediate problem is to see upon what the higher feelings themselves depend, and this we can approach from one or two different directions.

In the first place there arise *immediately* to mind, without any mediating processes of a psychological kind, certain other affective experiences besides the elementary ones of a pleasure and " unpleasure " kind. These are the emotions, appetites, and similar bodily conditioned " feelings." Emotions arise instinctively to mind. When baby hears a loud noise, fear creeps into its little mind (however dim the awareness may be for either the noise or the emotion). Similarly there are masses of bodily " feelings," of an auto-erotic kind, connected with almost every part of the body, and particularly with the sex and excretory organs, the mouth, breasts, and armpits.

HOW FEELINGS ARE BLENDED AND BEAUTIFIED

IT is supposed that just as cognitions tend to be felt as pleasurable or otherwise in some degree (first law), so these bodily-conditioned feelings are also experienced in different degrees of the same affect, and the result is experienced as a complex feeling. The two blend, so to speak, and produce the new feeling. With further complication, when complex feelings are experienced with reference to particular systems of ideas, still higher and more complicated feelings arise to mind. Thus, a dog may experience complex feelings, as when it is dispirited and cowed. Man, on the other hand, experiences still higher feelings in connection with his ideas, thoughts, wishes, and the like, as happens when he feels gratitude for the good turn that has been done him. Neither in the case of complex affects arising by a blending of simpler ones, nor in that of higher affects rising by a blending of affects with cognitive experiences, are we told, except in physiological terms, how the blending takes place.

Finally, it is as well to remember that feelings have profound effects on action. Exaggerated feelings appear to spur one to action. I know of a young man who was a brilliant success at College during the time that poverty struck him most. He drew his energy, it would seem, from anger that he felt against certain members of his family. Indeed, our social reformers tend to forget that it is not the person who has everything made easy for him who will make the best success of life.

FEELINGS AND IMAGERY

FEELINGS, too, have a decided effect on mental imagery: my most vivid, and especially my coloured dreams, are the few pleasurable dreams I have. It has been shown that those cognitions which are made under pleasurable circumstances tend to be remembered more than those either unpleasantly or indifferently felt—a hint to teachers, perhaps, to make the atmosphere of their classes and lessons as pleasurable as possible. But even cows are affected by soothing music: they give more milk if they are milked to the soft notes from a gramophone or wireless set. Unpleasant experiences, as we all know, tend to be forgotten.

There remains one further point of great interest, intimately concerned with moods, and peculiar to affects generally. It is that an affect can be *transferred* from one system of ideas to a wholly unrelated set. The gloom we feel on first arising in the morning can colour our thoughts and actions for the rest of the day.

MAINSPRINGS OF HUMAN ACTION : THE INSTINCTS

ONE more group of " feelings "—the emotions—remains to be discussed. But before we can do so we have to leave our introspective psychology and its supplementing measurement of abilities on one side and turn to many unintrospectible activities. We begin by examining what has been learnt about instincts. The word " instinct " has been given a multitude of meanings. The man-in-the-street will say that Mr. Baldwin has an " instinct " for describing proper English sentiments. If we stop walking without knowing why, to become suddenly aware that a cliff-edge yawns a foot in front of us, we say that we stopped " instinctively." Anything usual or mysterious is apt to be called " instinctive." There are some psychologists, too, who talk of the sex and life instincts even of single cells—the somatic and gonad cells, driven unceasingly as they are towards racial and individual survival. But we have already met instincts under the name of *unconditioned complex reflexes*.

For the reflexologist and behaviourist, as we have seen, these are complex systems of unconditioned (unlearnt) reflexes connected with the essentials of existence (with food and food-seeking), with *self-preservation* (pugnacity, defence, freedom, curiosity, play), and with *propagation* (sex and parental care). The sex instinct, for instance, is the sum-total of innumerable reflex systems connected with the sex organs, glands, and erogenous areas of the body, mouth, anus, and so forth. Some of these operate unceasingly in some degree, rendering the individual always in a state of prepared-ness, as though energy were being piled up for later use under appropriate stimulation.

There are other psychologists, however, who refuse to accept this mechanical theory of instincts. They agree that there are instincts connected with food, preservation and propagation ; and they agree that these are unlearnt. But they emphasise that instincts have a psychical nature, and not merely a mechanical one, Professor McDougall, for instance, stresses this. He holds that instincts are essentially teleological and hormic. Let us see what this means.

DOES "INSTINCT" MAKE THE SWALLOW FLY SOUTH?

IT is well known that birds, in due season, migrate across the miles of sea, as though aware of a "goal" ahead. McDougall believes that the bird is really aware, in however dim a fashion, of its present and past experiences, and of the goal to which it has to aim, the foreign district to which it has to fly. The facts are, according to McDougall, (1) that the complex reflex systems make the bird ready for the motor activities to be endured ; (2) that it is guided by an awareness, however vague, of the goal that it has to seek ; (3) that the activity once initiated tends to continue until the goal is reached ; (4) that the activity ceases when the goal is reached ; and (5) progress towards the goal brings with it pleasurable experiences, whilst thwarting and failure lead to disagreeable or unpleasant feelings.

Thus there is a certain solitary wasp, born alone and out of all contact with other wasps, which proceeds in the first moments of its maturity to kill spiders or insects of a particular species, and to place the prey in a prearranged straw stalk together with an egg, which in turn will develop into a solitary wasp and repeat the same instinctive cycle. The core of this instinct, according to McDougall, is that the wasp is aware, in however vague a fashion, of the end to be pursued, or of the separate steps towards it. The end to be pursued arises, as it were, as a " memory." With this single " thought " in its mind, so to speak, the insect pursues it to its instinctive conclusion. As the insect proceeds towards this goal or end-in-view, it may make unconscious " will " acts or series of such acts directed towards the goal. The total picture is that of an insect striving with a purpose towards an end that it has " remembered." This, in any case, is McDougall's " hormic " theory of instinct.

THE ELUSIVE QUALITY OF INSTINCTS

VERY few psychologists accept this teleological theory of instinct. It all seems to be too highly anthropomorphic, as though lowly insects have essentially human abilities. But, of course, they would be abilities of a very rudimentary (or highly specialised) form. For my own part, I agree with Professor McDougall that living behaviour cannot be explained completely in terms of the behaviourist's notions of a physical kind, and that we are left to make what use we can of the only other notions we have, those of a purely psychological kind, such as " awareness " and " volition." But man has no instincts in the sense that insects have them : rather he has tendencies and propensities only, reservoirs of energy on top of which all his wealth of cognition and volition can operate along lines laid down by social and individual educative forces.

McDougall believes that man has eighteen distinct propensities. Many propensities described by McDougall have been exhaustively investigated, and prove to be extremely complex things indeed. Perhaps it will be sufficient here to take the case of the parental propensity. McDougall only saw in this the beautiful care of a mother for her baby. But infanticide, if we look broadly at the history of man, has been almost as common as parental care. In Greece, babies were put on the hillside to brave the elements for life or death. Even the dog is as likely as not to eat its own puppies when they are born.

Many psychologists have therefore gone to the other extreme, saying that parental care in man is just a custom, a thing expected of us, and accordingly done under the force of social edicts. From this they jump still further afield, to say that there are no instincts at all, all being the result of learning and habit formation. But actually a whole book can be written about the innate forces, the cross-currents of emotion and fear and anxiety that enter into childbirth and parenthood.

A FORMULA TO EXPLAIN THE INSTINCTS

A REFLEX arc, as we have seen, can be represented by S→R. A stimulus (S) is given, and the response (R) follows, as when the knee is tapped (S) and the knee-jerk is the response (R). The same formula seems to apply for instincts. There is stimulation followed by some kind of motor response. The young lamb, we say, instinctively follows its dam. It sees the dam move away (the stimulation), and thereupon it follows (motor activity). The motor activity, however, is not necessarily part of the instinct proper—the lamb may skip, gambol, frisk, or walk with ungainly mien, as it will, so long as it reaches its objective—the dam. The core of the instinct is the *disposition* to follow.

What, then, is this disposition ? Is it a conative drive towards an end or " goal," both of which, the drive and an awareness of the goal to be reached, arise instinctively, mechanically, and invariably in the lamb's mind ? The behaviourist, of course, would remind us that the word " conation " is deluding us : what we want to call conation is, for him, just a complex chain of reflexes. The boomerang has no conation, but it reaches its " goal," nevertheless, purely by physical means : so, too, for the behaviourist all " conation " is equally purely a matter of reflexes.

Few psychologists would agree with McDougall that an awareness, an image or photograph, of the goal to be reached, rises instinctively to the lamb's mind. It is simpler to believe that as the dam moves away its lamb feels uneasy, and this uneasiness, it finds, is removed when it goes towards its mother. The instinctive formula then becomes S→F→R, the stimulus serving to raise a feeling (F), which, under a primitive urge to free itself from miscomfort, the lamb finds is removed by appropriate action (R). The core of the instinct is a *feeling*, and for the rest the animal learns to make appropriate motor responses. Many innate propensities in human beings seem to have this pattern : their core is a state of emotion. Professor McDougall has suggested, most brilliantly, that each of the instinctive human drives has attached to it in this way a primary (instinctive) emotion. The sex drive has lust as its emotional concomitant, whilst the parental drive has with it the *tender* emotion of parenthood.

The formula given above for reflexes, S→F→R, seems to accord well with the common view of action, no less than with these propensities. If I see danger ahead, I no doubt feel afraid, and take to flight accordingly, or act in some other appropriate way. If I am confronted with a truly horrible sight, say that of a child butchered on a roadway, a feeling of sickening disgust and horror rises to mind, and I try to withdraw from so frightful a scene. I have noticed something very akin to wonder in young children, and no doubt an appropriate feeling is experienced, after which the child continues to look fixedly at the thing occasioning the wonder. Similarly, of all the propensities it can be said, although sometimes with a decided stretch of the imagination, that first an emotion is raised, and after that appropriate action takes place.

But doubts come to mind. I may be hit, and feel hurt, and thereupon strike back. But I may strike my opponent immediately, and only afterwards feel the anger and hurt. If I see a lion at large I will probably take to my heels at once, and only when I am safe shall I be prostrate with fear. If I step unwittingly in front of a car on the roadway, I step back instantly, and the anger and relief are experienced only after the car has passed me and I am safe.

In the same way there are soldiers who fight fearlessly in action but are prostrate with fear when all danger is over. Nevertheless, McDougall's formula seems to represent the native or original state of affairs in human beings. We perceive ; this raises a state of feeling ; and we act. But we can also control our emotion, repressing it and keeping it out of consciousness. But it functions willy-nilly, and when the control is released the emotion is discharged. If we lose this control, then we would frequently be paralysed with the force of the emotion. It serves no useful end to face a lion when we are paralysed with fear ; it is better to run from it and be afraid afterwards.

The psycho-analyst uses the same notion that under stimulation certain emotions or feelings are raised, and should result in motor action. But instead, the tendencies to emotion are often repressed, and may remain repressed for years. If they remain repressed all is well, but the trouble occurs when the repression or control is ineffective and the emotion so long repressed bursts forth as depression, anxiety, melancholia, nervousness, and so forth, or when it leads to motor activity of an extraordinary or bizarre kind, like suicide.

INSTINCTS : THE DRIVING FORCES OF LIFE

IT is not surprising to learn that there are men and women who have to be taught what constitutes a sexual act, for this in man is no longer instinctual in its totality. The dull, dumb sexual instinct in a child is little more than the interest it takes in its nose, mouth, genital organs, and body generally. The baby first plays with its mother's nipple, then perhaps with its own navel, and later with its nose, mouth, genitals, and anus. These are the first actions of the sexual instinct. In this sense, and as we gather from the fantasy and interest shown about and in their parents, children have this sexual instinct in two phases—one from birth to 5 or 6 years of age, and the other from puberty onwards. At puberty the sexual instinct is not quite the simple and glamorous thing that McDougall would have us think it is.

The psycho-analysts hold, with Professor Freud, that there are two broad systems or sets of instincts—the sex-instincts and the ego or self-assertive instincts. We can appreciate the complexity of the sex-instincts when we recall all that enters into child-bearing alone. The ego-instincts are no less complex and elaborate. These two instincts are, for the analyst, the driving forces of life. They supply the energy that man uses in his thinking, his abilities, his learning. They are the petrol, as it were, to keep the motor running ; but they are also gyroscopes that give the direction in which man will expend this energy. All culture is but a way in which this energy is used.

EMOTIONS THAT HAVE OVERTHROWN EMPIRES :
LOVE, FEAR, RAGE

BUT not everyone will accept McDougall's list of emotions, nor their formation about general instincts. The behaviourist, Watson, holds that there are only three primary or elementary forms of emotion—love, fear, and rage.

The behaviourist does not regard these emotions as driving forces. Rather they are really useless, like most vestiges. They tend to delay action by throwing the individual into a state of chaos. Thus, when baby is experiencing love feelings it is not cognitively active. Baby's rage can become a paroxysm with the breath held until suffocation results and the body becomes as stiff as the rigors of death itself. Fear stupefies us, chains us to the ground, a quivering individual at the mercy of the real danger. Love, in its wider development, makes the young man a dithering creature, love-sick, incompetent, and impotent at work or play. That is, emotions are biologically useless, of no help in the struggle for existence. The world would get along much more efficiently, the behaviourist believes, if feelings and emotions were no longer born in us. Men would then be mere robots, creatures of habit and reason only.

But however emotions arise to mind, and whatever they are, they serve as nuclei about which man builds up his higher feelings and sentiments, as we saw in earlier sections. We can see, too, how readily an emotion can be transferred from its original to other stimuli. The baby hears a loud noise (however dim its awareness may be), and fear creeps instinctively into its little mind. Later, by a process of conditioning perhaps, the baby may learn to be afraid of darkness as well as of loud noises, and there may grow up in this way a network of ideas or cognitions, any one of which may act as a stimulus for the release of fear—a network, however, of a precise and clear-cut kind.

UNREASONABLE FEARS THAT PARALYSE THE MIND

EVERYONE has heard of the bizarre *phobias* from which some people suffer : one man is afraid of riding in trains, another of being confined in a room with a closed door, another of tunnels, another of wide open spaces, another of cats, and so on. One of my friends confesses to a phobia of this kind : she feels uncomfortable, apprehensive, when in an underground train, and the fear becomes almost uncontrollable if the train should stop between two stations. But it is the only " phobia " that she has.

After all, true associations between ideas are of this precise nature : not all ideas are associated in the way that, in my case, the " Spring Song " and the friend's suicide are associated [1]—in point of fact, there are very few such associations for most of us. It was John Locke who said that associations were abnormal and unusual rather than normal, and this, I think, is quite true. This applies, equally, to the association or conditioning (as the behaviourists would call it) of an idea with an affect. It is only dogs that one person is afraid of, only a closed railway carriage in another case.

[1] See page 25.

These examples are sufficient to indicate that there is a difference between sentiments and phobias : apart from the bizarre nature of the latter, they are much more clear-cut emotionally and ideationally than sentiments. In phobias we may be sure that the fears and anxieties have been transferred in a more or less automatic way from their original and instinctive sources, and it is the work of the psychopathologist to trace these fears back to their original sources.

Finally, we have to ask whether emotions can be measured. Are some people more emotional than others ? A few years ago it was thought by some experimentalists that they had found a most exact method for measuring a person's emotions. The method made use of what has become known as the psycho-galvanic reflex, perhaps the most striking experiment that one can perform in a psychological laboratory. The method consists of measuring the electrical resistance across a person's hand, from palm to the back of the hand. If we feel emotion, the sweat-glands are activated, and this alters the electrical resistance across the hand, so that we can determine just when, and to what extent, a person feels emotion by measuring the changes in resistance.

But what seemed to be so promising is now known to be otherwise : any mental activity, cognitive or affective, produces these same changes in resistance. Nevertheless, the psycho-galvanic reflex is quite useful for indicating emotional disturbances under certain conditions, even though it cannot be used to measure them. I believe, however, that some people are certainly more emotional than others.

FORCES WHICH REVEAL A MAN'S CHARACTER : MOTIVE AND WILL-POWER

CERTAIN laws of volition have been described in an earlier section, and notably the law of *determining tendency*. When we decide to do something—that is, from a volitional act—there ensue determining tendencies which tend to carry out the intention of the act, even without further volition to that effect. When I decide to post a letter on my way to the station to-morrow morning, I do not have to make a further volitional act about it : already tendencies are at work which will ensure that the letter will be posted in due course. These tendencies, it must be noted, are not the same things as "memories." I do not remember to post the letter, so much as in fact I am *driven* to post it, much as a swallow is driven relentlessly to warmer climates in the autumn.

Of course, some of these determining tendencies are stronger than others, or are even countered by others. If the determining tendency to post a letter is not very strong, I may " forget " to post it. Or, if there are inner motives for " forgetting " to post it—if, for instance, it is a letter to my dentist asking for an appointment for repairs to my teeth, and if there are reasons for keeping as far away from the dentist as possible, then the weak decision to post the letter may be impotent against this stronger counter-tendency.

The experiment performed by Dr. Kurt Lewin is an illuminating example of the distinction between the " memory " and the determining tendency. Children were asked to perform many separate tasks,[1] one after the other. Some were allowed to be completed, but others were interrupted before they could be completed. Afterwards it was found that the children could recall those tasks that had been interrupted twice as frequently as those that had been completed. There is a tendency, of course, to " remember " all the tasks, since they have been held cognitively in mind. But the tendency is stronger for those tasks which the child had decided to do, but had been unable to complete : that is, the determining tendency was still operative for these interrupted tasks. Once we decide to do a thing there are set up tendencies which seem to hold the decision subconsciously in mind in quite a distinct way, giving it preference, so to speak, over ordinary, cognitive retentivity.

A NEW LIGHT ON WILL-POWER

I HAVE already drawn a distinction between volition and *conation*. Conation is action and striving through or by volition, but the term is also used for the instinctive behaviour of insects and animals. It is as though, in these instincts, a decision had been made as to what the insect or animal had to do, what goals it had to strive towards, what motives it had to pursue, and had mapped out ways and means to these ends. It is this that mystifies us so much, that the insect, a mere flea or wasp, should act as though it had decided what to do. Volition itself, however, involves no action. It is a unique mental activity, altogether different from a cognition or affects.

[1] See page 20.

I mentioned earlier that most psychologists do not believe that we make these special acts, and that cognition and feeling explains all that is to be seen in striving, deciding, choosing, and the like. It is true, however, that volitional acts are not easy to observe : it is only after considerable practice that an individual can observe himself making decisions ; and I have no doubt that the behaviourist will never believe in the reality of a volitional act because he will never allow himself to observe it, much as an hysterical person does not allow herself to feel pain.

Again, although we speak every day of using our " will-power," or of " strong-willed " and " weak-willed " individuals, it is possible that the essential volitional acts are the same in intensity for everyone, strong-willed and weak-willed alike. What we call strong will is perhaps the tense expressions, the clenched hands and the lively feelings, and these hide from us the inner core, the clear-cut volitional act itself.

This lies like a tender plant under masses of weeds and stronger growths. All that we can say is that one person may look as though he is strong-willed, but that this is perhaps due to the way he displays his emotions and feelings, rather than to any true will-power. And, indeed, it is a common-place that it is the quiet and inexpressive person who is often most resolute in intention and its fulfilment. The strong, silent man of fiction may be drawn with a square jaw, but his volitional acts are the secret of his firmness, not his jaw.

It is impossible, however, to discuss volitional activity apart from the cognitive and affective settings. We cannot *will* about nothing. To make a volitional act at all we have to cognise or know objects that can be altered in some way by our action, or we must recall or remember such experiences, or we have to educe anew or think of something we have never experienced before but which we know can be so altered by our action. We have to realise, too, that we ourselves require this action.

Thus, perhaps one of the most important laws of psychology is this, that he who cognises most and most generally is likely to make the most numerous, and the most suitable, volitions. The less a person knows about himself and the universe outside him, the more must he be at the mercy of his instinctive tendencies, the less will he be truly able to exercise his " free-will." The exercise of free-will depends upon the fullest use of knowledge to free ourselves from unconscious motivation—the very thing that being psycho-analysed affords us. But this word *motive* brings us to the core of the volitional structures of the mind. Just as " memories " and knowledge are our cognitive structures, and just as sentiments and tastes are affective structures, so motives are the volitional structures.

MOTIVES AS THE MAINSPRINGS OF ACTION

WHAT, then, is a motive ? At the present moment I am writing these lines with a strong motive in mind—with several, perhaps, but the strongest is one that is driving me to complete this section on psychology by to-morrow morning. During the past week this has been a dominant motive. I realised that something can be, and has to be accomplished, through my voluntary action, and this realisation of a value that I can gain constitutes a motive. A motive is of the same nature as a determining tendency.

But there are different kinds of motives. We are not concerned, of course, with the ethical value of motives, with whether they are good ones or bad ones. Psychology knows no value of this kind. The person who is planning a minor war in an out-of-the-way republic for the sake of selling his machine-guns and ammunition has motives of a very high order psychologically, although ethically they are no doubt thoroughly despicable. The *lower* motives, psychologically, are merely those whose end is the satisfaction of immediate pleasure. One would call my present motive—one that is turning my attention towards supper—lowly. I see that it is desirable for me to have supper, I recognise that I want it, and I realise that I can go for it myself through my own volition. It is lowly because it serves an immediate end.

Higher motives, on the other hand, are more complex cognitively, and may stretch over a very long period of time. The young man or woman begins an academic career with a motive in mind : it is that which calls him to succeed in examinations, and to do so through his own action. There is no immediate pleasure so gained, and the value to be gained is a very general one. We can have *inner* motives, those we do not want others to see (besides many that we are quite unaware of ourselves), as well as *outer* ones, those which we are at pains to allow others to see.

A comparison should be made between sentiments and motives. Professor McDougall believes that sentiments are driving forces to action ; but he has confused, I think, motives and sentiments. Sentiments are quite interesting things, but in themselves they tend to be somewhat useless, like most affective experiences. They are luxuries that the truly rational person can scarcely afford—although, to be sure, they add variety and delight to life, and no doubt frequently serve to give a certain coherence to activity. But in motives we touch in a more intimate way, I think, the core of *character*. McDougall, we remember, wanted to explain character in terms of sentiments. But that person who acts by will and voluntary action, who has firmly founded motives (whatever their ethical value) must be considered to be the person of finest character. It is well known that a person's character often changes radically for the better in the course of a psycho-analysis, and the reason lies to a large extent in this matter of volition.

HOW HABIT AND PERSEVERANCE CEMENT OUR CHARACTERS

SEVERAL questions are now urgent. Can we improve our character, in the above sense ? Can we measure it ? Is character innate or acquired ? Let us take the questions in order. The formation of suitable *habits* may go a long way towards improving one's character. What we cannot gain by virtue of our present intention we might gain gradually by forming suitable habits to that end. Thus, the young man who wants to succeed academically, say, forms habits of work, habits of rising early in the morning, and so forth. These feed the higher motives, and help thereby to knit the character more firmly. Similarly the desirable goals of life can be shown to us, by our parents, and by our religious and moral no less than by our scholastic and physical teachers.

Can we measure a person's character ? Many attempts have been made. We draw a distinction in the first place between temperament and character. Temperament, we have already seen, is a result of affective structures of the mind : I mentioned earlier that tests of *fluency* supplied a measurement of temperament, and estimates of a person's *introversion* or *extraversion* come within the same affective field of the mind. But character is a volitional matter. Hundreds of tests have been made in America in attempts to measure character—the astonishing thing being that these tests were made by people who did not believe in volition at all ! By means of such tests we can test honesty, trustworthiness, reliability, and the like. Now, to act honestly implies

action by reason, habit, and will : there must be motives for
such actions, especially if immediate gain can accrue from
easily perpetrated dishonest acts. Or we can rate people for
traits of this kind and find which has, all-round, the best
character. Strangely enough, one of the best tests of character
is one that seems at first sight to have nothing to do with
character. We can readily pick out the unreliable, untrust-
worthy, and difficult child in a school by applying several tests
of the following kind :

A ZIGZAG TEST

(1) *Write as many capital Z's as you can, with good
quality, in 1 minute.*

(2) *Repeat for another minute.*

(3) *Now write as many reverse Z's as you can in a
minute—that is, write them all thus :*
Ƨ Ƨ Ƨ . . . .

(4) *Repeat for another minute.*

(5) *Now write straightforward Z's and Ƨ's alternately—
that is, write them for 1 minute :*
Z Ƨ Z Ƨ Z Ƨ . . . .

(6) *Repeat for 1 minute.*

A rest of 15 seconds is allowed between each minute's
writing. It is found that the highly difficult children fare
very poorly at the alternate writing at (5) and (6), compared
with their ability at the more straightforward writing. Children of poor character seem unable to write ZƧ rapidly.
But why this should be so is something of a mystery still.
The simplest theory is that this ZƧ-writing, being a little
more difficult to do, offers an obstacle to those whose motives
are not strong ones. The child of poor character cannot
surmount the difficulty under the circumstances of the test.

Finally, is character innate ? We can see how much it
depends upon habits, upon training, upon desirable motives
being shown us. It obviously depends, too, on our intelligence. The more intelligent a person, the more likely he is
to have a firm character, other things being equal. Yet
some people seem to go through life untaught and untutored
who have yet character in our sense of the word. It would
seem that, almost lost in the masses of cognitions, memories,
habits, sentiments, and the like, there is yet an indication that
some people are more prone to make decisions and to act
upon them persistently. The decision when made may not

be different to anyone else's, but the man of innate character makes them more frequently and on better grounds.

THE TOTAL PERSONALITY

To end this section I need only draw together the various threads of my argument, fitting them together to make my picture of a person's total personality. An individual has personality to the extent that he is different from others. He differs from others cognitively, affectively, and volitionally. He has certain abilities, and certain structures of the mind, and these differentiate him from other human beings and give him his individuality.

Of the structures, I may refer again to his knowledge, his retrospectible " memories " in the field of cognition. Subserving these structures he has certain abilities, machines of the mind, so to speak. Amongst these are his eductive ability, his special imagery facilities, and minor abilities constructed out of these and experience together. In the affective field he has sentiments, tastes, and his temperament.

Finally, there are our motives, conscious and subconscious. The latter include our innate propensities, whilst the former are the basis of all action, although fed, no doubt, by subconscious (or unconscious) motives. Motives are the volitional structures of the mind, and volition is the machine, so to speak, that produces them and sends them on their determined way. We have seen that *character* seems to be partly a structure of the mind, the person's motives, and partly the machine-like ability that makes it easier for one person to have firmer character than another. All these various structures and abilities or machines give the person his personality.

SOME BOOKS FOR FURTHER READING

For additional reading the following books are suggested. One might begin with A. W. P. Wolter's *The Evidence of our Senses* (Methuen), a most stimulating introductory book. *The Theory and Practice of Psychology*, by Dr. Wynn Jones (Macmillan), and *Psychology*, by Professor Woodworth (Methuen), are perhaps the best general books on the topics covered by the above account of psychology. R. H. Thouless's *The Control of the Mind* and *Straight and Crooked Thinking* (Hodder and Stoughton) are entertaining and valuable introductions to their subjects. On sentiments and the like one cannot do better than read Professor McDougall's *The Energies of Man* (Methuen) and *Psychology : The Study of Behaviour* (Home University Library, Thornton Butterworth Limited).

For more advanced students the following could be the basis of extended reading : C. Spearman's *Creative Mind* (Nisbet), R. Wheeler's *The Laws of Human Nature* (Nisbet), and the brilliant study by Professor Aveling, *Personality and Will* (Nisbet), which is difficult to read, but worth all one's effort and contemplation. Professor Lindworsky's *Experimental Psychology* gives a well-seasoned description of psychology : the book (published by Allen and Unwin) is not easy to follow, but is full of sound natural material. One might end one's days reading and studying Spearman's *The Nature of Cognition*, the classical work on cognition (Macmillan).

THE DISORDERED MIND : ITS STUDY AND CURE

by PATRICK SLATER, B.A.(Oxon)

*A*LTHOUGH there is not nowadays any need to apologise for an article on the unconscious mind, the subject having become part of everyday knowledge, yet one should perhaps make a reservation before this section. First of all, it should be remembered that there are a number of theories about the unconscious. It is too generally assumed that the term psychoanalysis covers them all. In fact, psycho-analysis is the name Freud has given to his method of analysing patients. Both Jung and Adler, who were at one time pupils of Freud, have formed schools of their own. In the following article the views of these three exponents of the study of the unconscious are stated. No comments are made about them, but the reader should not conclude from this that there are no criticisms to be made. So far from this being the case there are competent critics who do not subscribe to the notion of the unconscious. However, so many remarkable results have been obtained by the experiments of the leading exponents of this science that it certainly cannot be ignored by students of contemporary thought.

IN the previous sections we have learned something about how the mind works ; we have formed some idea of what energy it uses, of the way we perceive, the way we think, and the ways in which we tend to act. Now we must try to find out what happens when the mind becomes upset, what forces prevent it from working properly, and what is the right way of treating a sick mind in order to make it well.

Some children do badly in their school work because they are really stupid, but other children are just lazy, and could do quite well if they tried. When Binet and Simon made their first intelligence tests, it was for the purpose of separating the stupid children from the lazy ones ; because if a child is really stupid, it is not worth while giving him an education of the kind meant for clever children, but if a child is just lazy, then we must find some way of making him interested in his work—and once he is really interested, we shall expect to find him just as clever as the other boys.

So the first intelligence tests were made. And now that tests have been used and improved, and used again, for nearly thirty years, we have measures of intelligence which are accurate and reliable. These tests show us that intelligence is normally distributed. Stupid children are not in a class by themselves. When we separate them from clever children, we have to make a quite artificial dividing-line. To say that every child with an intelligence quotient [1] of less than seventy is mentally deficient, is like saying that every grown man who is less than four feet high is a pigmy. The dividing-line has to be made, but the exact spot where it is put is largely a matter of convenience.

But when we come to aberrations of the mind, the " normal " man is really an ideal. He is not the same as an average man. For it has been said that everyone is a little mad. And there are many different kinds of mental disorders ; some of them go through the strangest changes as they develop : they fade off into one another ; they may appear suddenly and abruptly, or creep upon us very slowly and gradually. If we took an average, we should find that the average man has a little of every possible kind of mental disorder ; he would not be at all like the " normal " man, who is supposed to be free from any kind of disorder.

GHOSTS AND FANCIES : THE PSYCHOSES

THE disorders which most frequently bring on temporary or lifelong insanity are the psychoses. One of the commonest and most serious of them is *Schizophrenia*. It is also one of the most tragic, for it often affects the young and promising, and leads to lifelong existence within asylum walls. The sufferer loses all interest in his ordinary life and work. He shows no affection for his relatives, he is not amused or moved to sorrow by any of the happenings around him. He appears to be completely absorbed in himself. While the outer world fails to interest him, he finds a ceaseless occupation for his thoughts in an inner world of fantasy. He may see visions and hear voices. He may form strange ideas of his own grandeur, or of the ill-will of those around him. His thinking becomes twisted, so that though he talks freely, his ideas are impossible to follow. Or he may remain listless and apathetic, scarcely speaking or moving for years on end, so that even his washing and feeding have to be done for him.

[1] See page 66.

HORROR ENVELOPING THE MIND

Yet somewhere beneath there remains a mind which is acute and master of itself. A sudden attack of pneumonia, for instance, may for a time awake the sleeping personality again ; he may show that he has not failed to notice what has gone on around him. And it is possible for a permanent cure to be effected.

Another common disorder is *Cyclothymia*, which appears in two forms—melancholia and mania. The occasion from which melancholia starts may seem natural enough—the loss of a relative, or a failure in love or ambition—but as it gets blacker, its morbid nature appears. The patient sits about in helpless despair, he speaks in slow and mournful tones, his thoughts are long delayed ; or he frets himself with countless worries, and accuses himself of exaggerated or fancied sins. He may refuse food because he is unworthy of the attention which he receives, or he may make desperate and in many cases successful attempts at suicide. Eventually, perhaps over the course of months, his gloom passes, and he is restored to his normal health and cheerfulness.

Mania, the other kind of *Cyclothymia*, is exactly the opposite condition. It may start as an unusual flow of good spirits, surprising alertness and brilliance ; and, with this, exaggerated optimism and self-esteem. The patient feels capable of anything, he keeps up a continual stream of activities, talking, laughing, cracking jokes, making arrangements and plans, ordering others about in the most dictatorial way. If crossed in his wishes, he may fly into a violent rage, and then as rapidly repent. He cannot understand that there is anything wrong with him, and fiercely resents the suggestion ; yet care is most necessary, for not only may he bring others into trouble through his hasty actions, but he may wear himself out with his ceaseless activity, which leaves him no time for food or sleep. Nearly all cases of this illness recover completely after a time.

That melancholia and mania are two phases of the same disorder is shown by the fact that often after the patient has recovered from one, he may succumb to a more or less mild attack of the other. Or the sufferer from one illness may have relatives who have suffered from the other.

THE METICULOUS MAN AND THE SHOWY WOMAN

OTHER disorders of the mind, the *neuroses*, seldom go so far as to make it necessary to shut the patient up in a hospital or asylum. One of the most interesting of the neuroses is the *obsession*. The man who is predisposed towards this disorder is apt to be hard and stern, with fixed opinions on a number of subjects. He must have everything in its proper place, neatly arranged. He shows a fondness for collecting things—anything from china *bric-a-brac* to brown paper and string. All his actions have to obey strict rules and regulations—he may, for instance, pick his steps along the street with the utmost care, so as to avoid treading on the cracks between the paving-stones.

In such a character the obsession may readily grow. He begins to feel uncertain whether everything is just the way it should be. He is not satisfied with seeing that everything is done correctly; he must do it over and over again, to make sure. Once he was scrupulously clean, now he is always washing and rewashing his hands. Behind him, driving him on, is a terrible fear, which he cannot understand. The only way that he can ward it off is by these incessant rituals, which allow him no time or rest.

Another common neurosis is *hysteria*. It, too, seems to go with a particular type of character. People of hysterical temperament are often unusually successful in society. They are alive to every change of mood in the company around them; they are easily moved to tears and laughter. They have a great desire for the crowd's admiration and attention, and they will spare no effort to reach the spot where the limelights are focused. They will readily change sides, wherever it is to their own advantage to do so. They are the great self-deceivers of the world, and will have a good reason for everything they do, no matter how selfish and contemptible. If crossed in their desires they become angry and petulant; they are grand at making a scene. Yet among such people are many great politicians, great actors and actresses, great revivalists.

In the morbid development of hysteria, the patient advances a stage further in his self-deception. One part of his mind seems to be completely shut off from another; even a whole part of his body may cease to exist for him, and there is an hysterical paralysis of an arm or a leg. Or the patient loses all memory of a large period of his life. In some rare cases the character becomes divided into two or more entirely different personalities, each of which in turn controls the actions of the body. One personality may play impish tricks on the other ; and the other, when it takes control, knows nothing of what the first has done.

The hysteric is profoundly sensitive to suggestion ; he copies physical disorders, of which he has seen or heard, to the life. His capacity for creating a scene may go so far as to produce convulsions that terrify the onlookers. Yet there is a motive for all that he does, and the advantage he obtains is often apparent to everyone but the patient himself. For this reason he is often treated as a poser, a hypocrite, a malingerer—an unjust attitude, for the patient's desires to impress and to deceive are not ones of which he is conscious himself.

Of all patients the hysteric is most easily influenced by hypnotism, and the great cures of this treatment, and other methods such as the miracle-working shrine at Lourdes, have been made on cases of hysteria. In treatment, the physician can readily impress the patient, through hypnotism or otherwise, with the fact that his illness is not real, and so drive it out. But such treatment cannot be guaranteed to produce permanent results. As long as the patient has something to gain by being ill, a relapse is liable to occur, or one illness may be cured only to be followed by another still more obstinate to treatment.

HOW MENTAL DISORDERS MAY BE CURED

IN this little survey we have been able to look at no more than a few of the commoner disorders of the mind. We have paid attention only to those kinds which are called "functional." No matter how closely we might examine the people who suffer from these disorders, we should not be able to discover anything wrong with their physical health, such as might have been responsible for setting up a disturbance in their minds.

In cases of advanced schizophrenia, physical changes may often be observed. The lines of the face become coarsened, the eyes become dulled, the fine indications of character disappear, as if the patient had sunk into a purely vegetable existence. But such changes can clearly be seen to be the results, not the causes, of the mental disorder. Again, an hysteric may perhaps appear to be completely paralysed in his right arm, yet when we come to examine the bones, the joints, the ligaments, the muscles, the veins, the nerves— nowhere are the physical symptoms of paralysis to be found,

The *Society Fraternally.*

West Ham Mental

To.
   the Viceroy of India

Hospital

The Dowager

Goodmayes

Empress of India

Ilford

States of India

Dr Sirs

   Ladies & Gentlemen

May I ask

   respecting the Case of

Veerasawmys Restaurant

99 Regent Street London W.

Whom I have written

yet respecting the

Curiosity of —— the Blood Blood.

I fainted when I found the

the Silver Ball.

Like many other persons I feel better - unwell.

Some days than others - illnesses being the

true case, Heart Diseases.—:

The facts of Heart Disease reminds me

of the Toumos - Black Prince Battleship

Question.

and esteems unto

Adam —

for I have had sores myself

but am better much

writing

do I press forward

in my Endeavour

So

London City and

The

   Mansion House Conquest

Sears

and the Royal Victoria & Albert

Restorfully.

Docks.

A Kidway.

MENTAL DERANGEMENT SHOWN IN A LETTER
Note the grandiose allusions and disconnection of thought.

no reason can be discovered why he should not use his arm if
he wanted to.

How far such a patient differs from one who is suffering
from general paralysis of the insane ! This is an " organic "
disorder, one which develops in the last stages of syphilis, as
the disease penetrates to the very marrow of the bones.
The patient's control over the movements of his limbs becomes more and more erratic, and as decay permeates the
fibres of the spinal cord and the brain, insanity ensues.

Even in these last terrible stages, modern science has found
methods of combating the dangers of organic insanity. Here
at least we know a great deal about the nature of the disease
and the stages of its development ; but how can we discover
the true causes of the functional disorders, where there is no
damage to the body, no poisons or infections to be found in
any of its systems ? What medicines, what treatments can
we prescribe ? We are faced with that challenge to
science :

> " Canst thou not minister to a mind diseas'd,
> Pluck from the memory a rooted sorrow,
> Raze out the written troubles of the brain,
> And with some sweet oblivious antidote
> Cleanse the stuff'd bosom of that perilous stuff
> Which weighs upon the heart ? "

Within limits, yes ! Cures can be effected, though hardly
by the means that Macbeth suggests. We know, now, that
the anxieties which prey upon the conscious mind are not so
deep or so difficult to alleviate as those which are thrust from
it and apparently forgotten. No drugs or opiates which
artificially blot out the painful feelings from the mind are
likely to effect a cure—forgetfulness is one of the greatest
obstacles against which the physician of the mind has to
struggle. The reply of the doctor then, as now, is :

> " Therein the patient
> Must minister to himself."

But our increasing insight into the causes of mental disorders
has brought with it the knowledge of many ways in which the
doctor can give valuable help to the patient.

Inherited mental deficiency, it is true, is something for
which no cure is known. But there is a world of difference
between the deficient and the insane or the neurotic. The

"AND THERE CAME OUT OF HER THREE DEVILS"

An old interpretation of insanity. In medieval times mental disorders were attributed to demoniacal possession.

mind of the deficient is not turned away from reality, nor is it divided against itself ; there is no reason why his life should not be as happy and as complete within its scope as those of cleverer men—indeed, according to Ecclesiastes, in much wisdom is much grief.

We must remember, too, that much of what appears as mental deficiency arises from circumstances which are capable of control. If through force of circumstances children are habitually underfed, their vitality becomes diminished, the quality of their school work falls off, their rate of learning becomes slower, and they exhibit all the signs of poor mental

ability. The cure for this is obvious enough. Unhappy
home life, too, or the mild forms of neurotic disorder which
frequently occur in children, may prevent them from con-
centrating, and prove to be the real causes which lie behind
an apparent weakness of intelligence ; and such disorders
can generally be given beneficial treatment.

THE METHOD OF PSYCHO-ANALYSIS

IN our study of the neurotic disorders and the insanities, we
find that the mind has often to struggle against itself ; that
the energy upon which it draws rises from hidden springs,
and that, at times, the dark forces in it may prove too strong
for conscious control, may rise like a swelling flood and sub-
merge the reason, or lead to long, exhausting, and indecisive
struggles, destroying the possibility of a normal and healthy
life. What are these dark forces ? How do they arise ? And
how can they be controlled ?

No thorough method of treatment can be devised unless
an answer can be found to these questions. Yet even without
knowing very much about them, we can do much to help the
patient to regain control over the hidden forces of his mind.
Although it is within the mind that the struggles take place
which manifest themselves as mental disorders, outside
influences such as misfortunes, disappointments, or family
quarrels may have been largely responsible for bringing on
the internal struggle. Patients may quite well be treated
by taking them away from these outside influences, giving them
rest of body and mind, treating them for any physical ailments
they may have, and thus nursing them back to mental health.
Many kinds of treatment may be used, from simple sympathy,
discussing his difficulties with the patient, giving him advice,
continual reassurance and encouragement, to a prolonged
psycho-analysis in special cases, where the mind can still be
influenced in this way, and nothing less will do.

Psycho-analysis is not suitable for the treatment of every
case of nervous disorder. In order to succeed, it must ally
itself with some force in the patient's mind which can be
turned into a genuine desire to become well. Such a force
can readily be found in cases of neurosis, where one force or
group of forces is in conflict with another. But we must not
regard our classification of different types of disorder as something hard and fast. Even where the diagnosis is different,
the patient may show some desire, such as an attachment to

a nurse or a doctor, which may be used as an avenue or approach into the recesses of the patient's mind, and pave the way to a cure. Psycho-analysis, as the most thorough of the methods of treatment, offers us the deepest insight into the ways in which the mind works.

THE CENSORED WORLD: FREUD AND THE UNCONSCIOUS

THERE are many things we do, many ideas that come into our heads, for which we do not consider ourselves responsible. We do not consider ourselves to blame when we make an occasional slip of the tongue or of the pen—then why do we make them ? Sometimes when we want to remember a name or a date, it completely escapes our memory. We know that in a few hours, when it is too late to be of any use, the name will come back—then why does it elude us now ?

Many people would say that this is all just a matter of chance. It is the merest coincidence that I forget some fact just at the moment when it happens to be important. It is just a matter of chance that my tongue tricks me into saying something that I did not mean, something that I would rather have left unsaid.

To say that this is chance is to say that there is no explanation, that there are no known forces which produce these events. But perhaps we say that they are a matter of chance because we do not want to have them explained. We do not want to know what forces might have produced them. It took a man of exceptional insight and courage, Sigmund Freud, to insist that every occurrence of this kind can be explained, and to find a way of explaining it.

Yet this is only one of the smallest parts of Freud's work. The ordinary man may forget a single name, or a date, for a few hours only ; the hysteric forgets complete episodes, possibly many years of his life. Why does this vast loss of memory occur ? Freud has shown that the forces which produce the small loss of memory are the same as those which produce the large.

There are other mental events which seem equally unaccountable—our dreams. They come upon us in strange, fantastic shapes, not of our own choosing. Each dream is an adventure, and each episode in it unexpected. Why does our fancy spin these tales at night ?

"Why did I dream last night of crossing a railway-track and walking up a lane?" If you had asked such a question at the beginning of this century, you might have got an answer of a sort—a theory of how dreams might occur, something which would have explained everything but why the dream was about railway-tracks and lanes, and why you dreamt it last night. But Freud's work on dreams has become so famous that by now, although we may not know what the causes of that dream were, we all know that they can be found, if the dream is properly analysed.

Any why does the obsessed man feel compelled to wash his hands many times a day, to do everything by twos or threes, to observe countless trivial rituals? Freud has succeeded in showing that the same forces which, in us, produce our dreams at night, govern the actions and rituals in the obsessed man, by which he relieves himself of his fear.

What are these strange forces? It would be tempting to hurry on at once to a description of them, and how they work; but there is something so new and strange about them that it is difficult to believe that they can really exist until we have seen the methods by which they have been discovered.

DREAMS THAT REVEAL OUR INNERMOST DESIRES

LET us take a dream of which Freud has offered a partial analysis, and see how its meaning is uncovered from the strange disguise in which it is presented.

> "*A young woman who had already been married for a number of years dreamt as follows: She was at the theatre with her husband, and one side of the stalls was empty. Her husband told her that Elise L. and her fiancé also wanted to come, but could only get bad seats, three for a florin and a half, and of course they could not take those. She replied that in her opinion they did not lose much by that.*"

Instead of trying to guess at once what is the meaning of the whole dream, let us take it bit by bit. What is the meaning of *the half-empty theatre*? The young wife explains that it has something to do with what happened to her a week before. She had been so anxious to see a certain play that she had paid an extra price so as to get her tickets early. But when she and her husband went, the stalls were half empty. Her husband had teased her about being in such a hurry to get her tickets. And what about the bad seats at *three for a florin and a half*? The money, 1 fl. 50, suggests quite a new idea. Her sister-in-law had had a present of 150 florins from her husband, and had rushed off in a hurry to spend it all on a piece of jewellery.

Why should both these events be brought together in the same dream? Is there any connection between them? Do not we notice a refrain, a kind of moral, running through both of them—" It is foolish to act in a hurry; one can do much better if one waits "? She had been in a hurry to get her tickets, her sister-in-law had been in a hurry to get her jewellery; both of them should have waited.

HOW FREUD ANALYSED A DREAM

AND where do Fraulein Elise L. and her fiancé come in? The young wife has already been married for some time; her friend, Elise, who is about the same age, has only just become engaged. Now we begin to suspect the meaning of the dream. Perhaps the idea behind it all is this: I was a fool to get married in such a hurry; I should have waited, like Elise, and got a better husband for myself.

Can we prove this? Is there any reason why *going to the theatre* should represent getting married? When first the young girl becomes interested in sex, she has to satisfy her curiosity by watching lovers when they are together, perhaps by catching a glimpse of her parents. Going to a theatre, seeing a show, expresses, by metaphor, one way of getting to know about sexual matters, and hence suggests another way—marriage. And there is another clue. Why are the tickets at *three for one florin and a half*? Why should Elise L. and her fiance want three tickets, when there are only two of them? What is the meaning of the number *three*? The young wife is quite unable to explain.

Freud has found, in quite a number of dreams, elements like this number three which cannot be explained by any recollections of the dreamer. But by comparing many dreams together, by tracing connections between dreams and primitive religious myths, even by gathering clues from popular catchwords, the meaning of such elements was gradually discovered. The sacred number three is so rich in religious, mythological, and superstitious associations that to trace them all might lead us any distance. But the most primitive of all trinities is that of the penis and the two testicles: and hence the number three has become a *symbol* of the male genitals. It is found over and over again, in different people's dreams, with this same meaning. And when the lady dreams that tickets to the theatre are being sold at three for a florin and a half, the thought at the back of her mind is that husbands are easy to get, and that she could have had a much better husband for the dowry that her father gave her.

From this example of how a dream is analysed, we can learn much. First of all, we can see how far we have to go from the original matter, the conscious ideas of the dream, in order to discover where its meaning is hidden. The dreamer has no idea what the dream means, and yet she has in her possession all, or nearly all, the facts which are needed in order to discover its meaning. This meaning behind the dream is what Freud calls the *latent dream*, while what is actually dreamt and remembered is called the *manifest dream*.

We see how many changes the meaning has to go through, how it has to be disguised, before it can become a dream. The idea of " being in a hurry " does not appear in the manifest dream at all ; it has been pushed out of place,[1] and only a few hints are left behind that it is there. And although all these little hints at the real thought are really quite separate from each other, yet they have been tied together [2] in the manifest dream, and a little story has been made out of them. We saw how first one meaning was found in the idea, " three for one and a half florins," and then, when we examined it a little farther, we found another. And in going to the theatre we found not one, but two different meanings. But we do not reject the first meaning when we accept the second. The dream cannot be fully understood unless we consider all the possible meanings of each dream element. Several meanings are often packed together [3] in one fragment of a dream.

But when we see how many complicated processes have gone into the making of this dream it seems as if, instead of understanding it more and more, we understand it less and less. The small problems are answered—we know how the parts of the dream really hang together, and what the meaning of the dream is—but larger problems immediately arise. Why are so many processes, so many disguises necessary ?

---

[1] *Displacement* (Freud).   [2] *Secondary Elaboration* (Freud).
[3] *Condensation* (Freud).

What prevents us from seeing at once what the dream means ?

WHY DREAMS PREVARICATE

LET us look over what has happened since we began trying to find out the meaning of this dream. Was it not rather bold to suppose, as we did when we started, that there was more in the dream than the dreamer remembered ? We allowed ourselves to suppose that there were things in the dreamer's own mind that were quite unknown to him. And it is lucky that we made this assumption, because we should not have got anywhere without it. " Of course," you will say, " I cannot keep everything in my mind all the time ; I just remember the important things and let the trivial things slide. No doubt I could remember them if I tried." But this is just exactly the opposite of what happens in the dream. All the trivial little details come into your mind, but the important matter, the real meaning of the dream, is held back and has to be dug out with the greatest difficulty. How can this have happened ?

When we compare the manifest dream with its hidden meaning, we can quite understand why the meaning should have been cut out. The dream, as it appears, is a harmless little story, that no one would mind dreaming. But how about its meaning ? Is wishing you had waited and got a better husband for yourself quite a harmless little wish ? Is it not something rather shocking, something that, even during the daytime, you would want to shut out of your mind ?

I am afraid you will have to agree that there must be two forces at the back of your mind that you know nothing about : one pulling this way, one pulling that ; one trying to force ideas into your mind, one trying to keep them out. And neither of them can claim a complete victory over the other. If one of them—the force which Freud calls the *Id* [1]—had been completely victorious, the whole of the latent dream would have entered your mind unaltered. If the other—the force which Freud calls the *Super-Ego* [2]—had won, the dream would never have been dreamt at all. But neither of them quite defeats the other : the Super-Ego manages to keep the real meaning of the dream out of your mind ; but the Id manages to slip a few of its suggestions past the Super-Ego— just enough to make up the substance of your dream. That is why the dream has to be broken up, twisted around, dis-

[1] *Id* (Latin)=That.   [2] *Super-Ego* (Latin)=Over-Self.

guised, and reshaped—in order to get past the Super-Ego.

Now we begin to be in a position where we can link up our knowledge about dreams with our knowledge about lapses of memory and slips of the tongue. We begin to think that it is not just chance that makes the hysteric forget large periods of his life. These forgotten periods are almost certainly the most important periods—some unconscious force must have driven them out of his memory. In order to find out what is wrong with him we must uncover those periods again. And similarly when we forget something that we want to remember —this must be because some unconscious force is keeping the memory away from us. There must be something about this memory which is repulsive to our Super-Ego. And when we make little slips of the tongue—when we mean to be polite, and really say something quite rude—there must be some unconscious force which has thrust the wrong words into our mouth. Perhaps, although we refused to acknowledge it to ourselves, we really wanted to be rude. This makes it all the more important to find out more about these unconscious forces. Whence do they spring ? Why are they opposed to one another ?

HOW CONFLICT ENTERS THE CHILD MIND

FREUD describes, among others, the dream of a child one year and ten months old. This little boy, Hermann, had to present someone with a basket of cherries as a birthday gift. He did it very unwillingly, and next morning he told his dream : " Hermann eaten all the cherries." Such children's dreams show clearly that there is no unconscious conflict in the young child. The dream has not been cut up, and had all its important matter removed, leaving it like a heavily censored article—no, it expresses the wish of the child simply and directly.

That grouping of two opposed forces at the back of the mind only develops as the child grows up, it is not born within him. The process which brings it about is not completed until the child is six or seven. In the baby there are no moral scruples ; it is in the same state as Adam in the Garden of Eden, knowing neither good nor evil. The child follows a quest for pleasure, and finds it first of all in its mouth—in sucking at its mother's breast, or sucking its finger, or its big toe, or a comforter, or anything else it can lay hands on.

Then presently it begins to find pleasures in other parts of its body—first of all in the anal regions and in the activities of excretion, and finally the genitals become the centre of its interest. Each part of the body is explored, and its appropriate pleasures discovered, before the baby begins to find a pleasure in its body as a whole.

While it is exploring the parts of its body, it is going through what Freud calls the *auto-erotic phase* [1] of development ; and when it begins to find its pleasures in its body as a whole, and in forming fanciful opinions about itself, it is entering the *narcissistic phase*.[2] Of course these phases are not separated from one another by a sharp, sudden dividing-line ; the child's interest is gradually transformed.

FORBIDDEN WISHES THAT MAY BE TRANSFORMED INTO NOBLE IDEALS

ITS development does not normally cease at the narcissistic phase. From its interest in itself, the child's search for pleasure becomes focused on people and things outside itself ; it passes into the third, last phase of *object-love*. The child's love of its parents at last begins to be a real motive power. And when this happens, the desire for pleasure—the *libido*—begins to be divided against itself. The first object of the boy's love is his mother ; and as his love for his mother develops, there grow up, beside it, hatred and jealousy for his father. These desires cannot be given a direct expression—the boy cannot follow the example of Œdipus, and kill his own father and marry his mother. But such desires exist within him, and they form what is called the *Œdipus complex*.

How can these desires become satisfied ? They cannot, unless they can be transformed. How can they be transformed and adapted to normal social life ? For they must, and they can. The boy's love for his mother, even the jealousy for his father which springs originally from the same source, may become a powerful, ennobling force. If he wishes to win his mother's love, to oust his father from her affections, how can the boy fulfil his wishes ? He must try to make of himself someone of whom his mother can be proud, he must try to take his father's place in the family by being like a grown man, taking responsibilities, proving his powers.

[1] From the Greek words *autos* (self) and *eros* (love).
[2] From the myth of Narcissus, who fell in love with his own reflection in a pool.

From wishing to win his mother's love, the boy comes to wish to make something great and noble out of himself ; he sets before himself an ideal of conduct ; and as his desires turn in this new direction, towards the achievement of this new ideal, his mother fades from the centre of his interest, and his desires, focused upon this ideal self, become the forces of the Super-Ego. Although his desires cannot be expressed in their primitive forms, yet by passing through this process—the process of *sublimation*, as it is called—they can become transformed and purified, and so attain expression.

But it would be difficult to imagine, and still harder to find, anyone in whom this transformation had been entirely successful. Not all the forces of the boy's love for his mother can become idealised and attached to the Super-Ego. Some of his desires become exalted and transformed ; others, robbed of anything good and valuable that they contained in their primitive forms, become thrust back ; they are not allowed to express themselves, and they form a group of forbidden wishes, incestuous desires for the mother, death-wishes against the father—the repressed forces of the Id. Of this part of our nature, Freud writes :

> " It (the Id) feels itself at one with all the demands of the sexual impulse, those which have long been condemned by our æsthetic training and those which are contrary to all the restraints imposed by morality. It chooses its objects unchecked by any inhibition, preferring indeed those which are forbidden : not merely the wife of another man, but, above all, the incestuous objects of choice which by common consent humanity holds sacred—the mother and the sister of men, the father and the brother of women. Hate, too, rages unrestrainedly ; wishes for revenge, and death-wishes, against those who in life are nearest and dearest—parents, brothers and sisters, husband or wife, or children—are by no means uncommon."

THE BURIED HISTORY OF OUR DESIRES

WE have glimpsed the two conflicting groups of hidden forces which carry on their work upon our conscious thoughts. We have some idea of what we should discover, if we were able, for a moment, to look beneath the surface of our minds. But such a thing is well-nigh impossible. Neither of these conflicting forces is known directly to us. Just as our idea of our body is really an idea of the surface of our skin—we cannot see the shape of our skeleton, the convolutions of our intestines, or the other things which lie beneath —so the desires of which we are aware are only the surface desires ; we know them at the point where they come into contact with reality, but we do not know, we can only guess through what fierce mental conflicts they may have passed before they reach the surface.

In the adult man, not only are these forces themselves hidden in the unconscious, but the whole period during which they developed disappears from memory, and we are faced with the remarkable phenemenon of *infantile amnesia*—that is to say, the fact that scarcely anyone can recall more than a few isolated, fragmentary incidents from the period before he was six or seven years old, the period before the two rival forces of the unconscious have become organised in their mature forms.

Yet primitive mythologies and religions, we find, are full of mystical images describing in a symbolic way the divided forces of the human mind. Above the human world, the world of the conscious mind, is pictured an ideal world, a heaven, and beneath, a world of outcast, evil forces, a hell. These images we find not only in the Christian religion, but in most other creeds—the Orphic creed reveals to us the Gods in Olympus and the Titans thrust down beneath the crust of the earth ; the Scandinavian Edda shows us the Gods and the heroes gathered together in Asgard ; and the Giants, the evil forces, driven out beyond the rim of the earth. How could anyone understand or believe in such fanciful pictures if he had not, in a manner of speaking, a heaven and a hell, as well as a conscious world, a God and a Devil, as well as a man, within him ?

It may seem, when we consider these facts, that we have done no more than give new scientific names to things of which we have long possessed a dim, unscientific apprehension. But this is not all. With our new knowledge we link up a new approach to the problems of human behaviour and a new practice in our method of dealing with them.

One of the most important functions of religion in the past has been to ally itself with the heavenly powers—that is to say, with the forces of the Super-Ego—and thereby to strengthen the forces of repression, to drive farther and farther away from our ken the desires of the Id, the real springs of human activity. We may say that such a method of continual

repression is full of dangers, in much the same way as a too
elaborate separation and stratification of classes in society is
dangerous. Repression leads only to an apparent, not a real
weakening of the repressed forces. They become explosive,
and the more tightly they are boxed in the more violent their
explosion is liable to be. By repressing them, we obscure
the symptoms of disorder, but we only increase the dangers.
The forces of the Id must be allowed to find expression, not
in violent, hysterical, and misdirected ways, but under conscious control and direction, so that their effects may not
be evil.

In a sense, therefore, the new method no longer seeks to
cast out the devil ; it seeks, instead, like some benevolent
magician, to raise up the devil, to look him in the face, to use
his strength for good. Lest such a metaphor should prove
misleading, let me add at once that the Super-Ego is certainly
not divine, nor the Id diabolic ; to imagine them endowed
with these qualities implies an attitude of self-idolatry, and
this is not wholesome.

HOW INNER CONFLICTS ARE EXPRESSED IN CONDUCT

WHAT, then, are the ways in which the rival forces of the
unconscious—the Super-Ego and the Id—influence our
conscious conduct ? The motive forces of action rise from
the Id, but only in so far as they agree with, or at least do not
conflict with, the ideals of the Super-Ego are they able to
reach the surface of consciousness. The forces of the Super-
Ego are not able, of themselves, to motivate our actions.
They restrain the impetuosities of the Id, they exercise a
censorship over its wishes ; they may at times prove over-
officious, obstructive, rigid, and unyielding, or at times
extremely lax and uncritical ; although they perform a
different activity, they are no less irrational than the forces of
the Id, and are no more capable of emerging on to the surface
of consciousness.

If Freud is right, the conscious mind possesses only the
function of discovering ways and means by which the unconscious motives may be fulfilled. It is neither able to
originate any spontaneous motive, nor able to exercise any
spontaneous control over the motives which penetrate to it
from the unconscious. On the one hand, our thoughts are
occupied with finding the means for giving expression to
the surface desires—in this way they serve the purposes of

the Id—and on the other hand they are occupied with finding good reasons, or at least passable excuses for what we do—in this way they justify the workings of the Super-Ego. Reasons are found after decisions are made, not before.

Freud's theory has been called one of strict *psychological determinism.* This means that it is a theory which finds the explanation of every mental event—such as thoughts, desires, fears, and anxieties, decisions, even dreams and slips of the tongue—in psychological causes, in the forces which operate on our minds unconsciously. It is " determinist," because it claims that none of these events is due to chance, but that each is the product of unconscious forces acting upon one another ; it is " psychological," because it claims that these forces reside within us, and that, when we wish to discover their nature, we must do so by examining mental, not physical, facts.

" GIVE ME THE FIRST SEVEN YEARS . . ."

LET us stop for a moment and consider what these theories imply from the point of view of the parent. To begin with, we must note how extremely important it is for the child to complete a successful psychological development during the first six or seven years of its life. An unsuccessful development over these years is the hardest thing in the world to remedy later on. To failures in this period almost all the neuroses, the psychoses, and the sexual perversions can be traced.

In the second place, we notice that the character of the child is undergoing many changes during this period. The task of the parent is to try to understand the child, and to help in its development. In its first year of life, for instance, the child is absolutely dependent upon its parents ; nothing could be more harmful than to try to force independence upon it so early in life. But by the third or fourth year the child has developed extreme self-confidence, even self-conceit ; then it would be equally harmful to try to break this down. It must be encouraged in its feelings of independence, though still it must be given a guarantee of security in its home.

Nor must we discourage the changing interests of the baby, though they may appear a trifle peculiar at times. For instance, there is no need to be horrified at its desire for sucking, if it does not suck anything very dirty. To stop the process of development at any point may hinder the success of the later stages. Above all, it is necessary to treat the child as someone with an entirely different character from the grown man, and not to expect adult behaviour from him, before he has formed an adult character. Fortunately there is a vigorous source of energy in the child, which enables him to overcome countless obstacles successfully in the course of his development.

What happens when development is unsuccessful? How are mental disorders brought on? Unusually such an unsuccessful development can be traced back to some sudden shock (*trauma*, as Freud calls it) in early childhood, before mature character has been formed. The child's desires are suddenly robbed of any outlet at a moment when they are intensely excited, and they remain pent up, never able to find a full release.

But we cannot say beforehand what kind of experience may cause this sudden shock. Even to start with, one child is quite different from another. The make-up that one child inherits from its parents is different, and the surroundings in which it has to live are different from those of another. And what acts as a deep and lasting shock to one child may leave another completely unaffected.

THE UNCONSCIOUS CAUSES OF CONSCIOUS DISORDER

PENT-UP desire, when it can find no outlet, becomes transformed into fear or guilt. When the child longs for its mother at night, and cannot have her, its longing becomes transformed into fear of the dark. And nightmares result from the transformation of desire into fear. We dream that some overwhelming force is menacing us, and we wake up suddenly, oppressed with monstrous, unearthly fears. This is because the wishes of the Id have threatened to thrust themselves openly upon us, our Super-Ego is not strong enough to resist them, and, as a last defence, we have been forced to break off our slumbers. The pent-up desires which are left behind when the shock is felt in childhood become a lasting source of fear and guilt, threatening to intrude upon our minds.

The symptoms of the neurotic offer a path of escape from fear and guilt. His mental life begins to centre around a problem which belongs to the time when the shock was felt— a problem which is no longer real. He must find a way out for his longings and his fears; but at the same time he must hold them back, because they threaten to overwhelm him. By a tremendous effort of will he thrusts a whole period of his life out of his memory—exactly that period which needs to be most fully understood, if his disorder is to be cured. Or he adopts apparently meaningless actions and rituals in order to allay his fears—but these actions and rituals, although meaningless in the sense that they have no real use in his life, are full of meaning to the psychologist, for they are the clues by which we can discover what was the nature of the shock which originally threw his development off the normal track.

In this way, neurotic symptoms are like dreams. The dream, too, gives a partial, inadequate expression to a forbidden desire. And the same methods which revealed the meaning of the dream from the fragments which reached consciousness will lead us from the symptoms of the neurotic to the unconscious disturbance which is the cause of his disorder.

There is no fundamental difference between hysteria and obsession. In each case the same hidden forces are at work, the same unconscious conflict exists. Whether the one disorder or the other results depends, not on the nature of the shock itself, but on the balance between the unconscious forces. In the hysterics, the forbidden desires of the Id are revealed in fantasies and symptoms ; in the obsessions, what we see most clearly is the struggle of the Super-Ego to dominate.

HELPING THE PATIENT TO " MINISTER TO HIMSELF "

BUT both disorders arise from the conflict of two opposing unconscious forces. What happens if development has been checked while the child is still in its earliest infancy, before the desire for pleasure has been divided into two opposing forces ? It is then that the way is prepared for the development of the psychoses and the sexual perversions. Since these disorders trace back to a time before the desire for pleasure had been divided against itself, there are no signs in them of any mental conflict. The patient appears to be perfectly satisfied with his own condition ; he becomes completely immersed in the pursuit of his own ideas and fantasies ; or he abandons himself to his misery ; or he has a boundless self-confidence ; or he feels no desire for normal sexual intercourse.

In Freud's method of treating mental disorders the patient is called upon to furnish his own cure. Just as Socrates led men to wisdom not by teaching them but by asking them questions, the analyst leads the patient to understand himself by pursuing his inquiries until nothing is left undiscovered. If the patient opposes himself to the analyst, and determines to hold back vital facts, the analyst is likely to discover this soon enough, but he cannot pursue his treatment until the patient is willing to co-operate again.

It would be possible to find out what is wrong with the patient very quickly by hypnotising him and obtaining the information during the trance. By this method a temporary cure can often be effected. But it will not last. The patient must discover for himself what is his trouble if he is to free himself of it for ever.

It is for this reason that psycho-analysis is more successful with the neuroses than with the other mental disorders. For where there is a conflict of desires, the patient can usually command enough resolution to pursue his cure to the end ; but in the psychoses the patient has surrendered himself to his disorder, and feels no interest in curing himself.

We can regard Freud's method of treatment from another point of view. In his disordered conduct the patient is reacting not to the situation in which he finds himself, but to a situation which belongs to the past—the situation which first checked the normal outlet of his desires. For the analyst, the ways in which the patient behaves are the clues which lead back to this past situation, and when all these clues have been traced back successfully, the analyst has solved his problem. When the patient fully understands the past situation, his energies remain pent up no longer, they are released ; and with their release the cure is effected.

MODERN MAN AND ANCIENT MYTH

FROM studying the ways in which men may become disordered in their minds, two important lines of thought have developed, which depart a long way from the opinions of Freud and his followers (*Psycho-analysis*). These two lines of thought were developed, one by Jung, most of whose work was done in Zurich, the other by Adler, who has worked, like Freud, mainly in Vienna. Jung distinguishes his theories by the name of *Analytical Psychology*, Adler his by the name of *Individual Psychology*.

It may seem strange, when we consider these theories in

DREAM SYMBOLS OF A PRISONER'S ESCAPE

turn, that the same observed facts (the symptoms of the mental disorders) should be capable of being interpreted in such different ways ; stranger still, that cures can be effected by such different methods of treatment.   The fact that many patients, especially hysterical patients, are extremely suscep- tible even to mild forms of suggestion may possibly have some- thing to do with this ; and it is possible, too, that all three methods of treatment are not equally efficacious.   It is even possible that the kind of treatment which any particular patient prefers may be determined for him by the nature of the disorder from which he suffers, so that in the long-run a selective distribution of patients occurs, to the advantage of all three methods.   To pass judgment on such matters is an extremely odious task, and it requires, if it is to be just and impartial, a profounder knowledge of the disorders themselves than is contained in any one theory.   The best we can do is to acquaint ourselves with the outstanding contributions of all three, and to leave the final judgment to the future.

Of course we were only able to touch on a part of Freud's work, and we tried to find what is of most general interest and importance.   It is not surprising, then, that we left many problems unconsidered.   Among them is one which grows more important when we come to consider the characteristic theories of Jung, and see how they differ from those of Freud.

Freud traces the mental disorders back to shocks received in early childhood.   In his treatment he aims at discovering the nature of these shocks, in order to set free the energy which has become tied up in them.   But while these shocks appear to Freud to be the most important causes of mental disorders, they cannot be the only causes.   Otherwise we should expect every mental disorder to start in early child- hood.   Mental disorders are in fact commoner among children than is usually supposed ; but a great many people who suffer from such disorders only begin to show symptoms much later in life, sometimes during the period of developing man- hood, between the the ages of twelve and twenty-one, and sometimes later still.

GOING BACK ALONG THE PATH OF CHILDHOOD

IF the causes of mental disorder lie in early childhood, why do the effects appear only late in life ? This problem seems, perhaps, a little more difficult than it is.   It does not mean that the shock theory is entirely wrong. But there must be other contributing causes, and these causes, though they serve to bring on the symptoms of disorder, may have only slight importance in themselves. If a boy has formed a neurotic attachment to his mother at the age of three, when would we expect him to show the first symptoms of mental disorder ? Not until it is time for him to leave the family and start on a career of his own. The shock which has prevented the child's desires from developing normally will not necessarily begin to show its effects at once—it will only affect his conduct when demands are made on him, as a man, which he should be, but is not able to fulfil.

Taking everything into consideration, then, there are three factors which help to bring on a neurosis : (i) the disposition that the child inherits from his parents, and the surroundings in which he lives ; (ii) the sudden shock, which we have described ; and (iii) the situation which brings the disorder to a head. Jung differs from Freud in the importance which he attaches to these different factors. To Freud, the second factor is what is all-important ; but Jung finds as much importance in the third factor as in the second.

Freud considers that the desire for pleasure, the libido, is essentially sexual. Even in his first activities of sucking, the pleasures of the child arise from voluptuous sensations just like those which he will derive later in life from mature sexual relations. As the child grows older the ways in which he is able to express and satisfy his desires become wider, they undergo a moral transformation, they lose their primitive sensuality : but still the normal satisfactions of his sexual needs may be the deepest pleasures of his life.

For Jung, on the contrary, the libido is a pure life-force. It is something akin to the Will in Schopenhauer's philosophy, that force which not only makes man live and reproduce, but makes the trees grow, the wind blow, the earth move round the sun—that force which is the reality behind our world of appearances. The libido may find a sexual expression at times, but it is not sexual in itself. The primitive desires of the child are not sexual. It is only as he approaches adolescence, as his body develops its sexual potentialities, that his desires also become tinged with sexuality.

How is it, then, that the early disturbances, which neurotic patients recall, nearly always centre around sexual matters ? Why do they confess to having felt incestuous desires for their parents ?— Why are the repressed forces, which struggle to be released, always of a highly sexual kind ?

Jung's answer is that these unfortunate experiences were not originally sexual ; their sexual tone is one that they have acquired in the recollection of the patient. Part of the life-force of the individual remains caught and held in these events ; but the greater part moves on, to encounter fresh problems. It is when some problem is encountered in the present, some obstacle is met too great to overcome, that neurosis develops. The whole of the life-force becomes held up by the present obstacle, and in order to overcome it must have fresh strength. Then it turns back into the past (*regression*) to gather up the strength which has remained imprisoned by past crises. The past crises acquire a new significance. The full energy of the adult, with its sexual tone, joins with the energy of the child ; and the childhood problems, infused with the energy of the adult, appear grotesquely sexualised.

WHERE JUNG DIFFERS FROM FREUD

JUNG, then, considers that disturbances in childhood are not very important in themselves. They gain their importance whe nthe energy of the adult becomes attached to them. Because of this, Jung's method of treatment comes to be different from Freud's. If, as in Freud's method, the entire effort is directed towards wiping out the effects of the past disturbance, the energy will be released from it, and it may move onward again and prove strong enough to overcome the obstacles of the present. But even with the new energy which has been released from the past, there may still be not enough strength to face the tasks of the present. Then we will find that, instead of moving on again, the energy moves further back ; a new crisis is disclosed, belonging to a still remoter past ; and the whole energy of the individual becomes fixed upon this in turn. So we may treat a patient for one disorder, and end by bringing on another.

When a man catches a cold, we may take his temperature, and find that it has gone up. We treat the temperature a; a symptom of the cold. But what causes the temperature ? Not the cold, but a fever, which is the body's reaction against the cold. In the same way, difficulties in the present bring on a disorder of the mind ; and, as symptoms of the disorder, we find repetitions of troubles belonging to the past. We do not try to cure a cold by driving out the fever, which is part of the cure. Nor should we treat the disorder of the neurotic by obliterating the symptoms which have their causes in the past. The patient must be able to overcome his present difficulties if he is to free himself of his disorder ; and the aim of treatment must be to bring this about.

MYTHS THAT ARE CLUES TO MEMORIES AND DREAMS

IN a previous section we discussed the symbol *three* when we were considering Freud's interpretation of a dream. There are many such symbols. For instance, a *house* is a regularly recurrent symbol for the body ; *water* for birth ; a *journey* for death. As evidence for these symbols, we find such popular expressions as " bats in the belfry," or " weak in the upper storey," used to describe slight mental peculiarities—both expressions imply a comparison of the body to a building. " The last journey " is a polite expression for death, and we speak delicately of the dead as the " departed." We find holy water used at christenings and baptisms, the two ceremonies which celebrate respectively being born of the flesh and being born of the spirit. " Crossing the Jordan " is a condensed symbol for death and re-birth. And we could find many other symbols commonly recurring.

We saw that such symbols cannot be explained by memories of the dreamer himself. They must be traced through popular idioms, through myths, and through religious ceremonials. They are ideas which do not belong to the individual but to the race. How do these ideas come into the mind of the individual ? Jung believes that they belong to the racial unconscious, which each individual inherits, just as he inherits a certain structure of body and of brain. He is predisposed to think in a particular way.

There are thus, in every man, ideas which belong not to himself alone, but to all humanity. They are not his ordinary daily thoughts ; he may go through the whole of his life without becoming aware of them. But they exist, an inner world which he can explore, and out of which he can bring to light ideas which have value for the whole world. Thus the great physicist, Robert Mayer, who gave to the world the theory of the conservation of energy, derived his original idea not by the observation and comparison of many facts, but through a discovery which seemed to take place in his own mind. He writes : " I kept to physics, clinging to the subject with such ardour that although it may seem ridiculous

to say so, I cared very little about the world we were in. . . .
A few flashes of thought that thrilled through me were immediately diligently pursued, leading again in their turn to
new subjects. Those times are passed, but subsequent quiet
examination of what then emerged has taught me that it was
a truth which cannot only be subjectively felt, but also
proved objectively."

It is this theory of the *racial unconscious* which has led
Freudians to denounce Jung roundly as a mystic. It may be
difficult to explain the origins of dream symbols ; but to
trace their origin to a " racial unconscious " is to explain
something obscure by something still more obscure—if you
accept the racial unconscious, then certainly the symbols are
explained, but you are left with the racial unconscious itself
to explain.

THE DREAMER AND THE MAN OF ACTION

ANOTHER theory suggested by Jung has met with more
general acceptance. It is his scheme for dividing people
up into various psychological types. First of all, Jung divides
mankind into two broad types—the introvert and the extravert.
In the introvert the libido or life energy directs itself inwards,
towards the inner world ; in the extravert, outwards—this
is the simple meaning of the terms. The true extravert
adapts himself quickly and unhesitatingly to his surroundings,
everything unknown seems to him alluring. The introvert is
shy, hesitating, cautious in his approach to the unknown.
He is more interested in names and meanings than in things.
" There are not a few," Jung writes, " who in all their actions
have but one consideration in mind ; namely, what do others
think of them ? There are those who can realise happiness
only when it excites the envy of others ; there are also individuals who wish for troubles, and even create them for themselves, in order to enjoy the sympathy of their fellow-men "—
these are pronounced extraverts. The introvert follows out
his own intentions, caring nothing for the opinion of others ;
he seeks values where others would not think of finding them ;
he forms his opinion of himself in sharp contrast with that
which others have of him.

THE FOUR GATES TO THE TEMPLE OF LIFE

BETWEEN the complete introvert and the complete extravert
lie the broad masses of more normal men. They combine

within themselves something of both types. " Conformity is one side of a man, uniqueness the other." The ordinary man may vary in his attitude, appearing introverted on one occasion, extraverted on another.

Within each of these two broad types, further type-differences may be found. Some men find the richest values of life in their sensations ; in the air they breathe, the sounds they hear—or even in the food they eat. Others find life's meaning in emotional experiences. A third group approach every experience with an elaborate machinery of thought ; they know no rest until they have grasped it firmly with their understanding. And a fourth enrich their lives with their intuitions—they see " something more " in every primrose. Each type has come to place his reliance on one main line of mental activity—sensation, feeling, thought, or intuition.

These four types cut across the introvert and extravert groups. Thus we might find someone who is a feeling-extravert, who is transported by every sunset ; or a feeling-introvert, who is passionately devoted to an ideal. And similarly with the other types.

There is much to be said for such a scheme of classification, and the broad division into introvert and extravert types has already been widely adopted, and has proved useful in many different spheres. The narrower division into sensation, feeling, thought, and intuition types has yet to find general favour ; although it is easy, when one thinks over one's different acquaintances, to find people who correspond well enough with one or another of these types.

LIFE AS A LONG STRUGGLE FOR POWER : ADLER

IT is well known that damage or weakness in one organ of the body may lead to over-development of another. Sometimes this happens between two similar organs, as when the loss of one kidney is followed by an enlargement of the other ; but a quite different organ may compensate, by its strength, for the weakness of another. When the lungs are feeble, and breathing becomes difficult, this puts a greater strain on the heart, and the heart becomes larger and stronger in order to meet the difficulty in breathing.

Adler's theories extend this principle of compensation so as to explain the peculiarities of different people's characters.

5

Every man's essential, most primitive desire, he holds, is to gain mastery over his fellows. He has to struggle against any bodily weakness he may have—as Kaiser Wilhelm II. had to overcome the weakness of his crippled arm—he has to struggle against the difficulties of his environment, against social disadvantages, against the failures in his own past. This struggle for mastery is common to all of us. The only way in which we differ from one another is in the uses we make of our own advantages and disadvantages, in the methods we adopt for putting ourselves on top. These methods are what form the character of the individual ; they go to make up his life-style.

Very early in life the child finds his own characteristic way of going about things, of getting hold of what he wants, of getting round his difficulties, and by the time he is five or six years old, everything he does, whether large or small, is worked out according to the same general pattern, his life style, and bears the full imprint of his character.

The weakness of one bodily organ can be off-set, not only by strengthening other bodily organs, but also by transforming the character, by an effort of will which converts weakness itself into strength. Beethoven, who was slightly deaf from childhood, and became deafer and deafer as he grew older, reacted against his deafness by musical composition. Demosthenes triumphed over a stammer, and trained himself to become one of the greatest orators of history. El Greco, the painter, suffered from an astigmatism in the eye. . . .

In the triumph over the weakness of his body, the individual not only regains a position of equality with his fellows, the strength of his effort carries him forward into a position of superiority. Adler even regards the whole evolution of man as a struggle against bodily weakness. For man's body is a weakly thing, it has not the tusks of the elephant, nor the claws of the tiger, nor even the tail of the monkey. His only advantage is in his brain. This he has carried to an astonishing degree of development, which has enabled him to triumph over the rest of Nature, and enslave it to his uses.

THE CASE OF THE HATED CHILD

BUT only in exceptional cases is a bodily weakness the chief obstacle which a man encounters in his pursuit of mastery. One man may compensate for the weakness of his intellect by cultivating strength of character—we often find the stupidest people are the most stubborn. The younger child of a family may find himself in a position of inferiority to his elder brother ; if his brother is good at sports, he will put them aside, and cultivate appreciation of the arts. Or a woman may find herself in a position of inferiority in an age when men command all the positions of importance, and yet she will gain power over all of them through skilful management of intrigues.

But compensation is not always successful. "*Everyone's goal is superiority, but in the case of those who lose their courage and self-confidence, it is diverted from the useful to the useless side of life,*" Adler writes in one of his books ; and elsewhere he says :

> "The spoiled child, being in a position where it receives too much from others, never proves its own powers to itself. Its goal, formed in accordance with experience, is to be the centre of the family, the focus of attention and care. The usual symptoms are : anger, discontent, disorderliness, anxiety, a struggle to avoid isolation. . . .
> "The hated child is in a worse position of never having been spoiled by anyone. Its goal is to escape and to get at a safe distance from others. Cruelty, slyness, and cowardice are some of the symptoms. Such a child is often unable to look one straight in the eyes, cannot speak, and hides its feelings in fear of abasement." [1]

Whereas the normal child succeeds in triumphing over his weakness, the neurotic child finds strength in his weaknesses themselves. He cultivates them ; he becomes ill. Instead of grappling with reality he flies from it, he finds an escape in his illness. He forms neurotic symptoms. He suffers from overwhelming anxieties, and achieves imaginary triumphs when he overcomes them. Instead of becoming socially useful, he finds his power through becoming a burden upon society. He uses his illnesses, his disturbances, as instruments for subjecting others to his will.

PUBLIC BENEFACTOR AND PUBLIC ENEMY

ADLER does not attach any great importance to the way in which different mental disorders have been divided up by medical science. The difference between hysteria and obsession is unimportant ; what is important is the difference

[1] All the quotations in this subsection are from Adler's writings.

between one man and another. The symptoms of the neurotic help to reveal one life-style, just as the actions of the normal man reveal another. The normal, social man pursues his goal of superiority through his daily activities, through the way he talks, the way he dresses, the work he does ; he shows it in the things he laughs at and in the things that aggravate him. The criminal pursues his goal of superiority by waging war on society, by defying and eluding the police, by gaining notoriety, by terrorising a neighbourhood. The neurotic pursues his goal by making doctors, relations, friends, and servants dance attendance upon him, by asserting his authority in trivial matters, by his precocious, unreasonable behaviour, by preying on the peace of mind of others. He exaggerates his troubles, he creates fictitious difficulties for himself, in order that his triumph over them may appear more melo-dramatic. The lunatic, shut up in his cell, compensates himself for his failure in life by imagining himself to be a great world figure, a saint, Mahomet, Napoleon, or Hitler.

In everyone, no matter how stupid or irrational his conduct may appear to others, there is a steady, unremitting pursuit of a single consistent plan of life. The whole of his conduct is organised around this central plan, and once we can discover it, we can find the logic in every one of his actions, we can see how they belong together. Everything falls into its place.

THE SOCIAL TRUST OF MOTHERHOOD

ADJUSTMENT to life, if it is to be successful, must reach success in each of life's three main problems—society, work, and love. Unless it is tempered with a finely-developed social feeling, " the goal of personal superiority is such that it invariably magnifies one of the three questions of life out of all proportion. We find that a person's ideal of success be-comes unnaturally limited to social notoriety, to business success, or to sexual conquest. Each disturbs the harmony of life by leaving many necessary demands unsatisfied, and then tries to compensate by still more frantic strivings in this narrowed sphere of action."

It is lack of social feeling that marks the difference between success and failure in the formation of a life-plan. " Suppose, for instance, that a boy is terrified by illness and death in his environment. He may allay his fears by the determination to be a doctor, and to fight against death. This is obviously a more social idea than that of being a gravedigger, who buries the others—a reaction which I have also found in a boy of that situation." And in a passage which may be said to summarise the essence of his teaching, Adler writes :

> "That which we call social feeling in Individual Psychology is the true and inevitable compensation for all the natural weaknesses of individual human beings. . . . Social feeling is not inborn ; it is an innate potentiality which has to be consciously developed ; the dominant purpose of education is to evoke it. . . . The most vital factor is the mother. It is in its mother that every child makes its first contact with a trustworthy fellow-being. . . . The art of motherhood is to give the child freedom and opportunity for success by its own efforts, so that it can establish its style of life and seek for its superiority in increasingly useful ways. Then gradually she must interest the child in other persons and in the wider environment of life. So far as she can discharge these two functions—of bestowing independence and of imparting a true initial understanding of the surrounding situation in the home and in the world—she will see the child develop social feeling, independence, and courage. And so far also will the child find its own goal in being a fellow-man and a friend, a good worker, and a true partner in love."

FURTHER READING ON PSYCHO-ANALYSIS

THE preceding article has dealt chiefly with the three great doctors who have founded the modern schools of abnormal psychology—Freud (psycho-analysis), Adler (individual psychology), and Jung (analytical psychology). It may be pointed out that the term psycho-analysis, strictly speaking, applies only to the researches of Freud and his school. It is well not to begin the study of the subject with the works of these writers. The best way is to get hold of a good general introduction. One of the best and most up-to-date of these is Ernest Jones's *Psycho-Analysis* (Benn's Sixpenny Library). Another good introduction is *Psycho-Analysis and its Derivatives*, by H. Crichton-Miller, M.D. (Home University Library, Thornton Butterworth, Limited). The historical aspect of the subject is treated in *A Hundred Years of Psychology* (Duckworth), by J. C. Flugel. R. S. Woodworth's *Contemporary Schools of Psychology* (Methuen) should be read before the student passes on to the main writings of the founders of the modern schools.

The most suitable work of Freud with which to begin is his *Introductory Lectures on Psycho-Analysis* (Allen and Unwin), which summarises a large part of his researches. Freud contributed additions to his theory in *The Ego and the Id* (Hogarth Press), in which he considerably expands his conception of the forces of the subconscious. Two most important books of Adler's are *Practice and Theory of Individual Psychology* (Kegan Paul), and *Understanding Human Nature* (Allen and Unwin). The most famous of Jung's works is certainly *Psychological Types* (International Library of Psychology, Philosophy, and Scientific Method). A more popularly presented book by the same author is *Modern Man in Search of a Soul* (Kegan Paul), which summarises most of Jung's theory.

WHERE IS GOODNESS TO BE FOUND?
THE PROBLEM OF CONDUCT

by

R. C. ROWSE, M.A., Warden of Percival Guildhouse, Rugby

THE branch of Philosophy which studies questions of goodness is called Ethics, or Moral Philosophy. The word Ethics is derived from the Greek word meaning character, which itself is connected with the word meaning custom. Morals, too, is derived from a word meaning custom, in this case Latin. So the very name gives us some indication of the field of study. It deals with the customs and practices of mankind considered from the point of view of their value rather than of their occurrence. Anthropology, which is a science and not a philosophy, deals with this latter aspect.

The question has probably already arisen in the mind of the reader: How does one judge the value of a custom? What does it mean when it is said that Ethics inquires into the value of customs? This is a really philosophical question: it is as a matter of fact the central problem of Moral Philosophy. In more technical terms we may say that Moral Philosophy is concerned with the inquiry into the nature of Goodness. It is important to notice that by Goodness we do not mean merely moral goodness in the narrow sense of the term, nor even morality as it is ordinarily understood. We mean its significance for human beings Moral Philosophy is not a tribunal which inquires whether an action has been performed in accordance with a certain law: it is the attempt to discover what is really valuable for mankind in the sphere of conduct. Then if it discovers this, it is possible to derive laws from it. We must insist that Moral Philosophy, despite its forbidding name, is not a mid-Victorian old spinster passing judgment on behaviour, but is a modern Socrates inquiring kindly, but with perseverance, into the nature of what we really want when we are most ourselves. For this is how we shall define Goodness.

The wise of all ages have concerned themselves with this question. Standards of conduct, petrified in customs, are to be found wherever there are groups of people. As time elapses, some of these customs grow out of date and become useless. But they are still enforced by the standard of conduct of the time. It is then that the more thoughtful people of the day begin to question them, and in time they may disappear, though they survive long after they have outlived their usefulness. Primitive taboos afford a good example. Another custom which is only just beginning to break down is that of going to war to settle international disputes. Many people consider that it is matter of honour to go to war ; others think that the method is now out of date, that a better way is open to us. This is an example of a custom in the process of breaking down, and it shows how very slow the process really is.

The fact that as the human race travels through the centuries—and, indeed, as the individual travels from place to place in the same century—different standards of conduct are to be found, leads people to inquire if there is not some more ultimate standard by which we can judge conduct.

OBEDIENCE AND ACHIEVEMENT : TWO GOALS OF MORAL CONDUCT

LOOKING back over the thought of centuries we discover two main types of answer to this problem. In nearly all primitive communities conduct is judged according to some law or rule. This is not, however, confined to primitive communities. There are modern thinkers who take as the standard of conduct a law—the law of God, the law given by Reason, the law of Conscience. There is, however, another school of thought that finds the standard in the achievement of some end. Actions, and even laws themselves, are good only if they are calculated to achieve a certain end which is desirable in itself. The commonest and most plausible form of this theory is that which regards happiness or pleasure as the end.

We usually use the words " Right " and " Good " to distinguish between these two methods of estimating action. In one case, the rightness of an action is the criterion : in the other, the goodness of the end. The greater part of Moral Philosophy is concerned with what we mean by " Right " and " Good." An illustration might be made out of the execution of the aristocrats in the French Revolution. If the *rightness of the action* were taken as the criterion, these executions were obviously wrong, for no one holds that killing in cold blood is in itself a good action. But if the *goodness of the end* were taken as the criterion, that is to say, if the deed were to be judged by the *ultimate* effect on the majority of the citizens by the executions, then, if the majority did benefit, the action would have been good itself. It is the root problem below the question so often asked : Do the ends justify the means ?

Closely connected with this distinction, though it cuts across it in some ways, is another, which is still one of the unsolved problems of Ethics, namely : *Do we judge an act by its intention or by its consequences?* Obviously, if we hold that obedience to law constitutes the goodness of an action, the moralist merely requires to cultivate a right spirit among the people. We can all obey a law if we want to. The trouble is that we do not always want to. On the other hand, if the achievement of a certain result is the criterion of action, we may try with the best will in the world, *i.e.* we may be as well-intentioned as it is possible to be, and yet for want of knowledge or skill not attain the end. Then, by definition, our action would not be good. We all know people who unselfishly try hard to do good but are always making a mess of anything they do. If we judge these people by their intentions, they are undoubtedly very good, if we judge them by consequences, they are undoubtedly very bad. It is impossible to judge a person by both these standards at once, and equally impossible to judge him by one only. If by goodness we mean that which is for the real interest of mankind, good intentions are not enough to secure it. Yet we cannot call a man good if he is a rascally knave and yet promotes the common good because it is his good.

THE LAW OF NATURE AND THE CALL OF CONSCIENCE

THESE are the two main difficulties in the search for the criterion of conduct, for the Good. We must now consider the principal views that thinkers have held on these questions. Let us consider first those views that look to some law as a guide to good conduct. On the balance, this type of view will be found to be the earlier of the two, both in the history of the race and in the history of the individual. Our first notions of right and wrong are that we must do as we are told and because we are told. We learn reasons why later, if at all.

Of the philosophical systems which have maintained that man's good lies in obedience to a law, we will consider the three most outstanding. There is firstly that of the *Stoics*, one of the later Greek schools. They held that throughout the world there was a law, the expression of the Divine Reason. Goodness consisted in living in accordance with this law, which was, of course, the law of Nature as well as of that part of Nature which is man. Therefore the rule of life was : *live in accordance with Nature*. Unfortunately the Stoics were not as definite as they might have been as to what this involved. This law, being a law of Reason, certainly meant keeping the emotions very much in the background. Also, as it was a universal law, it involved the brotherhood of all men—one of the first internationalist ethics. There are elements of permanent value in Stoicism, but the real unsatisfactoriness of it lies in its vagueness as to what is meant by " Nature." What nature have we to live up to—our animal nature or our divine nature ? It is useless to have a guide of conduct which itself needs to be explained.

Another important theory that holds that the criterion of action is its conformity to some law is that of Bishop Butler, an eighteenth-century thinker. For him the bar before which all moral questions are judged is the bar of Conscience. In order to understand this properly we must understand his view of human nature. This he regards as an organised whole made up of many parts, some of which are naturally subordinate to others, and the others naturally ruling the subordinate elements. The subordinate elements are our natural desires, affections, and feelings. There is nothing wrong about these : they are quite natural, and have their proper place. Wickedness does arise when these grow too big for their shoes and try to take a more important place than they deserve.

Above these elements of moral experience are to be found two organising principles—*Self-love* and *Benevolence*. Sometimes a particular appetite, *e.g.* the desire to eat, may be used for private purposes, *i.e.* to support life. Then it is organised in the system of Self-love. Self-love is not selfishness ; it is a necessary part in the task of keeping oneself alive, and after all a live human being is of more use than a dead one. But sometimes the desire to eat may be utilised for social purposes, *e.g.* at a tea-party, where the main purpose is to be good company. There the desire is organised in the system

of Benevolence. This is Butler's main view, though sometimes he suggests that Self-love should be subordinate to,
and not co-ordinate with, Benevolence.

Above these organised systems there is the supreme
principle of moral experience, Conscience. It is the judge
of all action : by it we know when we organise our life wrongly,
when, for instance, we let our passions sway our reasonable
Self-love or Benevolence instead of being ruled by them.
Butler, as a realist, regrets that very often Conscience is weak,
though even so we recognise that we ought to be ruled by it.
" Had it strength as it has right, had it power as it has manifest
authority, it would absolutely govern the world."

It is obvious that this theory has much in it that is attractive. It is clearly a law-theory and not an end-theory. But
it does not help us very much with our second difficulty,
namely : Do we judge an act by its consequences or by our
intentions ? If we could be sure that the individual conscience
never errs, the probelm would be solved. All we should
have to do would be to obey our conscience. But it is unfortunately a fact that some of the most conscientious of
people do much harm when trying their best to do good.
To do good in life we have not only to make sure that we are
obeying the dictates of conscience—that is not very difficult
and only requires practice—but we have also to make sure
that our conscience is not mistaken ; and that is very difficult.
It requires not merely moral earnestness, but prolonged
thought and comprehensive knowledge ; and even this will
not guarantee success.

KANT'S THEORY OF THE GOOD WILL

THE greatest of all law theories is that of Immanuel Kant
(1724-1804). He begins his treatment of morals with
the statement : " Nothing can possibly be conceived in the
world, or even out of it, which can be called good without
qualification, except a Good Will." All other things may
be good or bad according to the way they are used ; and this
depends upon the will. So the only ultimately good thing
is the will. Of course, by a good will Kant does not mean
the mere wish for good, but the putting forth of every effort
in our power.

The Good Will issues its orders in *categorical imperatives*,[1]
i.e. orders that must in no circumstances be disobeyed. A

[1] See also sections on Philosophy.

categorical imperative is best described in contrast to a hypothetical imperative. This latter issues orders in the form, " If you want to be healthy, rise early." One can always evade this command by saying, " But I don't want to be healthy." There is no answer to this. But a categorical imperative says, " Rise early," without any conditions, and there is no way of evading the command. The commands of morality are of this nature. If you disobey them you are wicked : you cannot excuse yourself, as you might if they were hypothetical.

Now, says Kant, " there is but one categorical imperative, namely, this : *Act only on that maxim whereby thou canst at the same time will that it should become a universal law.*" If, for example, you apply this criterion to promise-keeping, you see that if everybody were to make a promise not intending to keep it nobody would believe in promises, there would be no such thing as a promise. Therefore it is a duty always to keep promises. The same reasoning applies to all other duties, *e.g.* not to commit suicide, not to steal, to develop one's talents, etc. The essence of these duties is that they are categorical imperatives, they admit of no exceptions. The reason why we have to obey them is just that it is inconsistent not to do so. It is to make an exception in our own favour which we could not allow to everyone else. There is, of course, much more in Kant than this, but this is the essence of his moral theory.

Thus we see that Kant's ethics is a very pure example of a law-theory. We must obey the law because it is the law. It also solves our second difficulty, namely : Shall we judge action by motives or by consequences ? Kant states quite clearly that if we always act out of duty we can never be wrong, whatever the consequences. Morality is concerned only with motives : it is expediency that is concerned with consequences.

A QUESTION THAT STRIKES AT THE ROOT OF KANT'S THEORY

THERE is, however, one fundamental objection to all law-theories, even Kant's. This appears if we ask : *But why should I obey the law?* Or, if two laws conflict : *Which shall I obey ?* It is no help here to say obey the law because it is the law, for in this case both are laws. If you ask a Stoic : Why should I obey the law of Nature ? or Bishop Butler Why should I obey the law of conscience ? there is no answer, except to say that you ought to do so because it is your nature to do so. You may reply that it goes very much against your nature. If they retort that it should not do so, you may again ask why, and they have no further answer beyond another " ought not." A similar objection applies to Kant. If Kant tells you that you ought not to steal because by doing so you are implicitly denying the right to private property, you can always reply : " Why should there be private property ? " Or if he tells you that by making a false promise you are implicitly denying that promises should be kept, you can still ask why promises should be kept.

In all these cases you can legitimately ask : "What is the reason for the law ? " and then the answer must be : " Because it conduces to some end desirable in itself." It is obvious that the reasons for observing the rights of property, telling the truth, not committing suicide, are just that by so doing we help to make life in communities possible and more conducive to what we really want. What we really meant, *i.e.* the Good for us, is a state of life, not in the last analysis, life lived according to law. Therefore we shall now turn to consider the end-theories of Ethics, theories which consider the criterion of action to be whether or not it achieves a certain end.

But before doing so, we might note in passing one of the incidental psychological effects of law-theories upon people who do not see the reason for the law. It is characteristic of this type of theory to insist that the law must be obeyed because it is the law. Some of the more independent spirits may feel that, because no reason is given why the law should be obeyed, there is no such reason ; and consequently they rebel against it. We all know the child who when told not to touch something immediately touches it. That is the effect of issuing a command with which the person commanded is not in sympathy. The existence of this type of nature, together with an authoritarian Ethics, may account largely for the disrepute into which the word " morals " has fallen with many people. When moralists deplore the fact that morality to-day has fallen into disrepute, they should seriously consider whether this fact is not at least part of the cause.

ENDS THAT ARE DESIRABLE IN THEMSELVES

AN examination of law-theories of Ethics seems to indicate that they are incomplete in themselves, that the obstinate thinking which is philosophy has not been quite obstinate enough. They require an end-theory to complete them. We must look, therefore, for something which is desirable in itself and the attainment of which we consider good. There are clearly a number of such things, but the most obvious is pleasure. Everyone, it is said, desires pleasure, and, moreover, desires it for itself alone.

If you examine what people really want you will find that they want other things only as a means to pleasure. Take money, for instance, or power, or fame. These are not desired for their own sakes, but for the pleasure which they can command. If we have to choose between two courses of action we always choose that which will give us most pleasure, or least pain. Even the martyr, burning at the stake, is actuated by the same motives. For him it would be a greater pain to live with the knowledge that he had betrayed his faith than to endure for a short time the flames. He has reached such a degree of development that mental pains are more serious than those of the body. Thus the protagonists of this theory argue that if we examine our own conduct and that of everyone else we shall see that in the end we consider actions right in proportion as they tend to promote pleasure and wrong as they tend to promote pain.

This type of theory is called *Hedonism*, from the Greek word *hēdonē*, meaning pleasure. It has a long and illustrious list of thinkers as its protagonists, from Greek times to the present day. It has assumed various forms, *e.g.* psychological Hedonism, which holds that we do as a matter of fact always desire pleasure and cannot help so doing; ethical Hedonism, which holds that we ought to desire it; egoistic Hedonism, which holds that the individual's own pleasure is the criterion of Goodness; and universalistic Hedonism, usually called *Utilitarianism*, which takes the criterion of Goodness to be *the greatest happiness of the greatest number*.

The essence of Hedonism is the doctrine that pleasure is the only thing good in itself, and if we desire anything else it is only for its pleasure-giving or pain-avoiding qualities. It is not Hedonism to maintain that we desire pleasure for its own sake, while admitting that we may also desire other things for their own sakes. Hedonism finds the Good in pleasure and in nothing else unless it is a means to pleasure.

On reflection, this theory seems convincing, especially when we take into account modifications made by J. S. Mill

(1806–1873). By pleasure, Mill means not merely animal pleasures, but happiness in general and also the pleasures of such activities as music, art, philosophy. He even goes further and distinguishes between various kinds of pleasure. He admits that a person who has little culture and makes few demands upon enjoyment has a much better chance of having those few demands satisfied than has a person whose taste is cultured and makes high demands. But the pleasures of the educated man are better than those of the boor. " Few human creatures would consent to be changed into any of the lower animals for the promise of the fullest allowance of a beast's pleasures." " It is better to be a human being dissatisfied than a pig satisfied ; better to be Socrates dissatisfied than a fool satisfied. And if the fool, or the pig, are of a different opinion, it is because they only know their own side of the question. The other party to the comparison knows both sides." Now the theory is much more respectable than it at first appeared.

PLEASURE'S PLACE IN THE GOOD LIFE

MILL makes a second modification of Hedonism as it had been handed to him, which brings it still more into accord with the ordinary moral consciousness. To say that the best life is that which attains the greatest amount of pleasure is rather selfish. But Mill has a more worthy idea of morality than that. It is not the individual's own pleasure that is the standard of right and wrong, but the " general happiness," *i.e.* the happiness of all. Mill's argument for this is very simple—" each person's happiness is a good to that person, and the general happiness, therefore, a good to the aggregate of all persons."

It is obvious that there is something wrong here. If each of a hundred soldiers is six feet high, it does not follow that the company is six hundred feet high. The trouble is that one can no more add pleasure together than one can stand a hundred soldiers on each other's heads. If the argument for Hedonism is the egoistic one that each person desires his own happiness, no amount of egoists brought together can make the group altruistic ; they will still desire their own happiness and not the happiness of the group.

We are now beginning to see some of the difficulties inherent in Hedonism. In spite of its original attractiveness, it has two great defects. The more important of these is its great vagueness as to what it means by pleasure. If by pleasure we mean what the psychologist means—a feeling-tone, a definite sensation such as a dog may be imagined to feel when we scratch his ears—then obviously, however good pleasure may be, it is not the only thing good in itself.

If, on the other hand, we mean happiness, then Hedonism puts the cart before the horse. Happiness is a feeling of satisfaction we get when all is going well, that " something accomplished, something done " feeling. It is, as Aristotle said, the concomitant of perfected activity. We do not aim at happiness; we aim at certain particular ends, *e.g.* to make a success of business, to play tennis, to help other people, and if we succeed we feel happy.

It will not do to say that we only aim at these other things for the happiness they bring to us ; apart from the gross travesty of human nature, it is the essence of the situation that these particular things should be done for their own sakes. Everyone knows that if you play tennis with a view to enjoying every stroke, you do not enjoy it as much as if you put your whole energy into the game and forget about the pleasure. That, in fact, is the paradox of Hedonism ; the way to attain pleasure is not to aim at it, but to aim at doing something else well, when the pleasure comes, as it were, incidentally.

The second defect emerges when we consider Mill's introduction of the qualitative difference between pleasures. One feels that this brings the theory much more into accord with moral experience, but in doing so it gives up Hedonism. If we say that one pleasure is better than another, not merely that it is more pleasant, we are introducing a new standard of values, different from pleasure and by which we judge even pleasures themselves. It is no longer possible to say that pleasure is the sole thing good in itself.

It appears, then, that as an ethical theory, when we come to inquire into it closely, Hedonism is unsatisfactory. But it is not altogether false ; it would not have loomed so large in the history of Ethics if it had been. Though it is false to assert that pleasure is the only thing good in itself, it is quite true that it is one of the things that are good. It has its place in the good life.

Hedonism also has this advantage, that it is an end-theory of Ethics. It is more self-substantiating. There is some sense in asking why should I obey the law ? but there is much less or none at all in asking why should I seek pleasure ? The more usual question is : Why should I not seek pleasure ? The answer, as Mill unintentionally indicated, is that some pleasures are not as good as others, and these less good ones are not worthy of man.

MAN, KNOW THYSELF

WE must, therefore, set out once more on the search for a criterion of goodness that will stand examination. It seems clear that it must be an end desired for its own sake rather than a law authoritatively imposed. Let us try to look at the matter fairly without prejudices, as far as we can. On consideration, we shall find that what people really mean by their own good is that which satisfies their wants. Success, money, influence are considered good by many people for this reason. Some, who have seen the folly of selfishness, can conceive of a common good, and however they define it, it will be seen that its chief feature is that it satisfies the desire of the community in the most complete way. When we examine the various commandments of morality we shall see also the same principle underlying them all. They may now be out of date, but in their essence they are rules to enable the community as a whole to live together harmoniously and work out its own purposes.

We maintain, then, that the Good at its lowest is that which satisfies wants. When we consider what the wants of a human being are, we find that they have their origin in his nature. The sections on psychology in this book will give a fuller account of human nature. Here we merely insist that if we are to find the Good for man we must take into account what man is. He is a complex of wants, desires, ideals, emotions, etc.—a whole gallimaufry of experiences.

But he is more than this also ; he not only has experiences, but he orders and regulates them in some way. He is naturally an integrating force, he cannot help building up his experiences into systems—sometimes called sentiments. These systems have their ideals, and the man as a whole, the *ego*, relates these to each other, both consciously and unconsciously, until he has what we call a character or nature. A man's nature is just the way he has of organising experiences. An unkindly nature organises them in a system of hate and distrust, a kindly one in love, and so on.

If you ask any man to shake himself free from all cant

and hypocrisy and tell you what he conceives as his good, he will, if he can so free himself, tell you what would satisfy his particular nature as a whole. This, be it noted, is not a low, immoral pandering to desire ; it is not the satisfaction of any one desire, but of the man's whole nature. It is well-known that the satisfaction of particular desires does not satisfy the whole man—we all experience remorse. What was desired by one part of our nature was not *really* desired. It seems inescapable that what a man conceives as his real good is that which would really satisfy his whole nature.

We cannot, however, stop here. Men do not live in isolation, and what one man does always affects some one else. His own good is therefore inextricably bound up with the good of all other people by the inescapable *fact* that he is a member of Society. He may deplore it and struggle against it, but there it is, a fact. And when he has ceased to kick against the pricks he will come to realise that if he wants to achieve his own greatest desires he will have to do so in conjunction with others. He will see also that the others are far more of a help to him in this than a hindrance. No man liveth unto himself, and from his co-operation with others he gains more than he loses by adjusting his idea of good to the common good.

Thus our criterion of goodness becomes life itself, not mere life, but life at its fullest. We can find no external criterion with which to compare life. We are limited in our experience to life, and the only standard we can find is the fullest and most developed life of the individual in Society. It is the ideal of Jesus of Nazareth when He said : " I am come that they might have life, and have it more abundantly." It is the idea of the modern Humanists, however much they may misinterpret it in practice. We will name the ideal Self-Realisation following the two great thinkers, T. H. Green and F. H. Bradley, who developed the essence of this view at the end of last century. The criterion of Goodness is the richest and fullest development of all human possibilities, harmoniously expressed with regard both to the desires of the individual and of society.

THE THEORY OF SELF-REALISATION

IT now remains to relate this theory to the two difficulties which we noticed at the beginning of this inquiry. With regard to the first, it possesses the advantages of an end-theory and avoids the incompleteness of a law-theory. No one, once he has realised what it means, can ask why should he realise to the highest degree the possibilities of the human spirit ? The question is foolish, because everyone does, in fact, realise these possibilities to some extent in so far as he lives. In looking for a standard of Goodness, we merely look for a fuller degree of realisation. This surely escapes the charge of judging action and conduct by some extrinsic standard. The theory of Self-Realisation is an ultimate and self-substantiating theory.

But how does it solve the second difficulty, namely, do we judge an action by the intention of the agent or by the consequences of the action ? The answer is that we circumvent the difficulty. In judging of any act we ask : Was it the most complete and harmonious expression of the agent's nature of which he was capable at the time ? If he had thought more, read more, considered other people more, would he have done something different ? If so, it would not have been as good as it ought to have been. But if the answer is in the negative, we must say that the action was as good as it could have been. The agent was contributing what he could to the sum total of human experience ; and no man can do more.

The observant reader will notice that this view is the counterpart in the moral sphere of truth in the logical sphere, *i.e.* it is one which might be called the *Coherence Theory of Goodness*. Just as the truth of a judgment is determined by the adequacy with which it fulfils its place in a system and expresses Reality, so the goodness of an action is determined by its place in the scheme of life of the agent, and the adequacy with which it fills that place and expresses the purpose of the agent. One cannot live a consistently bad life, for that is a contradiction in terms. A bad life may be consistent with a selection of the facts of experience, but it is strikingly in contradiction with others. That is why we call it bad. The way to deal with a bad life is not to suppress it and start afresh—that is impossible—but to enlarge its scope, and sublimate the narrow and selfish purposes into a wider and more comprehensive plan where they work with the system and do not set up in opposition.

PLANNING FOR THE FUTURE OF SOCIETY

by WRIGHT WATTS MILLER, B.A.(Lond.), M.Ed.(Manchester)

I T is often debated whether education is a science or an art. It is not easy, however, to separate the conceptions *science* and *art* completely from each other. Advances in the sciences of chemistry and biology, for example, depend a good deal upon the individual skill, the practised art, of the glass-blower or the dissector ; advances in the arts of painting or music, on the other hand, have often grown out of (though they have not been created by) advances in the chemistry of oils and colours, or improvements in the resonance and compass of instruments.

Education is indubitably a science when it employs, for example, the discoveries of psychological science, rejecting perhaps at the same time certain popular beliefs based upon habit rather than evidence. Scientific observation, for instance, has proved that it is economical to learn poetry a verse at a time, or even several verses at a time, or again, that precocious children are likely to be distinguished above their fellows when they grow up ; popular practice, on the other hand, unscientifically prefers the wasteful learning line by line, and popular belief often shakes its head over precocious children, under the impression that they will " go off " when they are older.

But education is indubitably an art so far as its success depends, for example, upon the patience and forbearance and skill of the individual teachers who are persuading individual children to learn poetry, or any other subject under the sun. It is apparently impossible, and certainly unnecessary, to decide whether education is wholly a science or wholly an art. But it is of the highest importance to realise that education is a social science and a social art. It owes its existence to Society ; children do not learn poetry unless Society has decided, probably long ago, that poetry should be learned by all its members. Precocious children, again, are not encouraged in every society ; they may be regarded, and at some periods have been regarded, as dangerously eccentric persons, to be suppressed for the common

148

good. (The natural envy of the average members of Society is probably the reason for the lingering belief to-day that precocious children will come to no good.)

BEARING THE TORCH OF COMMUNAL LIFE

THE history of education throughout the world is largely the history of the development of Society. Where Society has remained stagnant, there has as a rule been little education ; where Society has become conscious of ideals to which to aspire, education has generally been highly developed. At the present time, it is so commonly recognised that Society depends on education, that it is often forgotten how closely education depends upon Society. Thus it is not uncommon to-day to expect radical reforms in education alone to bring about the ideal Society, and to blame the slow progress of civilisation on the schools and teachers. But against this should be remembered the radical changes in Society which have generally preceded radical changes in education in the past. It is illogical to demand radical changes in the future of education, and to refuse to envisage parallel and radical changes in the future of Society.

Good schools to-day frequently succeed in preparing their members for a world more perfectly developed than that which they have actually to enter on leaving school. This has been remarked of the products of institutions as widely different as nursery schools and Borstal. It is the shame of Society and not of the schools that this discrepancy should exist. But, in contrast, it should be remembered how commonly the aim of the whole education system, in many different countries and at many different periods, has been simply to adapt children as neatly as possible to the Society of which they were to become adult members.

All the educational systems that have ever existed may be divided into two classes according to their answer to the question : Do you believe in progress ? It is difficult for us to realise to-day that the idea of the possibility or desirability of progress in civilisation is not much more than four hundred years old, and has not been widely held anywhere as far back as two hundred years. Most people are aware that the idea of progress has only very recently begun to appeal to the Asiatic peoples, but even in Western Europe the currency of a phrase such as " the perfectibility of man " dates no further back than the late eighteenth century.

In the development of education, five main trends of thought may be observed. They are given here roughly in the chronological order of their first appearance, but they overlap a good deal, even in the history of education in a single country. Several ideas have often been prominent in the world of education at one time, sometimes in conflict, sometimes in harmony. In general, since the organisation of education has usually been in the hands of some of the most mature and established members of Society, the progress of education has tended, until very recent times, to lag behind many other kinds of progress which Society has made. In English education to-day all the following ideas have their clear and natural influence, though complete harmony among their separate claims has not yet been attained.

FROM RITUAL TO INTELLIGENCE TESTS: THE FIVE STAGES

1. THE PRIMITIVE STAGE: the vast early stage of the mere preparation of children for living in a Society expected to remain stable, and often ritualised to the last detail of ordinary existence. In modern England this ideal is still taken for granted in the education of children in good manners and many details of ordinary behaviour.

2. THE IDEAL STAGE attempted first, for a short time only, in Greece. Education was to help in realising an ideal state of Society—such as the Republic of Plato—which, however, once reached, was to be regarded as fixed, unalterable, and insurpassable. The revival of this ideal played a leading part in the great awakening of education throughout Western Europe during the Renaissance, and as the Humanist ideal it is the basis of our current ideas of culture as an ideal standard. It might also be said that primitive religious education was of the same ideal kind ; it prepared for a perfect though not a mortal state, within a noble framework of austere ideals, partly Hebrew, partly Greek, which have meant a great deal to English education and all English institutions.

3. THE INDIVIDUAL IDEAL, first preached by Rousseau. According to him the child left to develop quite naturally, with a minimum of interference from parent or teacher, must necessarily choose the highest when he sees it ; all evil in man must have arisen through the influence of bad social institutions. This ideal of non-interference has been proclaimed again and again by educators during the last and the

present century ; in the infant schools of to-day it is often a potent influence. The discovery of the theory of evolution (1859) lent great support to the ideal of individual perfectibility.

4. THE DEMOCRATIC IDEAL. In the Greek city-state a very high ideal of individual culture, both bodily and physical, was aimed at, always with the idea, however, that such culture should be of service to the community. But the " community " consisted of a body of comparatively well-trained persons for whom menial tasks were performed by large numbers of slaves or helots. Similarly, most attempts before the nineteenth century which appear to be attempts at democratic education are found to be in reality subject to severe limitations of class, religion, or function.

The great nations of the nineteenth century mostly established systems of democratic education in which, though birth and wealth still often retained privileges, equalisation of educational opportunity was for the first time attempted. In such a system it is always difficult to decide to what extent the individual is being educated for his own good and to what extent for that of the State. Humanist and individualist ideals have played a great part in democratic education, particularly during the last half century, but these ideals are perhaps more dependent upon the character of democracy itself than is often realised. Such aims of education as— " to make every child think for himself," or " to bring every child in contact with the best that has been thought and said " are found in practice to depend a good deal upon the ways in which the State believes a child ought to think or upon what the State in general believes to be " the best."

A violent reaction against these liberal ideals is seen in the perverted State Ideal paramount in the educational systems of Germany, Italy, Japan, and some other countries to-day. This ideal—which has arisen mainly through deduction from the doctrines of the German philosopher Hegel— subordinates the individual almost completely to the State —no longer a democracy—of which, however, he is still supposed to be an " individual " member.

5. IMPARTIAL SCIENTIFIC EXPERIMENT, especially the recent development of the science of psychology, has furnished valuable data to correct our ideas of what is desirable or not desirable, what is attainable with ease or with difficulty, in educational practice. The processes of learning and remem-

bering, the physical development of children, their diet, their attainments at specified ages—all have been the subject of valuable researches. Science, it should be noted, can furnish us with any number of educational tools, but it cannot tell us to what end we should use them ; that question only Society itself can answer.

INSTINCTIVE WISDOM OF SAVAGES

CHILDREN in a savage tribe undergo a system of education probably better adapted to its purpose than any in the world, even that of the Jesuits. The adult member of the tribe requires, as J. H. Driberg points out, a detailed education for two important ends—the maintenance of life and the perpetuation of his species. The most impressive stage of the savage child's education is, therefore, the initiation ceremony at puberty, when he receives, in nearly all tribes, a body of sex instruction and a code of principles for sexual behaviour more impressive and detailed than are given in any civilised country in the world. Strange though the sexual practices of savages may often appear to the white races, there is generally (or has at some earlier period been) sound tribal reasons for their existence.

But the entry into manhood or womanhood is not marked solely by the recognition of sexual maturity. The boys, as the future hunters and warriors of the tribe, and the girls, as the homemakers and tillers of the soil, have already been sharing the activities of the tribe, partly in play and partly in earnest. They have watched the flocks and herds, and at initiation are now examined on their knowledge of good and bad feeding-places, safe and unsafe water, diseases of animals, and defence against their enemies. They have flung children's spears and paddled children's canoes, and are now submitted to perhaps the most painful and searching tests of their ability to throw accurately, to bear pain, to stanch and cure wounds, to recover from an upset in a canoe, to harpoon accurately—all the acquirements which will be necessary to their very existence as adults, the existence of their families, and so the existence of the tribe.

During the initiation period the future warriors, hunters, or fishermen are made to fast for long periods, to eat the most repulsive food, to run immense distances, to bear elementary torture, and probably to submit to a few painful though minor surgical operations as a mark of their adult membership of the tribe. (Similar codes of severe and even nauseating initiation arise in civilised countries wherever there is a small, self-contained society of young persons ; the traditional codes of behaviour in most schools and colleges, created by their members and not by authority, are more severe than anything ever imposed upon the adult white man ; the initiation ceremonies of some of the American secret " fraternities " appear to be equally severe, but they cannot control the whole of an adult existence as a school code may that of a boy.)

Not only are the physical capabilities of the savage child trained and tested ; he may often be made to commit to memory long pieces of tribal lore, since very few tribes have any system of writing ; he may be instructed in the music of the tribe, and in what is of much greater importance—its ceremonial dances, which again assist the memory in preserving the ritual practices essential to the life of the tribe. The language of the tribe is impressed upon the child, among the Maoris, for instance, by long and often difficult exercises in naming things and in simple composition.

The legal, religious, and social practices of the tribe are impressed upon every child with the utmost severity, since the neglect or violation of any of these practices by the adult often means his death or suicide. A child at the initiation period is often allowed and encouraged, even forced, to break all the taboos of the tribe, so that the severe punishment he receives immediately afterwards may impress upon him for ever the wickedness of such crimes. The education of mental powers other than the memory is not so common or widely developed among savage tribes, but the powers of observation, at least, are often given a very thorough and acute training. The observation games played by Boy Scouts have actually been borrowed from the games which form part of the education of a Red Indian boy. The great politeness and charm of manner often observed among savages is also due in a large part to their education ; much of their code of good manners is part of a ritual fundamentally religious, and indistinguishable in importance, to them, from some other practices which to a white man have obviously religious significance. But apart from ritual, the growth of spontaneous courtesy is easy and indeed necessary in a society as small and intimate as that of the average savage tribe.

WESTERN CULTURE AND THE SOUTH SEA ISLANDS

IT is clear that the so-called savage tribes attach the highest importance to their educational rites and systems ; it is further clear that they have a natural awareness of the importance of the child, as future bearer of the torch of communal life, which is sometimes absent and often rather artificial in communities with a more complex civilisation. Corporal punishment is rare among savage tribes. The Sioux Indians say : " When a child is born, a star descends and appears on earth in human form." But the perfect adaptability of savage education to its tribal purpose is its fatal error. It preserves the life of the tribe indeed, often against natural odds of climate, wild animals, and other dangers which might seem invincible, but it preserves that life in a form so rigorously the same, so bound by stringent conventions in every direction, that it can only result in stagnation or degeneration. It may well provide a mode of life which will satisfy more of the fundamental needs of the individual than can be satisfied in some more civilised communities, but it negatives almost every possibility of improvement in the manner or degree of satisfaction.

How, then, has progress ever taken place ? Has education had no hand in progress ? Before answering this question we should first notice that the tribes to-day described as savage inhabit for the most part the least fertile and least suitable regions of the earth ; the savages of the regions most suitable for the development of civilisation have long since developed into, or been conquered by, the white races of Western Europe. Progress from the primitive Greek savage to the cultured Athenian was probably due both to the immigrations of various more civilised peoples into the Greek peninsula and to the fortunate accident of the appearance of several men of genius, and to the preservation of their teaching by the educational systems of those convenient units, the Greek city-states. Even in the golden age of Greece the leaders of thought were often in violent conflict with the remains of savage magic and other practices. Changes in environment appear also to have caused the rise of some civilisations from a savage state.

There seems no reason to doubt that similar progress might still be possible in the savage races of to-day if they were left completely out of touch with civilisation, which is now impossible, and if they were allowed time ; the habits of very few savages have been observed for more than three hundred years, and the meanings of their habits have scarcely been observed intelligently for fifty. We shall now never know the reasons for the rise of the great Aztec and Maya cultures in Mexico and Central America, since they were brutally destroyed in so short a time by the Spaniards.

Returning to the present day, we find that the modern savage is no exception to the processes by which civilisation and culture have normally spread during historical times—imitation, diffusion, and conquest. Primitive tribes under British rule in West Africa, for instance, or under Russian rule in Asia, are responding to systems of education embodying, even though in imperfect combination, some of the best of their own culture along with some of the best of Western culture. Other tribes originally mishandled and still for the most part misunderstood, in Australia, in North America, or in the South Seas, have often failed utterly to assimilate any but the worst elements of Western life, and have been so forcibly amputated from their own cultural bases that they are rapidly becoming extinct. Enlightened and suitably hybrid systems of education, under the guidance of sympathetic anthropologists, might even now save some of these tribes.

As our knowledge of savage tribes grows more intimate and sympathetic, there appear to be fewer and fewer fundamental differences between the savage and ourselves. We have, and have had for several centuries now, conscious systems of education, aimed at incorporating the best of the old with the natural desire for the new. The savage of to-day has rarely the chance of developing such a conscious system for himself, and by his white conquerors he has not always been given a fair deal in this respect.

THE UNCHANGING INSTITUTIONS OF THE EAST

THERE is a third possibility in the history of a savage tribe and of its education ; instead of degenerating and being destroyed by another civilisation, or evolving into a progressive civilisation of its own, it may reach a certain level of civilisation and then become fossilised, probably through some defects of the system it has created. Such a situation is presented by most of the Eastern countries, and China in particular. Stagnant though Eastern civilisations may

HARMONY AND THE SOUL OF ATHENIAN YOUTH

Music, poetry and mathematics, all related to each other, and proceeding out of the harmony of numbers, were the chief subjects in the schools of Athens. The picture is taken from the side of an ancient Greek vase.

pointed out the distinction and dignity of the Athenian public buildings, compared with the dwellings of private citizens, humble and uniform, however great their individual talents.

Into this society were born a few men of genius who performed immortal service to mankind in furnishing, not so much knowledge, as the tools to investigate knowledge, the kind of questions to be asked in order to acquire knowledge, and the nature of the " knowledge " which we wish to acquire. They were, in short, philosophers, and their discoveries were the discoveries of the power and limitations of human reason. The reasoning powers of savages are often extremely active and subtle, but they do not work in a free scheme of things ; the Greek philosophers were the first persons to attempt to investigate impartially the whole range of phenomena known to man. Socrates and Plato provided a workable way of distinguishing between real phenomena and ideal phenomena, and further of distinguishing between the ideas common to all men and the ideas existent in the mind of an individual man. Reason being thus freed, it was possible, for probably the first time in the world's history, to conceive of the existence of an ideal state towards which one might strive.

MASTERS, PUPILS AND PET ANIMALS

Another music-lesson scene from a Greek vase. Observe the homely, informal atmosphere of the class-room. There is nothing grim about this lesson.

MEN WHO NURTURED MANKIND'S NOBLEST IDEALS

PLATO'S *Republic* is one of the earliest of a Utopia. It is very largely an educational treatise, being an account not only of the perfect state, but as much, and even more, of the methods by which that state may be attained. Plato begins with the existing Athenian education, such as it was—courses in " music " (including poetry and much learning by heart) and in many kinds of bodily gymnastics. He then asks what is the best music and the best gymnastics for those who are to be the governors of the ideal state. (Before Plato's time the term " best " could have had only a very relative meaning in these connections.) Great as is the importance of gymnastics, however, he believes that the sound body cannot be trusted to produce the sound mind so much as the sound mind to produce the sound body. The sound mind will regulate the diet of its owner, stimulate him to needful exercise, and restrain him from the vices of over-exercise or of taking too much pleasure in the exercise and care of his body. The sound mind is to be obtained largely by feeding the young upon noble stories and noble examples, by giving them only the simplest and most austere poetry and music, and by developing in them a sense of beauty, harmony, and proportion, in general.

Plato's ideas were perpetuated in his Academy (the first institution in the world to bear that name), a school for statesmen which lasted in various forms for nine hundred years, and had a great influence upon the formative period of early Christian doctrine.   Knowledge was here studied for its own sake, and impractical though the curriculum may seem to the modern mind that likes to govern by rule-of-thumb, the courses, even in such abstract subjects as logic and geometry, attracted respect all over Greece.   Though Plato made no actual break in the history of Greek education, most Greek education after him showed his influence.   It was always regarded as a community matter ; the interests of the adult Hellenes were, it was patent to the school children, only an extension and maturing of the interests inculcated in school, instead of being totally unrelated, as so often occurs to-day.

But Hellenic education was still an education for a picked class ; the slaves and servants rarely come into the picture, or only as underpaid ushers, rather than as the recipients of education themselves !   The ideals of the small aristocracy which received education in Ancient Greece were some of the noblest ideals ever known, but they were not community ideals in the modern democratic sense.   Even among the aristocracy, great individual proficiency in a single direction was frowned upon ; the ideals, though morally such balanced and well-rounded ideals, were still those of the small tribe.   They were an ideal and immutable version of the state of affairs known to them, not an ideally different state.   The idea of completely free development of individual potentialities was not to come for about two thousand years.

EDUCATION AS A MEANS TO POWER

THE Romans, being empire-builders, considered themselves to be " practical " men.   They had a far better legal system than the Greeks, for instance, and were more enthusiastic for order, though they were, by contrast, much less interested in the principles of equity.   When the Romans came into cultural contact with the Greeks, late in the second century B.C., they already had their traditional education of the familiar tribal form—in hunting, fighting, patriarchal and tribal duties and ritual, and, above all, in law.   They had not the Greek gift for intellectual speculation, and they added little to the world's intellectual riches of such importance as the Greek discoveries in science and scientific method (actually more far-reaching in influence than Greek achievement in the arts).

But the Romans were keenly interested in government, and what they assimilated most avidly from the Greeks was the education in rhetoric—the science which would enable them to persuade and to have power over others. This type of education was best formulated in the *Institutes of Oratory* of Quintilian, a Roman of the end of the first century A.D. Apart from the formalism of his matter, Quintilian was a teacher full of humane spirit, and recommended gentleness and encouragement as the best fosterers of the young mind. The rules of his logic were taken mainly from Aristotle, and the inclusion of such subjects as geometry he had to justify to the hard-headed Romans only by their possible service in the cause of rhetoric. Further, it was clear to him that only if the orator were a truly virtuous and wise man could he be ultimately successful. Later generations may have often inclined more to the letter than the spirit of Quintilian's teaching, but it is of the very greatest importance in the history of education. For Rome, with its concentration on temporal power, spread so much second-hand Greek culture through the world, and imposed such a system of government on the greater part of the known world, that even after the fall of the Roman Empire Roman ideas remained paramount, preserved particularly by the Church.

The old rhetorical education became in great measure the education of the Middle Ages. Much of it survived in English public schools and universities until the nineteenth century, its influence upon our secondary school syllabuses is not yet defunct, and in every foreign university the old practice of disputation is still retained as part of the examination for one's degree.

EDUCATION IN THE DARK AGES : THE CHURCH CARRIES ON THE TORCH

IN the early Middle Ages a universal aspect appeared in education for the first time. While the education of the savage treated him purely as a member of the tribe, and the education of the Greeks, even at its highest, was always limited by the conception of the small city-state, the education of the Middle Ages treated man's soul as belonging to the universal Church, however much and however necessarily his body might be in thrall to the State of which he happened to be a member. It was from this liberating influence of Christianity that the modern idea of individualism was eventually to grow : man's soul was claimed for its own long before he could claim any earthly privileges. (In the savage tribe, it should by now be clear, a man's soul was, and is to-day,

LEARNING KEPT ALIVE IN THE MONASTERIES

Monks comparing scriptural texts. Drawn from stone carvings on a 13th-century French tomb.

regarded as neither his own nor a member of a universal society of souls ; it is regarded as a member of the tribe pure and simple, just as much as the man's body.)

But although Christianity provided the sheet-anchor of hope for men during the Dark Ages after the fall of the Roman Empire, learning was in a parlous condition. Not only were schools and scholars in many places actually exterminated ; there seemed to be little reason for learning in a world of such simple principles as that of the barbarians during the fifth, sixth, and seventh centuries. However, learning was kept nobly alive in more distant spots—notably in Ireland, whence Christianity spread to North England and produced great scholars such as Bede, and in the new Moslem world which assimilated much of the old Greek knowledge. In the Christian world, however, ideas of education, as of many other things, were severely limited by the prevailing belief that the world was to end in the year 1000—the Millennium. After this time the mystical, withdrawing outlook of the Church continued to be powerful, in obvious contrast to the rather brutal world of temporal affairs, but the best churchmen began to devote themselves to philosophy and the logical elucidation of theological questions, so far as these were susceptible to logical processes.

THE QUAINT STUDIES OF MEDIEVAL UNDERGRADUATES

THOSE who excelled in disputation and teaching began to form themselves into schools, and thus the first universities arose, the earliest at Bologna (which received its charter in 1155), and at Paris, and not much later at Oxford, Cambridge, Salamanca, and rapidly all over Europe. Students gathered in immense numbers to hear great teachers such as Abelard and to sharpen their wits against one another. And here, in the flourishing of scholastic philosophy, the influence of the old rhetorical education of Quintilian showed itself to be paramount. Quintilian's list of studies was preserved as "the seven liberal arts" (especially as the number seven is so often of mystic significance in the Bible), divided later into the Trivium—grammar, rhetoric, and dialectic, and the Quadrivium—music, arithmetic, geometry, and astronomy. But the first three, as with Quintilian, made up the real body of the work.

It is easy to jeer at the limitations of Scholastic philosophy and of mediæval learning in general ; the natural sciences were almost entirely neglected, and the principles of free observation and experiment which seem to us necessary for the pursuit of truth were scarcely thought of. The stock absurdity which it is customary to cite from the themes of medieval discussion is the problem : since angels are made of ethereal substance and therefore occupy no real space at all, how many of them can sit upon the point of a pin ? But even the discussion of such problems as this had its uses ; the great service done by the Schools of the Middle Ages was to train men in the logical methods which they must adopt in order to examine any kind of knowledge.

The Middle Ages made few practical or scientific discoveries : they devoted themselves to the authorities, mostly ecclesiastical, whom they knew, but they did perfect the methods of examining and using these authorities. They preserved a great deal of the thought of the ancient world when it was in danger of disappearing as completely as the old learning of the Mexicans or Peruvians, and they kept the minds of scholars in healthy exercise at a time when a meditative and solitary retreat from the world must often have seemed the only resource for a thinking man.

THE BREAKING OF THE CHAINS : THE RENAISSANCE

THE Renaissance was the culmination of the movement to recover ancient knowledge which had been slowly going on all through the Middle Ages ; but it was also the reawakening of a spirit of free inquiry, noble invention, and adventure in every field. Reason regained the place it had held for a short time among the best of the Greeks, and science had obviously to take the field against theology. An education of individual faculties was also obviously destined to develop, in contrast to the old education of the memory and of the faculties required to dispute about established authorities. But the battle between science and theology has not yet been fully fought out even in our own generation, though it is beginning to be realised that a final " victory " for either side is impossible and meaningless, and that a delimitation of fields, or of aspects, will be perhaps the ultimate result.

Similarly, the development of the new education fostered by the Renaissance suffered many setbacks, and has indeed only made really rapid strides during the last century or less. The Renaissance thus marks a turning-point rather than a period of great achievement in education. It is distinguished, however, by the names of many great teachers and thinkers on education—Rabelais, Erasmus, Luther, Melanchthon, and John Knox, Italians such as Vittorino da Feltre, the Spaniard Vives, and later Elyot, Ascham, and Bacon in England, and Comenius the Moravian. Some mention of the doctrines of Vittorino, Vives, Melanchthon,

Ey comence le grant codicille ᴂ te

THE MEDIEVAL GRADUATE

and Comenius will be sufficient to illustrate the types of educational thought in the Renaissance. The other distinguishing feature of the Renaissance was the actual founding of a great number of schools and universities. Not only were many of the most famous English schools, such as Eton and Winchester, founded at this time, but also many of the smaller " grammar " schools all over the country. And though few of these schools preserved for long much of the humane spirit of the Renaissance, except perhaps in their care for good manners, they remained the backbone of English education for two centuries.

A GREAT ITALIAN TEACHER WHO DID NOT RECOGNISE CLASS

VITTORINO DA FELTRE began his career as an educator in 1420, and three years later became tutor to the Marquis of Mantua's children. To these children he added others of the district, forming a school of ultimately sixty or seventy pupils, taken from all ranks of society. The poor scholars were supported by the Marquis or by Vittorino himself ; here was perhaps the first practical example of the Renaissance doctrine of equality of educational opportunity, not only between the different ranks of society, but between laymen and churchmen too. (Naturally enough this doctrine, even when put into practice by such noble Churchmen as Vittorino, ran parallel with the Reformation ideal that each man should judge for himself of truth in theological matters.) Vittorino drew his principles from the Church, from the Italian spirit of chivalry, and perhaps most of all from the evergreen Quintilian. It has already been remarked how Quintilian's ideal orator was really an ideal of the truly wise and virtuous man.

From Quintilian and from the ideals of chivalry Vittorino drew the conception that education was to prepare the young man for a life of action, not of meditation and study. His ideal man was a good citizen, and so he avoided the pagan excesses of some of the more unbalanced revivers of ancient learning, and was able, as few men of the Renaissance were, to reconcile the ideals of the Church with the culture of antiquity. The subject-matter of the studies in his school was mainly classical, but in no pedantic spirit. He revived the old Platonic doctrine of putting noble examples in history and biography in front of his pupils.

Greek was studied more at Mantua than in almost any

other Italian Renaissance school, much as it was prized by all the " new " teachers as the key to scientific and other knowledge.   For Greek to a fifteenth-century Italian was not only a literary study as it is to-day ; it was literally the language through which half the learning in existence was to be obtained.   There were no Outlines of History or Element-ary Geographies in one's own language then ; history had to be read in the Greek of Thucydides or the Latin of Livy, geography in the Greek of Strabo, science in the Greek of Aristotle or the Latin of the elder Pliny.   And, strange as it seems to-day, these and most other Greek authors, except Aristotle, had been neglected or looked at suspiciously during the whole of the Middle Ages, until the fall of Constantinople in 1453 and immigration of Greek scholars into Western and Central Europe helped reintroduce the language of Plato and Sophocles.

Two further predominant ideas in Renaissance education are illustrated by Vittorino's school at Mantua—the import-ance given to the education of the body, not only in violent exercise but also in ordinary deportment and gesture ; and the gentleness and sympathy displayed by Vittorino and his assistants, whereas to many mediæval teachers ignorance had been a kind of original sin to be flogged and bullied out of the bodies of the unfortunate children.   All Vittorino's ideals, it should be noted, except the ideal of social equality in education, can be found in the classics—Plato or Quintilian, and the practical application of these ideals during the Renaissance results in the first appearance in history of Humanism or humane culture.   The barbarous pedantry into which the study of the classics has often since fallen is in no way the fault of that culture, but of the pedants who have taken the letter for the spirit.

ILLUMINATION SPREADS OVER EUROPE

HUMANISM in Italy inspired men such as Erasmus in Holland, Grocyn and Cheke, the first teachers of Greek in England, Colet, the founder of St. Paul's School, and Sir Thomas More, whose *Utopia* is largely based upon Plato's *Republic*.   Melanchthon, a German, was a typical earnest humanist of the Northern Renaissance, Under the influence of Luther he made it his task to bring humane culture into the service of Protestantism, and particularly of German Protestantism.   He had fortunately more organising genius than many other humanists, and in North Germany changed the whole face of education by reforming the existing schools and universities and founding new ones. He realised what has often been forgotten by later evangelical reformers, that language is the key to doctrine, and literary studies therefore came first, in the cause of religion, in his schools. Mathematics and sciences were to be studied later. The ten years' course suggested in Melanchthon's high schools naturally proved too impractical for most parents, and his influence was felt more permanently in the German universities than the schools.

Vives (1492–1540) was a Spaniard who did much to inspire Loyola, the founder of the Jesuits. He was remarkable among the humanists for the attention he gave to psychology, observing how his pupils learned, and how association is of value to the memory ; for his respect for the mother-tongue as an instrument of teaching ; for his insistence on the importance of home education in the earliest stages ; and for his conviction that profound reform was necessary in the education of girls. From Vives and others the Jesuits must have learned much of their admirable technique. Though Jesuit education (beginning in 1542) was a product of the Counter-Reformation, and thus does not enter into the history of direct educational *progress*, it remains a model for its thoroughness and perfect adaptibility to its aim and to the needs of its time.

The Renaissance attitude was best expressed in England, rather late, by Francis Bacon, " the father of modern science." It was Bacon who most clearly and powerfully enunciated the principle of induction in the pursuit of knowledge—instead of the deductive principle and the appeal to authority. His *Advancement of Learning* (1605) is a landmark in the history of educational. method. He saw how we acquire knowledge slowly and with many checks and corrections, through our senses, and attacked the universities of his time for clinging to their mediæval sophistries. It was easy to deduce from his attitude that knowledge should be taught as well as acquired, inductively—the intellect playing upon the evidence furnished by the senses. Though Bacon did little himself in the actual field of education he greatly inspired others, the most important being the Bohemian Comenius, who has been called the father of modern education, as Bacon is of modern science.

ORBIS SENSUALIUM PICTUS,

A World of Things obvious to the Senses, drawn in Pictures

Invitation   I.   Invitatio

The Master and the Boy	Magister & Puer
M. Come, Boy, learn to be wise.	M. Veni, Puer, disce sapere.
P. What does this mean, *to be wise?*	P. Quid hoc est, *Sapere?*
M. To understand rightly.	M. Intelligere recte.

MASTER AND PUPIL

An illustration from the first children's picture lesson book, "Orbus Pictus" (The World in Pictures) *written by the great educational reformer, Comenius.*

THE "FATHER OF MODERN EDUCATION"

THE principles of Comenius may best be found in *The Great Didactic* (1632), which contains the scheme of education he adopted as an exiled Protestant pastor in the little community of Moravian brethren. He not only believed profoundly in universal education, but drew up, for the first

time, a scheme of universal education through four stages—
the home school, the primary school, the grammar school,
and the university—each stage to take four years. Comenius
perceived that the child's faculties develop in a certain natural
order, and that things come before books ; he was one of the
first educators to look at education objectively.

The Great Didactic was supplemented by the text-book
Orbis Pictus, which, with its amusing illustrations, represents
perhaps the first attempt to teach through pictures, in the
manner now commonly used for elementary lessons in a
foreign language. Underneath each picture is a good deal
of descriptive matter, both in Latin and the mother-tongue,
which can be easily grasped by careful observation of the
picture.

Not only did Comenius fully understand the receptive
processes of education ; he understood also how necessary
are the productive processes, and even suggested a school
where nothing but Latin should be talked, the boys learning
the language in their ordinary business at the desk, in the
workshop, in the church, even in acting plays in Latin.
Comenius' rules for the conduct of a class cannot be bettered
to-day : the teacher must never repeat a question, must
illustrate his talking always by objects or drawings, must
pick out individual scholars to see if they have been
attending, must keep his eye on the whole class at once,
and so on.

Though the educational treatises of Comenius were almost
overlooked until the nineteenth century, his excellent textbooks had their effect, and the German schools of Saxe-
Gotha and the American Common School, both of which
were set up during his life-time, almost certainly owed their
inspiration to his work. Like many of the world's great
teachers in other fields, Comenius did not see much of the
extent to which his influence would reach ; neither did that
influence spread itself directly and irresistibly ; it filtered
through almost unnoticed.

" VIRTUE, WISDOM, BREEDING, AND LEARNING "

THE great impulse of the Renaissance towards humane
studies appeared to come to little, mainly because the
world was not yet ready to receive it ; science was not established yet on any sound basis, and languages other than Latin
were still rather imperfectly developed. Towards the end of

the seventeenth century, however, science began to establish itself firmly with the help of Newton and some others, and the underlying philosophical principles of the Renaissance became clear in Descartes (who decided that the only fact he was sure of was his own existence—" I think, therefore I am "), and in the English philosopher and educator, John Locke (1632–1704).

Locke was one of the most practical of all philosophers. Going further even than Descartes, it seemed to him that his own feelings, rather than his own thoughts, were what he was surest of. Thus his idea of the world was the very antithesis of the mystical view ; he was content with the world of " experience." This view seems too strikingly simple to-day, but Locke nevertheless stands out as one of the founders of the study of psychology. Attaching this importance to the experiences we undergo, Locke naturally tended to believe that circumstance was responsible for the greater part of the traits, good or bad, in our characters, and he at first believed, though he later modified his belief, that " all men are by nature equal." It seemed in any case clear to him that the greater part of the difference between man and man could be modified by education. His *Thoughts Concerning Education* (1693) deal with the education necessary for a gentleman's son, a member of the governing class, who would be educated most probably by a private tutor, such as Locke himself had been.

The aims of education for Locke are virtue, wisdom, breeding, and learning. Virtue means a true notion of God, wisdom is the utilitarian notion of managing one's own business ably in the world, breeding is based on the principle " not to think meanly of ourselves, and not to think meanly of others," and learning comes last of all, as something into which children should by no means be bullied. Latin is necessary for a gentleman, but for no one else, and the natural sciences are better than the abstract studies, as metaphysics. Poetry is condemned in the extraordinary words : " Poetry and gaming, which usually go together, are alike in this too, that they seldom bring any advantage but to those that have nothing else to live on." Dancing, on the other hand, should be learnt, because it assists deportment, but music, again, is liable to become a waste of time. Manly exercises are necessary enough, but they also can be overdone, and carpentering or other crafts may be pursued with equal advantage, and indeed more practical point. A plain diet and regular, healthy habits are naturally insisted on, particularly for the younger children, The general aim of education is the training of character ; much learning may easily make a man top-heavy, but a wide smattering of a number of subjects is far from being despised, since it tends to general " culture."

Locke's views on education are thus typical of the empirical English way of taking things—better a working compromise than a beautiful ideal, or a " beautiful " piece of fanaticism ! Locke's direct influence on education was small, but on philosophy it was great. He wrote in a time when English society, copying the France of Louis XIV., was becoming " polite," but not-too-profound discussions of even the most serious topics might well take their place in elegant gatherings —but the discussions must not be too profound ! Thus Locke has little interest in art or even, fundamentally, in philosophy, and his idea of desirable motives in the handling of children is limited to the desire of praise and the hatred of blame. He is, in short, a man of the world, and the father of modern scepticism, and it was in this capacity that he influenced all the thought of the eighteenth century, though other minds greater than his developed and modified his philosophy.

UTOPIAS OF AN UNPRACTICAL GENIUS

THE ideas which originally fired the leaders of the French Revolution of 1789—of a return to a state of natural simplicity and equality—arose from sources which were far from being disreputable or proletarian. They were the philosophical ideas which were the natural outcome of the prevailing scepticism. " Politeness " and " wit " began to pall on some of the most enlightened members of polished eighteenth-century society, and they toyed in an unreal way with ideas of the " natural " man and the happy, unspoiled savage. Thus Marie Antoinette's playing at shepherdesses, and the equalitarian ideas of those who degraded her to " citizeness " and then guillotined her, both arose from the same source. The direct causes of the French Revolution were of course economic rather than philosophical, but the current ideas of the " natural " man had the greatest influence upon all educational ideas ever since, through the work of that unfortunate man of genius — Jean-Jacques Rousseau (1712–1778).

Rousseau was himself lazy, sensuous, and impatient of

discipline and restraint. Like many persons with these qualities, he tried to construct a world which would rationalise these defects for him and make him appear, on the contrary, virtuous. Genius, however, is always stronger than the defects of its possessor, and Rousseau's pleasant paradises which he invented in order to flatter himself have become creations of the highest importance to all educationists. Rousseau's principal books are four : *The Social Contract*, a sociological treatise which opens with the famous phrase " Man is born free, and is everywhere in chains " ; *The New Heloïse*, a sentimental novel ; *Emile*, a kind of reverie upon education ; and the *Confessions*, a very frank exposition of the author's wayward nature.

In *The New Heloïse* there is already a sketch of ideal education in Julie's bringing up of her family, never being hasty with them or worrying them, leaving them so far as at all possible to develop their own natures. *Emile* was published in 1762, and said by Rousseau to be the fruit of twenty years' meditation and three years' labour. It is an account of the education of a single child by a tutor, in the home, written in a vaguely fictional form, and based on a theory which had never before appeared in the history of education. No longer is the child to be educated as a member of a tribe or of a city-state, as a future governor or soldier or scholar or even as a member of the universal Church ; " the profession I would teach him is to live." The child is to become the man that Nature intended him to be. The revolutionary character of this doctrine is obvious. It has nowhere been followed to the letter, except perhaps in a few of the most modern experimental schools, but it has influenced not only educational but social doctrine all over the world since then.

THE CHILD OF NATURE

THE next question obviously is : What sort of a child, or man, did Nature intend the child to be, and how are we to know ? Rousseau wisely does not take a very particularised child for the purpose of his experiment ; he says : " At first I have said little about Emile, for my earliest maxims of education, though very different from those generally accepted, are so plain that it is hard for a man of sense to refuse to accept them, but as I advance my scholar appears upon the scene more frequently, and towards the end I never lose sight of him for a moment." Emile himself is thus often no more than a symbol, and the education he undergoes is the education Rousseau would desire for every child—an education truly " democratic " in one sense, though it is not an education for democracy.

Rousseau begins by reminding the world how the education of children has generally " sacrificed the present to an uncertain future," and destroyed much of the pleasure of being, almost as soon as the child has become conscious that he is alive. " The first of all blessings is not authority but liberty." Nature surely intended the young child for sensuous enjoyment, and if this enjoyment is interfered with by his education, then that education is at fault.

We see here the strange mixture of truth and dreamy falsehood typical of Rousseau. If he could persuade the world that the child Emile, under the care of its tutor (Rousseau himself, of course), would necessarily become the ideal and natural man, so much the better for the sensuous-living Rousseau himself. Most romantic writers have written by projecting their own desires and dreams outwards in this way. But Rousseau was perfectly right, long before the foundation of psychology as a science, in perceiving that the life of a small child is almost entirely a life of the senses, and that its education can only properly operate through those senses. In fact, Rousseau would have ordinary education kept back until twelve years of age, the child being occupied meanwhile with exercising his body and his senses, but his intellect being kept idle. The child should be kept from all vice and harm, but should have no positive principles taught him ; he should be free from society, from books, and from man, depending solely upon the world of things. It is just this principle which is employed to-day in the Montessori apparatus which teaches children incidentally to button their clothes or learn their letters, while apparently consisting only of pleasant puzzles for the child's eager fingers and eyes to solve. When the child discovers resistance, perhaps quite implacable, in inanimate or animate Nature, says Rousseau, he is learning his first moral lessons ; he should not learn these from the resistance or other behaviour of men, since men are imperfect and vitiated beings.

Rousseau recognises quite clearly the existence of morals, but he wants them to coincide as closely as possible with natural impulse. Children should receive punishment, for instance, to fit the crime, and as a naturally derived result of their crime, not because punishment in the abstract is " necessary " ; they should be bound by no necessity but the necessity imposed by circumstance. They may be taught, however, the one moral maxim : " Never hurt anybody."

"ROBINSON CRUSOE" AS THE CHILD'S PRIMER

AT the age of twelve Rousseau's Emile, or any child brought up on the same lines as Emile, should " know nothing by rote but much by experience," and if he is behind in some of the technique of school learning, he should be advanced in respect of judgment and understanding. He is now to prove the excellence of his early training by assimilating at a great pace the book-learning which has been so long withheld from him. Again, he is to follow his own bent as far as possible : " Let him not be taught science, but discover it ; let him know nothing because you have told him, but because he has learnt it for himself." This approach to learning, and particularly to the sciences, has often been practised since Rousseau's time, being known as the Heuristic method, the method of learning by discovery. The first book which Emile is allowed to read is *Robinson Crusoe*—a master text-book for the system of learning by doing !

The child should also learn a trade, and Rousseau's justi- fication of this is typical of the confused workings of his system of things. The trade is to be learned less for its own sake than for the sake of overcoming the popular prejudices against a life spent in following a trade or craft. (Rousseau foresaw indeed, vaguely, the coming of a revolution which might force every man to work with his hands.) Excellent though this intention may be in teaching a child a trade, it breaks away from the simple objective principles of Rousseau's earlier stages. The craft—carpentry is suggested as an ideal choice—is to be followed because manual labour approaches nearer to a state of Nature than other human occupations, because the life of the artisan is least of all dependent upon the vicious organisation of man's society, and because the hands " work for the development of the craftsman's mind." The craftsman must " work like a peasant " but " think like a philosopher." In such thoughts as these the social revolu- tionary speaks at least as vehemently as the educationist.

Social education should begin by drawing the child's attention to the necessity for co-operation among men working at different trades, but not till the age of fifteen should Emile really begin the acquaintance of men, and then mainly through history. Rousseau is now sorely tried to make the lessons of history appear always of moral value, and is reduced to recommending chiefly ancient and noble biographies, such as Plutarch's *Lives*. Religious education is introduced from the basis of the intuitions, while direct moral instruction is to be given on the subject of chastity. The usual empty moral precepts are scornfully rejected, however, and Rousseau advocates instruction in the evil results of debauchery, and the sublime happiness resulting from true and regulated passion, which would be approved by many advanced educators to-day.

The education of women, however, was to Rousseau something very different. To him feminine weaknesses were natural and to be cultivated, especially since woman's natural function was in any case to minister to man's delight. Since women are weak, they must be controlled, and restraint is to be the keynote of their education, though liberty was previously declared to be the natural right of man. Such unreliable creatures are women, indeed, that only the tutor (still Jean-Jacques Rousseau !) can be trusted to pick a mate for Emile when the time comes. As soon as Emile has conceived a violent passion for his Sophie and become engaged to her, the tutor once more intervenes. Emile must leave her for two years and travel about the world to learn to know men. Even when he at last settles down and has a son, Rousseau still makes him appeal to his tutor, whom he will need, he says, as long as he lives.

GREAT FORERUNNERS OF MODERN THEORY

Rousseau's ideas had a very wide and important vogue even during his own lifetime. Freed from the conceptions of formal society or formal religion, he was able, for the first time in history, to examine the problem of the education of the individual as it were anthropologically. What is the destiny of the creature Man ? " Liberty," answered Rousseau, and no society seemed to him desirable in which that liberty was infringed. He sketched a Utopia, but a Utopia evolved so much out of his own impulses that it was full of inconsistencies. Nevertheless, as an ideal its value can hardly be exaggerated. It was now left for others to work out the practical steps by which such an ideal might be

PORTRAIT OF PESTALOZZI

approached. The first to make an attempt was the Swiss schoolmaster Pestalozzi.

Pestalozzi's first experiment was the school at Neuhof, where he gathered local orphans in a community which was meant to be self-supporting and to inculcate the ideal principles of Rousseau. As a business experiment the school failed miserably (in 1780, only a few years after its foundation), but in the moment of his failure Pestalozzi was the more convinced of the rightness of his principles. He had rescued over a hundred children from poverty and neglect of every kind. All through his life his experiments seemed destined to misfortune—at Stans, where he cared for destitute children during the Napoleonic wars, at Burgdorf, and at the school he had for twenty years at Yverdon on Lake Neuchâtel. Yet he was visited and praised by all the greatest ones of his time who had any interest in education, though when he offered his scheme of national education to France, Napoleon said he had no time to " bother himself with the alphabet."

But, as Pestalozzi himself said at the end of his life, the real work he had done lay not so much in his unfortunate schools as in the principles which he practised. He put these principles into two books—*Leonard and Gertrude* and *How Gertrude Teaches Her Children*. Both these deal with the beautiful influence of an understanding mother, which was something that Rousseau had never enjoyed. While believing in " education according to nature," Pestalozzi did not cut off the child's contacts with mankind in the way that his master, Rousseau, had done. He believed that the child needed sensuous education for the development of his own nature, but also social education so that he could enter into proper relations with his family, his neighbours, and his fellow-citizens.

The simplicity and practicality of Pestalozzi's methods in securing these two kinds of education have earned him a great name as a teacher, pathetic though the picture of his life in general would appear to be. His Gertrude teaches her children names of objects by using them, arithmetic by counting steps, arranging objects, etc., and morals by gently reviewing the week's events on a Saturday night, the injuries done by brother to sister, etc. To Pestalozzi the fundamental point in educational technique seemed to be this : knowledge must at every stage be adapted to the powers and potentialities of the child, particularly at the beginning when the foundations were being laid. In his school at Stans, in particular, he was delighted with the results of this careful initiation ; the children grew conscious and proud of their own progress and wanted avidly to learn more. (This was very different from the exaggerated attempts of Rousseau at complete non-interference.)

Pestalozzi anticipated much of the discoveries of modern educational psychology, though being without exact scientific terms to express his discoveries, he was conscious often of inadequately conceiving his own ideas. He made a big advance upon Comenius, the greatest schoolmaster before him, in realising that not only does the range of objects around the child educate him, but his powers of apprehending those objects, through all the senses, can themselves be fostered and improved. He made an inexact but useful classification : the child perceives all the objects around him through the medium of their form, their number, and their name. Therefore counting, measuring, and speaking should be the basis of all instruction. He even anticipated the modern method of teaching reading through sounds rather than through the eye, and he attached much importance to drawing as a training in the apprehension of form.

All these methods of Pestalozzi's were intended particularly for the benefit of " the common people, who are forsaken and left to run wild," and " to open the doors of art, which are the doors of manliness, to the poor and weak of the land." It was this spirit that triumphed in the face of all the difficulties and inconsistencies and failures of Pestalozzi's schools. Those who came after him were able to restore authority to something like a just place in the scheme of education, but the full working-out of the inspiration of Pestalozzi and Rousseau is even yet not complete. Experimental psychology has only confirmed and stabilised many of the discoveries which they made, albeit imperfectly, by the light of nature.

PSYCHOLOGY ENTERS THE EDUCATIONAL FIELD

THE two greatest immediate followers of Pestalozzi were the Germans Herbart (1776–1841) and Froebel (1782–1852). Herbart, a philosopher rather than a practical teacher, was able to introduce scientific rule and order into the new ideas of education, while Froebel, a man gifted with sympathy and intuitions more like Pestalozzi's, was a practising teacher

perception and sympathy for their entire success; nevertheless the spirit actuating those methods has lessons for every teacher. It was never better expressed by Froebel than in his words : "All the child is ever to be and to become lies, however slightly indicated, in the child, and can be attained only through development from within outward." (Froebel died, it should be noted, before the enunciation of the Darwinian theory of evolution.)

Froebel's method was to discern, in children's play, how they were to be enabled to become all that they might become. The mediævalism of his symbolism, and his incoherent philosophy, may be neglected to-day. The success of his kindergartens even during his own day was so great that they were suppressed by the Prussian government in 1851 as dangerous to society; apparently they tended to evolve that dangerous product, an independent human being! (Froebel worked out methods applicable to the whole of school life, but most of his practice was with young children.) And to-day Froebel's infant-school methods have only been modified, rather than superseded, by the experiments and practice of Dr. Maria Montessori and others.

THE BEGINNINGS OF POPULAR EDUCATION

THIS section has so far been devoted to two forms of education alone—the tribal kind which grows up naturally and semi-consciously, and the isolated experiments of individual educators of genius. A third form begins to show itself in the eighteenth century—the conscious organisation of education, for altruistic motives, by societies other than religious, or by the State. This, of course, is the form which occurs most readily to the mind when education is mentioned to-day. There is no need for surprise at the late development of deliberately organised education in the history of mankind ; it has developed no later than a deliberate care for public hygiene, for the insane, for the rights of the working-man, for the equitable treatment of all religions before the law, or a dozen other of the problems which to-day swallow up, under the heading of "social services," sometimes even more of a nation's budget than is devoted to preparations for war.

As has already been pointed out, the first conscious organisation of education in Europe, on a wide scale, was due to the

Christian Church during the Middle Ages claiming immortal privileges for the soul of every created being, however much his body might remain enslaved. When a minimum of freedom had been won for the bodies and minds of men as well as their souls, the churches, particularly in the Protestant countries of the North—England and Germany—having adapted themselves to changing social circumstances, continued to be the inspiration, for a time, of big educational movements. This was more true of England than of Germany, where the church was often regarded as an arm of the State rather than its partner or guide. Germany, in consequence, has possibly the distinction, so far as can be ascertained, of producing the first municipal or State-organised schools in Europe, at Lübeck and Hamburg. These free cities were always far ahead of the rest of Germany, or of Europe for that matter, in social organisation, and set up schools, early in the fifteenth century, for instructing the children of their citizens in reading and writing and good manners. But the children of these city-states were the fortunate exceptions ; in less enlightened states, such as Prussia, for instance, they had to wait until the late eighteenth century for the establishment of schools, intended " for the support of the Christian religion and of an efficient police " !

France during the Revolution naturally displayed intense interest in popular education. The complaints drawn up for presentation to the States-General, or Parliament, in 1789, included a surprising number of pleas for educational reform, but the actual Revolutionary governments which succeeded the old States-General were too busy, with distress at home and enemies without, to make much progress with education. However, the idea of a national system of education was only strengthened when the Revolutionary committees were superseded by Napoleon, who himself established the universities as a State affair. The ideals of the French Revolution remained the ideals of reformers and " liberals " all over the Continent through the whole of the nineteenth century, and even later. (The Spanish Revolution of 1931 was based much more on these principles than on those of modern Socialism.) Consequently the ideal of a state system of education has been supreme in almost all Continental countries, and they nowadays all have systems something after the French model, of which it has been unkindly said that the Minister of Education at any moment of the school day knows what every pupil in

France is supposed to be doing. Such organisation, of course, does not exclude the possibility of intelligent and useful teaching, but it has never appealed to the English mind.

England had no State system of education, though she had thousands of schools, until 1871, and even to-day the State has less control over her education system than in probably any civilised country in the world. Foreign visitors are constantly surprised to discover, not only that Oxford and Cambridge and Eton and Harrow are controlled by the State in only a limited degree, but that elementary and secondary schools all over the country are allowed so much liberty in curriculum and organisation, and that the State shares their control with town councils, county councils, arbitrary boards of governors, university representatives, and others. There is indeed only one educational institution directly and solely controlled by the English Board of Education—the Royal College of Art, South Kensington.

THE FIRST ENGLISH SCHOOLS FOR THE PEOPLE

WE may now turn back to the history of popular education in England—a history of for the most part voluntary effort not to be paralleled elsewhere. Religious dissent has been responsible for many important developments in English history, and in English education it has played a great part, since the Church of England and the Nonconformist sects have always striven, since Cromwell's time, to spread their doctrines through schools of their own. Restrictive legislation has, of course, been a weapon that only the State church has been privileged to exercise ; at times Nonconformist academies have had to meet secretly if at all, and English Catholics desiring higher education had, until the middle of the nineteenth century, either to go abroad or make shift with a private tutor.

The first great educational body to be established in England was the Society for Promoting Christian Knowledge, in 1698. The Society undertook missionary work abroad, and preaching to Dissenters at home, but its main task was the setting up of parish schools, since it was " evident to common observation that the growth of vice and debauchery is greatly owing to the gross ignorance of the principles of the Christian Religion, especially among the poorer sort." Subscriptions were raised in an immense number of parishes, and the children were taught first to read, so that they might be properly instructed in the Catechism, then to spell, and finally " to write a fair legible hand, with the grounds of arithmetic, to fit them for services or apprentices." Girls might be taught sewing, but rarely writing or arithmetic.

By 1727 twenty-eight thousand children were being taught in these schools in England and Wales alone, and many similar charity schools existed in the colonies, Germany, Switzerland Sweden, and other Protestant countries. Unfortunately these numbers decreased hopelessly and the schools decayed within less than forty years, partly because the Church itself fell into a very low state, partly because they excluded dissenters, who, including as they did now the vast numbers of followers of the new Methodism, were too important a factor in the State to be cold-shouldered any longer.

The Industrial Revolution added so tremendously to the numbers of the " ignorant poor " that a movement strong enough to unite church and chapel was called for. It appeared in 1785 with the foundation by Robert Raikes of the Sunday Schools Union, a body (originally constituted with local committees half of Churchmen and half Nonconformists), whose influence even at the present day is of course outstanding among voluntary educational organisations. In the Sunday Schools the New Testament, instead of the Church Catechism, became the reading-book, and writing and arithmetic were also taught. One of the best features of the Sunday School was the opportunity it offered (and indeed still offers to-day) for adults other than professional teachers to take a hand in the elevation of their community.

THE STATE BEGINS TO TAKE A HAND

HOWEVER, it soon became clear that the most generous and enlightened voluntary effort could not provide either the funds or the adequately-equipped teachers for a national system of education, and from 1800 to 1870 the history of English education is the history of reluctant acceptance of one step after another towards a state-aided system. The reluctance was due partly to a laudable fear that a national system such as the French would suppress all opportunities for expression of religious or other dissent in the schools, but also to a very widespread fear that education would only ruin the poor by making them discontented with their station in life. It is nauseating to read to-day how even the philanthropic organisers of the charity schools constantly drew the attention of their pupils to the great goodness of the more fortunate classes in supporting these schools, and to the necessity of never forgetting the superior (and of course for them unattainable) advantages conferred by birth and wealth.

As early as 1802 Sir Robert Peel passed an Act compelling employers to provide education in the three R's and in the principles of religion for factory apprentices during their first four years of being indentured. The Act was practically a dead letter, however, and it was not until 1833, the year after the passing of the great Reform Bill, that Parliament first voted any public money at all—£20,000 at first—for the assistance of private subscriptions for the erection of schools.

During the intervening thirty years, however, great possibilities in popular education had been revealed by the diffusion of a discovery of apparently childish simplicity—the fact that the most advanced children might teach those less advanced, and they in their turn those who were just beginning. This was the famous Monitorial System, " discovered " by Bell in 1788 while in charge of an orphanage at Madras, and by Joseph Lancaster (it is presumed independently) at his school in the Borough, London, in 1807. " By this system," said Lancaster in the prospectus of his free school, " above one thousand children may be taught and governed by one master only." There are pictures in existence of the single master sitting on a high platform in an immense hall, surveying the head monitors on lesser platforms instructing classes before him, with lesser monitors farther down the hall instructing the youngest from no platform at all.

The defects of the system are painfully obvious, and many contemporaries testify to the crudeness of the monitors and the farce of much of the teaching. But no one had any other scheme for producing the large numbers of teachers which philanthropy required, and the experiments of Bell and Lancaster actually stimulated in Parliament a great deal of interest in the possibilities of popular education on a large scale. There was a further result : a society was formed in 1810 to propagate the methods of Lancaster, who, being a Quaker, favoured undenominational teaching of Christian principles. The society became four years later the British and Foreign Schools Society, which still controls a number of teachers' training colleges to-day.

In opposition to it some members of the S.P.C.K. founded

the National Society (on Church of England principles, of course), which still controls not only many training colleges, but a great number of " church schools " all over the country. The National Society also adopted the monitorial system, but naturally claimed its origin from the Churchman, Dr. Andrew Bell.

Robert Owen, the Socialist mill-owner of New Lanark, was interested in the monitorial system, but found that children in his factories could hardly assimilate instruction when they had already been at work for fourteen hours. So convinced was he that it is circumstances which form character, that he initiated at New Lanark, in 1815, the first infant school in England, so that children should be submitted to beneficent influences as soon as they could walk. He provided also for older children, and for adults, through evening classes, and his whole community, with its co-operative buying and other amenities, was called, " A New Institution for the Formation of Character." Only his infant schools remained after a few years, but they served as a model, even after their suppression by Owen's partners, for the London Infant School Society, founded in 1824, and indeed for all English infant schools for long afterwards.

EDUCATION BETWEEN THE TWO STOOLS OF CHURCH AND STATE

IN 1816 a government committee was appointed to inquire into the state of education of the English poor ; its report was not encouraging. Bill after bill was introduced to spend public money on education, but nothing was done until the grant of 1833. Six years later, as the grant had become an annual one, a permanent committee was appointed to super-intend the spending of the money. Its secretary was Sir James Kay-Shuttleworth, " the founder of English popular education," who had had much experience in observing State schools abroad. He saw at once that the monitorial system was inadequate, and when disappointed of government help for a teachers' training college, instigated two friends to set up one privately. During his secretaryship the education grant was raised, government inspectors of schools were appointed, and a government pupil-teacher system was established. So many schools had now been established, and by so many different bodies, that compulsory education seemed to many persons unnecessary. Much more than the three R's was now being taught in most schools.

to the trade unions and co-operative societies, many of which, especially the latter, had devoted part of their funds to education from very early days. Adult classes to-day receive assistance both from the Board of Education and from local education authorities.

The subjects studied to-day in these classes tend to be either economic and political in interest, or " cultural " subjects such as literature and the drama, where it is often easy to be superficial without knowing it. Science is rarely studied in these classes nowadays. This change of attitude from that of the Mechanics' Institutes is fundamental. It typifies the most important problem in English education to-day—education for the increasing leisure which, whether in well-paid spare hours or in the misery of unemployment, is undoubtedly to be the lot of more and more English men and women every year. Those who seek relaxation or recreation in these classes to-day seek something quite other than the " useful and interesting information " which was sufficient attraction during last century. If they are unemployed they are glad to find something they can do, in which they can forget themselves ; if they are in work, they are probably still seeking to forget both themselves and their work, They prefer on the whole to act, to sing or play or dance, to work with their hands, rather than to sit still and absorb.

It would be wrong to ignore the comparatively low level of achievement in these classes ; to exaggerate its quality would be to interfere with the hope of improving that quality. Where the quality is low it is due to the inadequacy of the elementary schooling of most members of adult classes, and to the fact that very few authorities, even those directly in touch with adult education, realise the profundity of the problem. As late as May 1934 a county education official was complaining that almost no one in his profession seemed to realise that education for the right use of leisure was going to be the problem of the future. " Culture in tabloid form " rightly repels the educated mind ; America has shown bad enough examples of attempts to grasp the " substance " of culture too quickly ; but the problem of diffusing culture has certainly to be faced.

The fact is that only a minority of persons engaged in English education, even to-day, are fully aware of the meaning of culture to a nation. The adult classes have been deliberately chosen to introduce this theme here because they have

no tradition of a false culture, such as a smattering of Latin
or Greek, because they have no examinations or other incentive to spur them on than the genuine interest of their
students, and because their members have more liberty in
choosing the subjects of their studies than any other kind of
student in the country. In most elementary and very many
secondary schools education is still vaguely felt to consist of
two things : the amassing of knowledge, and the building of
character. How admirably many English schools do build
up character need not be outlined here ; what is still very
widely ignored is the extent to which knowledge, if it is the
right kind of knowledge, must through culture build up character. The notorious defects of the English character in the
eyes of an intelligent Frenchman, for example, are due in the
main to this despising of the right function of the right kind
of knowledge. In answering the question : " What is the
right kind of knowledge ? " it would be difficult to improve on
the words of Matthew Arnold, the last great educationist whom
we shall consider.

A GREAT ENGLISH APOSTLE OF CULTURE

MATTHEW ARNOLD was a poet and critic who was by great
good fortune appointed a school inspector in 1851,
when English education was growing slowly out of the stage
of the three R's. He remained an inspector for more than
thirty years, and investigated schools in France and Germany
for the Government, besides publishing reports on elementary
schools from which may be gathered, as from all his educational
works, observations and reflections which are as significant
to-day, and are likely to continue as significant, as when they
were written. Of the curriculum he said : " We have no time
or strength to deal with half of the matters which are thrown
upon our minds ; they prove a useless load to us. . . . In
England the common notion seems to be that education is
advanced in two ways principally : by for ever adding fresh
matters of instruction, and by preventing uniformity. . . .
Wide ranging and the multiplication of matters to be investigated belong to private study, to the development of special
aptitudes in the individual learner, but separate from all this
should be kept the broad plain lines of study for almost
universal use. I say almost universal, because they must of
necessity vary a little with the varying conditions of men."
The almost religious enthusiasm for natural science dis-

played in Arnold's time, though not by Arnold, has fortunately somewhat cooled in our own day, now that science has progressed far enough to say with some clearness how much it does not know and what the problems are which it can never decide. The biological theory of evolution, enunciated by Darwin in 1859, inspired Huxley, one of the most powerful educationists of the age, and others, to lyrical defences of natural science, and the study of natural science, as the only key to free man from his chains. It is true enough that scientific discovery has freed man from some of the most irksome of his material chains, but, as is now lamented daily, it does not necessarily teach him how to use his freedom.

The adult students of to-day who reject the study of natural science for acting and choral singing have realised, even if imperfectly, the limitations of scientific studies for those not actually engaged in research; they are themselves a token that the theory of evolution is not only a theory of biological science. Liberal-minded persons in the later nineteenth century realised the evolutionary principle as so hopeful a thing that they attached almost magical importance to the study of natural science in consequence. But the evolutionary view of life is, as R. G. Collingwood has pointed out in our own day, as much a view of history as a view of science. The theory of evolution implies a compulsory acceptance of the idea of progress, and it is scarcely yet realised how inescapable and widespread the implications of this idea must be. In the world of education, for instance, there are still persons who would find the solution of our modern chaos in a return to the simplicity of the Middle Ages or of Ancient Greece, instead of trying to discover a system as well adapted to our complicated age as those systems were to their own times. Matthew Arnold was wiser; his whole life's work was a plea for those permanent values which may hand on culture from one age to the next, without interfering with progress and however great the apparent revolution in between.

LEARNING HOW TO LEARN

" WHAT a man seeks through his education," said Arnold, " is to get to know himself and the world; for this knowledge it is before all things necessary that he acquaint himself with the best which has been thought and said in the world." For Arnold literature, and especially the literature of Greece and Rome, was the essential portion of " the best which has been thought and said." He realised readily enough, however, the barrier of language, and English poetry was for him a sufficient instrument of culture, in the elementary schools at least. (It may be remembered that at this time the University of Cambridge did not yet confer degrees for English literature !) Arnold's complaints were not only against such things as the cape-and-bay method of teaching geography, but against the fundamental idea that a knowledge of natural science, as a mere mental possession, is itself of use without a training in the use of that knowledge.

" What a curious state of things it would be if every scholar who had passed through the course of our primary schools knew that, when a taper burns, the wax is converted into carbonic acid and water, and thought, at the same time, that a good paraphrase for *Canst thou not minister to a mind diseased* was *Can you not wait upon the lunatic !* To have the power of using these data of natural science, a man must have first been in some measure *moralised* ; and for moralising him it will not be found easy, I think, to dispense with those old agents, letters, poetry, religion. The fruitful use of natural science itself depends, in a very great degree, on having effected in the whole man, by means of letters, a rise in what the political economists call *the standard of life.*"

To Arnold the reason for learning grammar is not in order to memorise the definition of a noun, but in order to practise the difficult exercise of recognising nouns when met with ; the reason for learning poetry is not to train the memory, but so that great language shall have a formative effect on the character, and so that the " almost incredible scantiness " of the children's vocabulary may be remedied ; the reason for reading poetry is not because every Englishman " ought to know " the work of Wordsworth or Shakespeare, but because " the best, in literature, has the quality of being in itself formative ; of bringing out its own significance as we read it. It is better to read a masterpiece much, even if one does that only, than to read it a little, and to be told a great deal about its significance, and about the development and sense of the world from which it issues. Sometimes what one is told about the significance of a work, and about the development of a world, is extremely questionable."

7

BASIS OF CULTURE : THE MOTHER TONGUE ?

IN spite of the attempts by both the Board of Education and local authorities to humanise English teaching since the Great War, and in spite of the remarkable work done in individual schools, no one would claim that the average elementary school child to-day has more than an extremely scanty vocabulary, or that the average secondary school child knows the purpose of a great deal of the " science " he learns. We seem in many ways to have forgotten even the lesson of the Renaissance, when pious teachers such as Melanchthon realised that language (which includes literature) is the key to a true appreciation of religious doctrine and of all knowledge. But if this has been forgotten, it is not so much the teachers and education authorities who have forgotten it, as the public around them which realises so little of the importance of language.

As was said earlier, one cannot have a system of education very much better than the society in which it exists ; adjustments are necessarily gradual and painful. We seem to be in the position of " believing " in evolution but being unwilling to accept the instruments by which it must come. But the speed of progress increases, and, of necessity, year by year ; the pressure of economic circumstance, as well as the spread of enlightened educational thought, is forcing the problems of spare-time culture and mass culture upon everyone. The problem is in one way perhaps simpler than is sometimes believed ; the main instrument of culture, by which it is passed on from one generation to another, is the mother-tongue, and the literature of that tongue, and proper appreciation of English, difficult language as it is, is surely the basis of any true scheme of education, for children or adults.

Nothing is being said here of the remarkable experiments in education which are being so successfully made—in Montessori and other infant schools, in craft schools, in self-government, in self-education, in the stimulation of interest through the wireless and the cinema ; these belong to another section. The enterprise of individual teachers in England has certainly never been so great as to-day. If the lessons of the great educators—Plato, Rousseau, Froebel, Comenius—are still often forgotten, that is by no means altogether the fault of the teachers. There was no public system of education in England, it must be repeated, until 1870, and no very widespread public conscience about education until after that. Working-class parents have, within the memory of middle-aged persons, been led from downright indignation at the school's interference with their children to eager co-operation in all kinds of school activities.

English education is only at the beginning of the adjustments it must make in order to infuse the teachings of the great into so unwieldy an organisation as a national education system. The world is changing more rapidly than many people like or are able to realise, and the ideals of education necessarily change with it. When the plain citizen grumbles about the inefficiency of the schools to-day, he should be challenged to say what kind of a citizen he wants the schools to produce. Few people in the present viscous state of society have such a clear and *complete* idea, as they would have had in the Middle Ages or earlier, of what kind of a citizen the schools should produce ; the sickness of society is necessarily also the sickness of the schools.

MODERN EXPERIMENTS ABROAD

MANY foreign countries appear to be much more sure than England as to what kind of citizen they want their education systems to produce. In Japan, for instance, a few simple principles of unwavering loyalty to the State (symbolised by the Emperor) take the place of the religious teaching in the schools of other countries. In Russia and Italy the State has a monopoly of all textbooks, except a few importations. In Nazi Germany foreign books and books of liberal tendency are publicly burnt. In parts of the United States the teacher has the choice between dismissal and imprisonment, or teaching about biology what he knows to be a lie. In many American universities the professor of economics has to avoid giving a true account of the working of Socialist countries if he wishes to keep his chair. In Russia until very recently a professor of physics or chemistry ran the risk of being dismissed if he was not teaching " proletarian " physics or chemistry, whatever they may be.

All these absurdities are symptoms of the fact, almost universally true, that men in our times are still learning painfully to live together in large communities. Industrial and scientific progress have increased the size of communities so much beyond what has ever been known, and brought even these large communities so uncomfortably near to one another, that the most general tendency at the moment is the natural one of fear. Nearly every country seeks to turn out its foreign residents, to bar foreign imports, even to the discomfort of its own citizens, and to educate its children in a closely-knit loyalty in case they should be infected by any foreign virus, or be guilty of the mortal sin of questioning the inspired rightness of their government. In Italy " the Government demands that the school should be inspired with the ideals of Fascism—that it should be not merely not hostile to Fascism, but in no way out of sympathy with it or indifferent to it ; it demands that the whole school system in every grade and every phase of its teaching should educate Italian youth to understand Fascism, to renew themselves in Fascism, and to live in the historical atmosphere created by the Fascist Revolution." Parallels to this passage from a speech of Mussolini's could probably be found in speeches by the dictators of Russia, Poland, Turkey, Japan, Germany, or Austria.

Lamentable though the restriction of individual liberty must seem to an Englishman, there are, however, still lessons to be learned from the militarised systems of State education in foreign countries. They are attempting something that has never been attempted before ; if they fail, they will be warning enough ; if they succeed, they may suggest to us that mass education may be used for good ends as well as bad.

JAPAN'S EXPERIMENT IN A MATERIALIST EDUCATION

IT has long been common to quote Japan as the outstanding example of education creating a new nation in a generation or two. It is not so commonly known of what nature that education is. Judged by its results, it has undeniably produced a number of men distinguished in science, but no one as distinguished in literature, or in any of the arts, as the great ones who lived before the new education system. Native Japanese culture, indeed, where it is not already extinct, is notoriously not showing the same reinvigorated life which the native cultures exhibit to-day, in at least some respects, in West Africa, in China, in India, and in Mexico.

The greatest service the Japanese education system has performed for the average Japanese is to improve his general health and physique, but that is due, of course, in a large

measure to the improvement in his diet through the general
raising of the standard of living caused by Japan's remarkable
industrial progress. But if the body has improved, the
spirit seems to be strangely lacking. The reason for this
may be illustrated from the fundamental documents of the
education system—the preamble to the first education code
of the modern or Meiji era, in 1872 :

> " The only way in which an individual can raise
> himself, manage his property, and prosper in his busi-
> ness, and so accomplish his career, is by cultivating
> his morals, improving his intellect, and becoming
> proficient in arts ; the cultivation of morals, the im-
> provement of intellect, and proficiency in arts, cannot
> be attained except through learning . . . knowledge
> may be regarded as the capital for raising oneself ; who
> then can do without learning ? Those who wander
> about homeless, suffer from hunger, break up their
> houses, and ruin themselves, come to such pass
> because they are without learning."

The elementary schools are " to instil into youthful minds
the elements of moral and national education, and the knowledge and ability essential for the conduct of life, care being
taken at the same time to develop the physique of the
children."

The only element of native culture which seems to be
preserved in the Japanese education system is the old training,
formerly restricted to the upper class of Samurai, in self-
control, abstinence, and impassiveness (without any element
of either swaggering or cowardice) in face of every kind of
fortune, whether good or bad.

As to religion, the general spirit, apart from a great deal
of popular ritual, has been that any religion is good enough
so long as it is a religion—" all dangers and troubles are to
be endured without seeking the help of either those on earth
or those in heaven." The Emperor is thus a sufficient
symbol of authority, and it was the restoration of the principle
of implicit loyalty to the Emperor, as the patriarch of the
Japanese family, which made it so easy to carry out the swift
modernisation of Japan after 1872. (For some time before,
the Emperor's power had been usurped by various tyrannous
oligarchies.) Simple as the aims of Japanese education may
seem to us, the system often excites great admiration in other
natives of the East, who frankly envy the Japanese their
order, organisation, and certainty about things.

LEARNING BY EXPERIENCE : THE U.S.S.R.

ONE thing that can be said with safety about education in
Soviet Russia is that one or other feature of the present
account may quite possibly be out of date by the time this
book is printed, so rapid is the rate of change in Soviet
educational matters. The fundamentals, however, are not
likely to change unless and until the type of government in
Russia changes. The essential aim of primary education in
Soviet Russia has been described as " the indoctrination of
youth in the proletarian philosophy." Theory, in consequence, runs riot in Soviet education, as indeed in most
other aspects of life in Soviet Russia. At one time the
obsession with theory threatened to wreck all but the most
elementary kinds of Soviet education. The remarkable
thing, however, about modern Russia in general is the speed
with which she learns from her mistakes. In the course of
relatively few years she has learned, for instance, that the
principle of absolute self-government in schools does not
make either a successful school or good citizens ; that the
half-educated engineer who ruins the machinery under his
care is lacking, not in a knowledge of the proletarian philosophy
but in a knowledge of engineering ; and that the poet who
bellows loudest proletarian slogans is not necessarily the
best poet. All of which, of course, the foreigner may justly
remark, was known before. Yet there is undoubtedly much
to be said for the method of finding things out by experience.
It was as the result of experience that great modifications
were made in strictly pedagogical principles in the summer
of 1934. Direct Marxist teaching was abandoned during
the first years of school life, and the syllabus was restored
to something like the syllabus normally existing in educational
systems elsewhere.

The weakness of the Soviet educational system would seem
to be the exact opposite of the Japanese weakness, since it
suffers from too great a spiritual element rather than from
too little. In practice, however, the Communist philosophy
of dialectical materialism leads to an education so practical
that, to an Englishman, it may, at a superficial glance, appear
soulless. " The acquisition of theoretical knowledge alone,"
it has been said, " is regarded as the deadliest of sins—partly
on the assumption that it fosters a class mentality." In
order to guard against the danger of promoting purely

theoretical knowledge, each primary school is linked up, wherever possible, with a factory or other enterprise, where the pupil learns something at first-hand of productive labour. Here again the initial temptation to confound education with a narrowly vocational training has been overcome, though it would be rash to prophesy what form the principle of "polytechnisation," as it is called, will ultimately take.

SUMMING UP THE GREAT SOVIET EXPERIMENT

WHAT has Soviet education done ? It has, in the first place, almost completed the "liquidation" of illiteracy in Russia. An immense number—perhaps thirty millions—of adult citizens have been taught to read and write in their own languages—of which there are said to be more than a hundred in the Soviet Union, many of which had known no written forms at all until quite recently. The Soviet power has respected the national peculiarities of these diverse peoples, and, through its gift of elementary education, has done a great deal to win their adherence to Communism. It has made adult education compulsory (and, of course, like all other forms of education, free) for all ; and it has treated both sexes, all classes, and all religions alike, with the notable exception of the politically disfranchised sections, although the position of these has been greatly improved of late. Such a quasi-universal experiment in education has never been made elsewhere, and there is probably no country in the world in which enthusiasm for education as a social force is so powerful as in Russia. The worker, if he strives to educate himself, has little to gain for his own ends in the matter of "personal aggrandisement," but everything for the sake of the community of which he is a member. In view of the intensive industrialisation of the country under its planned economy, the technological bias in education, serving as it does the immediate interest of the State, is still rather pronounced. In consequence, it is perhaps true to say that Russia since the Revolution has produced some excellent scientists and some gifted administrators, but few really outstanding figures in literature, and not many more of above middle rank in any of the arts except that of the cinema, which is encouraged, amongst other things, for obvious propagandist purposes.

Soviet Russia has, in a sense, contributed little that is original to the technique of education, but her outlook on

as in China. It could not be claimed that Mexico—still less
China—is an entirely settled and comfortable place to live
in, but nevertheless in both Mexico and China there is a
spirit of living and progressive culture actuating education
more vividly than in many of the highly developed countries
of Western Europe.

In Mexico the problem was to bring the Indians into full
citizenship, and to get rid of the feeling, engendered in them
for four centuries, that they were members of a forever
inferior race. The avowed aim of the rural schools in Mexico
is to bring to light in the Indians " their talents, their intelligence, their fundamental goodness and nobility of character."
Similar sentiments have been expressed in other Latin-
American countries, and have even reached the force of law,
but have either become a dead letter, as in Ecuador, or
remained in the stage of vague idealism, as in Peru. In
Mexico the Indian population is, in any case, larger and less
scattered, and has preserved more of its original culture than
in other parts of Latin America. Village schools in the Indian
parts of Mexico have thus been able to make use of great
stores of unspoiled ' talent. Of parallel importance with
learning to read and write Spanish have been gardening,
painting, modelling, and agriculture in these schools. Each
school is a community of children learning to know the
world around them and to fit themselves for a place in that
simple world. This aim, the unconscious aim of savage
education, has perhaps never been achieved so successfully
through conscious effort as in Mexico. (The Mexicans are
dealing, it must be admitted, with circumstances much
simpler than those of the " technicums " in Russia.) America's greatest educationist, Professor Dewey, has said that
" no educational movement in the world presents a greater
spirit of intimate unity between school activities and those
of the community than in Mexico."

The greatest triumph of the Mexican village schools,
particularly among the Indians, has been in the open-air
painting classes. It is clear that the Indian possesses natural
and unspoiled vision (and perhaps a natural and unspoiled
musical ear as well) which is the envy of many a city-trained
artist in Europe. The teachers give no instruction in perspective ; they do not lead the children through artificial steps
of cube, sphere, and cone ; they keep them out-of-doors
and invite them to consider a tree, a cloud, a mountain, which

is genuinely picturesque. "Picturesque" means "fit to make a picture of," to them, not "sentimentally pretty," as the word is apt to mean in Europe. In picture-making, it seems to them that the picturesque is the sublime and the emotive the ridiculous. The work of their children is consequently characterised by an extraordinary purity of visual quality ; their pictures are real pictures and not pieces of half-literary work, as popular pictures which " tell a story " are in Europe. The work of these Indian children has been shown all over Europe, and received the highest and most wondering praise from European artists, while the naturalness of the methods employed by the teachers has caused them to be introduced into at least one British colony to replace the old formal type of drawing lesson which was ruining the artistic abilities of the native population.

PATHS INTO THE FUTURE

THE distant examples of Mexico and China have not been chosen capriciously to end this section. They have been chosen to illustrate from history of this very moment how the old educational doctrines may be successful and full of hope in modern countries, even while other countries are so hard pressed that they turn in desperation to the semi-enslavement of their citizens in order to preserve their bare existence. If there are lessons of organisation to be learned from education in Italy, Germany, or Russia to-day, there are far more important lessons to be learned from the efforts being made in such places as Mexico and China. These countries have re-discovered the old doctrines of the great educators that the child must come in contact with the best that has been thought and said in the world—the whole world—and for the rest, he must be led gently to develop, in a communal way of life, the best that is in himself. If a new culture should spontaneously develop in Russia or Italy or Japan it will be perhaps more surprising than any culture yet seen. It is more to be expected from Russia than Italy or Japan because the Russians are learning from their own mistakes. But it is at least as likely to develop in a country like China which has not lost sight of permanent values in education.

China and Mexico may, of course, be reduced to chaos and misery if world affairs continue to grow worse, though since they are primarily agricultural countries they will probably be able to hold out longer. But if they are so reduced, it will not be the fault of their education system, whereas if a country such as Germany should fall into chaos, it would very largely be because her citizens had ceased to be worthy of a good education system. It was never so true as to-day that the education of a society and its general social outlook are interdependent. The one can hardly move in any direction without the other.

FOR FURTHER READING

IT cannot be said that histories of education in general make bright reading, but some of the individual documents are as inspiring to-day as when they were first written. One should at least read Plato's *Republic*, Vives and Vittorino Da Feltre on education in modern editions, Bacon's *Advancement of Learning*, Locke's *Thoughts on Education*, Rousseau's *Emile*, and Arnold's *Culture and Anarchy* : these are not only historical landmarks, but permanent affirmations about culture. The problem of democratic culture has been admirably discussed in our own day by Delisle Burns in his *Leisure in the Modern World*. To a twentieth-century student some of the most interesting revelations about education are to be found in accounts of savage education, as in the anthropological works of Malinowski and Driberg, and in some parts of *The Golden Bough*. The place of Chinese family education is intimately described from the inside in Nora Waln's *House of Exile*. The best account of education in contemporary Russia is contained in the Webbs' book, *Soviet Communism : A New Civilisation*.

EDUCATION IN A CHANGING WORLD

by H. G. STEAD, Ph.D., M.Sc., F.C.P.,
Education Officer, Chesterfield

THE growth of the educational system in England has
been described in the previous section. In this section
we propose to examine the system at work around us,
tracing it in its various branches, and touching on the problems
that are its vital concern to-day. It will perhaps be as well
to begin by summarising briefly the forces in English education that have led up to the present position.

It has been said that there is no national system of education
in England, since the facilities that exist are neither truly
national nor do they form a system. At no time has there
been any effort made to impose upon the country complete
uniformity in the provision of educational facilities. The
process of development has been mainly one of trial and error,
and of the gradual incorporation of the results of voluntary
effort or experiment into the official system. Sometimes it
has been the *failure* of voluntary effort that has spurred the
State to take action. Only gradually, through a century and
a half, has there developed any real sense of the need for co-
ordination of the various parts of the system. In some
directions there is still overlapping and a lack of clarity of
thought. Administration is still in need of reform, and a
narrow conception of the meaning of education is still far too
prevalent.

As in many other fields of endeavour, it is true to say that
the English tradition is to experiment. In the main, such
experiments are not boldly planned attempts to meet some
new set of conditions. Rather are they " trial and error "
random shots, some of which prove successful, whilst others
are doomed to failure. Among the more successful experiments of English education are the infants' schools and the
development of advanced work in elementary schools, culminating in the reorganisation advocated by the Consultative Committee of the Board of Education. This committee,
which is one set up to consider educational questions referred
to it by the Board of Education, was in 1924 asked by the
Board " to consider and report upon the organisation, objec-

tive and curriculum of courses of study suitable for children who will remain in full-time attendance at schools, other than secondary schools, up to the age of fifteen." At this time the Chairman of the Committee was Sir W. Henry Hadow, C.B.E., and the Committee's report is usually known as the " Hadow Report." It contains a valuable historical survey of the problem, and the suggestions it makes are commonly referred to as the " Hadow Scheme."

The demands of the industrialists, the philanthropic and religious motives of individuals and societies, and the vision, ever widening, of the educationist have all played their part. They have all given something to the building of the system as we see it to-day. Unfortunately, conflicting motives have given rise to controversies which have retarded progress through prejudice and appeals to custom. From the eighteenth century onwards, elementary education has been bound up with the question of child labour. One of the earliest forms which the provision of elementary education took in this country was that of " Schools of Industry," in which children were to be inured from an early age to habits of industry, and given religious instruction in addition, in order to make them satisfied with their lot.

This conception of education has not yet passed. From Peel's Factory Act of 1802 up to the present time, the industrialist appears to have had only a narrow conception of the purpose of education. It has been, and in many cases still is, viewed by him as a process which has for its object merely the development of the ability to earn a livelihood. Ruskin's words, " You do not learn in order that you may live ; you live that you may learn," have been far too often forgotten.

RESCUING THE CHILD MIND FROM THE MOLOCH OF INDUSTRY

FROM one point of view, the development of education in this country has been the gradual winning from the claws of industry of vital years of the child's life, in order that some measure of education might be made possible. Early in the nineteenth century this process was seen at work, and in our own time the struggle still proceeds. Even now, the struggle for the years from fourteen to sixteen is in progress. There is common agreement that the Centres to be set up under the new Unemployment Bill will do something to prevent the physical and mental deterioration which so quickly and so certainly sets in in the unemployed adolescent. But it should be remembered that the Bill says, in effect, that the years from fourteen to eighteen are *primarily* to be devoted to Industry, and that it is only when no work is available that they are to be devoted (for the majority of adolescents) to education as something a little preferable to idleness but much less satisfactory than work. And much could be said about the type of education which is visualised by the Bill !

Gradually the years from eight to fourteen have been won for education, and gradually too the conception of education has widened. No longer can it be said that the elementary schools of this country have for their aim the " training of the poor for poverty." It is the transition of the elementary school from the stage when it was merely a school for the poor to the stage when it is becoming a school for all, that marks the gradual development of a national system. It is to the philanthropic and religious motives that we owe the early conception that education is a charity. Generally speaking, the charity schools preceded those set up by religious bodies. Those schools met the prevalent feeling of the time. They were cheap ; they reached a wide audience ; they did not teach too much ; they did not interfere unduly with labour. The sudden popularity of the Sunday School Movement in the early nineteenth century was due to the fact that the Sunday school satisfied two large classes. Those actuated by religious motives saw in them a means for the diffusion of religious knowledge : the industrialists saw a form of education which would help to maintain a docile attitude towards industrial development, and yet would not interfere with hours of work. The plant that grew from the seed was not the one which they anticipated !

Again, this idea that elementary education is a form of charity is by no means dead. The present movement in favour of nursery schools can be cited as an example. Again and again the argument is heard that such schools are required in " poor " areas, or for the children of " poor " parents. But there seems to be no sound reason why the development of a system of nursery schools in this country should start under the handicap which so adversely affected the early development of ordinary elementary schools—the notion that they are " schools for the poor." It would obviously be better to avoid a repetition of such old mistakes.

of education should be abolished and replaced by a horizontal one.

The old " elementary " system had been a self-contained unit—its scholars, with a few exceptions, began and ended their school life in the elementary school. There was the infant school, intended for children up to the age of about seven years, which had, thanks to the early work of Owen and his followers, developed on sound lines. Then there was the elementary school proper, which dealt with children of all ages from 7 to 14. The Hadow Report suggested a horizontal division at about the age of 11. All education below that age was, it argued, preparatory, primary, or, in the correct sense, elementary. *All* education above that age was in effect *secondary*, no matter in what type of institution it was given. It suggested that all schools should be reorganised on this basis into schools for children of over 11 years and those of under that age. The lower group was to be further subdivided into junior schools (7–11) and infant and nursery schools (2 or 3–7). In 1931 the Consultative Committee issued a further report on the primary (junior) school, and in 1933 one on infant and nursery schools.

SNARES THAT BESET THE WAY OF PROGRESS

MANY areas have reorganised their educational system in accordance with the principles of the Hadow Reports, although there is a wide diversity in the country in the extent to which the reorganisation is really effective. Even under a really progressive authority, certain administrative difficulties make it almost impossible to implement the first Hadow Report. This report, as has been pointed out, viewed *all* education of children of 11+ as essentially secondary in character. The inference is plain. All such schools should have common standards of staffing, accommodation, equipment, size of classes, playing fields, and so on. But the " secondary " schools already established (and those now in process of erection) come under the secondary school regulations, while the *senior* schools remain under the elementary ones. Until this anomaly is removed the basic conception of the Hadow Committee will remain an unrealised ideal.

Since all progressive authorities have made some effort to reorganise their systems as suggested by the Hadow Com-

mittee, and even the backward ones pay at least lip service
to its principles, the description which follows is that of a
reorganised system.   It deals only with schools under the
elementary code.   The relation of such schools to others
will be considered subsequently.   The system is indicated
below.

		Age Range.
Nursery Schools	. . .	2 – 5 years.
Infants' Schools .	. . .	5 – 7+ years.
Primary (Junior) Schools	. .	7+–11+ years.
Secondary (Senior) Schools .	.	11+–14 or 15 years.

There are one or two points which should be noted.
Nursery schools are not common—like much else in English
education they have their origin in the voluntary work of
devoted pioneers, in this case Miss Margaret MacMillan.
A few authorities have erected such schools and it may be
expected that the number will increase.   Some infants'
schools have nursery *classes* attached to them, into which
children are admitted between the ages of 3 and 5 years.

The senior schools are commonly of one of two types—
non-selective or selective.   The latter only admit children
who can successfully pass some form of entrance examination.   The former is what a Chinese lady once described as
a " twice-skimmed school "—once for pupils for the secondary
school and once for the selective school.   Some authorities
have no selective schools, and some again term such schools
Central Schools.   The varying nomenclature is confusing
to the layman, and it would be an advantage to all concerned
if a definite system of names could be agreed upon.   One
thing is definite.   No senior school under the elementary
regulations—no matter how high the standard of its work—
has yet succeeded in being admitted to the ranks of " secondary schools "—in spite of the recommendations of the Hadow
Committee.   A brief account of the last type of school
referred to above follows.

THE PROBLEM OF THE FIRST SEVEN YEARS

THE Report of the Hadow Committee upon the education
of children below the age of 7+ years, to which reference
has been made above, did not deal with the organisation of
such schools in the same thorough manner that it did with

those for children of 11+ in the original Hadow Report. The problem stated by the Board of Education for consideration by the Consultative Committee was "to consider and report upon the training and teaching of children attending nursery schools and infants' departments of public elementary schools, and the further development of such educational provision up to the age of 7+." In its Report the need for separate schools for children under the age of 7+ was re-emphasised, and the opinion expressed "that the nursery school is a desirable adjunct to the national system of education, and that, in districts where housing and general economic conditions are seriously below the average, a nursery school should, if possible, be provided." A further recommendation was to the effect that, where children under 5 were admitted to infants' schools or departments, nursery classes should eventually be the normal type of provision.

These findings were the subject of a note by Miss Freda Hawtry, Principal of the L.C.C. Avery Hill Teachers' Training College, and a member of the Committee, to the effect that there should be one type of provision for children between the ages of 2 and 7+. The organisation visualised by the Committee was of two types. In some areas there would be nursery schools providing for a *proportion only* of children between 2 and 5 years of age, and infants' schools providing for *all* children between 5 and 7 years. In other areas there would be nursery *classes* attached to existing infants' schools, and again catering for a proportion of children between the ages of 3 and 5, and infants' schools as before. The need for nursery classes or schools was not based upon educational grounds, but upon social ones.

Many educationists felt that the Consultative Committee shirked a vital issue, and either from timidity or under the undue influence of "economists," failed to deal with the education of children under 7 years of age with the same vision and consideration of basic principles that had been brought to bear upon the education of the adolescent. If nursery schools are "educationally desirable," and "exert a beneficial influence upon other schools," it is difficult to see why they should be restricted to certain areas only. At present they are to be found—

    (a) In very depressed areas, as a form of social ameliora-
        tion.

(b) In wealthy areas, where parents can afford to pay fees, which make the schools financially independent of local or government grants.

The intermediate classes are, in the main, entirely unprovided for. Again, there appears to be no natural dividing-line in the child's development corresponding to a school break at 5 years, and 2 years (from 5 to 7) is too short a period to spend in a school. For these reasons, it is the opinion of many experts that the only ultimate solution is the provision of a combined type of school for all children up to the age of 7. There are no essential differences in the methods used in good nursery schools and the best modern infants' schools. The object in each case is the development of good physical habits, sound sense training, and such medical care as will *prevent* avoidable defects and so lessen the volume of remedial work necessary at a later stage.

QUALITIES OF A GOOD INFANT SCHOOL

ECONOMIC, social, and administrative difficulties lie in the way of achieving the ideal. The cost of making provision for *all* children between the ages of 2 and 5 years is viewed with alarm by many. But against this must be set the fact that by the age of 5 years many bad habits, both mental and physical, have been formed and many defects have been developed which could have been avoided had the child been under uniform control. It is at least arguable that preventative work between these ages would save much expenditure on remedial measures at later ages.

Another common objection is that by the establishment of a complete system of such schools the responsibility of the parent would be undermined. For good or for evil, the State has taken upon itself the responsibility for much of the child's life, and it seems a short-sighted policy to neglect the most vital years. And, surely, the State has a duty to its future citizens—the duty of seeing that their development is as complete as it is possible to make it? The third obstacle is an administrative one. At present, nursery *schools* are under the medical branch of the Board of Education and are open to children of 2 years of age and upwards. Nursery *departments* are under the educational branch, and are only open to children of 3 years and above. This anomaly will have to be removed before real progress can be made.

The best of existing infants' schools are among the brightest spots in the English educational system. This is largely due to their history—they developed apart from the ordinary " all age " elementary school, and were never subjected to the conditions which prevented any real life in these schools. A good modern infants' school is a place where, through a variety of activities, and with carefully-devised apparatus, in well-lit, well-ventilated and brightly-decorated rooms, children learn their first simple lessons. Such lessons are rarely formal. Through free activity knowledge comes ; the teacher guides development rather than forcing it. By means of shopping games, the use of coloured counters and sticks and similar material, the elements of number are mastered. By dramatisation, games, and stories, power of expression is developed. Through various exercises, the control of hand muscles is achieved and the ability to write is gained. The whole object is to satisfy the growing curiosity of the young child, to encourage and direct his interests and, most important of all, to nourish that sense of wonder which is such a priceless possession and which, unfortunately, is so often lost.

TEACHING HOW TO LEARN : THE JUNIOR SCHOOLS

IN 1928 the Consultative Committee of the Board of Education commenced the consideration of " courses of study suitable for children (other than children in infants' departments) up to the age of 11 in elementary schools," and, as has already been stated, reported in 1931. The main feature of the report was its emphasis upon the fact that the period between the ages of 7 to 11 is a separate stage in a child's development, and that wherever possible schools for children between these ages should be organised as separate units. This was rightly viewed as " a new departure," bringing with it " new problems." " To-day, *primary* education is recognised as ending at about the age of 11 ; secondary education is that which follows." Such primary education, the Committee held, falls into two stages, " the first extending up to 7+, and the other comprising the period between the ages of 7+ and 11+."

The Report emphasised the point that " the curriculum of the primary school is to be thought of in terms of activity and experience, rather than of knowledge to be acquired and facts to be stored." This view should be inscribed over the entrance to every junior school !

It is clear that the junior school was intended to be one

of a new type—with a technique appropriate to the children for which it was devised. Its aim was to be the development of the child up to the age of eleven years in such a manner that he could profit by the secondary education given in the various types of senior schools. This aim was to be accomplished through devising activities suitable for children of this age-range, and by making it possible for them to pass through appropriate experiences. This point is important. It indicates a belief that education comes through experience and not by way of the acquisition of facts. It presupposes a knowledge of the physical and mental development of the child and the development of a curriculum based upon such knowledge. It suggests a widening view of the scope of education and of the appropriate methods. It should have opened the door to thought and experiment.

AN IDEAL THAT HAS NOT BEEN REALISED

IT has been stated that the English elementary school system consists of three units—infant and nursery schools, junior schools, and senior schools. It has also been suggested that the first of these groups is among the bright features of the system. On a later page reasons will be given for believing that the senior schools are making satisfactory progress. The junior school remains—the cause of anxiety to many educationists and a comparatively weak link in the chain. It is true that thought and consideration have been given to these schools and that experiment in methods is in progress. It is equally true that they have put the child of 11+ on the educational map. In the old " all-age " school he was largely a nonentity—lost in the middle of the school. Attention was carefully directed towards the entrants—if only from a critical point of view. The school was judged by its leavers—and so they received attention. But the boy or girl in the middle of the school was not so much in the limelight.

The coming of the junior school has changed this. The child of 11+ is the junior school *leaver*—the school is largely judged by his standard. But in spite of this, doubts remain. Many factors have affected adversely the development of this type of school. In the first place, it has been hailed as the legitimate successor of the older type of elementary school. It is true that in many cases, most unfortunately, it *has* inherited the old building, while new buildings have been

yet ripe for responsibility. It is to be doubted if any " prefect " system will work satisfactorily in a junior school.

PREPARING FOR THE PLUNGE INTO LIFE : SENIOR AND SELECTIVE SCHOOLS

THERE is a confusion in the naming of senior elementary schools, which is most unfortunate. As has been already indicated, the Hadow Committee viewed the education given to all children of 11+ as being essentially secondary in character. Administrative difficulties have prevented the practical application of this. Most areas have now senior elementary schools organised as separate units for children of 11+. Some areas have also selective senior schools (sometimes called central or intermediate schools), while occasionally the term " central school " is used to denote the senior school of the non-selective type. The age-range of the senior school is from 11+ to 14 or 15+.

From 1900 onwards many attempts were made to give some advanced instruction in elementary schools. The Hadow Committee reviewed all the types of provision that had been experimented with, and suggested the development, where circumstances warranted it, of the selective type of senior school. Admission is usually made on the basis of marks gained in the transfer examination commonly held at the conclusion of the junior school course. Although compulsion cannot be exercised, parents are usually asked to retain their children in such schools until they reach the age of 15+, or even 16, in order that they may complete the whole school course. The curriculum includes mathematics, science, and one or more modern languages, in addition to the more usual subjects. The aim of such schools is to give an education which shall fit the pupils for posts in industry and commerce.

The examination question again looms large in the future development of these schools. There is a feeling abroad that the secondary schools of the country are adversely affected by their worship at the shrine of the School-Leaving Certificate. Many argue that the new selective central schools have an opportunity to develop free from the incubus of such an examination. On the other hand, professional bodies demand such examinations for entrance purposes, and parents think that attendance at school until 15 or 16 should result in some certificate. The solution is difficult ; one possible solution will be referred to in the section dealing with secondary schools.

The secondary school and the selective senior (central) school are for the comparatively few. Most children between the ages of 11 and 14 will be found in the ordinary senior school. This reason alone makes up a most important unit in the system. One of the pleasing features of the reorganisation of the English elementary school system is the thought and experiment devoted to this type of school. It has had one great advantage—it has been enabled to make a clean start. It endeavours to provide a practical approach to education for the child who has not academic ability.

In the older days, the education given was, even in elementary schools, formal and academic. Ability to " do " arithmetic and to write a composition were the most desirable qualities. There were many who found no interest in formal arithmetic, or to whom the effort of expressing their thought in writing was torture. Long before they left school such children were ranked as failures, and in many cases they had developed a definite inferiority complex. They often formed a " hooligan " element at the top of the school, a source of trouble to the teachers, and were continually in disgrace. The school provided them with no interest and no outlet for their energies.

THE HOOLIGAN TURNED CRAFTSMAN

THE modern senior school is making an effort to provide an education for such children. In the best of such schools will be found a hall (fitted with a stage for dramatic work), a gymnasium, a woodwork and metalwork shop, a science room, an art room, and in the case of girls, a domestic-science room, all in addition to the usual classrooms. More and more of such schools are making provision for the use of the cinema and of broadcasting as adjuncts to the ordinary school facilities. All this is *not* a case of soft options, or a dodging of difficulties. Many children can express themselves in wood, metal, or colour when they fail to do so in words. Neither is it the case that less intelligent children academically are better craftsmen. To hold such a view is to libel all good craftsmen. Craft-work demands skill in planning, a knowledge of the properties of various media, and executive ability. These are desirable qualities to develop in any child. The fact is that there is an increasing recognition of the facts that there is more than one approach to knowledge, and that because we have followed one it is not to be held that that is the only possible one. The new senior schools have eliminated the " hooligan " type ; they have found outlets for energy untapped before, and—they are still in an experimental stage. They promise much for the future. Most important of all, they may give the country an educated democracy in place of a mass instructed populace.

INDUSTRY'S CONTRIBUTION TO EDUCATION: SECONDARY SCHOOLS

THE benefactors of individuals and of the guilds established in this country a number of schools which were subsequently to become the Public Schools and the Grammar Schools. It is difficult to determine exactly what factors decided the actual course of development. It appears that a reputation beyond the locality in which the school was situated was one important factor. Whatever the cause, the two types of schools developed from the common origin— public schools with a national reputation, which were in the main boarding schools, and the grammar schools which served a locality and which were mainly day schools. Provision for the advanced education of girls was practically non-existent.

It has been shown how industrial development had much to do with the gradual evolution of the elementary school system. The State secondary schools in this country came into being in an almost casual manner. The International Exhibition of 1851 led to the conviction in the minds of many people that a system of technical education had to be developed in this country if its industrial supremacy was to be maintained. From this, a system of secondary education developed, quite apart from the existing provision in public and grammar schools and from the elementary system. At first the need for a sound general education prior to a technical education was not recognised—technical and secondary education were confused. But gradually the need for further provision for secondary education was realised, and steps were taken to remedy the deficiency. In the first place, the basis of the instruction given in the technical schools (then termed Science and Art Departments) was widened ; then came the definitely secondary school.

During 1894–95 a Commission sat under Mr. (later Lord) Bryce " to consider the best methods of establishing a well-organised system of secondary education in England." Its report brought the question of secondary education into prominence, but the Commission could not, under its terms of reference, discuss the really vital question of the co-ordination of the elementary and secondary systems. The Act of 1902 placed upon the councils of counties and county boroughs the duty " to supply or aid the supply of education other than elementary, and to promote the general co-ordination of all forms of education." This Act marks the establishment of a State system of secondary education in England.

WHAT IS A SECONDARY SCHOOL?

THE first official definition of what constitutes a secondary school was given in the Board of Education Regulations for 1905. " A secondary school," the regulations stated, was one " which offers to its scholars a general education of a wider scope and higher grade than that of an elementary school, given through a complete progressive course of instruction continuing up to and beyond the age of 16." This definition has been modified subsequently, and now runs : " A secondary school must be a school for pupils who intend to remain at school for at least four years and up to at least the age of 16. It must provide a progressive course of general education of a kind and amount suited to an age-range of at least 12 to 17." The curriculum must include :

(1) English Language and Literature, including Geography and History.
(2) A Language other than English.
(3) Mathematics and Science, theoretical and practical.
(4) Drawing, and provision for Manual Work.
(5) Physical Exercises and Organised Games.
(6) Singing.
(7) Domestic Science for girls.

These definitions are based on two factors : age-range and curriculum content. The curriculum is derived mainly from the literary tradition of the old grammar school, and the tendency is to extend still more the scope of what is denoted by secondary education. This trend is clearly seen in the findings of the Hadow Committee on the education of the adolescent. Many of the new senior schools are secondary if the curriculum portion of the above definitions are taken as the criterion, and the age-range of such schools tends to approximate to that held to be the appropriate range for secondary schools.   Perhaps the only real criterion between the schools commonly termed secondary schools and the senior schools established under " Hadow " re-organisation is that the former is, or should be, an avenue to the university and training colleges of various types. This means that university standards and examinations each have an influence upon it.   It is admitted that many pupils never proceed to a university, but this remains its essential difference from other schools and is bound to affect its aims and development.   Out of the conflict between the claims of the university and the claims of those whose formal education will finish in the secondary school arise many of the problems of the secondary school and much of the criticism to which it is subjected.

OFFSHOOT OF THE SECONDARY SYSTEM

THE schools in this country which provide secondary education (in the commonly accepted sense of the words) may be divided into two classes : (1) Schools supported wholly or in part out of public funds and subject, therefore, to the regulations of the Board of Education. (2) Independent Schools.

The first of these classes is capable of a further division into : (a) Schools provided and maintained entirely by public funds. (b) Schools maintained in part by public funds.

Schools of the first type are known as Municipal Secondary Schools, while those of the second are the grammar and other endowed schools.   The independent schools are more difficult to classify.   The main subdivisions are : (a) Boys' Public Schools. (b) Preparatory Schools. (c) Other Boys' Schools. (d) Girls' Schools.

There are, in addition, a number of private schools which do not come under any of the categories mentioned above. Some of these are efficient ; some much the reverse.   All such schools may submit voluntarily to inspection by the Board of Education, and many do so, and are therefore described as " certified efficient " schools.   The complete system of provision of secondary education is, therefore, something as under :

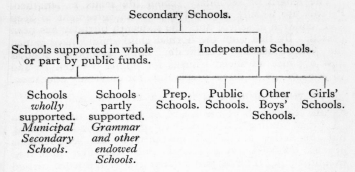

Secondary Schools.

Schools supported in whole or part by public funds.

Independent Schools.

Schools *wholly* supported. *Municipal Secondary Schools.*

Schools partly supported. *Grammar and other endowed Schools.*

Prep. Schools.

Public Schools.

Other Boys' Schools.

Girls' Schools.

It has been pointed out that there is a difference in the degree of assistance given from public funds to secondary schools. Some schools are entirely maintained by such funds together with fees. Others are aided to a greater or lesser extent. Provision for secondary education through such schools varies widely in different areas. In Middlesex the provision is about 13·5 places per 1000 children of the population between the ages of 11 and 16 ; in Sunderland, 4·5 per 1000 ; in Bradford, 19·5 per 1000, and in West Ham, 4·2 per 1000. Equally varied are the fees charged, although there has been a tendency to equalise these. In most cases the annual fees vary between 6 and 15 guineas, but in the majority of schools the limits are 9 and 15 guineas. For many people the inevitable goal of a State system is the general abolition of fees and a system of admission by merit only.

A certain number of free places must be open in State-aided secondary schools to ex-elementary school scholars. This obligation was imposed upon such schools by the Board of Education in 1907. Again, areas vary widely in the liberality and effectiveness of their scholarship schemes. The monetary value of the scholarships (more recently termed " special places ") usually varies with the parental income and the size of the family, etc. In most areas an income of £250 per annum is approximately the limit for a completely free place, but areas vary considerably in the scales they have adopted. In addition to these entrance scholarships most authorities award intermediate scholarships at a later stage of the secondary school career, and senior (or major) scholarships to selected children proceeding to a university.

The length of secondary school life tends to lengthen. Parents are usually required to sign an agreement to keep their children at school until the sixteenth birthday has been passed. By this time the normal child should have gained the School-Leaving Certificate. Most secondary schools now organise advanced courses for pupils between 16 and 18 years of age, in direct preparation for university education.

THE EXAMINATION BUGBEAR—IS IT NECESSARY?

THE regulations of the Board of Education determine in broad outline the curriculum of the secondary school, but the details are largely governed by the requirements of the School-Leaving Examination (the first approved examination). This is particularly true of the work carried out in the upper forms, and has led to the charge that the chief object of the schools is to force scholars through an examination rather than to educate them. The School-Leaving Certificate (and perhaps more definitely the Matriculation Certificate) is looked upon as a procrustean bed into which all children must be forced. It is certainly true that the examination requirements restrict unduly the freedom of the schools and over-emphasise the importance of certain subjects. It is admitted that non-examination subjects are dropped—even if they are the child's chief interest and delight. The problem is a thorny one—the demands of the universities, of the professions (for entrance), of employers, and of parents have all to be considered.

In any discussion of this topic one fact must not be overlooked. The secondary schools now deal with much larger numbers and a greater variety of type of mind than they did even a few years ago. Further, the conception of what constitutes secondary education is widening. No longer is it considered that only through foreign languages and mathematics can such an education be given. If due weight is given to these changing factors, it should be possible to devise an examination scheme which will meet the varied needs of differing pupils instead of forcing all pupils into the same mould.

Some of the most characteristic features of English secondary schools are to be found outside the confines of the ordinary curriculum. Many activities are developed which stimulate interests in activities outside those carried out within the classroom walls. Any good school will have its literary, debating, musical, dramatic, and scientific societies. It will be organised in houses with inter-house competitions. A school magazine will be published ; school camps and journeys will be organised, sometimes parties going as far afield as various parts of the Continent. It is no exaggeration to say that in such activities lies much of the value of secondary school education, as indeed it does of all education. The sympathy bred by contact one with another, the widening vision brought by contact with fresh people and fresh scenes, the development of powers of leadership, and the recognition of the value of service for the common good, should all be developed by the good school.

THE INFINITE VARIETY OF ENGLISH PRIVATE SCHOOLS

SIDE by side with the State system of secondary schools is a second system which has many points worthy of notice. The private schools of England range from the small school housed in a suburban villa to the greater public schools. They may be preparatory schools for junior children, senior schools for boys and girls up to the age of 18, or all-age schools. Some are single-sex schools and some are mixed, and in their efficiency there is just as wide variation. Some are inspected by the Board of Education and certified as efficient ; others exist only because of the snobbery of some parents.

The less efficient type of school is disappearing, but still exists in far too great numbers. The best of such schools often serve a valuable purpose, in so far as experimental work in new methods is often carried out in them. To say this is not to say that the State schools are bound by tradition. One has only to consider the experiments made in State elementary and secondary schools with the methods of the Parents' National Educational Union, the Dalton Plan, the Project method and the Froebel methods, to see that authority does not necessarily mean lack of freedom. But there are many independent schools which sponsor new methods and foster their development during the difficult early days. Many such schools are to be found represented in the New Education Fellowship, and have contributed much to the development of educational theory and practice. It is unfortunate that they have to be classed with schools actuated by motives of snobbery and based upon out-of-date theory.

8

NURSERIES FOR THE PROFESSIONS : THE PUBLIC SCHOOLS

IT is one of the ironies of the English language that the most select and private and independent schools in the country should be termed *public* schools. These schools, originated from ancient endowments, achieved a national reputation, and are now historical institutions. There is no definition of a public school ; an Act of 1864 mentions nine such schools, but others claim, or are granted, the name. All that can be said is that a public school is one not brought into being by any public authority and not subject to any direct public control.

They stand entirely outside the main system of national education. Some are inspected voluntarily by the universities of Oxford or Cambridge ; some by the Board of Education. They draw their pupils from preparatory schools or departments—usually at the age of 13+. The majority are boarding-schools, but some, such as St. Paul's, Clifton, Westminster, etc., have many day boys. They are all like in their non-local character. Tradition determines the type of many of their pupils. Boys of certain families attend the same school through successive generations, although there is a modern tendency to widen the field from which pupils are drawn. The majority of boys pass on to the university and ultimately into the professions, the Civil Service or the Colonial Service. The fees in these schools vary from the £10 per annum paid by 90 Foundation Scholars at Wellington (sons of deceased officers) and £31, 10s. per annum for 70 scholars at Winchester, to £250 per annum paid by most students at Eton. The average fee is about £175 per annum.

The traditional curriculum of these schools is a classical one, and much criticism has been levelled at them on account of this fact. This, again, is a tradition which is breaking down. A great deal of time is devoted to organised games. The question of the importance of games is a hotly debated one, and there seems good reason to suppose that too high a value is placed upon *success* in games. The games themselves may be beneficial—but the super-glorification of the young athlete is not.

But it is neither the intellectual nor the physical training which is given in them which is claimed to be the special virtue of the public schools. Rather is it the general outlook and spirit which the pupils acquire almost, as it were, by accident. Some claim that it is a narrow conception of good form, and a source of false pride. With many poorer minds this is probably true, but with the best it is a fine tradition. If a definite criticism can be made it is that individuality is not valued sufficiently. The training makes for conformity to rule, for similarity of thought and action. Only those of finer spirit *use* the tradition—others are apt *to be used* by it.

Granted much good in the public school system, the faults remain, faults which to some people seem to outweigh all the virtues. To the Socialist the system seems bad because it is made to equip the privileged classes to rule. Discipline and leadership are two of the qualities most insisted on. Then the boys are in most schools of this kind segregated and formed into a somewhat artificial society of their own, where aptitude at games is held to be the chief virtue.

In some of the great public schools social snobbishness is a powerful factor in the building of boys' characters. Of the moral atmosphere in a typical public school much has been written. Novels like *The Loom of Youth*, and such a play as *Young Woodley* have shown what may happen there to the normal boy who is hedged around with excessive sexual admonitions and restraints. Public schoolboys' attitude towards girls sometimes tends to become an unnatural mixture of idealism and coarseness as opposed to that natural comradeship supposed to be fostered at co-educational schools. In the past, the system has indirectly encouraged a good deal of cheating, a natural consequence of uncongenial work, the marking system, and a cynical attitude on the part of the boys (and not infrequently, it must be said, of the masters themselves) towards intellectual attainment. Yet while such criticisms remain true in many cases, the extensive reforms of recent years have made them less cogent than they used to be.

Recently the curriculum of such schools has been widened, with gratifying results. Literature (English) is now given an important place in most schools, and the importance of science is being increasingly recognised. In this respect, the work done by Sanderson whilst he was headmaster of Oundle School was of great importance. History is another subject to which more attention is now being directed.

AN EDUCATED DEMOCRACY : THE CRYING NEED OF OUR TIME

BELOW the public schools and intimately connected with them is a group of schools which fill a definite place in

English education. These are the preparatory schools, which usually take boys from 7 or 8 to 13 or 14 with the object of preparing them for the public schools. In some cases such schools combine with the preparatory branch an all-age school. From their nature, their organisation and work is conditioned by the requirements of the schools to which their pupils pass. These schools have practically all developed since about 1837. Parents began to feel that the more strenuous life of the public school was not suitable for boys of tender years, while the senior schools discouraged younger boys from entering. Whether they will remain a part of the English school system is doubtful. The more efficient State provision becomes, the smaller is the demand for such schools. The tendency is, perhaps, to abolish both preparatory departments and preparatory schools. The elements of education can be as well acquired elsewhere ; and segregation of a *class* at an early age is not a desirable measure.

It will have become apparent that there is, as yet, no complete system of secondary education in this country. Such provision as there is, is of diverse origins and of independent development. Steps have been taken to remedy this defect, but much yet remains to be achieved. The best that can be said is that the provision of such education is increasing, and that the conception of what constitutes it is developing. The classical tradition, the incubus of external examinations, and a certain (fast disappearing) element of snobbishness have delayed progress. But there is a healthy spirit abroad in English education to-day. The need of the hour is great ; sound educational methods alone can produce a people capable of dealing with the problems confronting our civilisation.

THE OLD AND THE NEW UNIVERSITIES

IN his *Essays on a Liberal Education*, Seeley wrote (1867), " Education in England is what the universities choose to make it." He proceeds to map out three main directions in which the influence of the universities is exerted. In the first place, the requirements of the university determine largely the curriculum of the upper part of most secondary schools. In the second place, many schoolmasters are trained by the universities, and tend to approve of the system by which they themselves were trained ; and thirdly, by virtue of their examining function, they influence considerably the work of those schools which do not send their pupils on to them. Changes may have taken place since Seeley put forward the above views. Training colleges for teachers have been instituted and the wisdom of allowing the curricula of schools to be determined by examining bodies has been challenged. But his words remain largely true.

The functions of universities are many and diverse. They are concerned with learning and research, with teaching and with culture. They have been charged with an undue regard for tradition and with a failure to adapt themselves to changing conditions. Questions of their efficiency, the value of their service to the community, and of their administration have been raised. Behind all this controversy there is in reality a cleavage of opinion about the proper function of the university. It is the old question of *value*, and the conflict is between the spiritual values (in the widest sense) and material ones. One school of thought would claim that the virtue of a university lies in a " way of life " ; the other would stress its importance for more practical purposes in the community. Put another way, the argument is whether universities are ends in themselves or means to an end. It is a controversy which has lasted as long as universities have existed, and one which bids fair to continue to be debated. And it is perhaps true to say that both the community and the universities have profited by it.

A fondness for setting up societies was one of the features of the twelfth-century renaissance. These frequently developed from the cathedral and other schools, and *Universitas* was such a society. It had no necessary connection at first with any definite place or building. It was in effect a guild or trade union licensed by the Pope to grant a licence to teach. The university was composed of masters, as at Paris, or of students, as at Bologna. It developed locally into a school resorted to by scholars from all parts.

The same general scheme of studies was recognised at all universities. There was a lower faculty of Arts and three higher faculties of Theology, Law, and Medicine. For a Bachelor's degree in Arts three years were required, while for a Master's degree in the same faculty, seven years was necessary. A Master's course in either Law or Medicine occupied six years ; in Theology twelve years. At first, taking both higher and lower faculties into account, the complete course extended over from thirteen to nineteen years, although these requirements were varied later. The full degree of Master made possible the issue of a licence to teach in the specified faculty.

DEEP-ROOTED IN THE PAST : THE OLDER UNIVERSITIES

THE foundation of Merton College, Oxford, by Walter de Merton, Bishop of Rochester, in 1263, marks the real beginning of universities in England. The statutes of 1274 show the full plan. Merton was the first autonomous institution, well-housed and endowed, and assured of perpetuity. From 1274 onwards, the new model served as an inspiration to a number of generous benefactors, and led to the development of Oxford and Cambridge as universities of colleges. Ten years later Peterhouse was founded at Cambridge, and a century later William of Wykeham, Bishop of Winchester, established his great foundation of New College, Oxford. At the same time, his method of providing for the teaching of the junior by the senior members of his foundation gave rise to the tutorial system.

For centuries higher education in England and Wales was confined almost exclusively to these two universities, and even their influence extended little beyond the Church of England. At Oxford, a dissenter could not matriculate or enjoy any privilege of university hall or college. At Cambridge he might become a student, but could not obtain a degree, could hold no office, receive no emolument, or take any part in the government of the university. The curriculum at both universities had narrowed, and distinctions were awarded by favouritism. At Cambridge the only honours examination was one in mathematics. The colleges had become more powerful than the university, and the professorial system had been almost entirely superseded by a system of college tutors.

Some attempts at internal reform preceded State action in 1850, when two Commissioners were appointed to inquire into the state, discipline, studies, and revenues of Oxford and Cambridge respectively. The Commissioners met with much obstruction in the progress of their inquiries. Information was refused them, and questions were left unanswered. But in spite of all difficulties, the Commissioners issued reports in 1852 ; and change could no longer be averted. Gradually the old restrictions and abuses were remedied and the curriculum widened. Broadly speaking, the criticisms of the last century have resulted in the old universities being confirmed in the medieval conception of a university as an autonomous guild of schools.

A SHOCK TO TRADITION : THE COMING OF THE UNDERGRADUETTE

TWO movements, similar, but not identical, led to the institution of women's colleges at the older universities. The one demanded a common standard of education for both sexes, while the other held that both instruction and examinations should be specially adapted to women, although not necessarily less difficult. In 1869 a college " designed to hold in relation to girls' schools and home teaching a position analogous to that occupied by the universities towards the public schools for boys " was established at Hitchin. The institution flourished, and was incorporated as Girton College in 1872, and removed to a building of its own within two miles of Cambridge in 1873. In 1869 the Local Examination Syndicate had instituted an examination for women over eighteen, and a Lectures Committee was formed to prepare girls for this special test. In 1871 a hostel for students attending the lectures was opened in Cambridge, and this developed into Newnham Hall, opened in 1875, which in turn became Newnham College in 1880. These two Cambridge colleges have been pioneers in the movement to secure higher education for women. In spite of their differing views as to the proper content of women's education, they have worked together in a common cause.

At Oxford, the Higher Local Examinations open to women only were authorised in 1875, and first held in 1877. In 1878 the Association for Promoting the Education of Women in Oxford was established, and in the same year Lady Margaret Hall was founded as a Church of England establishment. This was followed the next year by Somerville Hall, which is strictly undenominational.

From these origins, the place of women at the two older universities has become assured. Irksome restrictions have been successively removed and examinations opened to them. Their influence on university life has still to be assessed ; not sufficient time has yet elapsed since any measure of equality has been granted to them for it to be properly estimated.

In the seventeenth century the foundation of a university

in the north of England was often proposed, and in 1657 Cromwell approved of such a foundation at Durham. This scheme came to an end at the Restoration, and it was not until 1832 that the present University was established. Durham has always been somewhat crippled by the smallness of its resources.

Certain colleges are associated with the university. The College of Medicine at Newcastle, founded in 1851, became connected with Durham in 1852, and more closely associated in 1870. The original of Armstrong College was affiliated in 1871.

The university now incorporates eight colleges, and the constituent colleges conduct their own affairs in complete independence. The colleges have organic unity ; the university administrative unity. This raises problems concerning the very essence of a university. The comparison between the University of Durham and those of Oxford and Cambridge is illuminating, and raises questions of fundamental importance as to the proper function of a university.

AN EXAMINING UNIVERSITY : LONDON

THE University of London is an institution apart—unlike any other university in origin or function. As one writer puts it, " When a university has but one function to fulfil, the only question that can be asked about it is whether it fulfils this function well. It can no more suffer from the peculiar infirmities of Oxford and Cambridge than a skeleton can suffer from gout."

It was founded in 1839 as an examining body, in order to grant degrees to two London colleges founded ten years before—King's College and University College. In 1858 its examinations and degrees were thrown open to students generally, and the university thus became " external " in the fullest sense. In 1900 an internal organisation was added, and internal degrees instituted, a number of institutions being thus brought into federal union as " schools " of the university. Many colleges in the provinces which used the " external " facilities during the last century have now become independent universities, granting their own degrees. London has done much to mould the curricula and perhaps the spirit of modern universities.

Much about London University is open to criticism. It can be considered as merely an example of examination machinery, with neither " soul to be saved nor body to be kicked." But if it has never (except through a few of its colleges) given to its graduates that " way of life " which is one of the main functions of a university, it has led many to a genuine appreciation of learning. Its standard has always been high, and if the first incentive to study of some of its graduates was that of obtaining a degree, and through the degree an appointment, a real desire for knowledge developed in many of its examinees. Many of its graduates have yearned for the advantages that university life alone can give ; but they are far from lacking a love of wisdom. It may be that as modern universities increase in number the examining function of the university will diminish, but it will leave behind it in this field a record of which it may be justifiably proud.

THE NEW UNIVERSITIES : DO THEY GIVE A "MORE ABUNDANT LIFE"?

IN a variety of ways, dependent upon the needs of different localities and upon the means available, institutions have been developed in different parts of England which have ultimately received charters as universities. It is hardly possible to give a general description which shall be applicable to them all. They all possess constitutions, professional staffs, and buildings ; and residence is usually provided in recognised residential halls. Work of a university standard is carried on in day classes, but usually there are evening classes for those unable to attend during the day. Extramural work is often carried out in the surrounding areas, and usually men and women students are admitted on equal terms. Many of them were originally university colleges which utilised the examinations of the London University, subsequently receiving charters of their own. They provide " centres of intellectual enlightenment and culture " in industrial communities.

The chief danger that confronts them is that of becoming too dependent upon local interests and of carrying out research work for its " practical " ends rather than in the spirit of a real search for truth. The value of a university to a commercial community is apt to be measured in terms of cash returns rather than in terms of " more abundant life." There is, too, a danger lest the university become a mere administrative centre. Each shows a tendency to advance its frontiers, and institutions covet university connections. But the wider its realm, the less organic is the institution and the more immersed it becomes in the business of administration.

The true root of universities lies in a passion for knowledge, for expression, for controversy, and for teaching. The ideal is a high one. If in the rapid growth of the new universities the ideal has sometimes been obscured by less worthy aims, it must be remembered that they are still in the formative stage. If in the long history of the older universities tradition has sometimes stifled growth and proper development, it must be recalled that on other occasions they have kept the torch of wisdom alight in dark days.

THE COST OF A UNIVERSITY TRAINING

THE cost of a university education varies with the university. At Oxford or Cambridge, it is estimated that approximately £250 per annum is necessary, but this is reduced in a large number of cases by the grant of scholarships and allowances. The cost depends, too, on the college of which the student is a member. A really deserving student can usually obtain help if this is essential. At Birmingham, the average cost is £134 per annum ; at Bristol, £187 ; at the London School of Economics (London University), £129 ; at the Welsh Colleges, £118 ; and at Glasgow, £52. In every case there are numerous scholarships offered by the various colleges and faculties, and most local education authorities offer a number of major scholarships of varying value (£50 to £100 per annum) to promising students from their areas who desire to follow a university course.

TECHNICAL TRAINING AND MENTAL CULTURE

IN 1888, county councils were formed as administrative units by the Local Government Act of that year. They, and certain other councils, were given permission to raise a rate to assist the provision of Technical Education. The need for more technical education in an industrial age was recognised, and was met, to a certain extent, by the Technical Instruction Act of 1889. The need for secondary education had received no such formal recognition ; in fact, the two things appeared to be thoroughly confused in the minds of most people. It was by no means recognised that a sound general education is the essential basis of any system of technical instruction.

The 1889 Act not only enabled certain administrative bodies to aid technical instruction from the rates, but also placed at the disposal of these bodies certain excise money known as " whiskey money." The Science and Art Department quickly took advantage of the new position, reorganised its schemes of instruction, and included some literary subjects. It was not long before such courses covered practically every subject except the classics. The endowed schools were neglected and injured by the competition of the development of technical institutes.

Here, again, we get an example of the almost casual way in which the English education system has come into being. Industrial development had much to do with the gradual evolution of the elementary school system. An international exhibition had emphasised the need for technical institutes, and from this developed a system of secondary education quite apart from either the existing provision for such education (in the endowed and public schools) or the elementary system. The position was impossible, and, in 1892, the Science and Art Department ceased the payment of grants for most elementary science institutes. In 1898, drawing and manual institutes were transferred to the Education Department, and in 1899 the Department was incorporated in the new central authority set up in that year—the Board of Education.

PROVISION FOR WORK AFTER WORK : THE EVENING SCHOOLS

THE function of evening schools had changed considerably since the first days of the century, when they were merely elementary schools held during the evening. In those early days there had been a good deal of zeal and enthusiasm for them, and they gave much assistance to many who would otherwise have been denied any educational facilities. It is on record that at Wells the Bishop was engaged in teaching a class of navvies to read and to cypher, while at Rochdale, an inspector, who had intimated that the period of instruction had finished, was told by a member of the class, " Go thou on ; we want as much as we can get for the money."

Until 1861 teachers in day schools were forbidden to teach in evening schools as well, while from 1839 to 1860 only approximately £3000 was paid out of public funds as grant in aid of evening schools. The embargo on day teachers was withdrawn in the Revised Code of 1861, and a capitation grant, based upon average attendance, was established. In 1871 the grants were restricted to those between 12 and 18 years of age, and in 1876 the upper age was raised to 21 years. The work which these schools was doing is indicated by the fact that there was a rapid decline in the numbers attending them, subsequent to the erection of elementary schools under the Act of 1870. In 1870 there had been 73,375 on the rolls of evening schools ; by 1886 the number had dropped to 26,000.

In 1890, restrictions on the type of instruction were removed, and it was no longer necessary that they should be mainly elementary schools. A special code for such schools was issued in 1893. Attendance of scholars over 21 years of age was recognised, and no one was compelled to take the elementary subjects. The evening schools thus became, to a large extent, a means for the provision of secondary and technical education, and there was a rapid increase in attendance. By 1894 there were 266,683 scholars in 3742 schools.

TRAINING FOR WORK AND FITTING-OUT FOR LIFE

FROM such beginnings, re-enforced by enthusiasts working voluntarily outside the usual channels, there have been many and varied developments. Voluntary effort has done much to infuse the right spirit into the continued education of those who ceased to come under the influence of the State system of education at an early age. There are two distinct streams in such work. On the one hand, the definitely technical instruction is devised for the purpose of making workers in various occupations more skilled, and used by them largely as a means of securing promotion. On the other hand, there is provision for a definitely cultural stream, fostered by agencies and societies too numerous to mention, which has for its objective the widened outlook and the richer life. The one prepares men to earn a living —the other endeavours to make them fit to live. One is largely materialistic—the other, idealistic. Another division is between full-time and part-time provision.

The following diagram is an attempt to show the interrelation of the various parts. The classification is not rigid, nor is it suggested that all forms of technical and adult education are included. But it indicates roughly how the parts are

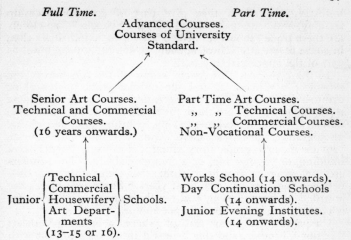

Full Time.   *Part Time.*

Advanced Courses.
Courses of University
Standard.

Senior Art Courses.   Part Time Art Courses.
Technical and Commercial   ,,   ,,   Technical Courses.
Courses.   ,,   ,,   Commercial Courses.
(16 years onwards.)   Non-Vocational Courses.

Junior ⎰Technical ⎱   Works School (14 onwards).
       ⎱Commercial⎰   Day Continuation Schools
Junior ⎰Housewifery⎱ Schools.   (14 onwards).
       ⎱Art Depart-⎰   Junior Evening Institutes.
        ments ⎱   (14 onwards).
       (13–15 or 16).

related to the whole, and how, gradually, some sort of system
has evolved from many diverse beginnings.

As will be seen from the diagram, full-time training in
commercial, technical, art, and domestic science subjects is
given to junior students (between the ages of 14 and 16) in
schools which have, in the main, a vocational aim. Continental countries have done more for provision for this type
of instruction than England. It is significant that it was in
the north of England that the demand for, and the supply of,
a type of education definitely related to commerce and industry
was first made. Skilled artisans were needed, and between
1905 and 1907 fifteen junior technical schools were founded.

But it was only in 1913 that this type of school was recognised as a distinct unit of the educational system, and not
until 1925 that the junior commercial schools, as such, came
into being. By 1931 there were 115 such schools—64 for
boys, 10 for girls, and 41 mixed. In the same year there
were 19,500 students in attendance.

THE YOUNG LONDONER'S OPPORTUNITIES

THE larger and more concentrated population of London
has led to a development there which is not possible in
less populous areas. Schools have been established, each of
which confines its activities to preparation for some particular

industry. In effect, they give part of an apprenticeship training, and are usually called " Trade Schools." So closely are these trade schools connected with specific industries that, in some cases, attendance at them is definitely recognised as part of the apprenticeship period.

In the provinces this specialisation of the function of the school is not possible, and the normal junior technical or commercial school is a *pre-apprenticeship* school. Amongst the London schools are those for bookbinding, boot and shoe industry, building, cabinetmaking, painting and decorating, photography, music trades, etc. Outside London, the courses provide general preparatory training for many branches of building, or engineering, or a commercial life. The scholars are, in general, recruited from the elementary school— between the ages of 13 and 14 years. Some free places are awarded by examination, and for the remaining places a fee is charged—usually about £3 per annum.

Frequently the junior institute shares a building with its " senior " brother, and this brings it into closer contact with industry and commerce than would otherwise be possible. Also, there is a " workshop " attitude about the building, which is of assistance when the boy actually enters industry. But it is doubtful whether this type of institution will continue to develop, excellent though its work has been. The main reasons are two. It was organised originally as a means of *supplementing* the instruction given in elementary schools, when the curriculum of such schools was confined to the tools of academic learning, and when the leaving age was 13 or 14. The tendency now to raise the school leaving age, and, more particularly, the changed outlook of the new senior (" Hadow ") schools have combined to make the junior institute less necessary than it was a generation or two ago. A good, well-equipped senior modern school (and the number is increasing) has its wood-work and metal-work shops, its art room and its science room, its gymnasium and (for girls) its domestic science room. It can do *all* that the pre-apprenticeship type of junior institute can do—probably a good deal more, for it does not specialise at too early an age. And it is doubtful if the " apprenticeship " type of school is entirely beneficial—even to the trades concerned. In a later section the question of tests for various forms of ability will be discussed.

One cannot imagine that boys can be selected at 13–14

years of age for definite trades with any certainty that the choice is sound. It is still more doubtful if it would be desirable to do it, even if it were possible. No educational system should endeavour to justify the epitaph, " born a man : died a greengrocer." It is possible that the wiser course of development will prove to be the extension of well-equipped senior schools where secondary education in its various branches can be developed, and where contact with varied types of minds makes for the wider outlook.

During 1935 the L.C.C. Education Committee reviewed the whole system of education under its control and planned an advance " on the whole front." Additional places in Secondary Schools are to be available for meritorious children, and facilities for technical education are to be extended and co-ordinated. Facilities for the cultivation of " leisure time " pursuits are to be widened, and the developments visualised should place within reach of the adolescent and adult Londoner a wealth of opportunities without parallel in the great cities of the world.

ART'S PLACE IN TECHNICAL EDUCATION

THE remarks which have been made with reference to junior technical and commercial schools are true of junior art departments. Prior to 1916 there were no such departments—by 1929 there were 36, with 1962 students. The work carried out is mainly of an applied nature ; i.e. it is closely connected with particular art industries, such as pottery and jewellery. Admission is usually by means of scholarships. It has been claimed that these departments are necessary because of the emphasis laid upon art drawing. This may have been true of the old elementary school, largely because of the deficiency, or entire lack, of suitable accommodation and equipment. With the new modern school, this argument loses its point. Good art rooms and good equipment are becoming more frequent, and well-qualified teachers are giving sound instruction. Co-operation between the local school of art and the senior schools of any district is very desirable ; in fact, it is essential. The school of art can do much to stimulate the art and craft work carried out in the schools. But it is again very doubtful if junior art departments can now be justified as separate institutions.

Girls are, of course, provided for in the Commercial Institute, in the Art Department, and in some trade schools.

But the Junior Housewifery Department has not been an outstanding success. Perhaps the reason is that domestic work is not often recognised as requiring special qualifications. Or it may be that many girls on leaving school endeavour to avoid it as far as possible. Factory work and commercial careers seem to be preferred to domestic. There remain three residential junior housewifery schools and a number of non-residential ones. The development of sound housewifery instruction in the new senior schools will do away with the *raison d'être* of this type of institution.

Reference has already been made to the variety which is to be found among English educational institutions. At no point is it possible to say that just *there* a new start was made. This is the case with respect to technical education, in the provision made for both junior and senior students. The development of trade and other full-time junior technical schools has been outlined. Side by side with these there is a system of part-time (evening, chiefly) education—a development mainly from the older type of evening schools.

The early history of the evening institute has already been traced. It provides vocational and non-vocational courses for approximately three-quarters of a million students, mainly between the ages of 14 and 16. Many of these students are taking courses preparatory to attending subsequently at some technical college. The courses are, then, in the main, conditioned by two factors—the standard of attainment reached by the elementary school leaver, and the requirements of the technical college. The former is of particular importance, for any overlapping of work or repetition of that already done, deadens enthusiasm and kills interest. The standard of attainment of the elementary school leaver is rising, and there is need for a very careful scrutiny of the work done in evening institutes if it is not to be ineffective, and, what is worse, devoid of interest for the scholar.

THE FACTOR OF FATIGUE

IT is unfortunate that many teachers in evening institutes come to their work fatigued by full-time employment elsewhere. It is equally unfortunate that many students are not in a fit state to benefit as much as they might by the facilities provided. Herein lies the weakness of much of the work attempted. The teachers are drawn from the ranks of day-school teachers and experts engaged in commerce and industry. The rate of pay is not excessive—in some instances it is meagre. Some day-school teachers undertake evening classes in their own day school from a genuine desire to carry their old pupils further on the path to the " good way of life." Others have an objection to the " outsider " handling the apparatus of which they are so proud. Others, again, are forced into it by their economic situation. The marvel is that, with tired pupils and tired teachers, the work reaches the level it does. Methods of eliminating the over-tired pupil will be discussed in this section. The over-tired teacher can only be eliminated by some method similar to that advocated in the section upon senior schools.

It has been argued frequently and with much force that the transition from school to work is too abrupt. The average boy of 14–15 years is not an adult. Neither is he any longer a child. To remove him entirely from whole-time schooling under the guidance of teachers to whole-time work amongst adults under different methods of discipline is to make the transfer from one category to the other too abrupt. For this reason " Works Schools " have been established by certain firms. The administrative details vary widely. In the case of some schools, the building is provided and maintained by the local education authority. In other cases, the employer both provides and maintains it, while provision by the employer and maintenance by the local education authority is another alternative.

The essential element is the direct contact between the employer and the employee-pupil, and between the school and the place of occupation. It has been claimed that three main benefits derive from such schools :

(a) The desire for further education is developed.

(b) Medical inspection and treatment is made possible.

(c) The transition from school to works discipline is made with less mental stress than would be the case otherwise.

There is very little doubt that these ends are achieved. The additional benefit derived by those who attend such schools is that they are enabled to study during normal working hours, and not at the end of a tiring day's work.

THE GEDDES AXE DESTROYS A PROMISING BRANCH

TOWARDS the end of the War reconstruction was in the air, and affected education in common with other fields of national activity. The Act of 1918 was the outcome of this desire to reconstruct our national life. One of its provisions required local education authorities to establish a system of free continuation schools for young persons between the ages of 14 and 18. Attendance was to be required between 8 a.m. and 7 p.m. for a total of 320 hours per annum. During the passage of the Bill through Parliament, the upper age was reduced to 16 years for the first seven years of operation of the Act, and local education authorities were given power to reduce the number of hours to 280. Provision was made for medical inspection and for assistance in choice of employment.

A wave of depression overwhelmed the country and brought with it the demand for retrenchment in the social services, known as the "Geddes Act." In addition, an impression that the continuation school handicapped young people in seeking employment got abroad. The two factors together destroyed the development of this type of school. One at Rugby remains the sole survivor of the storm, and continues to gather valuable experience of this type of educational facility.

The educational service was recovering slowly but surely from the effects of the Geddes Axe when the "crisis" of 1931 developed. Once more progress was arrested and many promising developments held up. The salaries of all teachers were reduced by 10 per cent., and authorities found it difficult to obtain the approval of the Board to new schools. The authorities claimed that there was instituted "an embargo on buildings." Although this was officially denied, the fact remains that very little was done to remedy obvious defects. In 1936 the Board of Education issued Circular 1444 which indicated that ordered progress was to be possible once more. A more detailed reference to this Circular is made subsequently.

The provision for adult education in this country is varied, and touches many interests, but it still remains chaotic. There are whole-time art, commercial, and technical courses, and similar part-time ones. Most of the provision is to be found in technical colleges, art schools and in the courses (whole and part-time) organised by university colleges and universities. A lot of it is definitely vocational, but much definitely cultural in aim exists. Local authorities and industry have combined to foster and develop this work. The

" Miners' Welfare Fund," for example, have generously contributed to the cost of provision in areas where mining is the predominant industry.   Adult schools, the Workers' Educational Association, rural community councils, and other bodies have all stimulated interest and taken a share in the cost and organisation of existing classes.   If there is still some overlapping, it is gradually disappearing as circumstances permit.

In the West Riding of Yorkshire, regional schemes have been developed and are working well.   Universities carry out much extra-mural work—extension lectures, extension courses, and shorter courses all being provided.   The subjects studied are many : economics, history, literature, psychology, biology are amongst them.   Of many such classes it is true to say that the main object of the students is that " better way of life " to which reference has already been made.   In the numerous technical colleges which have been erected (any town of considerable size has one), instruction bearing upon the needs of local industries is given.   Students are prepared to take higher posts—to qualify themselves for promotion.   The only real criticism that can be directed against this work is one that has been made already—the students come to it exhausted by a long day's work.

FALLOW FIELD : THE PROBLEM OF LEISURE

THE future will try these institutions severely.   There seems every reason to believe that hours of work will be progressively shortened if the effect of the multiplication of machinery is not to be an increasing number of totally unemployed persons.   Increased leisure may be a danger to both the individual and to the community of which he is a member if it be used wrongly.   It seems likely that preparation for leisure occupations will replace preparation for working hours as the main function of the various institutions which provide for adolescent and adult education.   Otherwise, the individual will be at the mercy of the commercialised forms of amusement—one of the mass demanding " circuses " from dictators.   The development of interests and the provision of suitable and desirable outlets for them is the need of an educated democracy, and the need is greater the greater the leisure time of the people.   The various bodies interested in the problems of adult education have much to consider and much to evolve if they are to solve the complex problems confronting them. But, if they fail, then culture dies, and mass thought and action replaces individuality.

The Ministry of Labour has the right to set up centres for the part-time instruction of unemployed adolescents, and a number have been established in areas where unemployment is widespread. The Act of 1933 makes it possible to extend this facility, and should there continue to be extensive unemployment, it seems likely that the number of centres will increase largely. These centres are under the Ministry of Labour, the Board of Education only acting in an advisory capacity. They have been highly praised—and acutely criticised. There is no doubt that they arrest to some extent that intellectual, physical, and moral deterioration which affects the unemployed adolescent. On the other hand, attendance is, of necessity, irregular—boys and girls come in and out of the centres as they obtain or lose posts. The buildings and equipment tend to be of a temporary nature, like the pupils, and the primary consideration is the job to be got, not the education and discipline to be absorbed. Employment is viewed as the best state ; unemployment as the worst.

Under proper guidance and controlled with vision these centres may develop into places of real educational and social value. To do this, it will be necessary to realise that shoddy buildings and cheap equipment are a mistake, while the curriculum will have to be widened. But it would appear that a raising of the school leaving age to 15 years, and the retention in school of children between 15 and 16 years who have no employment to go to, would be a more effective solution of the problem.

THE MODERN WAY WITH THE PROBLEM CHILD

ONE of the most significant developments in Education is the increasing amount of thought and attention devoted to the " problem " child. It is now recognised that such children require special consideration and treatment, and that very much can be done to relieve the burden caused by the defect and to discover the cause of backwardness and, by appropriate steps, eliminate it. The days have passed when defects removed children from the scope of education, and when backwardness was viewed as something which could not be remedied. Success with " problem " children should be accounted as one of the functions of an effective educational system. Success with normal children is comparatively easy to obtain ; " problem " children call for much greater effort from the teacher. But successful work with such children brings a correspondingly greater joy.

An immediate difficulty, one caused by current terminology, presents itself. There is no agreed standard either of defect or of backwardness. Views vary considerably as to what is connoted by the terms. It will serve as a useful introduction to this topic if the various terms in current use are briefly reviewed.

A consideration of the problem will show that retardation may be of one of two types. Retarded children are those who are not making the progress which their powers would lead one to expect. It should be noted that this definition is not concerned with the actual powers of the child. Retardation in this sense is a relative term. A child of poor ability may not be retarded if his progress is commensurate with his ability. A better endowed child is retarded if he is not making full use of his powers.

Dull children are those who, while not defective, are below the average in *ability*. Comparing this statement with the definition of retarded children given above, it is clear that a child may be dull without necessarily being retarded. If the dull child makes the progress of which it is capable it is not retarded.

Backward children are those below the average in attainment. The essential problem in the case of such children is to find the cause of the backwardness. It *may* be due to dullness, in which case the child has probably gone as far educationally as his attainments will permit. On the other hand, when the degree of backwardness does not correspond to the degree of dullness, then it is clear that something is wrong with his education, and that he is not realising to the full his potentialities. In other words the backward child may not be a dull child. Its backwardness may be due to some remedial factor.

THE DELICATE PROBLEM OF THE DEFECTIVE CHILD

DEFECTS are numerous in kind and varying in degree. They may be either physical or mental, and may be slight or grave. It is clear that both the nature and the degree of backwardness will affect the method and content of the education which is suitable for the child. In every case the defect will mean some variation from the normal method, and in many cases it will mean that the child must be dealt with in a special group taught by special methods using special apparatus. This is, in effect, a policy of segregation, and care is necessary in applying such a policy. A defective child amongst normal children is a subject of attention, and since young children are often unwittingly cruel, remarks passed may adversely affect the defective and cause him very real unhappiness. On the other hand, the segregation of defective children of various types in separate groups may lead to bitter disillusionment when the time comes for the child to take its place in the world outside the school. Teachers of such children are faced with a grave and difficult task and one which makes heavy demands upon their sympathy and understanding.

The first obvious division of such children is into physical defectives and mental defectives. This does not imply that the two are never found together—far from it. It is often the case that the physically defective child suffers from some mental defect as well and *vice versa*. But the classification makes discussion easier. It should always be remembered that the dividing line between groups of children is never a clear-cut one. One group fades almost imperceptibly into another, and often the border-line cases constitute the biggest problem.

It is commonly asserted that the number of mentally defective children is increasing, and that this increase is a *real* one and not due either to better methods of diagnosis or to a raising of the standard of normality. There is evidence that this statement is true, but much more thorough consideration needs to be given to the subject before it can be accepted as definite. There has been very little attempt made to separate the various types of defect, nor has it been considered how much apparent defect is remedial. Usually some group test of ability has been given to selected groups, general statistics collected, and generalisations made from them. But, to raise one objection only, it is problematical whether failure in intelligence tests is an infallible mark of defectiveness.

It appears that mental defect may be due to one or all of three causes. In the first place, there is inherent mental defect, due to some definite physical lesion. Then there is defect due to general mal-nourishment. If this is such that the body in general is working ineffectively, it seems reasonable to suppose that the brain will be affected. In the third case, there is the mal-adjusted child, the one unable to adjust itself to the speed or complexity of modern life. In some cases it is not so much the case that it is unable to adjust itself, as that it has not been taught how it *can* adjust itself. The defect here is emotional and social.

This tripartite division is not a rigid one, but it serves to emphasise one important fact. A good deal of what passes to-day for defect is remedial. There is always the temptation to say, " Poor child ! it is defective," and to leave it at that, assuming that the cause of the defect is something incapable of cure. Or, going a step farther, the sole concern is with the development of some form of education suitable for the defective child. The suggested division indicates that there are two types of defect—that due to general mal-nourishment and that due to mal-adjustment which can be remedied. This, again, serves to stress the first *duty* of the educationist towards such cases—that of diagnosis.

MAKING UP FOR THE HANDICAP

THE prevalence of what may be termed minor defects— defects of sight and hearing—has been discovered since medical inspection of scholars has become the general rule. The milder forms of such defect can usually be remedied sufficiently to enable the child to take its place in a class of normal children. It is when such defects become grave that special treatment becomes necessary, and in any case, a careful examination for a minor defect should always be made when backwardness is alleged.

Graver defects, such as total blindness, dumbness, or deafness obviously require special consideration ; and many special schools have been established to cater for the needs of such children. Some such schools deal only with a single defect—others take cases of multiple defect. It is the duty of education authorities to deal with such cases, and authorities which have not schools of their own, use, by arrangement, those set up by the larger authorities.

It should not be overlooked that other forms of defect may present just as much an obstacle to education as the more common ones of defective eyesight or hearing. An example of this is stammering. The stammerer tends to become an object of ridicule. He lacks opportunity for self-expression and may easily be rated of much lower mentality than his ability warrants. Many authorities have established classes for stammerers which are achieving remarkable results. It is an unspectacular piece of work, but a most effective one.

Other bodily defects may be such that special educative measures are necessary. Crippled limbs and spines prevent their unfortunate possessors from taking part in normal development, and education must provide adequate compensation for such children.

THE DEFECTIVE'S CHALLENGE TO SOCIETY

THE point has already been made that much alleged defectiveness is due to remedial causes. Far too many " experts " are prepared to think that they have adequately dealt with the case when they have labelled the defect and found a class or school which will admit the child. The sight of any defective child should be a challenge—a challenge to society as a whole, and to those charged with educational work in particular. Perhaps it is as well that we cannot see the minds of our defectives. The warped and crooked and stunted growth of many of them would fill us with horror— and perhaps with remorse. Every child alleged to be mentally defective should be subjected to a thorough individual examination by a competent expert. Its family history should be investigated and its school record carefully examined. Many children improve out of all knowledge when put upon a proper regular diet, or when made subject to a regular routine of life, including adequate rest. In other cases some emotional shock in early years is discovered to be the originating cause of the trouble.

The question of who should carry out such examinations raises several questions. In the case of physical defect there is no doubt as to the answer—the School Medical Officer is the appropriate person. The case of mental defectiveness is rather different. In the first place, a skilled psychologist is essential—and one who has had experience in dealing with children. It is not to be expected that the School Medical Officer can be an expert in all branches and, further, this is essentially a matter of mental development, not physical well-being, although the two always overlap. The teacher again is inclined to measure normality by ability to cover the traditional curriculum, and, again, is not usually a trained and experienced psychologist—alas ! Some few authorities have appointed a school psychologist to whom all difficult children are referred. Others make use of Child Guidance Clinics—some others utilise the services of the staff of the National Institute of Psychology. It seems possible to predict that, as a first step, an increasing number of Authorities will appoint their own trained expert. It is to be hoped that ultimately there will be on the staff of any school of average size a member who by training and inclination is able to deal with the continuous stream of problem children which are bound to pass through such a school. The amount of mental energy which could be so released would more than repay the outlay involved.

MENTAL DIETS FOR DEFECTIVE MINDS

CRITICAL study of the School curriculum has not been carried out, at least in this country, to the extent which the importance of the subject warrants. Starting with the 3 R's, other " subjects " have been added without any definite planning of the curriculum as a whole. Tradition has become the main reason for the retention of some subjects in the school course, and custom the authority for the relative amount of time devoted to each " subject."

There are two views current as to the type of curriculum suitable for dull or mentally defective children, and both of them are erroneous. The first is that such a curriculum should be similar to the ordinary curriculum in kind and vary only in the degree to which subjects are taken. The underlying assumption is that the brain of a defective child is of the same nature as that of the normal child and differs only in its range. This is an easy assumption to make, but a fallacious one. It leads to an " easy " curriculum, one for which the stimulus to effort has been eliminated. The dull and defective child is usually one whose development has not proceeded beyond a certain stage. At a chronological age of, say, 12, he may have the mentality of a child of nine. He will never catch up the child of normal intelligence, but there are many interests which can be given him which will add to the richness and fullness of his life. The idea that only those who can deal with the academic and abstract are fit subjects for education has to be abandoned. Many defective children can be taught through the concrete—the use of money through " shopping," the actual use of tools, reading for definite information, and, above all, they can be trained in routine activities. Gardening, the care of animals, singing, etc., all furnish scope for educating this type of child.

The second erroneous view of the curriculum is that " craft work ' can be done well by defective children. In the minds of many there seems to be a conviction that good craft ability and good academic ability are rarely found together. All scientific investigations are against this view. The defective child cannot do craft work in any true sense of the term. Craft work involves planning and forethought, consideration of appropriate material, and a " vision " of the completed job. The defective child can do *repetitive handwork—i.e.* having been taught a process he can repeat it, and often finds real joy and a sense of mastery in the repetition, where a more intelligent child would find only boredom. This should be borne in mind in planning curricula for defective children. Most of them have a sense of inferiority. To achieve success in something, no matter how simple, means as much, and perhaps more, to them than success in more difficult matters may bring to the ordinary person. The curriculum must be framed with this object in view. Much thought and experiment will be necessary before it can be said that this problem has been solved.

THE TEACHING OF PROBLEM CHILDREN

THE teaching of dull and defective children is an exacting task. They require much doing for them, and the teacher is apt to become dispirited on account of the apparently small return for the labour expended. Special classes tend to be staffed by " complacent " teachers—or by the latest arrival on the staff.

This is to be deplored. A special kind of ability is necessary in the teacher of problem children. The difficulty is to express in words exactly the factors which combine to produce this ability. There must be a love for children as individuals, and an insight into their difficulties and struggles. There must be faith in the value of the task, and the power to communicate this faith in possibility of success to the child. There must be skill in devising occupations and in stimulating interest and enthusiasm. There must be a wise and understanding sympathy. Above all, the main interest must lie in the child—not in the subjects taught. It is clear that such teachers cannot be selected at random. They must be carefully selected, appropriately trained, and stimulated and encouraged to view their task as one of great importance and one calling for all their highest powers.

Here one is confronted with difficulties. Some defective (physical) children are taught trades and ultimately placed in situations. Others (mentally defective) attend " Occupation Centres " or are looked after by various voluntary " after-care " or Welfare Committees. Work of some kind or another is found for many. But the major problems remain. We require much more knowledge and much less use of prejudiced opinion before these problems can be solved. Mere palliative work is of little use. It does not help the community if a kind-hearted person finds a job for a defective child, if as a result a normal child is not employed.

It may be questioned whether the expenditure of £60–£70 per annum on the defective child in a special school, and of only £12 per annum on a normal child is the act of a State ruled by wisdom. There is common agreement that all children, sub-normal, normal, or super-normal, should receive such an education as will enable them to utilise their abilities to the utmost, and as will bring them the richest and happiest lives of which they are capable. But more " biological engineering " is required—more planning, more *long-range* thinking—if the fundamental problems are to be solved. Expedients can never replace principles in the long run.

A PICTURE OF THE SYSTEM AT WORK

LET us try to get a picture of the system at work. Mr. Everyman lives in an area controlled by a progressive educational authority, which has a complete system operating in the area under its control. He has a son Tom and a daughter Mary. He and his wife are themselves educated to the extent that they understand the value of the Nursery School, the Medical Clinic, and the Child Guidance Clinic, and they are not so snobbish as to be willing to pay for an inferior education at the local " Private School for Sons of Gentlemen." (The assumptions are many—but necessary for a description of the ideal English system.)

One morning, shortly after Tom's second birthday, they present him at the local Nursery School. The teacher in charge takes notes of any information which the mother can give her—any childish ailments already contracted, and any

technical college, obtaining in due course a National Certificate in Electrical Engineering—and there we can safely part company with him, fairly certain that he is well on the way to make a success of his life.

STEPPING-STONES TO POSSIBLE PROFESSIONS

TOM has followed but one of the many paths open to him. Had he been successful in obtaining a place in the local Secondary School, the Local Education Authority would have inquired into his parents' means, and have fixed the proportion of the school fees to be paid by Tom's father.

At about sixteen years of age Tom would have taken the School Certificate and have done sufficiently well in his examination to have been granted exemption from University Matriculation examinations. The local authority might have granted him (if his circumstances warranted such a course) some further scholarship. Tom would then have been enabled to follow an advanced course for two years, culminating in obtaining the Higher School Certificate at the age of eighteen. At this age various alternatives would be open to him. He could enter for one of the examinations for admission to the Intermediate grades of the Civil Service, or he could proceed to college or to a university.

His choice would then depend almost entirely upon the profession he had chosen. If he had ambitions concerning the higher branches of the Civil Service, the Indian Civil Service, the Colonial Service, the legal profession, the Church, or higher posts in the Education Service, then Oxford or Cambridge would appeal to him. He might obtain a major scholarship from the local Education Authority (£50–£100 per annum) on the result of the Higher School Certificate examination, and in addition might sit for the Scholarship Examination conducted by the college which he desired to attend. Or he might desire to study Technology at one of the newer Universities (at which his major scholarship would be equally available). If he entered a Training College he would have to decide between the four-year and the two-year course (see Section on Careers [1]), and in either case could qualify for Board of Education grants towards the cost of the course. Or it may have been discovered at one of his Medical Examinations that he was unfortunate enough to be suffering from some definite physical or mental defect. He

[1] See page 278.

would then have been transferred to a school or class in which he could be given such education as his defect permitted, and have been taught some trade at which he was capable of earning a living.

Again, he may unfortunately have developed moral defects, and have appeared before the Juvenile Court. The latter would probably have referred him to the Child Guidance Clinic for a report, and upon the receipt of this may have decided that it was necessary that he should be sent to some " approved school " or training-ship ; one suitable to his needs being carefully selected. Here, again, he would be carefully trained and placed in some suitable occupation, and would be able to leave his youthful escapades behind him and become a worthy citizen.

Mary's career might have been somewhat similar. She might proceed to a Secondary School, to a University or Teachers' Training College, a School of Art or Music. Or, via the Selective Central School, she might have gone into some office or business and have attended classes at the Technical College on business routine, etc. Or, after a period in the ordinary Senior School, she might have obtained a post in some shop or factory, attending an Evening Institute and there have maintained her interest in the Drama, Art, or Music. Domestic Science classes would help her to be a good housewife in the future.

THE HEALTH OF THE SCHOOL CHILD

THE rapid development of the factory system in England, resulting in the congregating of masses of people in towns, led to attention being directed to problems concerning public health. Epidemic disease was rampant, and infant and child mortality very high.

Two aspects of the problem demanded special attention— the question of the development of a more hygienic environment, and that concerning the provision of pure food and water. After a series of minor Acts, the Public Health Act of 1875 dealt in a comprehensive manner with the problem, and in spite of numerous amending Acts, remains the principal Act under which local authorities work. The scope of the service has widened. The responsibility of the community to ensure satisfactory housing conditions for its members has been recognised. Measures have been taken to ensure the purity of water supplies and of food intended for human consumption. Drainage schemes have been developed. The standard of a satisfactory environment from the hygienic point of view tends to rise, and has in itself done much to improve the communal health. The notification of infectious diseases and the extension of hospital and clinic services have assisted in the fight against disease and an unnecessarily high death-rate.

Whole-time medical officers who were specialists in public hygiene were at work in most towns of any size by the beginning of the twentieth century. It soon became apparent that the rate of infantile mortality was unduly high, and that much disease and suffering was being caused through children receiving inadequate medical attention during the early years of their lives. Errors of dietary caused much waste of infant life, and one result was the appointment of Health Visitors, whose main duty was to visit homes and offer advice upon the upbringing of children.

But even this progress left very much still to be desired. It is often a war that shocks a nation out of its complacency, and national reconstruction often finds its origin in the heart-searchings caused by severe conflict. The South African War was no exception. It raised questions about the physique of the people, and Commissions were appointed to investigate the matter and report. One recommendation was that arrangements should be made for the routine medical inspection of school children. Later (1905) another committee reported upon the questions of the medical inspection and feeding of school children attending elementary schools. The main recommendations of this committee were incorporated in the Education (Administrative Provisions) Act, 1907. This placed upon local education authorities the duty of providing for the medical inspection of school children either immediately before, or at the time of, or immediately after, their admission to a public elementary school, and also at such other times as the Board of Education might direct. Three such routine medical inspections are now carried out —immediately after entry, midway through the school life, and before leaving.

ALLIES OF EDUCATION : THE MEDICAL SERVICES

AMONGST the provisions of the 1907 Act, to which reference has been made above, was one making it the duty of local education authorities to appoint School Medical Officers. It was foreseen that there might be a danger of isolation if the school medical services were separated from the general health services of the area, and the Board of Education recommended that the local medical officer of health should be appointed school medical officer, even in areas where the school population was of such a size that it was impossible for him to carry out the whole of the work himself. The co-ordination of the entire public health services was the ideal to be attained.

In addition to school medical officers and assistant school medical officers, the service required other workers. School nurses were appointed to assist in the routine inspections and to deal with minor ailments. These school nurses have been of inestimable value in the difficult task of " following up " treatment or advice given by the school medical officer. In many areas, the work of the school nurse is combined with that of the health visitor, and it is difficult to express the full value of the work done by these workers, particularly in rural or overcrowded areas. They visit expectant and nursing mothers, give advice regarding children of pre-school age, follow up the clinic treatment of school children, keep an eye upon the defective child. In other areas, the school nursing service is a distinct branch of the public health work, and following-up work is sometimes done by voluntary workers.

It has been pointed out that three medical inspections are required by the Board of Education during each child's school life. Some authorities provide for four. The gap between the routine inspections is obviously a long one, and it may be argued that such a gap defeats the objects of the inspections, in that disease may develop during the period between one inspection and the next. But it is common for the school medical officer and his assistants so to arrange their visits to any one school that they are in each school at least once each year and can then see any child considered by the school staff to be below normal as regards health. In addition, school clinics are held in most towns, often twice or thrice a week, and to these the teachers can refer any child suffering from a minor ailment, or any child who appears to be in ill-health. Again, each child is inspected by a nurse once every year for personal cleanliness ; and with her special training the nurse can often observe early signs of ill-health which less professional observers might miss.

9

THE FIGHT AGAINST INFECTIOUS DISEASE

IN 1930, approximately a million and a half children were inspected as part of the routine examinations referred to above. Of these it was found that approximately 300,000, or 21 per cent., required some form of treatment. Ten per cent. of those specially examined for eyesight were found to have some defect.

Authorities provide now for the treatment of minor ailments, dental defects, and defects of vision. They provide spectacles and deal with cases of enlarged tonsils and adenoids. Ringworm is treated by X-ray methods, and orthopædic cases are dealt with, and artificial sunlight treatment given where necessary.

In 1910 there were 30 school clinics, in 1930, 1741. During the same years dental treatment clinics grew from 14 to 1211. Other branches of the work show an equally great expansion. In all, some 922,000 minor defects were dealt with during 1930. Out of 14,500,000 examinations of children made by school nurses, 711,000 cases of uncleanliness were found.

These figures indicate the extent of the work ; they also stress the need for it. The percentage of defects found is still high, and the question of how much of this defect could be avoided by increased attention during the pre-school years is bound to arise.

Children are peculiarly susceptible to a number of infectious diseases, and an important part of the work of the school medical service is concerned with the control of epidemics should such occur. There is a general consensus of opinion in favour of keeping schools open during epidemics. At one time it was thought advisable to close them, and in very rural districts this may still be advisable. But in urban districts he risk of infection is just as great when schools are closed as when they are open. During an epidemic an early morning inspection will often remove suspicious cases from contact with other children, while if the children were not at school, the case might go undetected for several days. It is unfortunate that the keeping of a school open during an epidemic often involves a local authority in considerable loss in Government grant. Where the attendance falls below 60 per cent. the period for which it is below this figure can be excluded from the calculation of the average attendance for the year— the most important factor in the determination of the amount

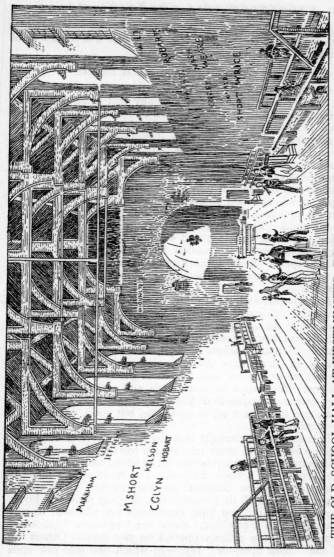

THE OLD SCHOOL HALL AT WESTMINSTER, WHERE ALL THE TEACHING WAS DONE

259

of grant payable. But any figure above 60 per cent. must be included and a severe epidemic may cause a serious loss of grant to a local authority.

THE NEW DRIVE FOR PHYSICAL FITNESS

THE diagnosis and treatment of defects can never be the sole or even the chief aim of any real health service in the schools. And it is a one-sided education which confines itself to matters of the mind and deals only casually with the development of the body. One of the most pleasing features of current educational practice is the development of sound ideas upon physical training. The days when a retired sergeant took a weekly " drill " class in most secondary schools has passed. A new spirit permeates the work in all types of schools. Its object is not the training of gymnasts, but the provision of reasonable exercise for the growing body of the child. The object is the co-ordination of all muscular effort. Games, dancing, and swimming all play their part. New syllabuses of instruction have been prepared by the Board experts. Local authorities have provided playing fields, and, in many cases, well-equipped gymnasia for the senior schools.

Much remains still to be done. There is a decided deficiency of playing fields still, but the need for suitable and controlled exercise as an ancillary to the more purely health services, is being increasingly recognised. Enormous strides have been made. Netball, cricket, football, and hockey are all being played in elementary schools, and played well. Athletic sports are organised, and one most pleasing feature is the rational dress worn by both boys and girls. The general turn-out and smartness of the competitors increases year by year, and must have an unconscious, but good, effect on the competitors.

It must not be thought that the health services constitute a thing apart from other educational forces. In many subtle and indirect ways other factors assist in the task of improving the physique of school children. The rapid strides made in school architecture constitute one such factor. Gone are the days of the dark, ill-lit, ill-ventilated, dismally painted schools. Now, large, airy, and light classrooms are planned, usually opening on to a corridor. Some are " open-air " schools—capable of being entirely opened on two sides. Others are of the " semi open-air " type—in which one side can open

AN UP-TO-DATE JUNIOR SCHOOL—IN THE HEALTH-GIVING RAYS OF THE SUN

entirely. Questions of heating and lighting have received attention, and there is no doubt that the improved type of building is bringing with it improved health for the children in attendance.

The provision of nursery schools has already been discussed. Here again is a service which can do much to improve the health of children and to prevent defects from occurring.

Some authorities have instituted definite open-air schools for children who require special treatment. In all there are some 141 such schools, having accommodation for some 13,000 scholars. There is much to be thought out before any very great extension of these schools is likely. A blind belief in the efficacy of fresh air will not lead one very far. Many physiological principles have to be considered, and these are receiving an increasing amount of attention.

The provision of school meals has been referred to. In 1930–31, 153 authorities provided over forty million meals for about 300,000 children at an average cost per meal of between 2½d. and 3d. In periods of industrial depression the need for such a service is obvious. It is no use waiting until the results of under-nutrition manifest themselves before taking action. The object of the service is to *prevent* more than to cure. Milk is being provided in increasing quantities ; and from observations made over lengthy periods is producing beneficial results.

School camps form another supplement to the health services. Camps vary from those of the hutment type to those of the tent type. Some are held in school-time, and lessons of the more formal type are held. Others are holiday camps, and the lessons are the informal ones—largely social—learnt in *any* well-organised camp. In every case the change of environment brings with it factors which make for improved health.

LOOKING TO THE FUTURE OF THE RACE : HEALTH TRAINING

IN the schools a continued training in habits of health is going on, and this is bound to have an effect, not only on this generation, but on future ones. Some of the training is direct—some is indirect. But it all has for its end the same purpose—the removal of *causes* of ill-health. Remedies for existing evils are necessary, but it is much more beneficial to look for the origin and to prevent the defect, than to attempt to cure it once it has developed. The concluding remarks in the Report of 1930 by Sir George Newman, the chief medical officer of the Board of Education, are noteworthy. He writes : " There is no more certain evidence of the keen interest and vitality in such a service than that which indicates both a spirit of research and a sense of the necessity for adaptation to new or recurring problems." " Happy is the man," said Vergil, " who knows the causes of things," and it is not extravagant to say that happy is the parent, the teacher, the school doctor, who not content with letting things drift along anyhow or anywhere, seeks for the causes of things, and on finding them, bends himself to control and direct them.

MAKING THE MOST OF A CHILD'S CAPACITIES

REFERENCE has already been made to the necessity for the development of what may be termed Biological Engineering. Much more definite knowledge of the nature of the material which is available for the building of human society and of the uses to which it can be put is necessary. A skilled architect uses his material in accordance with its peculiar properties. He realises that these properties vary, but that each type of material can be made to serve some one purpose most effectively. Biological engineering should do the same for human material.

At present, much avoidable suffering and unhappiness is caused by the haphazard manner by which the selection of individuals for various types of education and occupations is made. Any given post demands a certain level of general intelligence ; it also demands one or more specific ability, while, in addition, some peculiar temperament may be desirable. The possession of too high a level of general intelligence for a certain kind of work brings to the occupant of the post one type of unhappiness—restlessness and a general lack of satisfaction. A deficiency of intelligence leads to a feeling of continuous strain and a blind and rigid adherence to " rules." It is possible that temperament is of greater importance than intelligence in the consideration of vocational guidance.

A recognition of these facts has lead to the development of much research work, with the object of preventing bad misfits. The general problem can be stated very simply. Each individual reaches a certain level of general intelligence, and possesses also certain specific ability or abilities. In addition, he usually shows certain well-marked temperamental traits. Each job calls for a certain amount of general all-round intelligence, and also requires certain specific abilities in those engaged in it. The conditions under which it has to be done, and its nature, make it more congenial to those of one temperament than to others. The work will be done in the best manner, and the worker will be happiest when the factors demanded by the job are those possessed by the worker. This implies a double analysis—for the job must be analysed in order to determine the factors involved in it, and the individual must be analysed to determine his " make-up."

During recent years, the National Institute of Industrial Psychology has done invaluable pioneering work along these lines. It has (under Dr. C. S. Myers) trained a corps of research workers : it has sent trained investigators into factories of various types to engage in the difficult work of " job-analysts." It has placed its services at the disposal of local education authorities for the testing of children when necessary, and it maintains a service by which individuals can be examined and advised. It has investigated factory conditions, and has advised upon such problems as lighting, length of rest periods, temperature, etc., in relation to the efficiency and well-being of the employees. It is becoming increasingly recognised that it can render most valuable help to all engaged in industry and education. This is shown by the appeal made by one girl employed in a factory where psychological tests are used. She was inefficient and under notice of dismissal. But she asked to be " psychoed " first ! The abbreviation was the worker's own for " psychologised " —or being tested to see if she were more fitted for some other type of work.

DISCOVERING A CHILD'S NATURAL BENT : INTELLIGENCE TESTS

LARGELY owing to the work of Professor C. Spearman (University College of London) and his colleagues, there has been accepted more and more generally the view that the intelligence of any individual is due to two factors—(a) general intelligence, commonly denoted by the letter " g," and (b) one or more independent specific factors. To measure these factors, tests have been devised, and of such tests those for " g " have been developed farthest. There are two types of tests in general use—(a) individual tests, and (b) group tests.

The first developed from the investigation of Binet and Simon in Paris, and their work has been developed and revised by Terman (America) and Burt (England). Group tests were used by the American Army during the Great War, with the aim of forming mentally homogeneous units and so facilitating training. Since those days, the movement has spread, and now very many varieties of group tests are on the market. Those recommended by the National Institute of Industrial Psychology can be relied upon.

It must be remembered that the individual tests are the only ones which can be relied upon to give satisfactory individual results. They take longer to apply than group tests if carried out thoroughly, but give much more reliable results. Group tests are of value where a rapid mental survey of a whole group is required.

These tests measure general intelligence, i.e. the inborn level of intelligence of the individual. But any person possesses, as well, specific ability in certain directions—i.e. ability which is limited and not general, e.g. memory, verbal facility, manual dexterity, imagination, etc. Much research has been carried out upon such factors, and gradually they are being isolated, and satisfactory tests devised for their measurement. That they are of practical value has been demonstrated by the use to which they have been put in giving parents vocational guidance concerning their children.

A group of children attending London County Council Schools but approaching the school-leaving age were given a series of such tests, and upon the results were each given a card stating (a) the general level of ability of the child, (b) any specific abilities possessed, and (c) temperamental traits. There followed a definite recommendation as to employment and a statement that the card could be used as a " testimonial." The after-careers of the children so advised were followed, and the results compared with a similar group which had not been so advised. After a considerable interval, it was found that the majority of those in the "advised" group were still in their first post, and, what was even more pleasing, expressed themselves as being contented, whilst the opposite was true of the other group.

CLUES TO THE MYSTERY OF TEMPERAMENT

IT is a matter of common observation that two individuals of the same degree of intelligence may act in entirely different ways in the same situation, and that such variation in behaviour is due to what is loosely termed "temperament." The term is used to cover all tendencies which are concerned with feeling. They are marked by feeling rather than by intelligence, and by will rather than by skill.

That there are well-marked types of temperaments has been recognised since the days when ancient philosophers divided men into Sanguines, Cholerics, Phlegmatics, and Melancholics, each type being caused by an excess of some "humour." Subsequently, other systems of division have been suggested, of which perhaps the best known is that conceived by Jung,[1] whereby individuals are classed as either *extraverts* or *introverts*. The former find their main interest in things exterior to themselves ; the latter are more concerned with their own feelings and states of mind. This twofold division has been extended, and is at present the subject of much research. It is clear that there are several factors involved :

(a) *The strength of the passions*—the total amount of energy available.

(b) *The amount of energy graded or under control*—this is the basis of intelligence.

(c) *The strength of control*—whether strong or weak—this in some way is a factor of character.

Variation of these factors (and others) will lead to varying types of individuals with varying capacities.

TESTS FOR TEMPERAMENT

THE development of tests for temperament has not proceeded so far as that of tests for intelligence. Various tests have been devised, such as the *word association test*, the *psychogalvanic reaction test*, Dr. Downey's *will-temperament test*, and the *unfinished story test*.[2] For details of these, the reader should consult some standard work on psychology. The work of analysis of the factors involved must precede that of the invention of tests to measure the factors involved. But such tests as are now available enable the skilled investigator to form some idea of the temperament of the individual under test, and so to form some general idea of him as a personality. This is essential, for behaviour in response to the stimuli of the environment is never a purely intellectual reaction—it depends upon feelings as well.

[1] See page 128.   [2] See page 20.

HOW MISUNDERSTOOD CHILDREN BECOME SOCIETY'S "MISFITS"

THEORETICALLY, all children above a certain level of general intelligence (below that level are the idiots) are educable. In practice, it is found that attainments vary between very wide limits. Some reference to this has been made in the section upon the defective and retarded child. As is so often the case, there is need for definite information to replace the vague generalities with which so many observers have been satisfied in the past.

In this, as in so many other branches of child psychology, the pioneer was Professor Cyril Burt, who for many years held the post of Psychologist to the London County Council Education Committee. In his volume, *Mental and Scholastic Tests*, he gives tests for mental and scholastic ability, and stresses the importance of a correct technique in administering the tests, and the need for care in the interpretation of the results obtained. Any child who is not making such progress as its intelligence would warrant is a problem child—and the cause of the relatively low attainment has to be found and dealt with. Otherwise, there is a waste of mental ability— to the detriment of the individual and to the loss of society. Only under a perfect educational system in an ideal environment would capacity and attainment run parallel.

But even in an imperfect world much can be done to avoid the grosser mistakes and remedy the most glaring errors. It is to this end that the technique of mental testing is being developed. The steps are clear. There is needed (*a*) a sound psychological theory, (*b*) careful diagnosis and, (*c*) planned remedial measures. School clinics are now to be found in every town of any size. At present they are concerned with physical health only. Occasionally one finds a Psychological Clinic where parents may obtain advice regarding " difficult " children. Such clinics are usually voluntary—set up by pioneers. But their number will increase, and one can look forward confidently to the time when the Clinic will deal with all aspects of child development.

It is quite characteristic that the greatest use made of the tests described very summarily above have been in connection with Juvenile Delinquency. It is not until the young person " gets into trouble " that it is thought worth while to make use of modern developments as an aid to his individual development. The super-normal and normal children get less costly and less thorough treatment than the delinquent. For the average child in an elementary school, a year's education costs approximately £12 ; in a secondary school it is £30 ; and in a Home Office school £80–£100. The expenditure is a wise one, for often the potential criminal becomes a successful and satisfactory citizen. But similar treatment would turn many poorly developed children into even greater successes. As it is, it is not until the stigma of an appearance in Court is upon the child that the greater expenditure is thought worth while.

TREATMENT OF THE "YOUNG OFFENDER"

THE outlook of modern society as to what constitutes suitable treatment for juvenile offenders has undergone a significant change in recent years. The older view that retribution was the object of punishment has been replaced by one which sees in delinquency a symptom of faulty development. The duty of society is not to punish the young criminal for his lapses, or to protect itself against him, but to seek for the cause underlying his rebellion against the social code, and to remove it if it is at all possible to do so. The actual act of delinquency is a symptom, like the spots in measles. It is a sign of mal-adjustment ; it indicates a mental and a moral disease. And it is the *disease* which has to be treated ; when this is done the symptom will disappear. One example will make this plain.

A girl from a poor home who had won a scholarship to a secondary school was convicted of a number of thefts from her schoolfellows. Investigation showed that, while her scholarship provided for school fees, books, clothing, and meals, there were a number of other demands (subscriptions of various kinds, collections, presents) which were not met by the scholarship and which, owing to financial stress, the parents could not meet. The girl did not like to confess this—she had pride in her home and hated to " let her mother down," and children are often thoughtlessly cruel and snobbish. So she had " forgotten to bring it," and so on. Then, when pressed to produce it, she stole, and filled her life with fear of the consequences. The original motive here was a *good* one—pride in her home, a longing that it should not appear " inferior " to other homes. Properly educated, this motive could produce admirable results ; its misdirection led to crime.

This changed outlook of society upon the treatment of juvenile offenders is reflected in the Children and Young Persons Act of 1933. The spirit underlying the various pronouncements of the Home Office upon the administration of the Act is even more indicative of the intentions of its originators. The removal of Juvenile Courts so far as is possible from the immediate vicinity of the ordinary Courts, the ban upon uniformed police at these Courts, the stress placed upon guidance and assistance, and the provision made for the removal of children from bad environmental conditions are all signs of the new outlook.

Equally significant is the fact that the local education authority has much to do with the administration of the new Act. A special panel of magistrates, composed of suitable individuals, has to be formed for duty in the Juvenile Courts. The old " reformatory " schools are replaced by Home Office schools, carefully graded according to the ages of the children they admit. These schools, staffed by enthusiastic and far-seeing men and women, have a fine record of successes with the difficult cases sent to them.

FORCES THAT DRIVE CHILDREN TO CRIME

THE most thorough research work yet carried out upon this subject is that recorded by Dr. Cyril Burt in *The Young Delinquent*. In that volume, the reader will find individual cases discussed in detail, and statistics of a more general character. The keynote of the book is the statement that " it is not on the investigation of the offence, but on the investigation of the offender that the efforts of the psychologist must be primarily focused." This investigation of the offender must deal with every possible aspect, and be made from as many points of view as possible. Burt's scheme is as under :

(1) HISTORY.
  (A) Family History.
  (B) Personal History.

(2) PRESENT SITUATION.
  (A) Environment.
  (B) Personality.
      (i) Physical Characteristics.
      (ii) Mental Characteristics.
          (*a*) Intellectual.
          (*b*) Temperamental.

The mental characteristics are in each case divided into (1) *inborn factors*, and (2) *acquired factors*.

On the basis of his researches, Burt classifies juvenile offences as follows (numbers are per 100 delinquents of either sex) :

Type of Crime.					Boys.	Girls.
Sex	.	.	.	.	24·4	49·6
Anger	.	.	.	.	41·3	36·5
Acquisitiveness	.	.	.	.	91·9	46·0
Wandering	.	.	.	.	39·9	19·8
Grief	.	.	.	.	0·0	4·1
Secretiveness	.	.	.	.	4·9	13·6

(One individual may, of course, have perpetrated different offences.)

This table is of interest as showing the part played by the prominent instinctive tendencies in the causation of juvenile crime. In any civilised society the instinctive urges cannot be allowed free expression. There are two methods of dealing with them. They may be (*a*) repressed, (*b*) sublimated. The former course means that they are forced from the conscious mind, and denied any outlet. Sooner or later, the dammed-up stream breaks through the barrier, and some form of mental abnormality results. The second course means that alternative channels are formed, whereby the mental energy is utilised. It is this process of sublimation which is the basis of all successful education and of all re-education where the need for it becomes apparent.

ADULTS WITH CHILDREN'S MINDS

THE *average* mental ratio of the juvenile offender is about 89 (average mentality, 100). This indicates that at the age of 10 the child is equal mentally to a normal child of 9. As an adult, he will only have the mentality of a child of 13. These are average figures : the individual cases spread over the whole range of intelligence. But, even so, 82 per cent. are below average ability, and 28 per cent. are technically dull.

It is estimated that 9 out of every 10 juvenile delinquents are below the average in educational attainments, while 6 out of every 10 are so far below the normal standard as to be classifiable as " educationally backward." The educational ratio of the average juvenile delinquent is 81 (normal, 100), or, expressed differently, at the age of 10 he has the attainments of a normal child of 8.

The causes of this backwardness are many. In some cases, they are physical ; in others, it is due to some temperamental failing. But, very commonly, it is due to some moral source. In class, he is often referred to as the lazy child, the disobedient child, the unruly child. In other words, he has not developed any control over his impulses.

It is to be hoped that further analysis of the factors causing delinquency will result, not only in these receiving attention in the treatment of juvenile offenders, but will direct attention to them in the case of other children. Poor heredity, poor environment, faulty development, all play a part in developing delinquents. Equally, they play a part in preventing non-delinquent children from fulfilling their promise. It should not be necessary for a child to become a delinquent before a study is made of all the factors likely to aid to or arrest his development.

THE ENGLISH AND FRENCH SCHOOL CHILD— A CONTINENTAL COMPARISON

DURING the post-war years a considerable amount of educational stock-taking has been undertaken in most European countries. In those countries where definite political changes have taken place, violent changes in the educational process have been introduced in order to make it an instrument for establishing and furthering such changes. Amongst the larger countries, only England and France have escaped revolutionary changes, and a comparison of the systems of education of these countries will serve to emphasise certain aspects of both.

The term " public instruction " as used in France applies to national and secular provision as distinct from that given by private or religious organisations. Public instruction in France by no means covers the whole field of education. Religious teaching is considerable in all three grades— elementary, secondary, and higher. In fact, in some districts the number of pupils receiving education in schools controlled by religious organisations exceeds the number in the State schools.

Like England, France has its problem of dual control. For two centuries prior to the Revolution, the schooling of

tion based upon the elementary school course. If successful, they obtain a certificate entitled *Le certificat d'études primaires élémentaires*. In some larger towns what are in effect nursery departments (*jardins d'enfants*) have been established for children from 2–6 years of age.

Catholic schools are divided into three departments—primary, secondary, and superior. They receive no state subsidy and a number charge fees. They are maintained by church funds or private help. The Academy Inspector has the right to inspect them, but his supervision is confined to questions of morals and hygiene.

The curriculum of the French elementary school is very similar to that of the same grade of school in England. The main difference is that much less attention is paid to manual instruction than is usual in this country.

French pupils who have reached the age of 12 years and who have obtained the certificate referred to above, have two alternatives open to them if they wish to continue their education. Some elementary schools have attached to them supplementary courses, while in other areas there are separate higher elementary schools. The aim of both is to train boys and girls who may be expected to occupy positions of some responsibility—but not of the highest grade. The curriculum is a combination of general cultural subjects and instruction relating to the needs of local industries. General and specialised courses can be followed. A certificate is awarded upon the successful completion of the course. No pupil may remain in such a school after the age of 18 years is reached ; the usual leaving age is about 16. The larger schools prepare their pupils for the competitive entrance examination to the State Training Colleges for Teachers.

It is interesting to note that in some of its aspects the position in France is somewhat similar to that which existed in this country prior to the Hadow reorganisation. Here, many elementary schools had developed " Higher Tops "—the supplementary courses of the French schools. They embody an attempt to do higher work under conditions of inferior efficiency. There is no doubt that the better of such courses in France will develop into separate schools, and that the weaker ones will be abolished. The most interesting feature of the French higher elementary school is its close connection with local industries. More will be said on this point when considering technical education in France.

THE TEACHING PROFESSION AS A CLOSED CORPORATION

THE French pupil can pass direct from the higher elementary school to the Teachers' Training College. Admission to the latter is by competitive examination, and the State pays all expenses, including board and lodging. The prospective candidate has to promise to remain in the public service for ten years. There are two colleges for the training of teachers for service in the ordinary training colleges.

It should be noted that this system makes it possible for a child from the primary school to proceed by stages to the higher training colleges. But it makes the teaching profession a closed corporation, with all the defects of such a body. In England the tendency has been to recruit teachers from secondary schools and to develop training courses in universities rather than in isolated colleges. The French system prevents " wastage " during the course, in so far as there is no temptation to forsake the teaching profession for other professions on the way through college. But the segregation of teachers throughout their training cannot develop that breadth of vision which is so necessary if their work is to reach the highest standard.

There is nothing in the French system comparable to the English public school. The French system is highly centralised. French *lycées* are hardly ever privately endowed and are conducted on democratic lines. The teaching body is paid by the State, the buildings are maintained by the municipality.

There are two types of secondary institutions—*lycées* and colleges. In all, there are 130 of the former and 231 of the latter. The main difference between the two types of institution is that the colleges are maintained by the municipalities, while the *lycées* are entirely under State control. In addition to the State schools, there are independent secondary schools—preponderatingly Catholic.

As in England, the curriculum of the secondary school has recently been subjected to much criticism ; and the whole concept of secondary education is under review. The opposing forces of " liberality " and " utility " have since 1880 waged war upon one another and have not yet achieved a stable balance. One result of this has been the great development of technical education in France—which constitutes the most striking feature of the French system. To this development reference is made below. The examination requirements and the centralised control which exist in France make for uniformity amongst secondary schools, but cramp initiative. There is more freedom to experiment in this country.

HOW FRANCE'S DECREASING POPULATION IS FORCING EDUCATIONAL REFORM

THERE is a vital difference between the English and French views as to what is the function of a technical school. The English technical school does not set out to give its students manipulative dexterity in various occupations. Its function is to give students instruction in the scientific principles basic to their occupations. The complete training of the industrial worker is regarded in this country as a burden to be shared between the employer and the community. This has meant in practice that the employer has provided the workshop experience while the community, through its technical colleges, has given the complementary theoretical training.

In France, however, technical schools have been considered as apprenticeship schools—giving complete *training* in certain crafts. In Paris, between 1873 and 1899, there were established schools for the training of craftsmen in engineering, furniture manufacture, locksmith's work, printing and book production, etc. This example was followed in other parts of France—training in craftsmanship being the aim of the new institutions. In spite of this, it was estimated in 1901 that 90 per cent. of the young people engaged in industry received no serious vocational training. Before the Great War there were repeated discussions about this problem.

The natural desire to reconstruct which arose after the War, together with a consideration of population figures, which indicated a drop of at least 10 per cent. in thirty years, led to a revival of interest in the problem. It appeared that national prosperity could only be maintained by bringing the efficiency of every individual to its maximum point. In 1919 a Bill was passed which compels every employer (there are certain exemptions) to release young workers for not less than four hours and not more than eight hours a week during the ordinary working day, in order that they may make compulsory attendances at courses of instruction. The cost is provided in part by a special tax levied on all employers paying more than 10,000 francs per annum. The actual amount of tax is fixed by the Finance Law each year. At present it is ·2 per cent. of the total wage bill. In all, the tax produces about one hundred and sixty million francs and is expended upon Vocational Guidance work, the training of middle-grade workers, the training of research workers, and domestic instruction. There is no doubt that this tax increases the interest of French employers in problems of vocational training.

Trade schools admit children when they become exempt from attendance at primary schools (i.e. 13 years or 12+ if they have obtained the Primary School Certificate). There is no competition for entry to these schools. Of a higher grade than these schools are the National Schools, admitting students after a competitive examination (usually from the higher elementary schools) at 13–16 years. Of a still higher grade are the Schools of Arts and Crafts, with an age of admission of 16–19. Most entrants have attended the National Trade Schools or come direct from the higher elementary school.

A comparison of the English and French system of technical education brings out many points of interest. The French devote considerable attention to the question of vocational guidance, and in this respect England has much progress still to make. The French, again, give their young industrial workers instruction during the daytime, not in the evening after a long day's work. On the other hand, the English system is more flexible ; the English industrial system demands alertness, flexibility, and intelligence rather than specialised skill.

THE PROFESSIONS' LOSS AS INDUSTRY'S GAIN

AFTER the Third Republic, the whole system of university education in France had to be reconstructed. The university town bore about half the cost of the buildings ; but equipment and the salaries of the whole of the teaching and administrative staffs was a charge upon the State. This explains the State control of the university system. The head of the Academy is also head of the University, and is appointed by the Minister for Education. French universities retain the old four faculties of letters, science, law, and medicine, to which some centres have now added pharmacy. Except at Strasbourg, divinity—Catholic or Protestant—is studied in independent faculties. In France, university education suffers by competition from such institutions as the government schools for recruiting engineers, officers, military doctors, etc., and as the Central School of Arts and Manufactures.

The French system is more rigid than the English and is more definitely vocational. The method of training teachers does not make for progress, and universities are limited in their scope. But in the education of young industrial workers, England has much to learn from its neighbour. It is only by comparative study that the strong and the weak points of any system can be seen.

EDUCATION FOR CAREERS

FOR many years a fierce debate raged as to the relative merits of vocational and cultural education. Any form of education which had for its aim training for a specific occupation or profession was suspect to most educationists. If, as a by-product of the educative process, the person educated became more fitted for certain positions, all well and good, but the motive must at least be pure. There was fear lest the old epitaph, " Born a man : died a greengrocer," should be true of the products of the educational system.

Gradually it came to be recognised that much unnecessary heat had been engendered through a neglect to define the terms used. To the future lawyer or clergyman or schoolmaster, a study of Latin might be strictly vocational, whereas to the future civil servant it might equally well be cultural. And if the reason for teaching mathematics is that it develops the power of logical thought, a mathematical education might be considered vocational in relation to most walks in life. It is clear that it is not the content of a curriculum which makes it cultural or vocational, but the method of approach to the subjects.

The problem of education for careers is bound up with this question of vocational education. And again, wholesale condemnation of vocational education is as equally undesirable as whole-hearted advocacy of it. Much depends upon the age of entry into the profession. The later the age of entry.

the later will be the age at which it will be necessary to begin specific education for the career. In other words, the greater will be the possibility of giving a good *general* education before the specialised one is begun. This means that it will be more possible to adopt the very desirable course of making the individual a " man," before an attempt is made to make him into a " greengrocer." There is then more chance that he may be both a man and a greengrocer.

This is the whole argument in favour of deferring the age at which choice of a profession is made as long as circumstances permit. With some professions (clergy, barristers, upper civil service, consular, and colonial posts, graduate school teachers) it is possible to defer specific preparation until the conclusion of the normal university career. In the case of another large group of posts (non-graduate teachers, intermediate civil service, accountancy, etc.) specific training has to begin at about seventeen years of age. For a third group the age is still lower. It is clear that the degree of general education which can be given diminishes from the first-named group downward, and the " man " gets less and less chance as against the " greengrocer."

A WORLD WHERE WORK WOULD BE PLAY, AND PLAY LIFE

To admit this is not to decry the value of specific education for careers. In fact, if the time ever comes when vocational guidance is universal, it may well be that in his work the man will find himself, and the possibility of his greatest development—the " man " and the " greengrocer " will merge into one being. This is the ideal—expressed finely by the mad priest in Bernard Shaw's *John Bull's Other Island* : " I dream of a world where work is play and play is life ; three in one and one in three." With a proper system of vocational guidance, training for work would involve the development of all the latent capacities of the individual. The present-day danger is that the occupation is chosen not because of the suitability of the candidate for it, but because of tradition, or " respectability," or (commonly in these days of economic stress) because it furnishes a *safe* life. One can hardly blame the young adolescent who, seeing the extent of the unemployment problem, decides that the lower and intermediate branches of the Civil Service, or the teaching profession offer a position of safety, and decides that " safety first " shall be the guiding slogan in his choice of a career. And

of which appointments are made. The main classes of appointments are :

- (a) *Routine Posts:* Messengers, Telephonists, Telegraph-
  ists, Typists. Age on entry varies from 14–18 years.
- (b) *Clerical Class :* age on entry, 16–17 years.
- (c) *Executive class :* age on entry, 18–19 years.
- (d) *Administrative Class :* age on entry, 22–24 years.

In addition to these, there are the Customs and Excise
Service (19–21), the Indian Civil Service (21–24), Colonial
Service (19–22 or more), technical and special appointments
(open to candidates fully qualified in a profession—engineers,
doctors, etc.). As an example of how specialised and " vocational " a so-called " general " education can become, it may
be mentioned that special preparation for the Indian Civil
Service frequently commences at the age of 9 years, under
highly-skilled coaches.

LEARNING HOW TO TEACH

THE teaching profession claims a large proportion of
secondary school pupils each year. Largely owing to the
separate development of secondary and elementary education
in this country, there are two grades of teachers. There are
those who have had four years' training subsequent to leaving
the secondary school (three years' study for a degree, plus one
year professional training), and there are two-year trained
teachers who hold the Board of Education Certificate. Some
strange anomalies exist owing to a diversity in the secondary
and elementary school regulations. The four-year trained
teacher, if he has a degree and a teaching diploma, ranks as a
graduate in a secondary school and a trained teacher in an
elementary school. If he has a degree, but not a teaching
diploma, he still ranks as a graduate teacher in the secondary
school, but only as an uncertificated teacher in an elementary
school. The two-year trained teacher ranks as a certificated
teacher in elementary schools, but as a non-graduate in secondary schools. In other words, a graduate (without a diploma)
is in a better position than a certificated teacher in a secondary
school, but in an inferior position in an elementary school.
Since the salary payable depends upon status, it is clear that
the *four*-year course, leading to a degree plus teaching diploma,
is the best investment, since it leads to the most highly paid
posts in both secondary and elementary schools.

Four-year courses are organised in most universities and

university colleges. The two year courses are mainly given in special teachers' training colleges. The Board of Education gives grants to most recognised students and many local education authorities assist students from their areas where such additional help is necessary. Apart from the Board of Education grant, the cost varies from £50–£75 per annum, depending upon the university or college.

Provision is made for the training of teachers for various specialised branches of the teaching profession. Amongst these are nursery and kindergarten teachers, teachers of domestic subjects, physical training teachers, teachers of art and music, and teachers in schools for blind, deaf, dumb, and defective children.

SOLDIER, SAILOR, AND R.A.F. MAN

THE term "Services" is used to denote the Army, the Navy, and the Royal Air Force. Candidates for commissions in the Army and Royal Air Force must have had a good general education (usually at a public school) up to the age of 18–19 years. Assuming the entrance examination is passed, they then proceed to the Royal Military Academy (Artillery and Engineers), the Royal Military College (Infantry), or the Royal Air Force College. The training course lasts eighteen months, and the full cost is approximately £300 at the two first-mentioned institutions. There are, however, certain concessions, and some scholarships are awarded. At the Royal Air Force College the course lasts two years and the cost is £75 per annum, plus approximately another £100 for books, uniform, etc.

Entrance to the Royal Navy (commissioned officer) takes place as a cadet at 12–13 years, after a period in some preparatory school. (Some candidates are admitted up to 17½ years by special entry.) There follows a period of four years' training (8 months afloat) at the Royal Naval College, Dartmouth, the fees being approximately £175 per annum. This is followed by a qualifying period of 2⅓rd years as a midshipman. During this time pay is at the rate of £9 per annum, and parents are required to make a midshipman an allowance of £50 per annum.

It should be noted that in all the Forces there are openings for boys for training as artificers of various types, or in the clerical and accountancy branches, and that these furnish good opportunities and excellent training. Entry is usually at about

15–16 years of age, and keen competition has resulted in a raising of the standard. Many of those who now compete for these posts are secondary schoolboys, and with the increased facilities for promotion to the commissioned ranks the openings thus provided have much to recommend them.

THE WAY INTO COMMERCE AND INDUSTRY

Banking, Accountancy, Sales Management, Insurance, and secretarial occupations all demand a specialised education. The general procedure is for a secondary education up to about 16 or 17, to be followed by the gaining of some professional qualification during what are essentially years of apprenticeship. Most professional bodies demand some evidence of the preliminary general education (School Certificate or Matriculation Exemption). When this can be obtained prior to commencing work, it is clearly advantageous. Then there follows for bankers the examinations of the Institute of Bankers ; for insurance employees, those of the Chartered Insurance Institute or the Corporation of Insurance Brokers ; for secretarial work, those of the Chartered Institute of Secretaries or the Incorporated Secretaries' Association ; for accountants, those of the Institute of Chartered Accountants, or the Society of Incorporated Accountants and Auditors, the Institute of Cost and Works' Accountants, etc. and for salesmen, those of the Incorporated Sales Managers' Association. The possession of a professional qualification is the open door to promotion in these days.

There are other openings to which only a brief reference can be made. Amongst these are the legal profession (solicitors and barristers), engineering (civil, electrical, or mechanical), scientific workers (works' chemists, etc.), clergy (Established and Free Churches), and the municipal services. The latter absorbs an increasing number of well-qualified candidates, but the posts are so varied and the requirements so diverse that the best procedure is to enquire at some local municipal offices for information regarding local conditions and requirements. In every case, however, one thing is clear. Employers are demanding a rising standard of general education to precede specialised education for the career itself. And after that, the professional standard is also rising. More than ever is it apparent that a sound general and professional education is the only way to ensure a successful career. Influence counts less ; ability is ranked higher.

Modern life demands high standards. Sound vocational guidance and thorough training can give industry and the professions the personnel it needs.

LOOKING FORWARD

ONE section of this work has dealt with the views of pioneers and reformers—men and women with essentially the "forward" outlook. This section has necessarily been concerned mainly with the existing provision for education. From one point of view, existing educational theory and practice is a legacy of the past—it represents tradition—a good tradition it may be, but, nevertheless, maintaining its position as often by the force of custom as by the demands of reason. But it may also be viewed as a stage reached, as a point of departure upon a new venture.

It is often held that the school should be a microcosm—a miniature world in which is reflected the problems of the larger world without, and in which, as it were in play, the child looks for the solutions to questions which later on will confront him in reality. This analogy was not meant to be pressed too far. The school educates for a future state of Society, not the existing one. The educationist must certainly be in sympathy with, and be able to interpret, the movements which have together made our civilisation. But he must also have a vision of the future, for his pupils will be the citizens of twenty years ahead. More than ever is it important to remember this in post-War days. "Mankind," said General Smuts, "has struck its tents and is once more on the march." And to no one is the direction of its march and its objective of greater importance than to those concerned in the education of the future citizens. There is a definite need for a philosophy upon which education can be based. Teachers and parents alike are at fault here. There is much that is fundamentally contradictory in their work, and the school is far too often a microcosm of the world *as it is*—a prey to conflicting doubts and fears. The teacher may fail in his aim, but aim he must have—even before technique. If he fails, he can at least say with Morris's apprentice :

> Oh ! Master, pardon me, if yet in vain,
> Thou art my Master ; and I fail to bring
> Before men's eyes the vision of the thing
> My soul is filled with.

NEED FOR CO-OPERATION BETWEEN PARENT AND TEACHER

THERE is need for still closer contact between teachers and parents. Some teachers are what the late Sir John Adams used to call " Grace of God " teachers—those who require no philosophy or training. And many parents still believe that they know how to bring up children " by instinct." Between the two, there is a great gulf fixed. But much improvement has been made since the days (comparatively recently) when school gates were locked, after the children had assembled, for two reasons—to keep the children in and the parents out. Nowadays, most children go willingly and gladly to school, and parents co-operate with teachers. Open days, school concerts, and similar functions bring the two sets of people most concerned in education into close contact. But much more can be done. The development of some kind of Parent-Teacher-Old-Scholar Association, attached to each school, appears to be one desirable line of development.

One point will illustrate the difficulty under which many children suffer. For quite a large proportion of children have to cope with two languages, differing both in vocabulary and pronunciation—one used in school and one in the home. This is well illustrated by the note addressed to an education office by a parent: " Dear Sir,—The teacher at —— School called my child a fool in front of the class the other day. I object to this, as he never hears such language at home. And if she does it again, I will go to the School and knock her —— head off." In that area " fool " is an epithet, whilst the Pygmalion adjective is current coin. And yet, if there is one thing which is of value in life, it is good speech. No other knowledge has its value in making it possible for its possessor to pass from grade to grade without embarrassment. The present position is complicated by the growing importance of two modern adjuncts to formal education—the cinema and the wireless— Up to the present, the cinema has made for deterioration in speech, whilst broadcasting has tended to improve it.

AN UP-TO-DATE VISITOR THAT HAS COME TO STAY : THE CLASS-ROOM CINEMA

IT is certain that the cinema will come to play an increasing part in the educative process. At one time there were not wanting those who saw in it merely a means by which costs could be reduced. They had a fond vision of large masses of children being " educated " by watching pictures, and only a minimum of teachers being required. Fortunately, the fallacy of such a viewpoint has been seen. Recent years have seen a great improvement in apparatus devised for school use, whilst, with its increasing use, has come a demand for a better type of film. This demand is being met, and teachers and administrators alike are becoming increasingly alive to the potentialities of the cinema. The visual appeal is added to the auditory appeal. The apparatus which permits of the repetition of parts of the film which it is desired to emphasise, and of certain " shots " being used as " stills," and which is usable with sound films is necessary. It is certain that few schools will be erected in the future without being fully equipped in this respect. Not fewer teachers are required, but teachers with a new technique—teachers who are prepared to go that " little further " that makes the difference between stagnation and progress.

In this matter, the schools have a duty to perform, which they cannot shirk. It is no use educationists deploring the evil influences of much that is seen in the usual cinema. And it is equally futile to gibe at it as an example of a display of mass emotion. The cinema has come to stay. It has to be made into a force for culture and pleasure, an approach to life, and not a means of flight from life. It has to be made to serve a purpose, not to be an end in itself. It is no use to gibe at machines and mechanical appliances, and to make them the butt of sarcasm. If they have not brought culture to evil days, it is because individuals have not exercised efficient control.

> The fault, Dear Brutus, is not in our stars,
> But in ourselves, that we are underlings.

If the cinema is to be made that force for culture of which it is potentially capable, it is in the schools that the first steps must be taken. Then, in a generation maybe, a change in public taste can be effected.

EDUCATION BY THE BROADCAST LESSON

THE use of wireless in education is another development which it is safe to predict will become of increasing importance. Already, through its special school talks and the explanatory pamphlets which are issued, the B.B.C. has rendered valuable service to the schools. There are dangers, of course. Perhaps the most serious is that there will be developed listeners instead of thinkers. The term " listening-in " describes the process, and indicates the possible source of weakness. A skilled and well-read teacher is required in order that younger people in particular should derive the maximum benefit from wireless lessons.

Other dangerous elements suggest themselves. There is the danger lest " I heard it over the wireless " should become as much a reason for belief as " I saw it in the newspaper." There is the danger of passivity on the part of the pupils, and there is also the danger of a deadening uniformity pervading instruction. Again, question and answer, that most fruitful of educational methods, is necessarily absent. But, to admit all this is only to direct attention to the need for the skilled teacher to " fill in the gap." It is again a certainty that the use of the wireless will come to play an ever-increasing part in the educative process.

SCHOOL JOURNEYS AND CAMPS

ANOTHER development which will affect the future of education concerns those activities which are collectively known as " School Journeys." Each year an ever-increasing number of children proceed for a week or a fortnight or more to some fresh area and there study local history, biology, geography, etc. An increasing number of visits to factories and works are planned, with the result that much education takes place outside the actual walls of the schoolroom. Camps of all types are organised—holiday camps and camps held during school hours. Some are temporary tent camps ; others permanent or semi-permanent. In some cases, Youth Hostels are used, and there would appear to be the possibility of development in this direction. Such experiments show already that social education can be given through these channels—an education which is valuable and of increasing importance. Again, the opportunity to see other areas and other people widens the imagination of the children, and makes them less parochial.

THE FORWARD PATH

IT is clear that these developments—the cinema, the wireless, school journeys—are only typical of the new spirit which permeates education, and of the new outlook which that spirit brings with it. The school is no longer marked by the stone walls of the building, or the iron fences which surround the playground. No longer is the curriculum an academic one, and no longer is the intellect alone considered. Physical, mental, and spiritual—the educative process endeavours to develop each. It gives an intellectual education through the more academic subjects ; it develops the body through organised games and physical training ; by the drama, the cinema, and music, it furnishes the emotions with proper outlets, and it gives a social education in a variety of ways. It no longer talks of average pupils, and imagines that all children are alike. It takes account of individuality, and endeavours to develop it.

This is education at its best. Not yet has it been achieved, but it is the forward path that is being followed. If much still remains to be done, much has been achieved already. It is in the schools of to-day that the spirit to face the problems of to-morrow must be developed. It may not be desirable to go as far as the Chinese of old and execute the teacher of the murderer with the murderer, but the responsibility of the educator cannot be avoided. For him, the final prayer must always be :

> God in His mercy be good to me,
> For I made man.

And if that makes him feel that the task is too great—then let him seek some other less exacting occupation.

If the task is great, the reward is equal to it. Only through the sound education of the children and adolescents can real progress be made and civilisation be developed. Only when the educative process is a living one can its practitioner say with Burke :

> Methinks I see, as it were above the hilltops of time, the dawn of a better and a fairer day for the country and the people that I love so well.

LATEST DEVELOPMENTS

ON 6th January 1936, the Board of Education issued Circular 1444—" Administrative Programme of Educational Development." It points out that two proposals— (1) that relating to raising the School Leaving Age, and (2) that empowering local education authorities to give grants to voluntary schools—require legislation, and will be so dealt

10

with. The first proposal is that the school leaving age shall be raised to 15 years, but that exemptions shall be permitted between the ages of 14 and 15 where the child obtains beneficial employment or, in the case of girls, is urgently required at home for domestic duties. The Association of Education Committees and the National Union of Teachers have both expressed in no uncertain terms their objections to the granting of exemptions and their view that they will vitiate the value of the proposal to raise the age. They advocate a raising of the age for all children and the granting of adequate maintenance allowances in order to compensate for the loss of earnings. It appears likely that much controversy will centre round this issue. A system of exemptions means that in some areas, where juvenile labour is in demand, very few children will remain at school.

The second proposal is that local authorities shall be empowered to make grants to voluntary schools where such schools are necessary in order to reorganise the system in any area along the lines of the Hadow Report. This question, has, in the past, proved to be one which has given rise to much controversy. It is to be hoped that in the inevitable discussions which will follow this proposal there will be exhibited only a spirit of co-operation in the service of the young life of the country. The Circular goes on to point out that there are certain other proposals which can be implemented by administrative action. The points to which the attention of education authorities is directed may be summarised as follows. The provision of facilities for children under 5 should be surveyed and should be extended wherever necessary. Defective school buildings should be remedied, and over-large classes reduced in size. Where necessary, provision should be made for the transport of children.

In secondary schools the number of " special places " should be increased and the maximum limit on such places is to be removed. The number of state scholarships is increased from 300 to 360. More and better provision is to be made for technical education, and adult education is to be developed. The school medical service is to be overhauled and brought up to date, special attention being directed to dental, aural, and orthopædic work. The need for residential schools for debilitated children and those suffering, or convalescent, from acute rheumatism is emphasised, while the needs of defective children are to receive attention.

Special reference is made to the desirability of adequate facilities for physical education. This has been the subject of a further Circular (1445, issued on 13th January 1936). In this the importance of a well-planned scheme, which shall include provision for young people who have left school, is pointed out.

Circular 1444 increases the grant to local authorities for buildings and sites from 20 per cent. to 50 per cent., as from 1st January 1936. As from 1st April 1937, the grant on the cost of conveying children is to be raised from 20 per cent. to 40 per cent.

These Circulars should stimulate an advance on the whole educational front. It is to be regretted that the leaving age is not to be at least 15 for all children, but with careful thought and sound planning it should be possible to build a sound educational structure which will serve as a base from which further advances can be made subsequently.

KEEPING ABREAST OF EDUCATIONAL THEORY: SOME IMPORTANT BOOKS

FOR the reader who desires to study more closely any of the various phases of education, a number of books are available. *The Year Book of Education* (current edition), which has been edited by Lord Percy and published by Messrs. Evans Bros., provides a book of reference which is indispensable to the serious student. For information as to the administrative history of English education there is no more comprehensive work than *Local Administration in English Elementary Education*, by G. P. McHugh, published by Councils and Education Press. In the field of educational theory, Adams's *Evolution of Educational Theory*, published by Macmillans, remains a classic. For the general history of education, Monroe's *History of Education* cannot be surpassed.

These volumes will provide the general background. In addition, a number of other volumes deal ably with more restricted fields. Amongst volumes of the latter type may be mentioned such works as *History of Elementary Education*, by C. Birchenough (published by University Tutorial Press), *Educational Charters*, by A. F. Leach (Cambridge University

Press), *The Educational System of England and Wales*, by H. Ward (Cambridge University Press), and *Reports on Elementary Schools*, by Matthew Arnold (H.M. Stationery Office), which are all of importance. For a sound discussion of modern principles, Sir Percy Nunn's *Education : Its Data and First Principles* cannot be surpassed, while a vivid picture of experimental education can be got from *Towards a New Education*, a summary of the papers read at a Conference and published by the New Education Fellowship. The three Reports of the " Hadow Committee " contain useful historical material and also indicate future developments. It must always be remembered that a dynamic society demands a dynamic educational system, and for this reason the student must be alive to the necessity for reading critically current literature upon that subject.

THE STUDY OF MAN IN SOCIETY : POLITICAL SCIENCE

by ROSS NICHOLS, M.A.(Cantab.)

POLITICAL SCIENCE has been called abstract. The adjective is quite unjustified by its scope, which is the study of man in society, man in political relationship with his fellows, as a " political animal." To the extent to which the State is related to them—and to few is it unrelated—it deals with all human activities, questioning their social ethics and purpose for the community.

Unluckily, the study has in the past been too much confined to academic circles. For the man in the street, or even the average reader, it has not become a living interest, in the way in which he has latterly become interested in popular physics and biology of the kind dispensed by Sir James Jeans and J. B. S. Haldane. He has never learnt that an analysis of current problems of government, working from the experience of the past, might prove profitable ; political science has remained for him a name connected with a don's arm-chair.

Yet, in spite of some unhappy examples to the contrary, the study of political science does enable the student to analyse clearly current political developments and even to predict, within certain limits. Government is, after all, the most vital of human relationships. Without security and widely spread social relationships, man's life must be a savage thing —" nasty, brutish, and short." Hence knowledge of its assumptions and working is necessary to everyone ; and this knowledge is made systematic in political science.

Avoiding abstract definitions for the moment, let us ask ourselves what we normally mean in modern times by a nation. A nation, we might say off-hand, is a large community dwelling within recognised geographical limits, speaking the same language and sharing a common cultural and religious history. Taken singly, not one of these criteria will stand examination. True, we can find excellent working examples of each, but also glaring exceptions. A large community ; yes, but how large ? Aristotle in his day remarked that for a City State fifty citizens was perhaps too few, five thousand far too many. These numbers, of course, excluded women, slaves, mechanics, traders, and husbandmen. Where do we draw the line ? Do we consider that to begin where Aristotle left off, and start with Andorra, with its five thousand inhabitants, is beneath us ? Yet it is the oldest republic in Europe, its independence dating back to the Carlovingian times. Is Russia too large to consider as a single State ? And are we to consider the British Empire as one State, or a linked series ?

Leaving the question of size and considering the rest of our definition, we note Belgium as an obvious exception to unity of race, since Flemings and Walloons exist side by side in uneasy coalition. The U.S.A. and Russia are large-scale, Switzerland, with its four languages, is a small-scale, exception to unity of language as national bond. Again, though there is the notable positive example of France in the binding together of national sentiment by culture, we could hardly say of Jugoslavia or even the U.S.A. that the nation was so linked. If a nation must have geographical frontiers, are we to deny nationality to the Jewish people, which can scarcely be considered even now to have a country of its own, and which for centuries has existed merely as a cultural, religious, and ethnic entity amongst the nations of the world ? The Jews are an excellent example, again, of religion as a bond of nationality ; yet who will deny nationhood to Germany, torn for decades by religious strife in the Thirty Years' War, and still profoundly disunited between Roman Catholicism and the various Protestant sects ?

Yet, thoroughly pervious as our rough definition may prove in detail, we shall nevertheless expect a State to exhibit several of the bonds of unity we have mentioned. However, it is not until we turn to consider its purpose that there is to be found any adequate definition of the State. " The modern State," says Professor Laski, " is a territorial society divided into government and subjects, claiming, within its allotted physical area, a supremacy over all other institutions." The will of the State is merely one aspect of the interests of society, the will of the government as accepted by the body of citizens ; the State is merely an organisation to enable men to realise social good on the largest scale possible—" the final legal depository of the social will."

SWORD AND SCALES : THE FUNCTIONS OF THE STATE

WHY have the generality of men consented to owe obedience to the small group which in any State constitutes government ? Many volumes have been written on these "grounds of political obligation." We can merely mention a few theories. The oldest is the theory of the consent of the governed, which appears to have been held by Socrates, and which is the basis of the " social contract " of Rousseau. It is difficult, however, to hold that most governments, except, when elective, immediately after election, hold power by anything more than the passive sufferance of the people ; which is hardly what we mean by the word " consent." Fear was suggested by Hobbes as the keystone of social conduct, and habit by Maine. The first theory is merely inadequate ; the second fails to account for the achievement of a revolution which overturns habit. Utility is the contribution of the Benthamites ; but if we ask of some forms of State : " To whom are they useful ? " the only possible answer is, to the rulers, not the ruled. Russia before 1917 is a case in point.

There is, in fact, no rational explanation of political obedience. Political institutions have arisen from man's primitive needs, his need for sustenance, clothes, and shelter, his desires for mating and security. " The State comes into existence to maintain life," says Aristotle, " and continues to develop the good life." To trace its growth, therefore, is more profitable than to treat it as a rational structure, though we note the attempts made to rationalise it from time to time.

In origin, the European national State arose from the need for common defence and the need for the adjudication of disputes between members of the community. When the first petty baron ceased from a career of nothing but pillage and, settled in the local castle, bargained with the inhabitants of the region for a regular share of crops and services in return for defending them against any other exploiter and settling their quarrels, he was on a small scale creating a State. Actually, he was creating the manorial system ; and it was from an aggregation of such units that the medieval nation was formed. The bargain that he struck was perhaps as near an approach to the legendary *contrat social* between rulers and ruled as has occurred within historical time, outside the imagination of Rousseau.

With the coming of more modern times, the king ceased to be a chief amongst equals and became the embodiment of the State, the organ of its government, sole source of authority —the " Leviathan " of Hobbes. Justice and defence did not long remain the only functions of monarchies such as those of

Henry VIII. in England, Francis I. in France, or Ferdinand and Isabella in Spain. Sooner or later all came into conflict with the rival jurisdiction and temporal pretensions of the Catholic Church, and in the contest they were driven to define, if only by their actions, the absolutist claim for their sovereignty. No longer was the king the pope's delegate in governing men ; he claimed a separate right, derived separately from God. It was not wholly disconnected from the good of his people, but was hardly based upon it. It was only an accident that the conflict flared up first and most dramatically in England over a divorce question wherein Henry VIII. was morally in the wrong. A similar conflict between the spheres of civil and ecclesiastical dominion has since been a recurrent theme in the story of every country of Europe.

THE STATE AS GUARDIAN OF OUR LIBERTIES

THE history of the National State, then, has been one of increasing additions to its first functions. Into the sovereignty wrested from religion have been drawn most of the activities of civilised man, in one or another aspect. Freedom of association under the State's ægis has not been won without struggle. Against the anti-combination, anti-conspiracy, and other laws the principle was developed that whatever people are legally free to do as separate persons may be a valid object for an association. In application, the dictum leads to difficulties ; how, for instance, does a combination of people to boycott a single person stand ? Here the action of combination produces an effect quite different from that produced by individual action. Perhaps, however, we may leave it that the onus of proof now lies with those wishing to restrict combination.

Nowadays economic grouping is perhaps what we think of primarily when we consider associations within the State. As the old merchant gild system tended to split up into gilds of craftsmen in separate craft gilds, so in the revival of the collective system in industry, which we call trade unionism, the unions are always growing and branching off into more specialised groups. Development is complicated now by the fact that, owing to the dependence of modern industry on accumulated wealth of the past and on specialised direction, we have industry not merely divided perpendicularly, so to speak, by occupations, but also horizontally between employers and employed. The social warfare waged between capital and labour by means of lockouts and strikes can scarcely fail to interest the State as trustee of the general welfare. Not merely when a majority of citizens are affected by the services involved, as in the General Strike of 1926, but when any considerable section of citizens are involved, the State now tends to intervene sooner or later in the struggle.

Moreover, class-warfare tends to spread beyond any single State. The forces of capital are internationally linked ; labour receives sympathetic contributions from fellow-workers abroad. Never has this been seen more clearly than in the recent history of Austria, where the government in power appears to be closely allied to international finance, while the Vienna socialists receive help from their brethren elsewhere. The Labour Office at Geneva, moreover, begins to legislate over the heads of, though acting through, national governments.

TWO GREAT INSTITUTIONS AT VARIANCE: THE CONFLICTING CLAIMS OF CHURCH AND STATE

RELIGION is the form of association most profitably paralleled with trade unionism. In both a national church and a fully-grown trade-union system we have associations aiming to include all citizens ; both are supra-national, for the Church derives from cosmopolitan origins, and the unions aim at internationalism ; they are centralised in government —bishops on the one hand, trade-union secretaries on the other ; moreover, both claim from the State liberty of self-government, and members are not held responsible for corporate acts. Trade-union property is in effect sacrosanct, and church property mostly of august antiquity. Both organisations claim to stand for interests of widest application to human life ; the one for economic conditions of wage-earners generally, the other for the soul's eternal welfare.

It may be held that religion represents values more important than the State does. Certainly, from the first, Christianity held this to be so. Nevertheless, religion in its primitive stages usually represents the nation in its religious aspect. In Judaism, for example, race and religion are hardly distinguishable. In more modern times, the at-oneness of Church and State, the virtual control of one by the other, is typical of a lack of the deeper sense of religious values ; State control of the Church is the doctrine of politicians rather than of the devout. The prevalent view, however, seems to be that when acting in its own sphere the Church owes allegiance to a higher power than the State.   In its early stages the Christian Church's plea was for tolerance ; in the post-Constantine era not only did it achieve freedom, but it was a separate and powerful organisation parallel with the State.   When the State crumbled with the Empire, the Church remained without rival as an organisation until the setting-up first of the Holy Roman Emperors, then of national Kings.

The doctrine that a monarch should rule justly was nothing new ; but it was now expressed so as to limit the king's freedom.   Ideas of election and of a contract to rule well were introduced ; while in any case both the king and his officials were, as men, sons of the Church.   With the development of extreme papal claims, it came to be a question whether the Church was in the State, or the State a province of the Church.   The Church claimed not merely independence, but the right to determine the limits of its own jurisdiction ; it claimed not merely the right to discipline its members, but the assistance of the State in carrying out its objects of policy. On the actions of monarchs it claimed the right of pronouncing judgment on the elastic grounds of faith or morals.

THE DIFFICULT PROBLEM OF PASSIVE RESISTANCE

BY the time of the Council of Trent (1545) the Catholic Church is already legislating in a narrower sphere than these claims would imply, although nominally it is still regulating a Universal Church.   The revolted national Churches were mostly tied legally to the State, which thereby denied the supreme claim of the religious life.   Individualism had been born, though so far only in a national form ; the national Churches went their way, though decades were to elapse before anything resembling freedom of religious opinion for everybody was considered.

This individualism as fully developed is the side of religion perhaps most likely to come into conflict with the State. Rights to self-discipline and religious organisation, even when used for anti-democratic propaganda, can hardly be denied— though we have seen this happen in Germany recently, and the political influence of the Jesuits in various European States has led to their exclusion, for instance, from Switzerland.   But individualism of the conscientious Tolstoyan type, if it takes the form of passive resistance to governmental orders, presents government with the alternatives of physical violence to the unresisting—a thing the stomach even of professional soldiers cannot stand except in very limited quantity —or of indefinite imprisonment on negative charges. Some of the possibilities have been demonstrated on these lines in the non-co-operative campaigns, the technique of which was developed in Ireland, then practised on a large scale in India, where, at first at any rate, passive resistance proved a weapon of enormous moral force.

On the separate grounds of public morality and order it is also usually held that the State has the right to intervene in religious matters. Suppose a religion which ran frankly counter to the established social usages of the State—which proclaimed the necessity of bigamy in a monogamous country, or the wickedness of submitting to medical inspection in illness in a land where this was compulsory. Suppose, again, a revivalist movement of such fervour that whole squares and streets are blocked with adherents who proceed to find and burn all works of literature, other than the Bible, published since 1800. It would be difficult to maintain that in the face of such happenings the State should not override the rights of conscience in the interest of the majority of citizens.

Harping once more on our parallel between certain aspects of the Church and trade unions, it must be said that, once the full freedom of action which each would claim were granted, the State would in effect cease to be a State in the supreme sense and would come to resemble a federal system of divided powers. At times this has virtually occurred : for example, in Catholic Italy, when Papacy and Fascist State fought for control over education. Spain has recently been in the position of being rent in two, if not three, in a struggle wherein organised labour and Catholic reaction are the chief protagonists. On general grounds of personal freedom, membership of a supreme State is to be preferred to the distraction of double or treble conflicting allegiances of this kind. A group is more oppressive than a State.

Even within an organisation such as the co-operative store it is doubtful whether federalism works. Property distribution between the consumers and producers is a standing difficulty ; consumers' interests are likely to be emphatic, united and simple, while those of producers are manifold. One could, however, imagine a State wherein these varied interests were constitutionally represented, as was the inten-

tion in the unrealised proviso for an economic third chamber
in the constitution of the German Republic drawn up at
Weimar in 1919.

As things are, it is consumers' interests which the State
appropriately watches over ; clearly it has no standing other
than as mediator in struggles between Capital and Labour
unless a large section of the public is affected.   Unless and
until the State itself becomes employer, assuming to itself
" the means of production, distribution, and exchange," to
use the Socialist formula, this is bound to remain the position.

To a limited extent the State has indeed become employer,
though not, in Western Europe at any rate, of productive, but
of administrative labour.   At once has arisen a fresh set of
difficulties.   Who is to arbitrate between the supreme depository of the social will and comparatively small groups of its
employees ?   In the last resort, the State's control over them
is seen to be entirely arbitrary.   There was no pretence of
consultation of employees when the British " National "
Government, on *a priori* grounds and without demonstrated
proof of its statements, alleged the necessity of " wage cuts "
owing to financial emergency.   There was, in fact, little
attempt at resistance, since the employees, along with the
majority of the nation, believed in the reality of the emergency.

WHEN THE JUDGES PROTESTED AGAINST WAGE-CUTS

BUT the treatment of the one outstanding attempt at resistance was instructive.   His Majesty's judges have a wholly
different constitutional position from that of any other civil
servants.   In fact, their position dates from a time when the
conception of civil servant, as we know it, had hardly emerged.
By the Act of Settlement, judges hold office directly from the
Crown, on nomination of the Lord Chancellor, during good
behaviour ; they are removable only by resolution of both
Houses of Parliament.   Their salaries similarly have been
fixed early in our constitutional history on a scale making it
relatively certain that corruption will be unlikely to tempt
them.[1]   Yet these salaries were arbitrarily " cut," although
no effective governmental reply was forthcoming to the
dignified protest and statement of the special position of the
judiciary issued under the aegis of Lord Chief Justice Hewart.

Associations other than economic and religious ones can be

---

[1] The present salary of a judge is £5000 per annum, fixed by the
Judicature Act of 1873.

dealt with more briefly. There are scientific, educational, cultural, sporting, and social bodies, national and international. They call for little comment so far as political science is concerned. None of them attempts to set up any kind of *imperium in imperio* ; their influence is confined to special interests which they at times put forward for consideration by the State. They may even secure the election of a stray M.P. of their persuasion ; the anti-vaccinationist section in the House may waste much of its time by the introduction of futile measures which have no chance of success. In more hopeful causes, bills are relatively frequently passed owing to the persistence of some sectional interest embodied in an association. The " Tote " Bill was passed owing to pressure emanating from the Jockey Club ; restrictions on Sunday cinemas are largely due to the influence of brewing interests.

PLEASURE AND PAIN AS CRITERIA OF GOOD AND EVIL

AFTER this brief survey of the relationship of the State to some of the associations it contains, it will be well to cast our eyes back a little and ask what it was that hindered for so long the general recognition of the State's responsibility in all kinds of social matters, such as factory and wage regulation, in which we take for granted its action now. We shall find our attention arrested by exponents of a philosophy of very great interest and significance—Utilitarianism.

The Utilitarians may be regarded as the later and modified representatives of the theory of ruthless free trade and competition which conquered English policy after the publication of Adam Smith's *Nature and Causes of the Wealth of Nations*, 1776. Its positive merits lay in encouraging the abolition of irksome governmental regimentation in an age of expanding trade ; its defect was an inability to recognise that social conditions of overcrowding and sweated labour were of concern to the State. Jeremy Bentham (1747–1832) was a lawyer with a mind both critical and original. He held, as basic to his doctrine, that every sane person knows what is for his own good. The utility of any action is to be judged by its tendency to give happiness to the greatest number ; the criterion of happiness being pleasure (which he equates with good), its negative side pain (which he equates with evil).

Of these the average man can well judge. All seek pleasure ; even the holy ascetic is seeking spiritual pleasures

nothing more) in political theory. It is a powerful plea for individual freedom ; Mill wanted an area of conduct marked off from State and Social interference and reserved for the unfettered play of personality. The State and society were both, as he saw them, hostile to this. The view is partly to be explained in terms of Mill's own unhappy experiences in society.

One may criticise *Liberty* on the grounds that the so-called " self-regarding acts " that Mill reserves to the individual are not in fact entirely self-regarding ; that at any rate they have an effect on others, and hence must be of concern to society. Drunkenness and idleness, for example, if carried more than a very little way, obviously affect a citizen's social usefulness. But supposing one could make a satisfactory list of a number of acts which, without damage to the interests of the community, might be left without interference by it : would this really be a satisfactory way of defining liberty ? It would, in fact, be the kind of misleading half-truth characteristic of an ingenious mind rather than a profound one, not fulfilling the content of the word " liberty " as generally understood. More satisfactory is the equally Utilitarian conception of an " individualistic minimum " of areas of governmental interference ; all not so scheduled being free to the development of the citizen or the citizen as organised in society. Mill, however, disliked society, as before hinted, regarding its usages as oppressive ; hence his views in *Liberty*.

The book has become the gospel of anti-social individualists ; it profoundly influenced Kropotkin in his formulation of the principles of anarchy ; it has inspired Tolstoy and Gandhi. This world-influence is due rather to the literary qualities of the book than to its logical process, which develops brilliantly from unsound premises to a visionary conclusion.

In general, however, the Utilitarians were very typically English in addressing their minds to the practical problems of government as they saw it. In particular, they were untroubled by speculations about the origin and nature of the State. Their function for it may be summarised by saying that they wished it to prevent interference, and emphatically not to develop and sustain the citizen.

THE STATE AS A MONSTROUS JUGGERNAUT

IT will be convenient to deal next with the philosophy of the State which stands over against individualism in the sharpest contrast, exalting the State at the expense of the citizens who compose it. Whether regarding the State as fundamentally power, force, or instinct, the view exalting the State connected with the names of Hegel, Treitschke, and Fichte regards the good of the State as the object of society, and individual values as more or less subordinate.

Fichte (1762–1814) was a follower of Kant ; he was concerned with exalting Germany for its racial and linguistic purity—quite in the current Nazi manner. The State he conceived as power, the citizen as a mere cell in its organism, which grows by continuous extension of the sphere of government through inventive developments of national economy. Externally, the State's policy was to be that of simple acquisition. Universal empire is therefore the object, and any " balance of power " a mere second-best. The most civilised States are the most militant, and the destiny of great States is to absorb smaller ones. It is well, however, to promise peace in order that enemies may be unprepared.

The view contrasts on the one side with the Greek, in which an ideal State is always sharply limited in scale, never infinite ; on the other side with Hobbes' " Natural State." Whereas Hobbes' natural man or State is a mere creature of instinct, Fichte's is intellectualised and deliberate.

The State for Fichte is not so much immoral as non-moral, or rather with new morals. The State is the embodiment of right, and is itself the moral law. Fichte does not, however, deify the State ; he merely takes the State as he finds it and rationalises it.

Hegel (1834–96) makes the State an absolute end in itself, and identifies it with God's action in the world. A follower of Plato, he asserts the State to be prior to the individual, and objects to the Church because it substitutes God for the State. The State owes its existence to the Reformation. Philosophically, he held reality to be what is rational ; Reason acting in the world is the absolute God ; this is embodied in the State, wherein Reason realises itself as Will. The individual has his true activities in the State only. Hence any idea of a contract theory is wholly inadequate.

World history is the only judge of the particular State, which establishes universal truths in its legislative, judicial, and executive measures. The " Prince's " function is to unite and give meaning to the whole process in a constitutional monarchy. States are only developed through conflict ;

plain : it was the action taken by the body of citizens to end a State which had failed to serve a specific end, a new State being constituted by the consequent change in the distribution of power. This clearness, like most of the Greek clearness, is due to the teleological view—the habit of having in mind the defined purpose for which an organisation exists.

A PHILOSOPHER WHO DIGNIFIED THE INDIVIDUAL : ROUSSEAU

ROUSSEAU (1712–78), the most influential of all modern political philosophers except Marx, stands for the extreme development of the theory of natural rights without corresponding duties. Politically, he held that the citizen in a democratic State constantly exercises his rights. The people become sovereign in the act of institution of the State, and so remain ; they do not, as in Hobbes, after instituting a government embodying right, retire leaving it the field of affairs. Each member of the " collective moral body," which in various aspects goes by the names of State, Sovereign, Power, or People, is both sovereign and subject. The State cannot have interests contrary to those of its citizen-parts, for all individuals can be placed under an obligation to the sovereign by a public vote. The individual has exchanged his " natural right " for the guarantee of society ; hence justice, not instinct, becomes the guide of his actions, and in obedience to such self-imposed law he is morally free.

This is the central point of Rousseau's system, at which the individual becomes the State. It is never quite clear in Rousseau when he is equating *volonté générale* (the General Will)—his sanction for a law or act of government—with *volonté de tous* (the Will of All). The last phrase means, with him, government by majority of equal wills ; whereas the first appears to mean general consent.

One may query whether individual wills which are, for example, subconsciously seeking their own and not the general good, can be said to embody the " general will." Yet, once we have admitted disqualifications, it might be possible also to rule out the majority of the citizen body, as not actuated by the true and conscious " general will " that Rousseau appears to mean. Concerning this phrase there have been endless speculations. " General will " has been interpreted as the will of one or of a small group, which after argument, has been adopted by the majority ; as the Will of God ; as the coming into consciousness at moments of crisis of a general

ROUSSEAU BOTANISING IN HIS COUNTRY RETREAT

Moving into society, these values are partially realised in associations ; bodily conditions of life in terms of wages and hours become the affair of trade or employers' unions ; universities, learned societies, and lecture bodies spring up, and public amusements flourish ; public art develops, if only in the form of municipal galleries and pudibund public statuary. Men establish theistic cults, build temples and churches to a god or gods.

PROVISIONS THE STATE HAS YET TO MAKE

THE State's functions in guaranteeing rights, or, as we may prefer to say, satisfying needs, have been steadily widened by the growth of a sense of social justice. The State, it is generally agreed, should as far as possible guarantee life itself. Our maternity and child welfare schemes, our national health insurance, are guarantees of the kind. The provision of maintenance in the absence of work has been recognised since Tudor times, as an obligation of the State, though exercised through parish authorities, boards of guardians, or poor-law officers. Neither of these forms of guarantee has yet gone as far as humanity might dictate. It is very recently indeed that children's health has been benefited constructively by extra food from the State, instead of being merely looked after when undermined. Free, or nearly free, milk for the schools is one of the educational matters upon which the National Government can be congratulated. Again, even putting aside the just claim for full pay if society cannot provide work, it is not yet recognised that to keep a large section of the population at a level of living that provides —if the dole indeed does provide—a bare minimum of subsistence, is false economy. Education is another right we have learnt to seek from the State.[1]

Closely connected with education is the demand for the opening of all careers to free competition. This is a matter for society rather than for the State ; all Civil Service posts in Britain are open to competition without social distinction, the Diplomatic Service being the last to abolish any trace of caste privilege (during Mr. MacDonald's tenure of the Foreign Office). In the past, quick promotion for talent has been one of the baits tempting consent to absolute government ; Napoleon, himself the careerist paramount, saw to it that ability should find its reward, if possible.

[1] See section entitled *Education in a Changing World*.

PLATO'S VISION OF JUSTICE AND ORDER

MOST of the above values, which we usually now term rights, would in the past have been labelled benevolence ; individualists have assigned many of them to the sphere of private action, and denied the State's competence. We now come to a right recognised from the first as fundamental to society, one of the two primary interests of the State : the right to justice.

For Plato, justice meant the balance of power and appropriate functioning of classes in the State. The Sophists had said that the State was an organisation for the gratification of the rulers ; Plato called such a State perverted, a " spoils system," and set up the ideal of justice in a State which should counter ignorance and selfishness by free education (a reformed version of the extant kind) and communism. These positive features were to condition the proper distribution of function, which constituted justice in the State. Functions of classes were to correspond with the three principles of the human mind—the combative, domineering, and creative instincts ; there were to be warriors, rulers, and husbandmen. Rulers were to be educated until the age of fifty. Aristotle includes priests in his corresponding list, which it will thus be seen is nearly identical with the Indian. The idea of making such an analysis is not the only link between Plato and the philosophy of the Far East ; for his model the great democrat paradoxically looked to oligarchic and monarchical Sparta, where public education and meals and the communisation of property were really practised. Plato's State is at once collectivist and aristocratic.

Justice in the narrower and more usual sense Plato defined as the keeping of laws which are rules of conduct enacted by the dominant class according to the type of State. Laws were thus necessarily always being modified as unjust, as the balance of classes in the State altered. (This view reads to us as curiously modern, almost Marxist.) At any given time law is derived from previous times ; laws are only recognised if in accordance with tradition. Nevertheless, the principles are to be ascertained by reason and revealed by conscience. Laws, in fact, are never ideal, and always need interpretation.

Aristotle agrees with Plato in treating justice as the bond between men that constitutes a State. Concerning laws, he again agrees, but, with his more conservative bias, nevertheless tends to exalt them. Laws must be supreme, the magistrates their only interpreters. He seriously questions whether any changes should ever be made in a country's laws, and concludes that great caution is needed in doing so ; and that it is better to leave some errors rather than risk the growth of the habit of disobedience. " For a law has no power to command obedience except that of habit."

Concerning the administration of justice, Aristotle lists eight types of courts, and four methods of appointing judges, *i.e.* selecting citizens as a temporary bench of judges. He animadverts on the use made of the courts by party passions, especially of their use by demagogues to ruin the rich.

Plato's last work was the *Laws*, detailing the enactments which a constitution such as he had envisaged in the *Republic* would require, though in some ways the *Laws* represents the harsher outlook of old age. Plato will not, for example, allow poets to enter the ideal State of the *Laws*, though he had assigned them a function in the *Republic*.

Aristotle, while agreeing with Plato on public educational policy, objects to his communism on the ground that private property enables men to be generous ; it is only its abuse that is wrong. The communisation of women at certain seasons and the system of universal relationships so based, which Plato proposed, would, Aristotle remarked, merely destroy affection, which is necessarily a possessive and concentrated thing and cannot be spread indefinitely over a large group of " brothers " or " sisters " of the communal kind.

THE DEFENCE OF PROPERTY

To move to other conceptions of justice, let us take first the definition that it consists in the maintenance of rights, at first defining rights, in the lawyer's phrase, as that which the law defends a man in using. We have discussed natural or social rights above ; we will merely mention as borderline cases between justice and law the performance of contracts, the claims of natural relationships on property, and claims due to custom. We will now take the concrete matter of property. What constitutes property ?

Locke's definition is : That with which a man has mixed his labour. While more definite as a phrase than " produce of labour," it leaves out of account the fact that we are no longer living under pioneer conditions, and own much for which we have not directly toiled. Sidgwick (*Elements of Politics*) gives " normal expectations," which is broader, but throws the onus of definition on to general opinion. It is clearly better than the " policeman " view of the State's functions we first suggested. But general opinion may be contrary to general welfare or to the ideal of justice. The notion of equality enters here with decisive effect. It applies, certainly, only to the administration of law ; but it is difficult to pick holes in the general contention that a law should fulfil the definition that what is required or forbidden is so of all men.

Applying this to property, which includes the life that gives value to the property, there is the right of all to protection from enemies external to the State and from social enemies within. This clearly implies the upkeep of competent police forces. In the sphere of taxation, equality has come to mean not taxation by capitation, but in proportion to the amount of property owned. The amount thus paid has been said to be proportioned to the benefits received from the State in protection of that property. When we inquire, however, whether all forms of property, of equal cash value, require equal protection, one can only answer, " No." No such perceptible effort is required of the State to safeguard a balance at the bank as is made to safeguard a country-house full of valuables. The basis, therefore, of taxation is, in fact, capacity to pay.

THE STATE ACKNOWLEDGES A DEBT TO THE PARENT

THE assessment of this, however, may lead to inequalities. Take the case of two men of equal income, one unmarried, the other with a wife and eight children. On a capitation basis, the latter would pay nine times what the former would pay ; on a basis of capacity to pay, the converse would occur. Actually, income-tax is graded in such cases in favour of the domestically burdened man, though not, of course, in the instance given above, to the extent of charging him only one-ninth of the amount paid by the single man. The State, that is, recognises a new value besides equality—social benefit ; it considers that B's family is of more value to the nation than A's motor-car.

From this point of view of social utility the State would be justified in assessing taxation by discriminating between sources of income—taxing more heavily, for example, income derived from extortionate rents from slum property ; or money made by gambles on the stock exchange, especially from selling out on speculation ; or by the watering of capital. It already does so between ways in which money is expended.

Equality so far has appeared rather as a guiding idea than as a precise rule for application. " Equality modified by fitness and desert " is Sidgwick's definition of ideal justice. In society equality of possession is, so far as Western Europe is concerned at any rate, at present impracticable. Only equality of duties—for example, in compulsory military service, jury service, or the obligation to assist the course of justice—is possible in such directions. Equality of opportunity, again, can only be partially promoted by the State ; it can but ensure equal education and open competitive examination—systems acting on diverse human material with varying results. Defective material may perhaps be more specially catered for in the future and nursed up to the average ; outstanding material cannot be prevented from remaining outstanding, though it may be hindered. Equality before the laws remains the one sphere wherein the ideal is fulfilled.

The kinds of law that coincide with justice, says Sidgwick, are those that define and secure the rights of individuals. Rights include the equal distribution of desirable objects and means of pleasure, liberties, privileges, burdens, restraints, and pains. Since this is no more a legal than an economic treatise, we here leave the question, merely remarking *en passant* that Sidgwick in the first item shows himself a thoroughgoing communist by anticipation. We shall proceed to examine the dealings of the State, through the specialised instrument of the law, with unsocial conduct of the kind that comes within its orbit.

The State's right to punish the individual is usually justified on the grounds of maintaining individual rights, *e.g.* to life and property, by giving an exemplary punishment to an offender sufficiently salutary to prevent others from behaving similarly. There are, further, the maintenance of public order, and the infliction of retribution sufficient to satisfy public feeling. In practice, these three grounds are often difficult to separate.

Taking the last ground first, it will be seen to be ultimately a moral question. It assumes that the person punished understands the nature of the rights he has infringed, or the obligat n he has not fulfilled. Green writes : *Ignorance is no defence in law . . . the right or obligation being one of which the agent might have been aware, and the violation of right being one which he might have prevented.* It is notorious that even lawyers do not know all the ins and outs of that marvellous edifice, British Law ; yet the average citizen is assumed to know his legal obligations in all circumstances. This ground further assumes that the public opinion which is to be satisfied is itself just ; furthermore, that retribution is in itself a good.

PSYCHOLOGY'S CLASSIFICATION OF THE CRIMINAL MIND

IF we are thus to base punishment upon satisfaction of a herd instinct, it is plain that we are obliged to admit the possibility that the offender may also have acted under an instinct, which we must then proceed to evaluate. In order to do so we shall have to know his life history and mental history. Starting in this way, we may soon discover that *tout comprendre c'est tout pardonner.* Early influences in the stratum of society from which criminals are usually drawn are poor ; they emanate from a specialised sphere of public opinion whose values are not those of the generality of citizens. Many law-breakers, again, appear to have been moved to commit the act by virtually irresistible emotions. The law itself now indirectly acknowledges the possibility of this. Others, without being actual morons, have little sense of the consequences of their actions. Opposed to these are the intellectual criminals, whose minds have been warped ; those who may regard themselves as warring upon a society which has wronged them. Of a higher type, then, are those, such as pro-feminist agitators or conscientious objectors, who hold a conviction that the law is in some respect wrong. All these must in justice be separated from the deliberate and calculating criminal if the psychological ground of punishment is to be upheld.

We return to our first ground, prevention of future violation of rights by the exemplary deterrence of possible offenders. This is in fact the soundest ground of the three, and may be held to include in itself the second, the maintenance of order, which, except perhaps in cases of " protective arrest," an act officially unknown to British Law, is mostly a matter of setting examples. No punishment prevents an offence already committed ; it can merely try to remedy it, if the case admits of remedy, and try to render less likely the doing of a similar wrong in future. The extent to which extenuating circumstances are allowable appears to vary with public opinion as embodied in twelve good men and true. Even in law, circumstances alter cases, as generally happens in matters of conduct outside its purview. A starving man steals a loaf; the act cannot be regarded as on all-fours with the same act in a beleaguered and starving garrison where upon the maintenance of strict rationing depend the lives and whole morale of the force.

CAPITAL PUNISHMENT IN THE DOCK

THERE are good reasons why punishment should not and cannot be proportioned to the degree of moral obliquity of the act punished. The degree is in fact not ascertainable; and, if it were, the State is only concerned with punishing acts which it has specifically declared worthy of punishment, and only rarely inquires into motives. In earlier days it never did so; " the law trieth not the heart of man " was the pious mediæval principle, which left that inquiry to the Church. There are whole areas of behaviour in which the law does not recognise punishment as appropriate, or perhaps expedient. Fornication is the classic instance. While the act of fornication makes debts incurred from it not recoverable at law, and while it makes habitual female offenders liable to be charged as common prostitutes, and employers of such liable to heavy penalties, the action itself remains immune from the law, except in so far as public decency and order are concerned. Law in the past has always failed when it has experimented with the abolition of prostitution; it has been brought into contempt by reason of non-observance in this application, and has had to be altered. The attempt to enforce the Volstead Act in America had similar results.

In both examples a widespread social habit was challenged by law ahead of and contrary to public opinion; in both, the flouting of the particular law led to a widespread deterioration in respect for the law generally. We may deduce that a law must in effect have the tacit assent of the majority of citizens before it will work—at least if it be a law affecting general conduct. One might, however, urge against this opinion the still-endured restrictions on the sale of chocolates and tobacco in England, and that on the sale of liquor, a relic of D.O.R.A. never yet removed, and certainly endured unwillingly.

The questions at issue in the matter of the State's right to punish are seen most clearly if considered in relation to the extreme sanction—the death penalty. For the infliction of death, Green puts the case that, for purposes of deterrence of others, " association of the extremest terror may be necessary." Moreover, the crime punished, murder, may show the perpetrator to be permanently incapable of the exercise of rights.

Returning to our original three grounds for punishment, the first, deterrence, is dubious as applied to judicial execution. For maximum effect, obviously, it should take place in public, as until recently in France. Actually, this has been found to have undesirable effects, not necessarily deterrent. The sufferer becomes something of a public figure and hero to the weaker-minded spectators. An unpleasant sadism is evident amongst the crowds at such spectacles. The sight of bloodshed has an effect of releasing the submerged killing instinct present in most people. Reports in the public press of the grisly details often produce public sympathy ; and subsequent crimes often show the influence of a past crime that has received publicity. Conversely, if executions take place in decorous privacy and with little publicity, the effect of deterrence is at least lessened.

Actually, there are reasons for thinking that the deterrent effect of the death penalty has been much exaggerated. Figures showing murder percentages have not notably increased in countries that have abolished it. Judge Kavanagh's evidence before a Select Committee of the House of Commons merely showed that capital punishment was better than none. It did not show that the death penalty was a more effective deterrent than other penalties swiftly and regularly enforced. " Certainty, not severity, of punishment is the essential factor." On the other side, Lord Darling may be quoted ; he has supported the death penalty by the lesson of the French President, Grévy, whose invariable commutation of the sentence led, it seems, to an outbreak of homicide.

A LIFE FOR A LIFE : SATISFYING PUBLIC OPINION

OUR third ground of punishment (we have incidentally dealt with the second), the infliction of retribution and the satisfaction of public feeling, is that on which capital punishment is most easily justifiable. That to try a man

before a constituted authority is better than to lynch him
has usually been held an irrefutable argument ; though the
negroes in the Scottsboro' case might well wish they had
been instantly lynched rather than have had to endure the
series of partial trials and delays which have recently dis-
graced American justice. A certain retributive satisfaction
is undoubtedly experienced when a murderer of an unpleasant
type is finally deprived of the life of which he had deprived
another. It is, of course, impossible to pretend that such
a view can be reconciled to Christian principles, though it be
held in a Christian country.

We saw earlier that, if the motive of a satisfied instinct is
to be our ground, the instincts of the criminal must also be
weighed. Many criminologists now hold that the murderer,
other than the man who may kill in hot blood, is a man with
a characteristic kink, allied to egomaniac vanity. That is
not to say that he is certifiable under the lunacy laws, but
that he has a definite bias, often unrecognised until a crime
is committed.

Concerning reparation, it cannot be held that the death
of a second human being compensates for that of the first,
though it may afford pleasure to the relatives of the victim.
The principle of reparation would be better carried out by
the murderer spending his time working for the support of
the relatives dependent on his late victim.

There has further to be considered in the special matter
of capital punishment the effect on the servants of the law
of carrying out the sentence. A public hangman, if his
duties are known, is likely to be shunned socially. That
the post does satisfy sadistic cravings is shown by the fact
that on occasions when it becomes vacant numbers of highly
respectable, even wealthy, persons apply for it, obviously
from the motive of satisfying suppressed sadism. The
suicide of the best-known British hangman of recent times,
owing, it was said, to the effect on his mind of the execution
of a woman, throws further light on the possible effects of
his employment upon the law's agent in the death penalty.
This is only one aspect of the more general question of
the brutalising effect upon gaolers of carrying out legal
punishment.

If a conclusion must be reached, the right one on an
unprejudiced survey of the facts appears to be that public
feeling, and the feelings of relatives of the murdered man,

ought to be sufficiently satisfied with the removal of the murderer from spheres wherein he can do harm. The State is concerned to prevent crime. If a murderer be held to be unbalanced in the sense we have indicated as probable, then a mere term of imprisonment, at the end of which he is again let loose upon society, is clearly insufficient. The sight of a murderer digging potatoes in the next-door garden, armed with a lethal-looking garden-fork, is one which might well decrease the value of house property in the neighbourhood. Society has a right to demand that the irresponsible offender be removed permanently from its purview. Criminals themselves are not without rights. Amongst other objects of punishment we must not forget the remedial.

GERMS OF MORAL CORRUPTION THAT BREED IN PRISON WALLS

PRISONS in the past have been the most notorious breeders of crime. The association of young offenders with " old lags," the brutalising atmosphere of the average prison, with its gaolers drawn from the less intelligent strata of the community, have been fruitful causes of evil, and are still to some extent, though some separation is now made between young and old prisoners, and conditions of life have been made more tolerable. Upon whether one regards imprisonment as retributive or remedial will depend his opinion whether conditions should be further improved. Clearly, if prisons are to be considered places of expiation, they should not be improved further than they already have been in England ; certain prisoners, as it is, view them as happy refuges from their condition of life outside.

If one regards society's duty to be to reclaim human wreckage so far as may be, and make it again socially serviceable, then he will take a very different view. If criminals are considered as showing on the whole a feeble mentality—and this is generally recognised—one cannot imagine a worse environment for mental cases or even for those with a kink than the average prison. But offenders may be considered class by class.

Those who commit murder or violence under extreme emotion seem almost to be sufficiently punished by the reaction following. It may almost be said that they themselves are also victims. Criminals with profound social convictions may prove to be mere orators wishing to attract attention by an overt act, fanatics of the anti-vaccinationist

sense represent a number of others would have seemed to them illogical. Democracy, or polity, to use Aristotle's actual word for the system, was for them a matter of direct voting on specific questions by all those privileged to be citizens. The Greek City State was like the primitive type of Swiss canton. In the one the sea, in the other the mountains, separated each community from other communities ; the actual assembly of all citizens was thus possible on account of small numbers, and the ascertaining of the will of the majority presented no difficulties.

The modern Western idea of representation grew, as before remarked, out of the ecclesiastical system of government, from provincial synods of the Church. The notion of one person representing a number is in reality a mystical idea. In practice we have to take our choice between the election of a representative because we approve of his personal qualities, or because he represents opinions and intentions we would see put into effect ; we have to choose between a personality and a delegate. The two may happen to coincide ; or they may not. The most distinguished English exponent of the personality thesis was Edmund Burke (1729–97). In effect, English elections until very recent times have been affairs of choosing the best fellow, since the English political mind has not readily taken to choice by political programme. In this, as in other ways, our mentality is changing. The trade-union movement is governed exclusively by the delegate system. Each branch representative at a national conference may count for the number of members in that branch. This is the logical method, once the principle is admitted.

Governments to-day form a museum of methods of choice for their legislative bodies. Electorates vary from suffrage commonly called universal to suffrage so restricted as to be almost worthless. It must first be remarked that suffrage is never universal. No political theorist could maintain that votes deposited by young children or idiots had rational value. Exclusion, however, is generally carried far beyond these two classes. Nowhere are legal minors allowed votes ; in most states the whole female population is excluded ; in many dependencies the majority of the native population under white rule is denied the vote, or it is confined to the literate minority of natives. Governments have frequently shown themselves queasy over admitting in set terms the restriction of their electorates. A good example is the French constitution of 1791 which, anxious to combine the notion of sovereignty by the people with a franchise drastically curtailed, distinguished between those with and without political rights as *active* and *passive* citizens.

A fraction of the populace, ranging from one-fifth downwards, are entitled to vote in democratic countries now. The law of 1874 grants the vote to all male French citizens over twenty-one years of age. The pre-war German Reichstag granted it to all resident males of the Empire of twenty-five and over. The post-war Republican Constitution granted franchise to all men and women of twenty and over—a basis which is still retained, except for " non-Aryans," under the nazi régime.

THE VARIED LOT OF THE AMERICAN CITIZEN

THE United States leaves the qualifications for the electorate to its component States ; the varying qualifications necessary for State suffrage are also those needed for federal voting, except that, by the 19th Amendment to the Federal Constitution, all women over twenty-one have federal votes. The only general condition otherwise imposed is that the right to vote is not to be denied or abridged because of race, colour, or previous servitude. The twenty-two States agree in excluding those under twenty-one years of age ; four of them grant women the suffrage ; most only grant votes to citizens of the U.S.A., though some do so to aliens who have declared their intention to qualify as citizens. Residence necessary to qualify varies from three months (Maine) to two years (Alabama). Exclusions generally comprise the insane, idiots, and felons ; most States exclude paupers, some the Chinese specifically, in spite of the federal constitution as noted above. Similarly there are laws in the Southern States intended to prevent negroid voting ; for example, in Louisiana only citizens who are literate, or who own $300 worth of assessed property, or whose fathers were entitled to vote in 1867, are allowed the franchise.

In Great Britain the growth of the suffrage has been slow and complex. Until recently no single uniform law has regulated it ; each measure has only partially repealed previous laws. The great Act of the last century was the Act of 1832, which gave tenants as well as owners of land the county franchise, and borough franchise to those rate-paying householders of premises worth £10 a year or over.

In 1867 reform was carried farther ; there was household suffrage in boroughs, £12 household in counties, while lodgers paying £10 rental also had votes. Generally, this Act enfranchised working men, as distinct from the middle-class, who alone benefited from the 1832 Act.

The Act of 1884 set up a fairly democratic suffrage ; the voter must be a male of twenty-one years or over, the owner or lessee of premises of a yearly value varying with tenure, or alternatively must occupy or lodge in fixed premises of a certain value or on which rates have been paid. This did not abolish remnants of previous laws—qualification, for example, by being a born and resident freeman, a liveryman of a city company, or a graduate on the electoral roll of a university. Aliens not naturalised and members of the peerage, as well as idiots and convicted felons, were considered incapable of the franchise. In the 1918 Act the franchise was extended to women over thirty who were householders or wives of householders, and women were made eligible for membership of the Commons. In 1928 Baldwin's Act removed the invidious age proviso from female suffrage, reducing the qualifying age to twenty-one, and rectified various other anomalies.

THE GATHERING OF THE POLITICAL CLANS : THE PARTY SYSTEM

CONCERNING the political organisation of the electorate, there is much to be said of its working in England, where it has taken the form of the growth of parties. Constitutionally, the State knows nothing of parties. Yet all countries which have set up parliamentary government have created something that is meaningless without them. Party government has been called the most natural and the most unnatural of phenomena. On one side it is held that the party struggle is a natural expression of the combative instinct ; on the other, that the state of chronic impenetrability to the arguments of opponents which is demanded of the loyal party man is a sin against the light of reason, and prevents the natural division of opinion.

Conservative organisation may be dated from the formation of the Carlton Club before the 1832 Act ; Liberal organisation from the starting of the Reform Club in 1836. Both sides compiled lists of voters through registration societies. They were placed in the hands of patronage secretaries. Party whips appeared in the House ; they managed party

funds. These developments had occurred by the middle of the century.

The free-trade campaign gave a great stimulus to the parties ; the Anti-Corn Law League gave examples of the management of the electorate. It was the second Reform Bill that was the turning-point. Additions to the rolls of electors were huge ; in Manchester there were no fewer than 30,000 new electors. The personal touch, in the old sense, now became a thing of the past in elections.

At Birmingham a new piece of party machinery was set up by Joseph Chamberlain in the party council of delegates from branches. Another new element in the country's political life appeared with the secret ballot set up by the Ballot Act of 1872. The Liberals, who had apparently hitherto held power in Birmingham by undue influence over the electorate, were now defeated there.

If voters could not now be directly influenced, propaganda must needs be started. Accordingly the National Liberal Federation was founded. It had control over Liberal M.P.s in the party interest, and acted as intermediary between the Liberal branches throughout the country and the party leaders, forming a kind of sounding-board for local party opinion. A revolt against this programme method, whereby M.P.s had to toe the line to the party whips, was initiated by Cohen, who wished to revert to Burke's conception of the semi-detached relationship of a representative to his constituents. It was useless ; the party caucus drew up the Newcastle Programme, to which candidates in the Liberal interest had to subscribe in advance ; and M.P.s approximated definitely towards being delegates rather than representatives.

Since then, strict party voting has increasingly been the rule ; whips are rarely taken off. Lowell, in his *Government of England*, puts 90 per cent. as the average of strict party voting to voting as a whole.

The relationship between the party leaders and the local party organisations might obviously be easily embarrassed by irresponsible proposals passed by mass meetings. The National Liberal Federation has not in fact always seen eye to eye with its chiefs. The Home Rule question in 1886 brought about the reconciliation of one cleavage. Since then, mass meetings have been more and more strictly controlled by the leaders. Local federations have issued no more threats to headquarters since a national party meeting has become annual.

THE POWER BEHIND THE PARTY

THE Conservatives in 1883 formed a National Union of Federations. They, too, quarrelled with their leaders, but more successfully. Their first leader was Randolph Churchill. Then Joseph Chamberlain forced a protectionist policy upon his leaders in 1905, without, however, dislodging his chief, that skilful tactician Balfour, from his position. When the ordeal by election resulted in defeat for the policy, a cry was raised, not for its jettisoning, but for the clearance from the party of non-protectionists. This resulted in Balfour himself being expelled from the Club, and the leaders were definitely brought to heel.

Lowell speaks of both the movements we have traced as the rise and fall of the caucus, but it seems clear that it was the caucus system that eventually won. M.Ps. in effect are now under the domination of both the party caucus and their leader. What is the relation of the caucus to local voters ? Broadly, it determines the issues to be decided in elections, organises voters and, though now less frequently, selects as well as approves of the party candidates. Numbers here mean little ; it is always a small group that runs the local organisation. The whole machine functions only at actual election times. The average cost of an election is £700 to £900, supplied from a central fund or capacious private pockets. The Labour Party alone raises the money locally. The lowest sum spent by a successful candidate is £95 (James Maxton).

THE "SYSTEM" SYSTEM IN THE U.S.A.

IN the United States the two great parties have ever since the Civil War been two large and intricately organised rival systems rather than parties divided sharply on questions of principle and policy. From the convention for selection of party candidates that grew up in the eighteen-twenties has developed a hierarchy of local primaries, regional and State conventions, and national conventions, the last of no fewer than 994 delegates. The manifold elections in the U.S.A. do not encourage the average citizen to attend the primary ; and the whole organisation tends to fall into the hands of party rings and bosses of the kind that are rarely scrupulous. Save in times of crisis, the American people are unluckily inclined to allow political power to remain in such hands.

On the Continent, the system of small party groups does not encourage the growth of great political organisation of the Anglo-American type. Any widespread movement, indeed, tends to transcend or ignore the political groups. *Action Française* in its palmy days consisted mainly of those who refused association with the Third Republic, and neither nazism nor fascism can be called a great party group in the constitutional sense, since they are movements which have set up their own constitutions in totalitarian States. We shall return to the consideration of the group system in politics later.

While dealing with this matter of the organisation of electoral opinion, we may glance at education in this connection. In England education has hitherto been treated as a sphere of political neutrality ; with rare exceptions, educationists conscientiously refrain from indoctrinating their pupils. But within the last decade there has come to be a more and more marked tendency in other countries to merge the individual in the State's purpose by deliberate political teaching. The Young Communists have been followed by the Italian *Ballíla* and the junior nazi organisations ; schools have been made propaganda centres.

Now, the State may have the right to implant principles of conduct ; and if a State be based on authoritarian doctrine, nothing could in any case prevent this from reaching the young. Any lingering regard for liberty, however, is outraged by the spectacle. If government is granted to be even partially based on the explicit consent of the governed, it can only be asked of what possible moral value is a consent that is given under the influence of experience that has been allowed to know only one side of the question. What, in fact, is the moral worth of a conditioned reflex ? And if the majority of citizens in the future prove to have been so trained, what validity has government by consent in such a country at all ? It may indeed be " broad-based upon the people's will " without the wills being free enough to have value at all.

GIVING MINORITIES A LOOK IN : PROPORTIONAL REPRESENTATION

THE problem of the representation of the wishes of minority groups is another point here arising. Put in the simplest

to distort the proportion of opinion in the direction of providing
workable and distinct parties. This is in sharp contrast to
that of France. Whether the rise of a third party in Britain
represents the beginning of a break-up of this classic clarity
is a matter for speculation. As Professor Laski writes in this
connection :

> " Proportional Representation, where it has been
> tried, has not noticeably improved the standards of
> public life. In Belgium it tended to eliminate in-
> dependence. In Switzerland it has so much multiplied
> the tiny groups that no coherent opinion has been
> able to emerge. That always implies weak govern-
> ment."

KEEPING THE M.P. UP TO THE MARK

SUPPOSE that your member of Parliament, instead of remaining a good conservative or anti-vaccinationist, becomes
converted to communism or the virtues of vaccine. Is the
electorate to have any remedy ? It has been until recently
the British tradition that no private member may take office
under the Crown without a fresh by-election ; there is nothing
compelling him to submit himself to that ordeal if he changes
his opinions. True, he usually does so voluntarily, but he
need not. The device of the Recall is framed to meet this
need. It is suggested [1] that, not before a year has elapsed
from a general election and not later than a year before the
next is due, on the demand of at least half the constituents,
a by-election should be held at which a two-thirds majority
might decide not to retain the member's services.

There is something to be said for this safeguard. It will
obviously make a member tread more warily and be more
careful to reflect what he knows of the wishes of his supporters. Unless, however, it be hedged about with such
substantial safeguards, the proposal seems mischievous. The
constituency has made its choice ; if it has chosen ill, it should
take the risk. Manifestly, if a member, whose duties necessarily take him away from his constituency to the capital, is
to be subject in his absence to a campaign of irresponsible
abuse with the object of obtaining a fresh election, he may
become too much afraid of electoral opinion to express freely
his own on controversial matters. A sense of insecurity is
not a good basis for efficient work.

[1] Professor Laski, *Grammar of Politics*, p. 320.

If, however, the safeguards were sufficient, it would certainly be a salutary check on an M.P. to know that if his conduct seriously outraged general opinion he might in the last resort find himself superseded. There is no reason why a constituency should be misrepresented for perhaps three years out of four. That the Constitution has decided that five years is the appropriate term for a chamber's life, during which it is unlikely to become seriously out of touch with opinion, does not imply that any particular M.P. is free to behave in a manner politically outrageous. For his general conduct, an M.P. is now responsible in most respects before the law like any other citizen, except for a certain exemption from libel laws necessary for free debate in the House. (This statement needs the qualification that a member cannot be arrested for an offence below the rank of felony.) Why should he be free to act as he pleases politically ?

Other pieces of machinery have been devised for the more flexible registration of electoral opinion. Supposing that the elected legislature fails, or ceases to represent the opinion of the electorate on one or more important matters—cannot some means be devised for giving effect to majority opinion on a particular measure ? For this purpose the method known as the Initiative can be used. On the petition of a certain proportion of voters, a Bill may be obligatorily introduced to the chamber ; if it fail to pass, on another petition it may be referred to the direct vote of the people. There is also the complementary process, the Referendum, by which a measure which has passed the legislature may, on petition, be referred for ratification or rejection to the electorate.

Both devices now have a considerable history behind them. In the North American State of Oregon, one house of the legislature can by majority refer a constitutional amendment to the people for decision as an extra question at the normal biennial elections. Legislation can be initiated by 8 per cent. of the voters, and may be initiated by even 5 per cent. On the matter at issue in either case an informative voters' pamphlet is issued, partly paid for and distributed by the State.

The electorate has proved to be less interested in measures than men ; the more questions are directly submitted, the fewer find approval. No fewer than thirty-four measures were submitted in 1913–14 ; the number proved a burden on the voters' attention, though the voting appeared to be intelligent, owing to the pamphlet and press propaganda. Party issues bulk smaller in these bills. Petitions for initiation are signed rather indiscriminately in crowded areas ; paid circulators take and send them round. Strong local interests are commonly the motive ; emphasis laid on these is perhaps the Initiative's best quality. By one or other device, measures for increasing popular control, constitutional amendments, creation of new offices and functions, imposition of taxation, criminal laws, liquor control bills, and bills for social welfare, have been passed. Authorship of Petitions is usually anonymous ; some organisation is always the effective agent. For good or ill, therefore, initiative has not passed to the citizens, but to organisations.

A SMALL COUNTRY WITH A GREAT DEMOCRATIC TRADITION

IN Switzerland, 50,000 voters may initiate an alteration in the Constitution, which must be submitted to popular vote. As almost any law can be brought under the head of " constitutional," in effect this means that most measures can be so initiated. All amendments definitely altering the federal constitution must be submitted to a plebiscite, canton by canton. Any law, if 30,000 citizens or eight cantons appeal against it, can be referred to a simple majority of the whole electorate—not decided cantonally.

In effect, as in Oregon, party views are discounted in the measures dealt with ; capable legislation is the sole criterion. The same effects are observed in the cantons themselves where they have adopted the devices—all but three have adopted Initiative. Between 1874 and 1896, thirty-eight popular votes were taken. Opinion is divided on their merits. The recent unwise anti-gambling federal law, passed by direct vote, has been a burden hard to displace, rather like the Volstead Law in U.S.A. A directly voted cantonal law against the Jewish method of slaughter [1] is a good example of misuse.

Concerning the working of Initiative and Referendum, it is to be observed that their tendency is generally conserva-

---

[1] The method of slaughter of animals consists in severing the neck arteries with a sharp knife, and is at least as painless as Gentile methods, unconsciousness being almost instantly produced. The casting of the animal into the right position has, however, in the past led to allegations of cruelty, now rendered baseless by the adoption of the casting-pen method.

tive. Only some half of the electorate commonly vote. The measures submitted are often the work of fanatics obviously destined to rebuff. The inherent difficulty in these devices is that they are far too crude for the complication of modern legislation, which is much more than a mere matter of eliciting yes or no to a question of principle. There is no means of amending and altering measures submitted, as in a legislature. The application of a principle in a law involves technical administrative clauses not to be drafted or easily comprehended by the average citizen.

Actually, as an interim test of how national feeling is moving, that excellent barometer, the by-election, keeps the government of the day in touch with fluctuations of opinion. Governments are extremely sensitive to by-elections, especially after the second year of office. In them the current issues of the day are usually taken as platforms. So long as the casualty list among private members remains high, it may be doubted whether Initiative and Referendum would add very much to English public life in the sense of airing any new ideas which had much chance of acceptance.

THE WHEELS OF GOVERNMENT IN MOTION

WE have given relatively large space to the matter of representation and its machinery. It is time to turn to the thing elected, the legislature, the executive it appoints, and their relationship with the judiciary and administrative officialdom. Our survey will for brevity be virtually confined to three states—Great Britain, U.S.A., and France.

Manifestly the whole tripartite division of government is highly artificial, if regarded as an absolute. All three functions may be united in some form of absolutism. The first category, legislature, may be partially and limitedly executive, as in the U.S.A., where appointments are directly made ; or may overlap with judicial functions, as in the British House of Lords.

What shape shall the legislature assume ? The fact that in most countries it is two-chamber is largely historical accident, due to British example—itself partly an accident. If the chambers have equal powers there is deadlock, as in 1832, save for creation of new peers. Generally speaking, upper chambers are conservative. If nominated, not hereditary, they possess little authority. " The Canadian Senate

is a body which scarcely commands its own confidence"
(Laski). Broadly, they may revise or postpone measures,
as in Britain and Norway. The first function is better done
by expert committees ; as to the second, its use is not evident ;
modern legislative processes are too slow rather than too fast.
A blockage of measures desired by the elective chamber
has proved impossible in Britain and, short of this, there
seems no function at all for a second chamber.

Taking our government, therefore, to be in effect single-
chamber, even if traces of an upper chamber be still extant,
its membership should plainly be free to all. Such tussles
as occurred in the "Wilkes and Liberty" incident, in 1769,
when John Wilkes's election was twice declared void by the
House on the ground of his having been expelled for libel,
should be constitutionally impossible. Easy access to membership gave us the younger Pitt. Under modern conditions
it might, however, be possible to suggest some apprenticeship
in local government as a desirable preliminary.

Absolute freedom in debate and unlimited eligibility for re-
election are other essentials : long experience in the House
gave England the unique personalities of Burke (thirty years
in the House) and Gladstone (sixty).

A period of five years has been found most practical for
the life of the chamber, though it should be elected within
a shorter period at the discretion of the executive of a majority
of the House. Sufficient check on the holding of causeless
elections is found in the fate of prime ministers who have
risked them, as Baldwin did in 1923. The dangers of a
longer life for chambers are illustrated by the melancholy
fate of President Wilson, who returned from Europe to find
himself powerless. The size of the chamber should evidently
not be over five hundred. The British Commons, at over
six hundred, is too large.

A CASE FOR REFORM : THE CABINET'S "CONFIDENCE TRICK"

THE law-making process itself varies with countries. In
the U.S.A., the legislature has no initiative, and the
Bills passed are moreover applied by a separate constitutional
power. The executive is not directly controlled ; the two
spheres may be under different party control. A certain
lack of reality and dramatic appeal is evident under these
conditions. In France, Bills introduced are so freely amended
by commissions as frequently to reappear in unrecognisable

forms. Even finance Bills are thus crippled. The average French ministry's life is so short that it has no time for an adequate programme of legislation. In Great Britain, the government presents a programme of legislation—not excluding Bills introduced by private members—and is in particular wholly responsible for money Bills. Thus, a visible group of men, and one in particular, the minister in charge of it, or the member introducing it, is answerable for any particular measure. The executive can make any question one of confidence (*i.e.* one involving the fate of the Government); a power often used arbitrarily, which needs reform.

There is need, too, for facilities for the gaining of information by private members by means other than questions to ministers, whose responses are frequently guarded to the point of inarticulation. Private members, if under present conditions they are to form more than a registering body, must not be tied by the vote of no-confidence method to such an extent that the amendment of measures in detail is impossible. In 1900 the Balfour administration actually made the question whether pillar-boxes should be red or green a matter of confidence. The reasonable way out would seem to be to entrust to the Speaker the certification of measures as implying or not implying votes of confidence, as he at present certifies money Bills.

The executive, whose functions overlap with those of the legislature in so far as it makes administrative orders that imply legislative powers, and with the judiciary in respect of the office of Lord Chancellor, is usually a committee of the elective chamber. In the U.S.A. it is not, nor is it present in that chamber; with results indicated above (see p. 336). It must not be so large in proportion to the chamber as to swamp or seriously influence its division of opinion. The presence of the executive in the legislature has the effect of enabling men fit for future office to emerge in debate and in committee work; M.Ps. who may be future ministers are thus grounded in affairs.

Politically, the executive is known as the cabinet. In the U.S.A. the head of the State is a member; in France and Britain not. The American President dominates his cabinet to an extent which makes co-operation nearly impossible; the Prime Ministers in Britain and France, on the other hand, have primacy without dominance. They are free to select their cabinets—not obliged to give offices to prominent

Scotland, Wales, and the West of England. Actually, local affairs of relative unimportance occupy but a tiny fraction of the Commons's time ; alternatively, local affairs of real importance are also of national interest—for example, health. For federal States the problem is different ; the U.S.A. and pre-Nazi Germany are models which work or worked well. So far as Britain is concerned, the House of Commons is peculiarly jealous of any rival administration, as was plainly shown during the Prayer-Book controversy (1929). Any regional legislature would before long find itself at loggerheads with the House ; friction and ill-feeling may safely be predicted.

LOOPHOLES AND ANOMALIES IN THE LAW OF ENGLAND

WE pass to the judiciary. We have already mentioned in passing the tenure of office by British judges. Their function blurs with that of the legislature when they declare law not specifically enacted by statute. The personnel of the bench need not be absolutely differentiated from the executive, but it is desirable ; the Lord Chancellorship is an anomaly, and successful attorneys-general are not necessarily good judges. Appointment is elective in the U.S.A., a method not notably an improvement on the British. To declare opinion, judges must necessarily have a case brought before them ; an apparent limitation in effect void, since a test case can in most matters be brought.

Administration has increasingly entrenched upon judicial ground. A *droit administratif*, whose absence was the pride of earlier legal writers (see Dicey's *Law of the Constitution*), has, in effect, developed. By the highest tribunal it has been decided that " when a government department assumes quasi-judicial functions, the absence of express enactment means that the department is free to embark upon what procedure seems best to it ; nor will the courts inquire whether such procedure results, or could result, in justice " (Laski). Under such conditions, in the U.S.A. an American-born Japanese can be excluded from the country by the Secretary for Labour on his return from a visit to Canada. In England, Insurance Commissioners are in some ways beyond the reach of law ; and a regulation made under the Defence of the Realm Act is held to nullify the Habeas Corpus Act. On this whole theme Lord Hewart's *The New Despotism* may profitably be read.

Safeguards against this type of encroachment are to be

found in the specific recovery of powers by the legislature, and in not excluding from the ambit of the courts the definition of the area of administrative prerogative. From the viewpoint of the administration itself, prior consultation of interests involved in proposed regulations is the obvious course.

All acts of the executive should be questionable in the courts. It should be impossible for the British Admiralty to infringe a patent granted to a private citizen when infringement by another private citizen would incur heavy damages. The increased use of the committee system would in many directions increase the efficiency of government, by influence rather than specific law-promotion. Public services might well follow the example of the Post Office and have consultative councils for purposes of contact with the public. Within the legislature, committees might be means of further organising the specialised knowledge of M.P.s ; in committees civil servants may be made vocal and explanatory at the minister's discretion, and the public itself can be called in evidence. To committees it might well be possible to refer private members' bills, on petition of a certain quorum of M.P.s, for technical and administrative emendation.

Finally, a written constitution, not alterable by less than a two-thirds majority of the legislature, is desirable for the safeguarding of certain fundamental rights, such as the Habeas Corpus Act and the right to free speech, which should not be left to the hazards of a party vote or administrative high-handedness. This written constitution should not go to the length of paralysing legislation, as frequently happens in the U.S.A. ; there the will of Congress is frequently balked by the Supreme Court, which has constitutional power not to disallow a measure only on specific grounds, but also if it is held not to be " reasonable." Reason in the persons of a bench of elderly judges, politically appointed, is apt to take reactionary form.

DESPOTS AND PUPPETS : HEADS OF STATE

ONE matter remains—the titular headship of the modern constitutional State. The head of the State is held to embody the representation of its unity. In France, he is an elder party politician considered sufficiently " safe " to lay numberless foundation-stones and make Sunday speeches without disgracing the nation. Maine remarked that no one occupies a more pitiable position ; he neither reigns nor governs. Poincaré, moreover, usurped the President's functions even in the minor directions we have named. There is, in fact, a certain duplication of functions between President and Prime Minister, made evident in President Millerand's dealings with Briand and Poincaré. The President's most important function is to choose the next Prime Minister—often a difficult task under the group system.

In England, the choice is usually obvious. The English sovereign has a prestige which lifts him above direct comparison with any politician. He may in fact be a considerable, even a decisive, influence in politics ; in the formation of the National Government the Throne played a considerable part. As the inheritor of a political tradition, as a highly specialised lifelong public servant, the monarch frequently has better knowledge than his ministers, while his personal popularity often has a stabilising effect upon a régime. In brief, while technically it is the Prime Minister who advises the Crown, frequently it is the Crown which advises the minister, especially on foreign affairs.

Abroad, the presidential fever is still strong ; in France the Presidency is the highest ambition of the moderate politician ; in the U.S.A., in spite of the number of Presidents who have died in office from overwork, the Presidency is in keen competition as the supreme executive power as well as the highest honorific post. Some of the prerogatives of Royalty have recently surrounded it ; a presidential invitation is, in the English manner, almost a command, while the President's person is treated with increasing marks of respect. In Switzerland, the office passes between the federal ministers in order of seniority. Both here and in the U.S.A. it is to be noted that an office has been found for the head of the State besides the function of embodying the State.

POLITICAL PHILOSOPHIES OF ALL AGES

HAVING dealt, however summarily, with conceptions of State and individual justice, general will and its modulations, and machinery of government, we now come to a brief review of some political philosophies not yet touched upon ; first, and most notable, the cyclic theory of politics. Here it is necessary to refer once more to Aristotle. The accompanying table of cycles shows his development from Plato's less generalised analysis.

PLATO

Aristocracy . . . . rule of " the best."

Timocracy . . . . rule of a military class—
" honour."

Oligarchy. . . . . rule of " the few."

Democracy . . . . " mob " rule.

Tyranny. . . . . rule of one irresponsible man.

ARISTOTLE

" *Normal* " *Form.*   " *Perverted* " *Form.*

Rule of one person

Monarchy   Tyranny.

Rule of the few

Aristocracy   Oligarchy.

Rule of the many

Polity   Democracy
    (sometimes rendered   (sometimes rendered
    as " democracy ")   as " ochlocracy ").

A government, he held, starting perhaps as a hereditary monarchy, by degeneration of successive monarchs, becomes a tyranny. The more powerful members of the community unite to overthrow the king, and form an aristocratic government. This, degenerating and losing public spirit, falls into being an oligarchy. The citizens, rebelling, form a " polity," or democracy as we should now say. Pushed to extremes, the " polity " converts into an oppression of the rich by the poor, or " democracy," a meaning it is best to confine in modern terminology to ochlocracy. The resultant confusion and loss of values and discrimination is brought to an end with emergence of some powerful warrior-statesman who once more sets up a monarchy, and the cycle starts again.

Aristotle's analysis is strikingly confirmed by the histories

of the Greek City States in centuries preceding the Pelo-
ponnesian War. In modern times political progressions of
the kind are not unknown. The most dramatic has been the
French Revolution—tyranny overthrown by what was at
first group rule ; then this set of property-holding voters of
the 1791 constitution, *i.e.* an oligarchy, was very soon overthrown by the setting-up of a republic with theoretically
universal suffrage. The anarchic period of this (1793–99)
was ended by the emergence of military despotism under
Napoleon Bonaparte. More recently, democracies which
might be regarded as being corrupted have been changed
almost overnight into absolutisms, under one or another
constitutional form, in Italy and Germany, Austria and
Jugoslavia.

A GERMAN PHILOSOPHER PREDICTS THE FINAL DECAY OF THE WEST

WITHOUT having attached themselves to the definite
sequence of Aristotle, recent thinkers have been recurring to the cyclic idea. Dr. W. R. Inge has eloquently
pointed out (in *The Idea of Progress*, Romanes Lecture) that
the idea of unlimited progress is unhistorical ; that the idea
of a millennium without miracle led to the French Revolution,
and survived into an industrial revolution which gave a
society that " has mistaken comfort for civilisation," given
rise to further millennial visions, and resulted in a complexity
that is not necessarily an evolution at all. " Ancient civilisations were destroyed by imported barbarians, we breed our
own." The progress idea in this unlimited form is due to
the historian, " a natural snob who . . . approves the
winning side." In truth, civilisation comes and goes in
cycles. There may be perfectibilities, however, attainable
within them, but limited aims are necessary to attain the
limited ideals that alone are practical.

Something similar is indicated by the German philosopher,
Oswald Spengler, in his famous *Decline of the West*, and other
works. With a wealth of detail, and examples drawn from
remote and ancient civilisations supplementing those of contemporary States, he demonstrates the inevitable processes
of rise, fruition, and decay, century after century, with
striking parallels between the culture and institutions characteristic of these phases as seen in various civilisations.
Western Europe he considers to be far on the cycle of decline.

The cyclic theory may be illustrated from English and

French history. After the rise of monarchy verging towards tyranny in the English State under Tudors and Stuarts— Hobbes's " Leviathan "—came the rise of the great Whig and Tory houses and their control of government (oligarchy), broadening slowly into democracy. In France, the definitely tyrannical rule of the monarchy and its systematic weakening of the aristocracy was followed, not by the natural intermediate sequence of aristocracy, but by a violent and painful arrival at virtual democracy almost immediately ; this because the fit few did not exist.

There are reasons for doubting the soundness of the cyclic analysis on the ground that modern States are, as Inge remarked, increasingly complex, hence different in kind from their predecessors. The increasingly detailed machinery of the modern State, like a vulnerable and long boundary in States of older date, calls for vigorous centralised control, for the emergence of a State with a creative purpose which assumes a vigorous initiative in the formation of new governmental devices. Newer inventions, such as wireless, fall increasingly quickly under State control, and contrast with the State's inertia over railway construction, or canals, where in the second example varieties of size of the most chaotic kind, in width, depth, height of bridges and size of locks, occurred for lack of the slightest governmental regulation. New inventions increasingly demand international collaboration, as again, in wireless and in aviation.

Spengler and his cyclic theory, in a word, may make successive rise and decline seem probable, but cannot effectively predict, since the conditions are changed and continue to change in ways which may check and divert tendencies.

The philosophy of Count Hermann Keyserling, like Spengler a philosopher only in vogue since the war, is embodied in his *Travel-Diary of a Philosopher*, *Europe*, and other works. Writing with far greater literary skill than Spengler, he advocates a heightening of the sense of human values and differentiations of types. He seeks to set up between the nations a comparison in values for humanity as a whole. " A nation can achieve significance for humanity only in certain respects ; namely, in those wherein its special aptitudes fit it to become the appointed organ for all humanity. . . . I examine the individual nations from the point of view of Europe as a whole." This he proceeds to do, finding in France the prototype of sexual love, in Switzerland the

culmination of the problem of the loss of values in an undis-
criminating democracy (ochlocracy), and so on. As between
classes he tends to think in terms of caste, with stress on the
aristocratic ideal and the forces of leadership.

Keyserling's influence has been and is profound ; from it
derives most of what is intellectually reputable in the Nazi
philosophy, which caricatures his leadership principle. As
the broader, more immediate and material problems of government gradually solve themselves, much more is bound to be
heard of the philosophy of type values as between human
beings. Possibly the study of the social merits and defects
of the workings of the Indian caste system may have more
to contribute to politics of the future than, as heirs to a
supposedly superior political heritage, we are at present
inclined to admit.

LIFE AS " DUTY, STRUGGLE, AND CONQUEST "

THE philosophy of Fascism is, again, auctoritarian. These
quotations are from the authorised translation of Mussolini's own statement of the philosophic basis of the movement
(*The Political and Social Doctrine of Fascism*, translated by
Jane Soames).

> " The Fascist conceives of life as duty and struggle
> and conquest . . . class-war is denied. . . . Fascism
> denies the validity of the equation, ' well-being equals
> happiness.' . . . Fascism affirms the immutable,
> beneficial, and fruitful inequality of mankind, which
> can never be levelled through the mere operation of
> a mechanical process such as universal suffrage. . . .
> Fascism supersedes the antithesis, monarchy, or re-
> publicanism . . . to-day it can be seen that there are
> republics innately reactionary . . . and monarchies
> which incorporate the most ardent social and political
> hopes of the future. . . . If democracy may be con-
> ceived in diverse forms . . . Fascism may write itself
> down as ' an organised, centralised, and authoritative
> democracy.' . . . The Liberal faith must shut the
> doors of its deserted temples ; this will be a century
> of authority. . . . When the conception of the State
> declines, and disunifying and centrifugal tendencies
> prevail . . . the nations . . . are in their decline.
> . . . The Fascist State has drawn into itself even the
> economic activities of the nation . . . its influence
> reaches every aspect of the national life and includes
> . . . all the political, economic, and spiritual forces of

the nation. . . . War alone brings up to its highest tension all human energy and puts the stamp of nobility upon the peoples who have the courage to meet it."

This will suffice as representative of a mass of similar utterances among the various European dictatorships, marking the return to Hegelianism. So far as Germany is concerned, the return is even less rational. " The Fuehrer's will is law " is the official pronouncement.

Of new political philosophies in practice two outstanding examples are not here dealt with. Neither the New Deal in the U.S.A. nor the Marxist philosophy as modified in the U.S.S.R. system lends itself to analysis in terms of political philosophy older than itself. In place of the mere democracies and autocracies shown by the world of pre-war days, we have now Communism, Constitutional Dictatorships, and Fascism in one or other form. For an authoritative group, energetically affecting events and educating its public by ceaseless propaganda to public ends, there is in fact no previous parallel ; especially when, as in Italy, there is a largely vestigial monarchy and a chamber elected by farcical means. In the U.S.A. we have the spectacle of virtual dictatorship set up without the destruction of any of the apparent constitution of the State ; a feat in which Americans may take considerably less pride when the precarious nature of President Roosevelt's tenure of power leads to the enfeeblement of his whole scheme, which evidently needs fifteen or twenty years' secure lease of power if any lasting change is to be made. This is not to be contemplated if Congress is to be left in its present turmoil of parties.

UNITY OR ISOLATION? OMENS FOR THE FUTURE

WHAT of the future ? We look outward and onwards from the Nation State. The States as entities are in closer contact with one another daily ; normally, interdependence would by this time have welded the world into an economic whole. Instead, the States are in a condition of attempted economic self-sufficiency in which an exacerbated sense of nationalism equates " buying foreign " with treachery to the patriotic cause, and considers giving more than it receives a mark of healthy national economy (" sound trade balance "). The peace treaties are largely responsible for this in Europe ; elsewhere, as with Japan, it is a case of mania for expansion.

If, in spite of this temporary obsession, nations are indeed moving towards larger entities, we may be sure of one thing ; that, just as the Nation State has proved to be neither the City State on a larger scale nor an aggregation of such States, so, owing to the entry of new factors unforeseeable now, a United States of Europe would not be a Nation State on a larger scale, nor would the example of the Federations of the U.S.A. or U.S.S.R. prove helpful guides. In one matter of machinery, however, the experience of the first might be useful. The whole lack of prestige of the League of Nations to-day lies in two fatal weaknesses : that it has an assembly of representatives of nations and not of peoples, and that unanimity is required before any substantial decision can be taken. In American federation, Congress is directly elected, traversing all local State elections—the States are represented in the Senate. And no unanimity is required.

Precursors of the League are of interest to recall. Dante dreamt of a World State governed by the Church. George of Podibrad, King of Bohemia, suggested a parliament of Christian kings and princes for all Europe. This Bohemian plan was reiterated by Sully in the time of Elizabeth ; he prepared a Great Design to set up a council of Europe to avoid the need of the cost of armaments. Penn, Bentham, and others toyed with the idea in later times. The first international conference took place in 1851 ; it was to fight the spread of infectious diseases. Eventually, in 1893, certain effective rules were agreed to for fighting cholera and plague. In 1874 came the Universal Postal Union. A long step forward was that to the formation of the Permanent Court of Arbitration at the Hague, 1899 ; the direct predecessor of Wilson's League set up by the Covenant attached to the Versailles Treaty.

IS THE PARLIAMENTARY SYSTEM TOO SLOW?

POSSIBLY it is true that, as orthodox Marxists hold, the State is a temporary thing, " destined to wither away." Figuratively, it may be called a lake, destined, like all lakes, to disappear, and to let its human water flow directly to the universal sea of the World State. In a world perfectly governed by a unitary organisation, interest might well sink away rom politics altogether, and rise—if it be considered rising—

to the political atmosphere of indifferentist pre-republican China. It would seem, however, that for a long time yet philosophic anarchy of the indifferentist type is likely to lead, not to a blessed non-political Eden, but, as in China, to the rule of the unscrupulous few. Endless vigilance on the part of the general public, especially with the proliferation of departments and the increased complexity of their ambits, is still the chief safeguard of political rights. These will need guardianship as much under a constructive Socialist régime as under any absolutist State.

G. D. H. Cole, in his *Theories and Forms of Political Organisation*, gives the following grounds for believing that old-fashioned party election methods are unsuited to the modern type of government : " States and governments are called upon to be more active and vigorous in the formation and pursuit of policies and plans of action ; and the careful checks and balances of the old parliamentary system are felt as a severe and sometimes crippling restraint on swift or decisive action." To change a system effectively, a government must have assured tenure ; and it is, the author thinks, impossible in any country to achieve Socialism through mere party means. " If Socialism is to come, I believe it will involve transitionally some form of dictatorship, and, when that is over, a system of administration far more closely resembling Sovietism than Parliamentarianism." The ways and means antecedent to this state of things are, Cole holds, unpredictable.

In this atmosphere there is evidently plenty of work for the citizen concerned for the maximum of toleration. " The case for toleration is founded in the last resort upon belief in human rationality " (C. E. M. Joad, *Liberty To-day*) ; and the history of the setting-up of dictatorships, whether of the proletariat or the absolutist group, does not encourage belief in the probability that reason will be the only motive appealed to.

On the other hand, " unless the supporters of liberty and democracy . . . can use the liberty which remains to them to offer a constructive policy to satisfy the aspirations of the generation now coming to maturity, they will succumb to the forces which have destroyed democracy on the Continent."

THE SOCIETY OF THE FUTURE : WHAT WILL IT BE LIKE?

POLITICAL Science is, like many other studies, in a state of transition. In the nineteenth century it was too greatly an affair of economic surroundings and personal viewpoint ; it waited upon events, and interpreted them through prejudice. Marx, who found himself in straitened circumstances, with a wife and large family, turned to the economic interpretation of history ; J. R. Green, nursed in liberalism, was capable of seeing in the British State just as it was the ideal of political organisation, with but a quibble here and there.

The science has been an affair of analysis of the legal order plus a certain infusion of psychology. The first merely tends to a theoretic justification of the *status quo ante* ; it takes the sources of reference of that power and compares with social facts. The sources of rights, however, provide no criteria of themselves. For instance, the basis of British law is the fiction of legal equality, defended and expounded by the older political scientists. An unbiased and new study would query this, and ask whether in fact prosecution and defence were on a plane of equity. The psychological basis of the science is, as before indicated, inadequate. Wallas merely indicates that co-operation, love, and thinking are desirable things ; McDougall inclines to think that human beings are more efficient if organised, but has little to suggest in detail ; Rivers, with his anthropological outlook, emphasises the need to recognise and satisfy primitive traits, but the fitting of these into the modern cultural environment is a questionable enterprise which seems the more impractical the more we learn of the extraordinary social traits of the untutored savages.

The older science, then, has been in effect the interpretation of material necessarily historical in terms of law and psychology. Newer political studies may take at once more practical and less ambitious forms, and question the actual administration, how it operates, its adjustment of means to ends. Political science will question the effectiveness of Factory Acts without a sufficient inspectorate ; ask if the device of a war cabinet in the war years was efficient for its purposes ; more generally, query the modern revival of " natural rights " and establish at what level, given a certain average income in society, they should be satisfied. On the question of scale, it will perhaps decide that the idealisation of the vote is inappropriate in States over a certain size ; that in the great modern State a Common Will is really impossible of attainment in any real sense, and, if ascertainable, impracticable ; that, in consequence, administration must needs fall to a class apart, since those who like public life form in fact a small minority and the majority finds satisfaction in private ways ; that therefore a main problem for the future is to make the varied actions of this detailed administration, which is too complex for public under-standing, correspond with the multiple popular will on various subjects at which it now makes a vague guess.

If liberty is still taken to mean a lack of restriction on the individual, it is completely dead, since the State everywhere interferes. But if it means the fruitful interaction of State and personal functions, on a plane of economic equality, it can be secured once that plane is secured. Looking at the world as a whole, economic factors press towards a unity ultimately political ; when that is achieved, political science will have a fresh scope in inquiring into the appropriate size of its units, since national status will then surely be found a cumbersome burden.

The future probably rests with some form of stratified democracy on caste lines, not with the undifferentiated egalitarian democracy of Bentham. Our democratic general-isations are found to be untrue both of the Far East and in the Far West ; Africa is a museum of governmental methods other than our own.

Political science, in short, will tend to be less general, more quantitative and qualitative. It will determine the size of committees in the light of their purpose ; it will question the means of choice of judges and bishops. Facts are not democratic and equal, but form hierarchies that need measure-ment. Teleology, the questioning of means in terms of ends, is the chief instrument in the laboratory of Political Science.

SOME BOOKS ON POLITICAL SCIENCE

IT is to be feared that there is no one short general book for the ordinary reader which gives theories and facts in Political Science in any adequate proportion. C. E. M. Joad's *Introduction to Modern Political Theory* (Oxford University Press) is perhaps the best ; some may prefer Professor H. J. Laski's *Introduction to Politics* (Allen and Unwin), or his *On the Study of Politics* (Milford)—both brief introductory essays. Attractive books in dialogue form, wherein some of the principles of Political Science are debated, are *A Modern Symposium* and *After Two Thousand Years* (both

Allen and Unwin), by G. Lowes Dickenson—the latter a dialogue with Plato.

Among the more solid books of text-book type, Professor Laski's *Grammar of Politics* (Allen and Unwin) is outstanding ; Professor Leacock's *Elements of Political Science* (Constable) and Sidgwick's *Elements of Politics* (Macmillan) are somewhat dated. Of books giving brief treatments of the main political theorists, the best are those by W. A. Dunning, whose various books on political theories range from ancient to recent times. Professor Ernest Barker's *Political Thought in England, 1848–1914*, revised 1928, and Professor Laski's *Political Thought from Locke to Bentham* (both Home University Library, Thornton Butterworth Limited) cover that phase of political thought admirably.

Those who wish to trace the growth of British political institutions will find A. B. White's *The Making of the English Constitution* clear and not too full on the medieval period, while J. A. R. Marriott's *English Political Institutions* (Clarendon Press) is excellent and brief on the modern side. An excellent, though not quite up to date, survey of governments is F. A. Ogg's *Governments of Europe* (Macmillan). The only entirely up-to-date volume on that matter is necessarily the current *Statesman's Year-Book*.

On particular aspects of Political Science, J. L. Dickenson's *Justice and Liberty* (J. M. Dent) and *The Meaning of Good* can be recommended as clear and interesting ; while his *Greek View of Life* (Methuen) gives the background against which it is necessary to set Greek philosophy to understand it. Professor Laski's *Dangers of Obedience* (Harper) is a stimulating study in civics, while his *Sovereignty* and *Authority in the Modern State* attack squarely the great problem of the location of governmental function in the complex twentieth-century Nation State. The same author's *Democracy in Crisis* (Allen and Unwin) sounds an impressive call to activity to all citizens of goodwill ; and Lord Hewart's *The New Despotism* attacks that growth of bureaucracy which needs watching so carefully under modern conditions. An excellent brief list of the more outstanding texts of Political Science will be found at the end of Professor Laski's *Introduction to Politics* (Allen and Unwin) ; C. E. M. Joad's *Liberty To-day* (Watts) is a restatement in the light of modern conditions of the fundamental principles of liberty and democracy.

THE NATURE OF REALITY :
PHILOSOPHY'S PROBLEM

*by R. C. ROWSE, M.A., Warden of Percival
Guildhouse, Rugby*

MANY people are apt to be rather impressed by a Philosopher. When they see him decked out in his robes and hear him uttering dignified speeches they think that here is some rare creature that is not as mortals are. They forget that Philosophy says what everyone knows in language that no one can understand, as Prof. Muirhead has confessed. After all, the Philosopher is an ordinary man, dealing with ordinary things. That is the point of the first half of Prof. Muirhead's statement. The Philosopher is a very ordinary man, only more so, as an Irishman might remark. The " more so " is the point of the latter half of the Professor's cryptic remark, and we shall now proceed to explain it.

Philosophy is based on a fact, and is one method of response to that fact. The fact is that here we are, conscious, sentient, active human beings in the midst of a vast number of events which we call the world. A stone may be in a very similar environment, but, so far as we know, is not troubled by it. For it is not conscious, and this consciousness, which we as human beings all possess, is a necessary condition of there being any Philosophy. We react to our environment in a way which inert matter does not.

There are a number of ways of reacting ; we may do so practically, which is probably the most common way. If we were to find ourselves in a cart behind a runaway horse the most usual response to the situation would be to try and get out of the cart as safely as possible, perhaps by stopping the horse first. But this practical response is not the only possible one. An artist in the cart might be entranced by the beautiful act of the horse with flying mane and tail and sit back and admire. A philosopher might meditate upon the brevity of human life, how easily brought to an end by accident, and might even start a long train of thought about the place of Necessity and Contingency in human life. The example, of course, is exaggerated for the purpose of illustration. But it suggests two important points. Imagine a person not in a runaway cart, but on the threshold of life and a career. There are three main ways in which one can meet the challenge of events.

THE THREE SIGN-BOARDS AT LIFE'S STARTING-POINT

(1) One may say that life is a practical affair, here we are faced with life and we must do something about it. A man must live, so he sets out on a career of practical activity. This man is the worker or the business man.

(2) A man may be impressed with the beauty of the world. As the poet sang:

> *The world is so full of a number of things,*
> *I am sure we should all be as happy as kings.*[1]

There are beautiful pictures to be seen, beautiful symphonies to hear, Nature herself, if you are lucky enough to live near her, is full of beautiful sights and sounds. Such a man enjoys all the feelings that beauty in whatever shape or form can stir up in him. He is the artist, the poet, the man of sensibility.

(3) Finally, a man on the threshold of life may not wish to plunge into it straight away in a busy round of activities, nor give himself up to the contemplation of the beauty in the world, but he may wish to sit back and survey it, think about it, ponder deeply over its significance. This man is the Philosopher, whose approach to Reality (or to the World) is intellectual.

Our first man did, our second felt, our third thinks. These are three ways of reacting to our environment, all of which are to be found in experience. However, as our example of the runaway horse and cart would suggest, we should not find anybody who embodied these three types in their purity. An artist would not merely admire the situation, nor a philosopher reflect upon it : if they had any sense they would *do* something to avert the catastrophe as well.

None of us is really entirely concerned with one of these three main ways of accepting the universe to the exclusion of the other two : we say we are one or the other in so far as one of these predominates in our attitude of mind.

We have said that Philosophy is an intellectual method of

[1] R. L. Stevenson.

dealing with Reality, or the World. But it is not the only intellectual method. Our ordinary everyday knowledge, the knowledge of common sense, is another. And so in the scientific approach. So in order the better to understand what Philosophy is, we must differentiate it from these two.

THE TANGLED SKEIN OF OUR BELIEFS

THE Common Knowledge of the ordinary man possesses the following three characteristics :

(1) In the first place, it usually has some practical bearing. We may know that the sun is between $91\frac{1}{2}$ and $94\frac{1}{2}$ million miles from the earth, which seems to have no immediate practical application, but such items of information are sporadic and most of our knowledge is closely connected with our practice, *e.g.* we may know much more about gardening, motor-cars, and even our neighbours.

(2) In the second place, it is often self-contradictory. It is a commonplace that the beliefs we confess on Sunday are inconsistent with those confessed on Monday. Our religious beliefs, just because they deal with ultimate and fundamental matters, are usually full of inconsistencies. We pray to a God whom we acknowledge to be omniscient (*i.e.* all-knowing), kind, and omnipotent (all-powerful), informing Him of the state of the world or of our souls, and telling Him what to do about it. The rich heritage of our proverbs can be divided into contradictory pairs, *e.g. Look before you leap ; Nothing venture, nothing win ; Penny wise, pound foolish ; Take care of the pence, the pounds will take care of themselves,* etc. It needs very little observation to catch ourselves or others in some contradiction.

(3) The third characteristic of our everyday knowledge is that it is extremely ill-founded. We can give no reason for many of our most firmly-held beliefs beyond the statement that " it must be so," which very little reflection will show to be no reason at all. We are members of a Christian Church because our parents were, but we should find it very difficult to prove that Christianity is an ethically superior religion. Our politics we take in the same manner. The common stock of our everyday knowledge has its roots in the same soil as that from which we derive our language, our food, and our other habits, namely, our environment. In

youth our reaction to knowledge is to accept it, and we find it difficult to lose the habit even with training, witness the belief in anything " in print." This belief in authority is a part cause of the contradictions in our knowledge, for we can easily believe two contradictory authorities if we do not bring them together.

These three characteristics of our everyday knowledge make many of the more thinking members of society dissatisfied with it. Instead of being content with our haphazard hit-and-miss knowledge they approach the subject scientifically.

SCIENCE'S ARDUOUS QUEST

THE outstanding characteristics of Science are dealt with in the section entitled *What we know about the World : The Problem of Science.* For present purposes, it will suffice to say that the chief characteristics of the scientific approach are : Science assumes the existence of a consistent outside universe, and that the observer's ego, though not necessarily reasonable, is consistent from one set of observations to another. The scientist would say, for example : " It seems to be, as a result of my observations, that A and B cause C. And, if I assume that my reasoning is true and this proposition has a relation to the reality of the phenomena, it enables me to predict that C and D will cause E. This prediction can be verified by experiment with the same degree of certainty as that with which I measured the reaction of $A + B = C$. On these grounds I begin to believe that my observations of phenomena have at least some contact with the nature of the phenomena themselves." Warily though he must tread, the scientist yet assumes that by experiment, observations, and hard thinking man can discover the nature of the universe.

WHAT PHILOSOPHY IS

WE have now examined the main characteristics of the common-sense and scientific method of dealing with Reality, or the World. It remains to point out the distinguishing features of the philosophic approach. This, too, is an intellectual apprehension of Reality. Unlike common sense, it is not practical. Nor are its conclusions so immediately capable of being applied as are those of Science. It is an attempt to understand simply for the sake of understanding. For instance, it does not make much difference to our ordinary life whether the whole world is an idea in the mind of God or a self-subsisting reality. We may hold with Bishop Berkeley that there is no such thing as matter in the ordinary sense of the word, and that everything that exists is an idea. But brick walls will still be hard, food nourishing, etc. No sane philosopher wishes to deny these facts ; he merely tries to understand them. It is failure to realise this that makes some people assert that Philosophy is a useless study. The study of Philosophy need be of no use at all, except in understanding.

Secondly, Philosophy is like Science in that it is systematic and attempts to remove by reason the contradictions and inconsistencies that experience provides. It is becoming the fashion now to glory in inconsistency, and to consider consistency as petty or a sign of unconscious dishonesty. But this is mere defeatism. We are so constituted that we cannot rest content when faced by a contradiction, and this element in our constitution is the source of Philosophy. It is true that consistency may be achieved by excluding inharmonious elements, and it is this sort of consistency that is rightly deplored to-day. But it does not therefore follow that no other consistency is possible and that the inharmonious elements cannot be synthetised, or brought together, in a wider whole.

But Philosophy carries this process of systematisation even farther. The sciences limit themselves to a definite set of facts, *e.g.* physics deals with certain properties of matter and energy. In this sense they are abstract. In this sense Philosophy is concrete. It attempts to see things steadily, and see them whole. Accepting the deliverances of the special sciences, it attempts to synthesise them and see what light this throws upon Reality. Where Science splits up its problems in order to understand, Philosophy puts them together again.[1] Both processes are necessary.

PHILOSOPHY AS "THE SPECTATOR OF ALL TIME AND EXISTENCE"

THE concreteness of Philosophy is to be contrasted with the abstractness of Science in another way. Not only does Philosophy attempt to look at Reality as a whole, to be " the spectator of all time and existence " in Plato's phrase,

[1] Cf. Herbert Spencer, *First Principles*, chapter entitled " Philosophy Defined," for an exaggerated example of this.

but it attempts to view even the particular things of experience in their completeness. For instance, chemistry can tell us a lot about John Smith, and so can biology and psychology. But John Smith is more than an organism, or even than a psychological subject. Each special science abstracts its special interest from John Smith. Philosophy builds him together again. But John is more than a compilation of the deliverances of these sciences; he is more than his medical certificate and intelligence quotient. He is a human being with hopes and fears, loves and hates. It is here that a new topic enters the realm of Philosophy—the topic of values. Science recognises only one value, namely Truth, and takes no notice of others. That is why vivisection is perfectly justifiable from a scientific point of view. But the question remains whether the scientific point of view is ultimate. Facts for the scientist are neither good nor bad, beautiful nor ugly; they are just facts. But the philosopher has to consider values, for he could never claim to see things whole if he left them out.

The scope of Philosophy should now be clear. Its scope is the whole world of experience. Philosophy is not so much a special subject with its own subject-matter as a special way of looking at the common subject-matter of everyday experience. In this sense it says what everyone knows. It is an exaggeration to say that it does so in language which no one can understand. The truth that this suggests is that it speaks in a language unfamiliar to the untrained mind because (1) it is more precise and more systematic; (2) it deals with common problems in an ultimate and more fundamental manner. This analysis of the nature of Philosophy will give us our scheme for the rest of the outline.

One of the main divisions of philosophy is the inquiry into the nature of knowledge—called *epistemology*. Arising out of this is the inquiry into the certainty of knowledge, *i.e.* the question of *Truth* and *Error*. These two points are concerned with the fundamental assumption of Science and common sense, the faith in Reason and Knowledge. We next pass on to an inquiry into the categorical notions. These are (1) The nature of *Causality*. (2) The Concept of *Matter*, and (3) its correlative, the Concept of *Mind*. (4) The notions of *Space* and *Time*.

Finally, some attention must be given to values. (1) *Moral.* (2) *Æsthetic.* (3) *Intellectual*—Truth and Error.

The *Naturalist,* 1	*Physicus,* 1

Vieweth all the works of God in the World.

Speculatur omnia Dei Opera in Mundo.

The *Supernaturalist,* 2

Metaphysicus, 2

Searches out the *Causes* and *Effects* of things.

Perscrutatur *Causas,* & rerum *Effecta.*

The *Arithmetician*

Arithmeticus

Reckoneth *numbers,* by adding, subtracting, multiplying, and dividing ; and that either by *Cyphers,*
   3. on a *Slate,*
   or by *Counters,* 4.
   upon a *Desk.*
Country people reckon, 5.
With *figures of tens,* X.

Computat *numeros,* addendo, subtrahendo, multiplicando, dividendo : idque **vel** *Cyphris,* 3
   in *Palimocesto,*
   vel *Calculis,* 4.
   super *Abacum.*
Rustici numerant, 5.
Decussibus, X.

AN ILLUSTRATION FOR PHILOSOPHY OUT OF AN OLD PICTURE LESSON BOOK

THE LANGUAGE PHILOSOPHERS USE

PERHAPS it would be opportune at this point to explain a few technical terms. Philosophy is a general term which stands for the sort of studies outlined in this section. It is of the same order of terms as Science, and has its subdivisions. These are Metaphysics, Moral Philosophy, and Æsthetics. Metaphysics is a term which is often used loosely, and is sometimes employed as a synonym for Philosophy itself. The name gives no indication of the nature of the subject, for it really means " after the Physics," and is so called because the book in which Aristotle dealt with ultimate questions was placed by early editors of his works after the Physics. Metaphysics is the general inquiry into ultimate problems. It is subdivided according to these problems. The term *Ontology* (theory of Being) denotes inquiries into the nature of Reality, and *Cosmology* is very similar, being the inquiry into the nature of the Universe. *Epistemology* (Greek *epistēmē* means knowledge) is the theory of knowledge, and again is a subdivision of Metaphysics.

The content of these particular studies must be gathered from what follows ; here it will suffice to have indicated their relation to each other.

DIGGING FOR THE ROOTS OF KNOWLEDGE

THE need for a Philosophy, we have said, arises from the necessity of resolving the many contradictions which beset us in experience. It is an implicit presupposition of the human mind, not only of metaphysics, that Reality is not self-contradictory. The proof of this presupposition is a *reductio ad absurdum*. If two contradictory statements could be made with equal truth about one and the same thing at the same time and in the same respect, then, of course, these statements could mean nothing. A thing would be no more what it is than what it is not, and so knowledge would be impossible. But in order to say that knowledge is impossible one must have knowledge of at least one fact, namely, that knowledge is impossible. And this is absurd. Therefore our hypothesis must have been absurd. Therefore its contradictory must be true. This contradictory is that Reality is not self-contradictory.

Now if Reality is not self-contradictory there is something very like it that is self-contradictory. This we may call appearance. Things, indeed, are not what they seem. A straight stick half-immersed in water looks bent; railway lines appear to converge in the distance; colours, and even shapes, change with varying lights and perspectives. Yet we believe that the stick remains straight, we hope the railway lines remain parallel, and we believe that light and distance make no difference to the table in reality. It is only the appearance of the things that has altered, and it has altered owing, we believe, to some change in the relations between the object perceived and the conscious subject that perceives it.

A consideration of these and many other common instances of illusion must, I think, lead us to the inescapable conclusion that consciousness plays an important part in our knowledge of the qualities of things. By this I mean not only the obvious assertion that were we not conscious we should not know anything, but the less commonly realised assertion that were our powers of perception different the things we perceived would be different—in short, that consciousness is not merely a passive mirroring of Reality but it is constitutive of Reality. What Reality is depends at least partly upon what we are.

But we must not go too quickly. While no one could deny that the state of the conscious subject must affect the manner in which Reality *appears* to him, it goes against common sense to maintain that it affects Reality as it is. We believe, with Bishop Butler, that " everything is what it is, and not another thing." A colour-blind man may see everything as grey, but that does not make everything grey. The real question in dispute is not whether perceiving affects appearance—we all know it does that—but whether it affects Reality.

APPEARANCE AND REALITY

EVERY one of us knows this distinction. But few have ever troubled themselves to ask, *How can we distinguish between the thing as it appears and the thing as it really is ?* The asking of this question is a sign of philosophical interest, and the attempt to answer it leads straight to the heart of philosophy. This is just another illustration of the fact that philosophy lies not far from everyday human experience.

Let us take the example of the straight stick half immersed in water. It appears bent. We say it appears bent, not it is bent, and if we ask why, we may give various reasons, *e.g.*

it is absurd to suppose that it bends straight every time it is put in and taken out of water ; or we know from other experiments that light rays are bent when passed through water. All our reasons come in the end to this, that for all practical purposes we must consider the stick to be straight, otherwise it would not do what it does. The only purpose for which we need to consider it as bent is for perception, *e.g.* if we were drawing a straight stick in water we should draw it as bending at the surface of the water. But we know in many cases that we do not see things as they are, and so are ready to discredit the evidence of perception.

The chief difficulty that meets someone trying to draw still life is to draw it as it appears, not as it is. We often find that children try to draw a horse with four complete legs because they know that a horse should have four complete legs if it is to perform its function properly. Or they draw the side view of a face showing both eyes, because most faces have two eyes. They do not realise that one does not see four complete legs on a horse or two eyes in a profile view. Even adults have difficulty in drawing a square-topped table, just because it does not appear square. If any reader still thinks that things are what they seem, let him try to draw things as they are, and he will see that they will not then appear to be what they are, and if he wants them to look real he must pay great attention to accurate observation, i.e. to draw them as they appear.

It must by now be obvious that things are not what they seem to the eye, that seeing is not believing, and a similar case can be made for things not being as they appear to any of the five senses. Thus we are led to say that sense perception can give us no knowledge of things as they really are, *i.e.* of Reality.

If we hastily adopt this position we are indeed in a difficulty, for whence can we get any knowledge except from the senses ? Reason and understanding can give us no material of knowledge : they can work upon the facts given by the senses, but without this material they can do nothing. You cannot really think about nothing without making it something. The abstract reasoning of the quantum theory which seems unrelated to sense perception could not ever have made a start without data given by the senses. The British Empiricists [1] and Kant were right when they said, " All knowledge

[1] See page 422 *et seq.*

begins with experience," and by experience they meant sense-experience.

FITTING IN WITH ALL THE FACTS OF EXPERIENCE

Now we have arrived at the position that the knowledge given by the senses is knowledge of appearances only, and yet any knowledge of Reality must arise from the senses. It is clear that reality and appearance must be closely connected, that reality is derived from appearance. It must be quite clear, however, that we must give up the view that Appearance is reality, that things are what they seem. This is the view of naïve Realism, and for it there is no justification.

The question now arises, " What is the relation between Appearance and Reality ? " If the table which we see, a rhomboid sort of figure, is square in spite of its appearance, what do we mean by saying that it really is square ? We cannot mean that it would be square if it existed in a world in which no-one knew of it, because (a) if no-one knew of it no-one would know what it was like, and (b) in any case we mean that it is square even when it appears in perspective. We really mean that to regard it as square best fits in with the rest of our knowledge. We know that if we measure it we shall find that it has the characteristics of a square ; that if we want to find the area of its surface we should treat it as a square ; we know that we could not put it into a round hole, etc. etc. In fact, we call it a square table because, for all theoretical and practical needs, that description best accords with our other knowledge. We find as our knowledge grows greater that even the perspectives of the table are due to its being square. In fact, when we say it is *really* square we mean that such a description fits in with all the rest of our knowledge, and to say it was anything else would make knowledge a chaos. The test is a simple one, to which in recent years we have become accustomed ; it is the test of a crossword puzzle. In a good crossword puzzle every letter is what it is because every other letter is what it is. So in our experience the real nature of anything is that nature which enables it to fill satisfactorily any need of the intellect that it is called upon to fill.

There are some interesting points about this view of reality which should be noticed. In the first place, when we say that a thing is real we do not mean that we can see, feel, or touch it. We sometimes think that a ghost is unreal because we cannot touch it, and a lamp-post is real because we can touch it. We see now that a ghost is unreal because it will not fit in with our ideas about the nature of the world. If it does fit in with someone's view of the world, it is real to that person. If you ask, " But is it ultimately real ? " you can only find the answer by getting an ultimate view of the world.

In the second place, it must be more clear that Reality is what it is because we are what we are. In a sense we make a thing real, in so far as nothing can be real unless it is a part of somebody's world. It would be misleading to say that we each make our own world, because we must make it according to the material supplied to us by experience, and we have little control over this. But it would be equally misleading to maintain that anything can be real by itself. A thing is what it is only in relation to other things, and to perceive this relation a conscious mind is required.

THE PROBLEM OF TRUTH AND ERROR

THE foregoing inquiry into the nature of our knowledge is only half complete. It attempts to explain and estimate the various factors involved in knowledge, or awareness. But so far it has not made any pretensions to discriminate between true knowledge and error or mistake. It should be noticed that this sense of the word Truth is slightly different from that most commonly employed in everyday life. By Truth we usually mean telling the truth, *i.e.* not saying that things are otherwise than we know them to be. But this is obviously a secondary notion : before we can " tell the truth " in this sense we must " know the truth " in the epistemological sense, i.e. know how things are. This is why Plato can make the arresting statement that it is worse for a man to tell a lie unwittingly, i.e. to make a mistake, than to do so intentionally. It is worse from the epistemological point of view, though not from the moral.

Theories of Truth are, of course, closely allied to theories of Knowledge. Thus it is obvious what Truth is for the believer in the theory of Representative Perception. This theory maintains that we gain our knowledge of the world through what are called " ideas." For instance, when one sees the Queen's Hall what really happens is that the Queen's Hall makes an impression on the mind and through this the Hall is known. This impression is called an "idea." On this view that we are not in direct touch with things, but that we know them only through the ideas we have of them, it is clear that our knowledge is true if the ideas faith-fully represent the objects they purport to represent. But this is open to all the objections to which Representative Perception is open, *e.g.* how do we know what Reality is like, except through our ideas ? We cannot compare two things unless we can know them both. Alternatively, if we do know both the Reality and our ideas, is not a mistake rather a question for the moralist than the metaphysician, for nothing short of gross carelessness or wanton deception could enable us to harbour a false view.

I am afraid this is "a short way" with believers in the Correspondence Theory. They often make the defence that this criticism misses the point. We must distinguish, they say, between questions of the *nature* of Truth, and of the *test* of Truth. It is the nature of Truth to be the correspondence of our knowledge with the facts, for this is what we mean by Truth. But for the reasons given, this cannot be used as a test for Truth, for which we may have to refer to the Coherence Theory. The above criticism they accept, but it applies only as against a test of Truth. But its nature remains un-assailed, and they call the whole populace to witness that what people mean by Truth is correspondence with fact. But to me this merely seems to place the issue a stage further back. How does one know what is and what is not a fact ? Did not the early Fathers call divine authority to their aid to maintain the "fact" that the sun went round the earth ? It is not so simple as it seems to discover fact. And when you have discovered it, you have discovered Truth. The error of the Correspondence Theory of Truth is just that it fails to realise the unity of Truth and Fact. It sets up a dualism in Reality and presupposes a certain metaphysical priority on the part of the world of objects. The real answer to these assumptions must come later when our own view of Truth is expounded.

"I THINK, THEREFORE I AM"

MANY Realists have taken up a Correspondence Theory of Truth. But there are other theories possible for one of that persuasion. Descartes (1596–1650) set out on his philosophical pilgrimage with a serious attempt to find some indubitable fact, upon which as a basis he would build up by reasoning as incontrovertible as that of mathematics a system of judgments. Then if his starting-point were true, and his reasoning correct, his conclusions would necessarily be true. The only judgment he could find as a basis was, *I think, therefore I am*, and from this he was able to rebuild the whole world. Unfortunately his starting-point was not unambiguous nor were the successive steps in his reasoning quite as conclusive as he might have wished. What was the " I " that thought ? Here the whole question of personal identity is raised, which cannot be solved merely by the dogmatic statement that one cannot doubt it. People have done so. Self-evidence, in the sense of a statement carrying its meaning on its face, is not a test of Truth.

For a naïve Realist, one who believes that Reality is directly present to mind and that consciousness of a fact makes no difference to the fact, there seems no course possible except to deny error. How can one be mistaken if reality reveals itself directly to us ? Realism breaks down when faced with error and illusion.

Another theory of Truth which has gained some hold in America is the Pragmatic Theory. William James was its leading exponent, and now Prof. Dewey has taken it up and improved upon it. In this country Pragmatism has been chiefly associated with the Humanism of Dr. F. C. S. Schiller, and it is now receiving a wide but unsystematic expression in the wave of modern Humanism. Humanism is so called because it attempts to make all standards relative to man. What is true enough for human needs is all the truth there is. Thus, if it is accurate enough for all practical purposes to consider the circumference of a circle as three and one-seventh times the diameter, then the circumference *is* three and one-seventh times the diameter, in spite of all the mathematicians who would work it out further. Humanism goes further than mere contradiction of the Sabbatarian fallacy, namely, that the Sabbath was made for man and not man for the Sabbath. It says that everything was made for man. As Protagoras said two thousand three hundred years ago, " Man is the measure of all things." The general idea of Pragmatism is that what makes anything true is not conformity to an objective world, but fitness to meet a subjective need. Thus Wm. James, in the *Meaning of Truth*, pp. 51-2, says, " If it can make no practical difference which of two statements be true, they are really one statement in two verbal forms. If it can make no practical difference whether a given statement be true or false then the statement has no real meaning. In neither case is there anything to quarrel about." This is extremely vague, but is usually interpreted as meaning that a belief is true if it works. Prof. Dewey says, " The true means the verified, and means nothing else " (*Reconstruction in Phil.*, p. 160), and by " verified " he means verified by experience, *i.e.* that which works.

This view certainly does not overlook the part played by the conscious subject in the obtaining of knowledge. But does it not invert the order of connection between Truth and expediency ? Is it not the case that a thing " works " because it is true, and not that it is true because it works ? Truth appears to be the logically prior characteristic. Then, in the second place, what does the word " works " mean in the case of Truth ? Does it mean that a judgment is true if it satisfies some need—a need of some practical or theoretical situation ? Does it mean that if we find as a matter of fact that to believe that $2 \times 2 = 4$ always works, *i.e.* satisfies the requirements of the situation, then $2 \times 2 = 4$ is true ? The answer to this would be that there have been times in my accounting when I have wished that $2 \times 2 = 6$, and that judgment would have worked, while $2 \times 2 = 4$ will not. But I have not been allowed to incorporate this judgment, even though it would have worked, because it was not true. The pragmatist's answer to this would be that such a solution would not work ultimately.

If it be said that $2 \times 2 = 6$ is false because it does not satisfy the theoretical requirements of the situation, we are nearer a true account of the business, but this hardly appears to be Pragmatic.

"WHERE IS WISDOM TO BE FOUND ?"

THE criterion of fitness to meet a theoretical need seems rather to point to Coherence as the criterion of Truth. This has at least the great advantage of not demanding a dualistic view of the universe, for dualism, we have seen, seems to raise insuperable difficulties. The Coherence Theory can find Truth in the interrelation of judgments, without appeal to external objects. This is an advantage, for when we come to think of what we know, we find we are limited to judgments, and we know nothing which is not a judgment, however rudimentary. (I am speaking now of cognitive experience, *i.e.* experience of the mind, not of the emotions).

The Correspondence Theory considered Truth to consist in a correspondence between judgments and reality. But the Coherence Theory finds it to consist in a quality of judgments which we may call their adequacy to express Reality. To the ordinary mind no distinction is intended by the difference in formulæ. But we can accept the latter, though not the former.

This implies that judgments can express Reality with varying degrees of accuracy, and very little reflection is required to show that this is so. With greater experience and knowledge comes a fuller understanding of what is apprehended. Anyone who has learned a foreign language will realise this. The first words have to be learned parrot-fashion, taken on trust, and there seems to be no rhyme or reason in them. But as one progresses, word-forms reappear in different contexts and combinations, and one begins to *understand* what one formerly learned by heart. These first words now have a new significance ; by seeing the various uses made of them we get a new idea of them.

The learning of languages is a good example of this, but the same principle holds good of any systematic knowledge, and what knowledge is not systematic ? It is true of geometry. At first the axioms are taken on trust, but as one advances in the study one sees how they are not merely arbitrary, but are necessary to the rest of the system. The student of co-ordinate geometry gets a fuller revelation of how all things fit together and explain each other. And it is to be hoped that as the reader progresses in this book he will see how later parts throw light on earlier ones. In the end it is not difficult to see how the simple judgment $3 \times 3 = 9$ expresses more to the Professor of Mathematics than to the child learning his " three-times." To the one it is a symbol of the whole numerical system, and he sees why 3×3 must equal 9 ; to the other it is a fact to be learned by heart and cannot be arrived at by reasoning. Surely it means more to the Professor ; it expresses Reality more adequately.

THE WILL-O'-THE-WISP OF CERTAINTY

IF it be true, as it seems to be, that new knowledge increases the significance of what we already know, *e.g.* that our knowledge of the movements of the heavenly bodies affects our knowledge of the tides at Southampton, then it must be true that the more complete our knowledge becomes, the more adequately does it express each part in the system. For, indeed, what is the meaning of anything but its position in its system ? When asked to explain anything, we explain its relations to things we already know, and say nothing about the thing itself, e.g. if you do not know what an Ibis is and go to the *Concise Oxford Dictionary* to find out you will read : IBIS—" stork-like bird found in lakes and swamps of warm climates." That is, the bird is like a stork, but it is not a stork. It is found in certain places, but it is not these places. The description of an ibis does not tell you what the bird is but tells you its relation to other things you know—in this case, other birds and countries. It is obvious that this is all we can do in description and explanation. This means that in order to know what anything is you must know what a lot of other things are. You could not explain *anything* to a man who knew *nothing* ; you would have nothing to explain it by. If this is true at least part of the Coherence Theory is true, namely, that our knowledge of anything depends upon our knowledge of other things. By carrying out this process of explanation further you will see that in the end we should need to know everything in order to explain anything completely. Thus the conclusion is that he who would attain to complete Truth would need to be, as Plato said, the spectator of all time and existence.

This is a result which has led many to turn away from Coherence in disgust. They set out to look for Truth and find it for ever eluding their grasp. This, however, is not the fault of the Theory, but of the Reality. We must admit that all our judgments are fallible, and that what we consider to be most certain results of long ages of thought may after all be either mistaken or require re-interpretation. He would be a bold man who would deny this, as well as a bad philosopher. In such a predicament, though it may be disappointing to discover that we may still be lying in heathen darkness, it is infinitely better to recognise it than to turn to the worship of false gods merely to pursue the *ignis fatuus* of certainty. Rather, we believe that we have a certain amount of Truth and that by our efforts we may gain more. The only corrective of thought is more thinking, ever wider and more comprehensive. And this, it would appear, besides satisfying the Coherence Theory, is in fact the way in which philosophers go about to show each other the truth or error of their ways. By their *practice* ye shall know them.

It would be unfair to make up our minds on this point until we have given it much more attention. And fortunately it is not my business to give solutions to the problems of Philosophy. I shall be quite satisfied if I have brought them clearly before the reader.

We must now turn to the question of Causation—that the same cause always produced the same effect. It is clear that Causation, and not Causality alone, is a necessary postulate of Science. But no scientist, as scientist, ever attempts to justify this principle upon which the whole of his magnificent superstructure is built. This is what we mean when we say that the problems of Philosophy are more ultimate than those of Science.

When we look for proofs of Causation again we find a singular dearth of satisfactory ones. It is equally impossible to prove it from experience as it is to prove the principle of Causality. It is even more doubtful whether it is a category of the understanding in Kant's sense, for the categories are *a priori*, *i.e.* free from any content derived from experience. But to say that the same cause always has the *same* effect implies a definite sense content which must come from experience.

Nor can the principle be proved from the Uniformity of Nature, for it is only another formulation of that principle, and the question remains, on what does the principle of the Uniformity of Nature depend ? But though it cannot be proved, this principle that the same cause always has the same effect seems to be an assumption which it is necessary to make in order for knowledge to be possible. We cannot yet say that it is altogether justified in experience—Sir James Jeans seems to have been able to consider its opposite true—but so far it has been justified. What will emerge in the future progress of knowledge we know not, and dare not speculate too far.

THE UNIVERSE AS A COMPLETE WHOLE

THE third question, What do we mean by Cause ? is as difficult to answer as the two preceding ones. Someone pulls the trigger of a gun, and it goes off. We say the cause of the firing of the gun was the pulling of the trigger. But was it ? Triggers have been pulled many a time without any firing. It was also necessary that the gun should be loaded. And even that is not quite sufficient. The powder must be dry, there must be oxygen in the atmosphere, and there are numerous other conditions which require to be satisfied before we get the desired effect. And each of these conditions depends upon other conditions, e.g. the amount of oxygen in the air in the last resort depends upon the whole series of facts investigated by physics, chemistry, meteorology, etc. etc.

In short, to the production of the smallest report of the tiniest toy pistol there has gone the co-operation of all the detail of the entire universe immediately preceding the effect. Nay, more, since it is true that the present would not be what it is if the past had not been what it was, it is true that the past would not have been what it was were not the present what it is, *i.e.* there is a relation of reciprocity between past and present. Therefore the present state of the Universe is not altogether independent of the future, and to the cause of the firing of our little pistol we have to add all the content of future æons of time as well as of past and present.

Now it is clear that when the ordinary man speaks of a cause he does not mean the whole of the Universe. He usually distinguishes between the cause of an event and the conditions of it. But though this distinction is convenient, is there really any such distinction in Nature? It is possible to make any of the conditions the cause by varying the order of procedure. If we mean by cause " that without which the event called the effect would not come about," then the whole state of the Universe is the cause. This is really the theory that lies behind the scientific conception of Causality. In the end it becomes just another statement of the Principle of the Uniformity of Nature, and as such is a working hypothesis which has no proof. When the scientist says A causes B, all he means is that a law can be stated according to which A is uniformly connected with B.

But does not the plain man mean more than this? He usually thinks that a cause must be active. A thing doesn't explode into change unless something other than itself forces it out of its quiescence. We do not observe this force, of course ; all that we see is the succeeding events that the scientist sees. The chief arguments for the Activity Theory of Causality are derived from experience of willing and intro- spection. In acting we are conscious of producing an effect, and we definitely originate something. These theorists, then, hold either that all Causality is ultimately personal (human or

interested in light waves of a certain frequency, but those are not colours. A blind man could understand what that meant, though he had never seen a colour and could not imagine one. But soon even this view of the physical universe as made up of colourless, soundless, odourless bodies possessing only shape, size, motion, and number, has to be modified. A stone is not really what it seems to be : it is a mass of molecules, atoms, electrons, protons, and perhaps other -ons, too. Sir James Jeans describes the view of the world to which this approach leads : " Thirty years ago we thought, or assumed, we were heading towards an ultimate reality of a mechanical kind. It seemed to consist of a fortuitous jumble of atoms which was destined to perform meaningless dances for a time under the action of blind, purposeless forces, and then fall back to form a dead world." [1] All other content of the world—colour, beauty, emotions, values—is gone as merely subjective, and Reality becomes a fortuitous jumble of atoms. And in the last thirty years that has gone too, and ultimate reality has become a system of mathematical equations. And the scientists are not even sure about that.

Thus our search for Matter has not been very successful. We went to the physicists, who professed to deal with Matter, and they successively threw overboard all the qualities by which we recognised it, and left us with very little. So let us turn to Mind, and look for mental reality. Here we should expect to find all the qualities which the physicist rejected. But no. We go to the psychologist and ask to be shown Mind. He replies that he cannot show us any Mind in its purity, but Mind as he sees it is always in contact with Matter. As Hume puts it : [2] " For my part, when I enter most intimately into what I call myself, I always stumble upon some particular perception or other of heat or cold, light or shade, love or hatred, pain or pleasure. I never catch myself at any time without a perception, and never can observe anything but the perception." Or, again, in the same chapter : " What we call a mind is nothing but a heap or collection of ideas and supposed, though falsely, to be endowed with a perfect simplicity and identity." And Hume is not obviously wrong. We can give little meaning to Mind beyond activity—the mind is an active synthesizing principle, but is never seen alone. It always has some non-mental content to synthesize.

[1] *The Mysterious Universe*, p. 148.   [2] *Treatise* I. IV. 6.

So here we find Matter and Mind making a division in Reality. Matter sends it all over to Mind and Mind returns it to Matter. One can understand the remark, " What is Matter ?—never mind. What is Mind ?—no matter." But we cannot renounce the search so easily. We must believe in both Matter and Mind, and yet yet we find it difficult to believe in them both together, and we cannot find them separate. We know no Matter except by a mind, and we can find no mind separated from Matter.

This is really the solution of the problem, though the plain man, and even the philosophers, must make it harder. They first split the Universe right across into two divisions—Mind, Spirit, Soul, on the one hand, and Matter or Body on the other. Then they make futile efforts to bring them together again. There are three main types of Theory to effect this. To make the exposition simpler, let us consider the question of the relation between the Mind and the Body, which is a special case of the relation between Mind and Matter.

The first of these three theories is *Epiphenomenalism.*[1]

CAN THE SOUL BE SEPARATED FROM THE BODY?

THIS view holds that all bodily and physiological changes take place according to the laws of cause and effect, *i.e.* according to the laws of Nature. But the mind is no part of Nature in this sense and does not enter into the causal system. But though this is so, states of consciousness accompany certain bodily conditions, though they make no difference to the causal sequence of bodily events. They are, as it were, by-products—epiphenomena.

There are grave objections to this view. In the first place it makes a serious attack upon our whole method of understanding the world. If there is something (consciousness) which is an effect and not a cause we shall have to revise our whole notion of Causality : our physical universe would lose its regularity and become chaotic and not subject to law. Put in another way the criticism becomes that the theory violates the principle of conservation of energy—there are some effects which are not in their turn causes, and so some energy is lost.

These difficulties are not necessarily insuperable objections, for the law of the Uniformity of Nature and the law of the

[1] From Greek *epi*, " in addition to," and *phenomenon*, " object of perception."

of Philosophy, and Zeno of Elea (who lived about 450 B.C.)
has placed some of them on record for all time.   The puzzles
of Zeno were concerned with motion and the difficulty of
conceiving the infinite nature of Time and Space.   The best
known of his puzzles concerns Achilles and the Tortoise,
who were to run a race.   The course was to be 100 yards, and
the Tortoise, being the slower runner, was to have 10 yards
start.   Achilles runs 100 times as fast as the Tortoise.   The
signal is given and they are off.   In a few moments Achilles
has reached the spot where the Tortoise was, but by that time
the Tortoise has gone 1/10th of a yard ahead.   Achilles makes
a great effort, and reaches the point where the Tortoise was
when he (Achilles) had covered 10 yards.   But again the
Tortoise is not there, he is 1/1000th of a yard ahead.   And so
on.   You can keep dividing by 100 but you will never reach
zero, and so the Tortoise will always be a fraction of a yard
ahead.   (Incidentally, at this rate they will never reach the goal.)

Zeno did not wish to deny that the fastest runner in Greece
could pass a tortoise in a race.   What he wanted to show was
that we cannot conceive how it is done—motion presents
insoluble problems to the thinker.   The argument of the
Flying Arrow supports this.   An arrow flying through the air
must at any given moment occupy a certain space.   But in
order to do so it cannot be in motion, for if it were it would not
be occupying that space.   And as an arrow even in flight
always occupies some space it can never be in motion.   This
again is absurd, but it is not easy to show how to escape the
conclusion.   The difficulty is concerned with the attempt to
show how a finite object—an arrow, can be related to the
infinite divisibility of Time and Space.

There are other problems connected with the infinite in
the sense of limitless :   we can never imagine a Time which had
no moment preceding it, just as we can imagine no beginning
or end to Space.   This is rather puzzling, because we feel there
must have been a beginning to Time, though we know there
cannot be, just as we feel there must be a limit to the Universe
somewhere, though we know there cannot be.   The very
notion of limit involves something beyond the limit, between
which and the limited the limit is a boundary.

This problem seems definitely to point to some such solution as we have been suggesting in regard to the contradictions
involved in the other presuppositions of Common Sense,
namely, that Space and Time are results of ways in which our

mind works rather than anything in themselves. Space, for instance, is not anything: objects have spatial characteristics and relations, but empty Space is just a bung-hole without the barrel, nothing at all. Thus it is foolish to think of empty Space stretching out miles away from this planet. When we do this, what we are really doing is to *imagine* a point miles away in Space. But from this it does not follow that there really is such a point, and if there is not, then there is no space there. It was a view something like this that Kant held. Space and Time he called forms of intuition, *i.e.* ways in which the mind must perceive if it is to perceive anything at all. It is true that he sometimes spoke of them also as pure intuitions or perceptions, but that was when he fell away from his more consistent view.

SMASHING UP OUR CONCEPTIONS OF THE UNIVERSE : EINSTEIN'S THEORY

BUT this Kantian view is not the only view, and it is unacceptable to many people. It is, for example, unacceptable to philosophical realists. It is also unacceptable to the scientist, whose researches into spatial relations of the Universe demand a different conception. The traditional view of Space and Time, and that upon which the law of gravitation as at present formulated is based is that Space and Time are some sort of entity. Galileo and Newton were both convinced that Space and Time were real existents forming a framework in which all events took place. Newton spoke of " absolute space, by virtue of its own nature and without reference to any external object which always remains the same and is immovable," and he described time in a corresponding fashion.

This is the view upon which science and particularly physics and geometry were based. But that is now having to give way to a new conception, that of Space-Time, in the place of Space and Time. The arguments for this theory are of a highly technical nature, since the need for it has arisen out of later researches in mathematics and physics. But a sufficiently simple account of its conclusions can be given for present purposes. The first point of this modern theory is that Space and Time, instead of being separate entities, are really two sides of one fact, namely, Motion. We cannot fully consider the one without the other, for they are connected as the inside and outside of a box.

The second point of this theory is the relativity of Space-Time to the observer. This should be quite obvious to those who have read so far in this book. If the perception of anything whatsoever is not unaffected by the percipient we should rather expect Space-Time to be relative to the spatial and temporal characteristics of the percipient. Those who have any difficulty in this need only think of a train standing in a station from which another train is leaving. One often thinks one is moving when instead it is the other train.

So much is simple and mere common sense. But it involves the further contention that if objects are thus variable according to the relative positions of observer and object, so also are standards of measurement. The standard yard-stick which is the official standard determining what a yard is, is no longer so constant and fixed as we think. It is true that it will always seem to be the same when measured by another stick, because both are in the same system of reference. But in another environment it will alter in length. Thus simultaneity, succession, length, etc., have no absolute meaning which is eternally the same in every place and time, as Newton thought.

What precisely is the significance of all this it is rather too early to say yet. But it does appear that considerations of Space and Time strike another blow at a naïve Realism, and suggest once more the importance of the part played by mind in the discovery of the nature of Reality. Reality is shot through and through with mind, and to arrive at the nature of the ultimate Reality we shall have to pursue thought processes further rather than attempt to withdraw mind from Reality on the ground that it falsifies it.

GOODNESS, BEAUTY, AND TRUTH

WHEN in the Introduction to this section on Philosophy we were distinguishing the various intellectual approaches to Reality, we said that Science did not examine values, whereas Philosophy did. Science may of course take note of values. For example, there is a science, as distinct from a philosophy, of Ethics. But the science of Ethics strictly so called is concerned only with the factual side of behaviour and not with the value side of it. Thus the scientist inquires what views upon conduct people have held and practised, but he does not inquire into their intrinsic value. The science of

Psychology inquires how in fact minds do actually operate; Philosophy inquires as to the value of these operations—truth and error. Psychologists can gain much information from erroneous thinking, hallucinations, and abnormal psychology. All these are facts, and any fact is grist for the scientist's mill.

Thus there is a distinction between judgments of fact and judgments of value. We must not say that the two classes are mutually exclusive, for it may be that values are facts too. But one can distinguish between the existence of a thing and its significance for human beings. This latter is its value. There are, of course, many values. Health, money, love, rare pictures, even cigarette cards have a value. So in order to clear the ground we must group values into classes. We may make first of all two wide classes—a class of things valuable for the sake of something other than themselves—extrinsic values. Thus money, for instance, has no intrinsic value : it is valuable only for the things it can buy. But happiness is valuable in itself. Anybody would wish to be happy even if it were of no further use to him or others.

It is clear that of these two classes intrinsic values are the more fundamental. It is as means to them that the extrinsic values have their value. A consideration of such extrinsic or instrumental values is concerned chiefly with expediency— do they or do they not lead to something valuable in itself ?— and the question becomes merely one of discovering causes and effects. Philosophy is concerned with the examination of the final values to which these are means.

These intrinsic values have traditionally been grouped under three headings—Goodness, Beauty, and Truth. This corresponded with the three-fold division of the mind—the Will, values for which were Goodness; the Emotions, whose values were Beauty; and the Intellect, in which sphere Truth was the value. But these theorists who thus based their classification tended to separate these three aspects of the mind too sharply and drew it into disrepute. Nevertheless, as a rough basis of classification this will serve. In any case, it is useful for our purposes, and under it in some way we can include all intrinsic values.

IS MAN FREE TO ACT AS HE LIKES?

OUR purpose in this section is just to indicate the nature of the problems of Goodness and their place in the scheme

of Philosophy so that we may in this outline be able to see
things whole and see them steadily.

The fundamental questions of Moral Philosophy centre
round Goodness, or value in the sphere of conduct.

These problems concern (1) the Nature of Goodness, (2)
the Metaphysical implications of Goodness—(a) Freedom of
the Will, (b) the implications of Freedom as affecting our
view of the Universe.

We need not here repeat what has been said about the
nature of Goodness in the section on Ethics, beyond saying
that the particular view adopted by the present writer is the
counterpart in the moral sphere of Truth in the logical sphere,
i.e. one which might be called a Coherence Theory of Goodness.   Just as the truth of a judgment is determined by the
adequacy with which it fulfils its place in a system and expresses Reality, so the goodness of an act is determined by
its place in the scheme of life of the agent and the adequacy
with which it fills that place and expresses the purpose of the
agent.   It would be maintained that one cannot live a consistently bad life, for that is a contradiction in terms.   A bad
life may be consistent with a selection of the facts of experience, but it is strikingly in contradiction with others.   That
is why we call it bad.   The way to deal with a bad life is not
to suppress it and start afresh—that is impossible—but to
widen its scope and sublimate the narrow and selfish purposes
into a wider and more comprehensive plan where they work
with the system and do not set up in opposition.

The question of the freedom of the will has always puzzled
people, and has not yet lost its interest for the expert and
amateur alike.   Philosophical controversy has usually ranged
itself round one or other of the rival standards of Determinism or Indeterminism.   The Indeterminist maintains that
in order for us to be free our acts of will must have no cause.
They are not parts of the physical universe in which the law
of cause and effect holds strictly ; but are defined against
them as being everything that they are not.   In any moral
situation choice may be exercised, and in choice there are
always genuine possibilities, any of which might be followed.

This theory has one virtue—it recognises that if there is
to be such a thing as morality, the strict law of Causality which
holds for the physical Universe cannot apply to acts of will.
Man is so far free—*free from* the Determinism that rigidly
encloses Nature.   But this is a negative freedom, and is by

itself incomplete. For we have no principle to determine the will—its possibilities are practically infinite. If we choose one alternative rather than the other, for no reason at all, we are unaccountable, capricious, even mad. Sheer Indeterminism is not freedom ; it is madness.

THE UNDERLYING PURPOSE

WHERE Indeterminism has made its mistake is in supposing that the only alternative to physical Determinism is Indeterminism of the kind it describes. But this is not true. There is a third possibility, namely, that the will may be determined by itself and not by anything external. Freedom would then mean self-determinism. This is what most people mean by freedom, it is doing what you like, not on any momentary whim, but according to a purpose. This theory also allows for the influence of character upon actions, which Indeterminism does not. We should not call an act really free unless it were a true expression of the character of the agent. Whenever we say " I shouldn't have thought it of him," we think that something has caused him to change his mind so that in that particular action he was not free.

This theory admits of degrees of freedom—a man is free in so far as his actions express his particular character, and this can be done to various degrees. Nor is it any diminution of our freedom that our acts may often be predictable. All that this fact means is that the person who successfully predicts our action knows our character so well and that we are true to it. To object to such prediction being possible is comparable to the objection of the savage to revealing his name to a stranger, lest by so doing he should put himself in the stranger's power.

The foregoing is just the barest outline of the path along which freedom is to be found. We must turn now to consider what effect such a view must have upon our conception of the Universe. Must it split the Universe into two halves—one ruled by the strict laws of physical Causation and the other by the laws of freedom of self-determination ? This was the view of Kant. On the old view of physical Causation every state of the Universe was caused by a preceding state ; the Determination was from behind. But in psychical causality the determination is from ahead : we are attracted onwards by some purpose or ideal which is not yet actual, and that is the cause. This type of Causation we may call teleological, because it is determination by the purpose. It should now be obvious that we would prefer not to have this cleft in Reality, for our whole purpose as philosophers has been to avoid the contradictions to which such dualisms lead and to see things as a unified whole. Some little assistance towards obtaining this unified view has been afforded by our analysis of physical Causality. There we saw (1) that the cause of any event was by no means so simple as a single event preceding it, but was in effect the whole system of events of which it was a part : (2) that Causality was a categorical notion—a way of looking at events.

If we expand our notion of psychical Causality to include a whole system of purposes and ends we bring it more into line with the amended notion of physical Causality. And when we finally bear in mind that both these notions—psychical and physical Causality—are categories of the mind, we do see at last some opportunity for the rapprochement of the two halves of the dualism. It is not maintained that the dualism is transcended, but only that there is now open a more hopeful way for its transcendence. If this rapprochement can be effected we shall then be assured that there is as legitimate a place in the universe for good, and values generally, as there is for fact and the material of the physicist.

WHAT PHILOSOPHERS HAVE THOUGHT ABOUT BEAUTY

PROBLEMS about Beauty are a never-failing source of argument and discussion where intelligent and well-informed people meet. Many people have made their first excursions into the realms of Philosophy *via* such problems. We will outline the problems under three main headings : (a) the nature of Beauty, (b) the appreciation of Beauty, (c) the relation between Beauty and other values, especially moral values.

There have been many theories as to the nature of Beauty, but they can all be roughly divided into two groups. The most commonly held view is probably that Beauty exists in the eyes of the beholder only. This has obvious advantages in explaining the divergences of opinion of acknowledged artistic experts. It also has the disadvantage of setting up an unbridgeable dualism—the physical world on the one hand, empty of all values, and the psychical world on the other. This view is charmingly expressed in George Meredith's " Song of the Songless " :

They have no song, the sedges dry,
   And still they sing.
It is within my heart they sing,
   As I pass by.
Within my heart they touch a string,
   They wake a sigh.
There is but sound of sedges dry,
   In me they sing.

The difficulty of this view is that we should not all be content to acknowledge that the sedges sing only in us : we should want to take our beloved to hear them sing. But how could we if they have no song ? Those who are most insistent that Beauty exists in the eyes of the beholders only will often trip themselves up by trying to point out Beauty in things, and condemning other things as being such that no one could possibly by any stretch of imagination see Beauty in them. Further, how could there be any artistic progress if Beauty was a private experience in the mind of an individual ? The mere idea of progress involves a standard or criterion, and such standard cannot be merely subjective.

And so we swing round to consider the opposite view, that Beauty is objective, *i.e.* exists in things whether it is seen or not. We can bring up against this view the formidable battery of arguments which we directed against Realism as a theory of knowledge. It is meaningless to talk of unperceivable Beauty. Also such a theory has placed upon it the task of explaining why people do not see the Beauty that is there, and especially why experts differ so as to whether it is present. Nor can it explain progress in appreciation of Beauty : if Beauty exists in things how is it that the taste of a nation changes over long ages ? One would expect that it would be seen straight away or not at all. There is here the old question of how to explain error on a Realist theory. But the objective theories of Beauty have this advantage, that they do account for the fact that Beauty " strikes " us, that we do not consciously make it. In perceiving Beauty we feel constrained to see it : we do not feel that it is a creation of our individual minds.

SCHOOLING OURSELVES TO APPRECIATE BEAUTY

As neither the extreme objective view nor the extreme subjective view is satisfactory, we must seek elsewhere a solution. It is evidence of the rightness of our epistemo-

logical theory that it here also affords help. It is a bad formulation of the question to ask whether Beauty exists in objects
or in the mind. We know no object separate from a mind,
nor any mind that has not some object. All our knowledge
is essentially related to Mind. We see something, *e.g.* a
picture, which attracts our attention and the contemplation of
which gives us a particular sort of pleasure which we call
æsthetic. It is so far beautiful. That satisfies the element of
value in an objective theory of Beauty—it is presented to us
and not made by us.

But later we see more pictures, and also sunsets, and hear
music and gradually our experience of Beauty is enlarged and
we come to have a truer view of it. Our first crude notions
become refined. This is essentially what the amateur does.
He finds, *e.g.*, that he likes the music of Schubert, and hears
as much as he can of it. So far he knows a certain type of
Beauty, but when he comes to hear Beethoven he gets a new
idea, not only of Beethoven, but also of Schubert. And so
his conception of Beauty is extended. The wider his experience and the greater his insight into that experience, the more
valid do his opinions become, until finally, absolute Beauty
is that which would appeal æsthetically to the man who could
see all beautiful things in their interrelations and would
synthetise, hold together in a union that was organic and
profound, the whole realm of beautiful objects. Beauty is
to that part of experience which we call æsthetic what Truth
is to that part of experience that we call logical. Each is the
value which satisfies the equation set by experience.

This conclusion may be disappointing to some who hoped
to be told what Beauty was. But it is all that Philosophy can
offer. It is the poet's or artist's business to produce Beauty :
ours is only to think about it. No physicist could show a
man who had never seen the colour yellow what yellow is,
though he could tell him much about it. Neither a blind
physicist nor a man acquainted with yellow but not with the
theory of light knows all about yellow. For complete knowledge experience and thought are necessarily fused. And so
it is with Beauty. The artist who can recognise Beauty but
knows nothing of æsthetics does not really know Beauty, as
Plato pointed out. On the other hand, however clever a man
may be at the philosophy of Beauty, he will never know much
about it until he has experienced Beauty. Thought can
enrich experience, and is constitutive of it, but it can never

be a substitute for it. The principle of the Coherence Theory of Goodness, Beauty, or Truth is the same as that expressed by Jesus of Nazareth as the principle of religious knowledge— "If any man will do his will, he shall know of the doctrine." Experience, controlled by thought, is the only criterion.

BEAUTY'S TWO PORTALS: MIND AND SENSE

WE have already given the greater part of our answer to the second question, namely, the appreciation of Beauty. But one point remains to be cleared up. Is the method of appreciating Beauty intellectual or emotional? It is a bad question, but must be answered, because there is growing up in modern Humanism a tendency to discountenance Reason. The question is bad because it separates two things which are not separable, though they are distinguishable. There is no act of mind that is intellectual only, or emotional only, or conative [1] (*i.e.* to do with the will or action) only, but every act has all three aspects. The writer of even the driest treatise on metaphysics cannot eliminate all emotion from his reasoning, and the most sensual emotionalist must be aware of objects, which awareness is the beginning of cognition. It is true that in some of our acts and experiences we are primarily emotional, in others primarily intellectual (cognitive), and in others primarily conative. The question now becomes, are we in æsthetic experience primarily intellectual or primarily emotional?

The answer, I think, is this. The æsthetic experience belongs rather to the order of experiences which are predominantly emotional. Many people extend their æsthetic experience within this emotional system only. In such cases the mind subconsciously integrates these experiences so that the Coherence is here a result of subconscious mental effort. In other cases, of course, the person consciously thinks and puzzles out the problems for himself. But the process is essentially the same in both cases. Thinking is just a process of systematisation of experience, and as the experience in question is æsthetic, and therefore primarily emotional, the process whereby we arrive at Beauty is thus an emotional one. But it is most important to note that the process is identical in principle with the intellectual process of arriving at truth; the difference lies in the material with which the mind deals in the two cases. Therefore it is misleading to

[1] See page 92.

say that one cannot dispute about tastes.   One can, and the
process is the same as that whereby one disputes about
reasoning : to correct false taste as to correct false opinions,
one seeks to correct or complete the system which is the
background of the taste or opinion.

TRUTH, BEAUTY, GOODNESS : WHICH IS THE GREATEST?

THIS title is included here merely to indicate that Truth is
one of the values of experience, and as such is material
for philosophical examination.   It is included to complete
the scheme on which this essay is worked out.

This apparent duplication of the section on Truth is,
however, indicative of the method of philosophy.   One can
begin to philosophise from any point of experience.   A bent
stick in water, a difference of opinion about a new building
to be erected, a conflict between what one wishes to do and
what one feels one ought to do—any of these may arouse
trains of thought that will not be satisfied until they have
raked over the whole field of philosophy, and not even then
will their curiosity entirely rest.   Philosophy should clarify
problems, but we can hardly expect it to solve all problems.
Only a full life, rich in experience and thought, can afford
us any really satisfactory answer to the problems of philosophy;
and those answers are not for young men or beginners in
philosophy.

But once started on the path of philosophy the student
requires to follow it out in all its branches, for each branch
throws light on all others.   We thought it best to outline our
theory of Truth first, because it is implicit in all the reasoning
of this book.   But our grounds for holding it should now be
stronger because we have seen its relations to other problems.
That is what is meant by the systematic nature of knowledge.
The search for unity in the diversity of experience is the spring
of philosophy and the force that drives men along its difficult
way.

One question, and that an important one for philosophy,
remains.   What is the relation between these three values ?
Are they each supreme in their own sphere, or are they three
different facets of the one Reality ?   It is clear that in ordinary
life they can and do conflict.   The conflict is obvious between
Morality and Art.   There are people who condemn nude
figures, obscene literature, etc.   On which side will the
philosopher take his stand ?   Croce, a modern philosopher

of importance and an expert on æsthetics, is on the side of
the artist. Those, he says, who criticise art from the standpoint of morals should relinquish art criticism, about which
they apparently know nothing, for morality, about which
they claim to know more. This rebuke is often deserved,
but it implies that art cannot legitimately be judged from a
moral point of view. What justification is there for it ?

But Goodness and Beauty are not the only values that can
come into conflict. Goodness and Truth can, too. One cannot doubt the sincerity of many religious people who will not
believe in the doctrine of Evolution, for example. Goodness,
when most zealously pursued, is often in conflict with Truth.
Again, which side of the conflict should the philosopher
support ?

It is quite obvious that he cannot support either with any
more justification than the other. As in most of these insoluble problems, he has to point out that the question should
never have been asked. The question assumes that these
values may conflict, whereas they cannot really do so, but only
appear to do so. This is clear in the latter example we gave.
If a man's moral beliefs conflict with his scientific ones, then
one or both of these beliefs is false. He may have a false conception of goodness, or evolution. And similarly in the
example of morality and art. It is not maintained that my
moral values do not conflict with my intellectual ones. They
may. It is maintained that moral values do not conflict with
intellectual or æsthetic, *i.e.* if the values are real values.

The reason for this is that these three values are really only
facets of one Reality. A value is the power Reality possesses
of satisfying some fundamental human need. If the need is
for intellectual satisfaction, only truth will satisfy : if it is
practical, only moral goodness (in its widest sense) can
satisfy it ; and if æsthetic, only beauty can satisfy it. These
values are attained when we experience Reality adequately in
one or other of these three ways. Philosophy is not concerned
to attain the experience of beauty : its business is to understand it, and other things, *i.e.* attain the experience of Truth.

"THOSE WHO LOVE TO LOOK UPON THE TRUTH"

THERE is no conclusion to philosophy, for each time one
goes over familiar ground one does so with a rather
different outlook, and this affects what is seen. But after this
introduction to the subject a few words can be said with

advantage about philosophy as a whole. One can only understand what philosophy is by actually philosophising. The purpose of the section on philosophy in this outline is just to map out in a rough way the field that can be explored by those who have the pertinacity to follow up their inquiries. And after such an introduction we can look back over this map and draw conclusions that would have been unintelligible without it.

The business of philosophy is to discover the Truth, for philosophy is an intellectual approach to Reality. But the Truth is not easy to discover : the road to it is difficult and calls out all one's energy, not merely of thought, but of life. Because one's thought is the crystallisation of one's experience ; one cannot think truly and act badly. Philosophy is in the end a way of life. The early followers of Pythagoras realised this, and right down the ages philosophy has reflected the cultural and spiritual background of its time.

Philosophy to-day seems to be taking a new turn, not without significance. In the first place there is a lack of the clear, large, synoptic vision—there is no Plato or Kant among us to-day. Instead we fiddle about with pettifogging details, arguing how many meanings the word " good " has or what a motive is. We shall never solve these until we get a larger frame of reference, a system which illuminates and orientates the detail.

The second characteristic of the modern tendencies in philosophy is that they point increasingly towards the individual and his welfare. There is a general movement in favour of Humanism. This is a valuable element in present-day civilisation, which seems to be adequately reflected in its philosophy. But in our concern for the well-being of the individual we must not forget that even that well-being is bound up with Truth. Anything that is false cannot be ultimately for the individual's benefit. The philosopher's devotion is to Truth, for he believes that in that concept are included all others of importance, and without it nothing can be permanent.

Plato's answer to those who asked him who were the real philosophers was, " Those who love to look upon the Truth." That alone is the philosopher's creed, and with this creed does he survey all time and all existence.

THE HISTORY OF PHILOSOPHY

by R. C. ROWSE, M.A., Warden of Percival Guildhouse, Rugby

TAKEN in its very broadest outlines, the history of philosophic thought is clear and simple. There are only three outstanding periods : the *classical Greek*, that of *Descartes*, and that of *Kant*. The first and most remarkable in the history of the human mind is the period in which Greek philosophy flourished. Greek philosophy was at its height in the fifth and fourth centuries B.C. This " peak " period was of course preceded by a period of preparation, and followed by a period of decay. But, taken as a whole, the Glory that was Greece in these centuries, not only in philosophy but in art and general culture as well, has never been surpassed in any time since. After the Greek efflorescence it was a long time before any new and important steps were taken in philosophical thought. Philosophers were mainly concerned with adapting Greek philosophy to the conditions of their own life and thought, rather than with setting out to find a philosophy of their own.

The second great period came when men of courage and independent thought went to experience for their facts and hammered out their own philosophy from life. This attempt is considered to mark the birth of modern philosophy, and was first made by René Descartes (1596–1650). He found a number of vigorous thinkers ready to carry on his work, and from him developed two schools of thinkers who gave new life to philosophy. But in less than two hundred years these two lines of thought had worked themselves out. Each had reduced itself to a position from which it could not move further. It is always difficult to get out of a mess, and all the more so when this mess has been created by men of first-class intellect. Therefore all the more credit is due to Immanuel Kant (1724–1804), whose master mind, following both schools of thought a great part of their way, was able to see where they had gone wrong and how they might be reunited in a useful channel along which progress was once again possible.

It is perhaps too soon after Kant to discern another school

Leukippos. Of Pythagoras himself not much is known, though we do know something of the *Pythagoreans*, the group of thinkers who associated themselves with Pythagoras. The Pythagoreans were primarily a religious sect, aiming at purification by means of strange rites and taboos. But a part of their doctrine was of philosophical importance.

Every secondary schoolboy has heard of Pythagoras' Theorem in geometry, which is a statement of the relative lengths of the sides of a right-angled triangle. However big or however small you draw a right-angled triangle the sides will always be in the same proportion to each other. The Pythagoreans made a number of discoveries of interesting proportions in many spheres—especially arithmetic, geometry, music, and medicine. Thus, if we stretch a string and pluck it, we get a certain note. If we stop that string halfway down, and pluck it, we get a note an octave higher. If we stop it two-thirds of the way we get the fourth, and three-quarters gives us the fifth. Thus the Pythagoreans came to see that the relations between the notes of the scale (though they did not use our scale) could be expressed in numbers.

Again, in medicine, it is important to observe the due proportion of things. Too much heat or too little heat can cause a man's death, and so with food and drugs. The health of the body may be considered as a harmony of opposites,[1] heat keeping cold in check—too much being prevented by too little. Here, again, amounts and numbers seem to be the key to the science of medicine. Wherever you go you find that at the root of all things is proportion and numbers. In his elation at these discoveries Pythagoras exclaimed, " All things are numbers." This Pythagorean doctrine had a considerable effect upon the more abstract thinking of Plato.

" THE MANY CHANGE AND PASS "

TWO other thinkers, Herakleitos and Parmenides, are interesting for the extremeness of their positions. Herakleitos must have been a most interesting man. A proud and aristocratic noble of Ephesus, he wrote in an obscure and prophetic style. His writings earned him the nickname of *Herakleitos the Dark*.

Herakleitos' thought is well summed up in the statement, *Everything is in a state of flux, nothing remains the same.* In

[1] It is due to the Pythagoreans that we find the same word " tonic " used both in medicine and in music.

common with many other thinkers of the time he held that the primary stuff of the world, for which Thales was seeking, was not water or air, for one element alone could not explain all the differences in the world, but consisted of four elements : the wet, the dry, the cold, and the hot.

Everything in the world was passing from one of these states to another. Things were becoming either wetter or drier, hotter or colder. Summer and winter, night and day, life and death, were all alternating with one another. We are, therefore, not the same for two moments together—we are a little older, our body has altered its composition just a little, our minds have had new experiences which have changed them, however imperceptibly. All things are like a river, the water of which is constantly passing on and new water taking its place. In fact Herakleitos did say, " You cannot step twice into the same river." Some one capped this with the remark that you cannot step even once into the river, for when you have stepped in you are not quite the same as you were a moment earlier before you stepped in. A debtor once tried to turn this philosophy to account by arguing that as he was not the same person as the one who had contracted the debt, it would be wrong to ask him to pay it. History does not record whether he was successful or not.

The absurdity of this doctrine that all is change must be quite clear, but it is a very difficult matter to avoid this conclusion. The clearest refutation of it was given by Kant, over 2200 years later, when he showed that it is only something permanent that can change.

THE ONE REMAINS

PARMENIDES, the contemporary of Herakleitos, taught a diametrically opposed doctrine. He too was looking for the real matter or stuff of the world. This he called, innocently enough, " that which is." Now, obviously, " that which is not " cannot exist. We cannot even think of it, because it is nothing to be thought about. It just is not there. There can therefore be no such thing as empty space. There can be no such thing as " nothing," because " nothing " is that which is not.

Now if there is no empty space there can be no movement, for where could matter move to ? It cannot move to a place where there is already matter, for there is not room, and it cannot move to a place where there is no matter, for there is no such place. But if there is no such thing as movement, there can be no change, and no development. The continual flux of Herakleitos is unthinkable. Really, the world becomes a finite, round, motionless, solid whole. This conclusion too is unsatisfactory. It would be a very interesting and philosophically valuable exercise for the reader to try to solve it satisfactorily.

Of Leukippos, the last of the pre-Socratic philosophers we shall mention, we shall not say much. But he cannot be passed over in silence, for by pure speculation he arrived at a theory of the world essentially similar to Dalton's atomic theory. The atomic theory thus discovered by the Greeks had to wait over 2000 years for its confirmation, made possible by the advance of science and the perfecting of scientific instruments.

SOCRATES, A GREAT TEACHER

IMPORTANT as the earlier Greek philosophers were, they are all insignificant in comparison with Socrates. He made a tremendous impression upon the people round him—a tribute both to his personality and his doctrines. As a result, we have more information about Socrates than we have about any other Greek philosopher. Unfortunately scholars are not agreed as to the accuracy of all this evidence. But a good case can be made out for accepting Plato's account as substantially correct, modified a little perhaps for artistic effect, and if this is so we know a great deal about the life and teaching of Socrates.

He was born in Athens about 469 B.C. and was put to death in 399. His father Sophroniskos was a sculptor and his mother Phainarete a midwife. They were in quite comfortable circumstances, and of good birth. When he was getting on in years Socrates married Xanthippe, who is traditionally reported to have been shrewish, though Plato does not give this impression. They had three sons. Little is known of Socrates as a husband and father : in Athens of this time the domestic side of life was not considered as important as the public.

His personal appearance was not prepossessing. Short, with a big head, snub nose and protruding eyes, he was likened to a satyr. But his personality was most impressive. The three outstanding features of his character were his intense moral earnestness and strength of will, a certain mystical idealism, and a shrewd practicalness. It is not often that idealism and pre-eminent practical common sense are found in the same person, but when they are, that person is always outstanding. Socrates' strength of character is not only seen in his life, but is reflected in his teaching that virtue is knowledge, *i.e.* that all we need in order to be good is to know what is good. This was undoubtedly the case in his own life : his problem was to discover what goodness is ; he appeared to find no difficulty in doing it. At the end of his life when he discovered that it was right for him to take the poison offered him by the State, although an easy means of escape was open to him, he had no temptation to escape but awaited the gaoler who brought the poison and talked calmly of philosophy.

Before this, in 406 B.C., it was his turn to be president of the committee that had to judge the generals for failing to recover the bodies of the dead after the battle of Arginusæ. There was a very strong popular clamour that the generals should be tried *en bloc*, which was against the law ; but in spite of pressure Socrates refused to put the question to the meeting, a very courageous action in view of the ugly temper of the gathering.

One more example of his integrity is shown by his behaviour when ordered, along with four others, by the Thirty Tyrants to arrest Leon of Salamis that he might be put to death. The others went, but Socrates returned home. But for the subsequent overthrow of the Thirty, things would have gone hard with Socrates for this.

WISEST IN THAT HE KNEW HIS IGNORANCE

SOCRATES had also certain very exceptional and peculiar traits. He himself remarked on the special gift of Providence which he called his " voice " or " dæmon." This was a sort of mystical or warning voice that told him on occasion not to do certain things. What resembles it most closely in normal experience would appear to be conscience, with these two differences—the " voice " never told him what to do, but only that he was not to do something which he had intended to do—*i.e.* it was always negative, and, secondly, it appeared to be much more personal than our conscience. It was not merely a feeling that he ought not to do something, but a definite command not to do so.

Besides possessing this voice, Socrates was subject to ecstatic trances. He had been known to stand motionless for twenty-four hours apparently wrapped in thought. The most famous instance of this occurred at the siege of Potidea, where he stood in one of these trances from early morning right through the day and through a hard frost at night until the next morning, when he just said a prayer and went about as if nothing had happened.

With all his special characteristics one could not say that Socrates was a " crank." His practical common sense as well as his sense of humour saved him from this. Everyone must have heard of the famous Socratic " irony," an irony that was not unkind but was rather a sense of proportion. At the heart of this irony lay his conviction, honestly held, that really he knew very little. When he was informed by the oracle that he was the wisest of all men, he could not believe it, and went to the wise men in various walks of life to prove that the oracle had made a mistake. He found on talking with them that while it was still true that he knew nothing, the men who were reputed to be wise knew nothing either, so that he was the wiser in that he knew he knew nothing, while the others did not. The subjects which they discussed on these occasions were usually fundamental and ultimate questions, such as what is goodness, what is justice, wisdom, etc. ?

Socrates' life came to an end in 399 B.C., when he was 70. He was condemned to death on a charge of not worshipping the gods the State worshipped and of corrupting the youth by introducing new gods. It is quite obvious that this cannot have been the real offence, for no one took seriously the gods of Greek mythology. Many dramatists had ridiculed the gods, even at the festivals of the gods themselves, and no one took any offence at it. There is perhaps more substance in the charge of corrupting the youth, not by introducing new gods, but by his political teaching.

Socrates was opposed to democratic government because it rested on the principle that seemed foolish to him, that anyone could govern the country, whether he had skill and training or not. As against this Socrates taught that the business of ruling was a most difficult one, requiring picked men (or women) who would be carefully trained for the work from childhood, and this of course was inconsistent with Greek democracy. Also, as we have seen, he had already refused to carry out the illegal orders of the Government. He could not, however, be charged on these political grounds.

because of a political amnesty that had been proclaimed, and as a result the ostensible charge was put forward. Nor do I think that the court wished to put Socrates to death. He could quite easily have got off with a fine and exile (which was all that the Government required), but his behaviour at the trial made that impossible. The account of his trial and death is well worth reading, and can be found in four of Plato's dialogues. The *Euthyphro*, *Apology*, *Crito*, and *Phædo*.

MEN MUST PURSUE THE GOOD

THE fullest account of the teaching of Socrates is given by Plato in his dialogues. But unfortunately it is impossible accurately to distinguish the teaching of Plato from that of his master. We may, however, ascribe to Socrates the initiation of the doctrine of Forms (see under Plato) and the simple statement of it in the earlier dialogues.

We have already referred to his central moral doctrine, that Virtue is Knowledge. It is a curious idea to us to-day. We can think of many men who possess great knowledge, but are not particularly good. Yet, if virtue really is knowledge, these men must be accounted virtuous. Socrates must have been encouraged in this view partly by his own very strong will. But the real centre of his belief was in human nature—in the attractiveness of being good. He believed that if men really knew what they were doing they would always choose the good, for that alone can make them happy. If they deliberately choose to be evil it is because they think it is a short cut to happiness. But they will find that the short cut is a *cul-de-sac*. It is their ignorance that makes them put their trust in evil-doing. All men wish to achieve one and the same end, namely, happiness ; the wise man chooses the path of virtue which leads him there, while the fool in his ignorance chooses the path of vice, believing that it is a better road to the same goal. In this sense virtue is knowledge.

Closely connected with this view is also another well-known belief of Socrates, that " the unexamined life is not worthy to be lived by man." He had a great faith in adult education, and clearly saw the need for it. His life was the putting into practice of this faith. He spent his time inquiring into human life and its qualities, all that we should now call the spiritual and mental side of life, in the wider meaning of these terms. Believing that virtue is knowledge, it was incumbent upon him to spread abroad knowledge. His humility, how-

touch it or smell it, or perceive it with any of the senses. It cannot be perceived, it can only be thought. Plato believed not only that it *can* be thought, but that it *must* be thought. He would say : we find a painting beautiful, a sunset beautiful, a person's face beautiful, and so on. Now, what have all these things in common which makes us apply the same word " beautiful " to them all ? There is nothing visible in common : it must be something thought. It is, we might say, the *element* of beauty that is present in them all. And so it is with many of our other general conceptions. What have a kitchen chair, a dentist's chair, and an arm-chair in common ? Nothing you can lay your hands on, but a certain quality that we may call " chairness." A thing is a chair if it expresses the idea of a chair whatever it is made of and whatever shape it is. Plato held that all things expressed their " idea " and are what they are because this " idea " is present to them, *i.e.* they all have a general principle of which they are one manifestation or embodiment.

So far we can follow him. But he also held as an essential part of his doctrine that these ideas really existed not only in the mind, but in the real world. For this reason modern philosophers prefer to use the term Form instead of Idea, because in its ordinary signification an idea has no existence apart from a mind which thinks it. But for Plato a Form exists as a part of the real world whether anybody thinks it or not. It does not float about in some sort of shadowy half-existence, but actually gives the world what reality the world possesses.

Plato did not invent this doctrine merely because he thought it sounded interesting : he had reasons for it. The reason was his distrust of what knowledge our five senses afforded us. We have already seen when dealing with the Problems of Philosophy [1] that this is true. Mere feeling is a poor test of the temperature of bodies, for if you immerse one hand in cold water and the other in hot, and then put them both into the one bowl of warm water, it will feel different to each hand. Feeling is relative, and so is size as revealed either by the sense of touch or of sight. A schoolmaster, who loomed immense when we were young, may seem small and insignificant when we are grown up. A size six screw may seem very small to a carpenter, but enormous to a watchmaker. In fact, the whole of our experience is riddled with

[1] See page 361 *et seq.*

contradictions of this kind. A thing is no more small than it is big, beautiful than it is ugly, good than it is bad. But a world of things that are thus indefinite and changing cannot be real : a real thing, if it is small, cannot be big.

ENDURING FORMS BEHIND THE WORLD OF SENSE

A ND so Plato was led to consider the world of our everyday-sense experience as a shifting shadow show of unreality ; he had to look for reality in a world where things were constant. This he found in the Forms. A Form does not change, beauty itself, real beauty, is always beautiful, although particular examples may fade away. A Form is, for knowledge, an intellectual constant, and, for metaphysics, a constant component of the real world.

By some such thinking as this, Plato was led to formulate what is now known as the " theory of ideas " or " forms." There are two major questions which he had then to settle. One is, what is the relation between the world of Forms, which is the world of real existence or being, and the world of everyday experiences, which is what he called the world of becoming, or change ? The other is : what are the relations between the Forms themselves ? The answer to this latter question constitutes an undoubted addition to the doctrine he derived from Socrates, and is purely Platonic, but it is too difficult for a brief outline like this. To the question of the relation of the Forms to the things of everyday experience, Plato gave a number of answers. He said that an object " participated " in a Form, or that a Form was present to it. A penny is round, hard, and flat, because the Forms of roundness, hardness, and flatness are present to it. It is, if you like, the meeting-place of these Forms.

It is clear that these Forms are the fundamental principles, the backbone of knowledge and existence. Plato also believed in a more ultimate Form still, which he called the Form of the Good—not to be confused with the idea of moral goodness. This was a Form of Forms, the most ultimate principle of all. In Book VII. of the *Republic* he attempts to describe this, which he admits is impossible to describe adequately. So he does it in a simile. He compares the Form of the Good to the sun in its sphere. Just as the sun, by giving light, enables us to see things, so the Form of the Good enables us

did think that he had mapped out the main divisions of knowledge. These were :

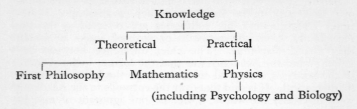

The difference between theoretical and practical knowledge lies chiefly in their aims.   Theoretical knowledge seeks knowledge for its own sake : good examples are to be found in many of the subjects taught at a university—philosophy, theory of mathematics, theoretical physics and chemistry, etc.   Practical knowledge also seeks to know, but it wants to know with a view to doing something.   The applied mathematics of the engineer, the applied physics of the electrician, etc., are good examples of this division of the subject.

Aristotle also notices another distinction between these two types of knowledge : the former dealing with the things of the mind, such as $2 \times 2 = 4$, leads to universal conclusions—results that are always true.   The latter deals with the things of this world which everybody knows are to some extent unaccountable.   There is an element of chance, of contingency in these events, and so the conclusions of practical knowledge are only generally true : there may be exceptions to them here and there.   The realm of practical knowledge was subdivided by Aristotle's successors into three main divisions. *Politics* (management of State), *Economics* (management of the household), and *Ethics* (management of the individual life), and it is obvious that in these matters there cannot be the same certainty as, for example, in mathematics.

First Philosophy is perhaps the only other item in this scheme that calls for comment here.   In Aristotle's day the term philosophy was used for all theoretical knowledge ; so to distinguish one part of it that was more ultimate than the rest, Aristotle applied the adjective " first."   It is logically prior to the rest.   This included what is now called metaphysics, the nature of reality, of God, and of cause, since God is the supreme Cause.

THE INVENTOR OF LOGIC

ARISTOTLE prefaced the whole of his works with two introductory studies—*Logic*, which dealt with the general
principles of reasoning used in any subject whatsoever—and
Theory of Knowledge.   Aristotelian Logic still forms the
greater part of modern treatment of the subject (except perhaps
some mathematical logic), and until comparatively recently
it was handed down unchanged as the final word on the
subject.   Of the theory of knowledge, we may say that it was
very similar to Plato's doctrine of the Forms, in spite of the
fact that Aristotle never misses an opportunity of attacking
this doctrine of Plato's.   Aristotle was never satisfied with
Plato's attempts to bring the world of sense-experience and
the Forms together (there are signs that Plato was not satisfied
either), and he dissociates himself from the view that the
Forms exist in a world by themselves.

ARISTOTLE'S ANSWER TO THALES' QUESTION

ARISTOTLE begins his investigation into the nature of what
is by distinguishing two characteristics that everything
possesses.   Everything is composed of a subject-matter
arranged in a certain way.   These two Aristotle calls matter
and form.   The matter of a chair is the wood from which it
is made ; the form is the principle on which it is constructed.
This is the case not only with material things, but also with
intangible things.   Character is composed of the matter, *i.e.*
all the thoughts, desires, and tendencies of a man's nature,
organised in a certain way, which is the form, the scheme of
life.   We never find these two separate : we never find
matter which has no form, or a form which is not expressed
in some matter, except God who is, of course, outside the
Universe.   This doctrine is also applied to things which grow
and develop ; for these Aristotle uses the words Potential
and Actual.   An acorn is potentially an oak, and an oak is the
actualisation of the potentialities of the acorn.

These distinctions are useful when we come to consider
the cause of the universe, *i.e.* when we try to answer Thales'
question, " What is it ? "   Thales' answer, namely, water,
was incomplete.   It mentioned only the matter and not the
form, *i.e.* it did not describe the law or principle according
to which water had become the world.   In considering the
cause of anything, Aristotle says we must consider four

meanings of the term. There is first the material cause, the stuff out of which the thing is made. Then there is the formal cause, *i.e.* the principle or law according to which the matter has been worked up or arranged. Thirdly, there is the efficient cause—the power that makes the process begin. Lastly, there is the final cause, or the end which the thing is made to serve. These causes are well illustrated in the making of a statue. The *material cause* is the marble from which it is made; the *formal cause*, the rules which the sculptor follows to achieve his end ; the *efficient cause* is the sculptor ; and the *final cause* is the end which he had in view in making the statue, *e.g.* his idea of a beautiful person which he is realising in marble.

Applied to Thales' question the answer becomes that the world is made up of matter, or nature, originally given and not created. The formal cause is just the principle on which the world has evolved, the natural laws of development of things which the physicist studies. The efficient cause, or agent, is motion, which he conceives as eternal. If it were to stop once, the whole world would stop. The source of eternal motion is God, the Unmoved Mover. God did not create the matter of the universe : He only keeps it going. The final cause is of course the state of perfection of the world, the world at its best, the idea of the perfect universe which our universe expresses, however inadequately.

After Aristotle there was no peak in the range of philosophy for eighteen hundred years. Schools of thinkers sprang up with their doctrines, but none achieved eminence in comparison with the heights of the three great Greeks. The most famous post-Aristotelian schools were those of the *Stoics* and the *Epicureans*, better known for their moral theory than for their metaphysics. The Stoics in particular existed for a number of years and spread to Rome, where they included among their number the famous Roman Emperor Marcus Aurelius. The element of Stoicism which is best known to-day is, of course, fortitude in bearing pain, but this was only part of the original doctrine. Equanimity in general was preached. Owing to the break-up of the Greek city-states a cosmopolitanism hitherto foreign to Greek Philosophy became an essential part of Stoicism. This was due to the belief that all men were brethren in that they all possessed reason. Their rule for the guidance of life was *live according to Nature*, which meant for man, live according to reason.

Reason is to be found as the essential element of the universe. It is also the essence of man : it is because the emotions of man are non-rational that the wise man does not heed them.

The Epicureans (followers of Epicurus, 341–270 B.C.) embraced a *Hedonistic* view of morality, namely, a belief that pleasure is the only thing good for its own sake.   In practice they meant the more refined pleasures of a cultured taste, though their theory did not allow them to distinguish between pleasures.   But their continued existence was due chiefly to their atomic theory of the universe, which received its most noble expression in the poem, *On the Nature of Things*, by Lucretius, a Roman who lived from 98–55 B.C.

With these schools Greek Philosophy gradually petered out.   The inspiration which had flourished in Socrates, Plato, and Aristotle had gone, and the glory of Greece in its years of independence had also faded as the memory of the independence of the city states was lost.   A new inspiration and a new soil were required for the flower to burst forth again, and these were not found until the fifteenth century.

PHILOSOPHY IN THE DOLDRUMS

IN our first rough survey of the field of philosophy the first two outstanding areas were those of the Glory that was Greece and the new field of inquiry opened up by Descartes. The most important event in the general history of this period was, of course, the advent of Christianity.   Now, Christianity as taught by Jesus was not a philosophical system : it was not even moral philosophy, it was a practical way of life.   For it, thinking in the philosophical sense is not as important as *believing* and *doing* : in fact, thinking may be dangerous, and may interfere with these.   Therefore philosophy, *i.e.* free unfettered speculation, was not encouraged, and as the Christians grew stronger it was actively discouraged. In A.D. 529 the Emperor Justinian closed all the schools of philosophy.

The only outstanding name among the early Christian Fathers that we need mention is that of St. Augustine (A.D. 354–430).   He was not converted to Christianity until he was thirty-three, and until that time he had done much thinking and teaching.   His writings belong chiefly to his Christian

period and are concerned with various theological controversies. The philosophy of all the Christian Fathers was of
this theological type, and the wider problems which had
exercised the minds of the great Greeks were forgotten.

Philosophical problems again began to be studied in the
ninth century, largely as a result of the enlightened interest
of Charles the Great, who in the previous century had founded
schools in France. Later, in the eleventh and twelfth centuries, the Universities of Paris, Bologna, Oxford, and Cambridge were founded, and they gave a further impetus to
learning. Among the earlier scholastics the most famous
names are those of St. Anselm (1033–1109) and Peter Abelard
(1079–1142). Of the later, St. Thomas Aquinas (1225–1274)
is the most eminent, and at the present time there is a revival
of interest in his works. Early Christian theology still held
free speculation in check, and thinkers still appealed to
revelation and (the bolder ones) to Reason rather than to
experience. But in spite of these limitations there was an
advance upon patristic philosophy, *i.e.* the philosophy of the
earlier Fathers. Aquinas took up the Aristotelian doctrine
of Form and Matter and employed it in the service of Christian
philosophy, multiplying greatly the number of " forms "
that can exist separate from matter.

The question, started by Aristotle, of the relation between
a universal and the particular objects which it includes,
between the form and the matter, became a central feature of
Scholastic philosophy, and divided philosophers into two
schools—*Nominalists* and *Realists*. The question is this.
We know that particular things, *e.g.* men, exist. But what
about the universal term, humanity ? No one has ever seen
humanity : one sees only men. It would seem then that
" humanity " is only a name for a collection of men, and so
on with all universal terms. People who believed this were
called nominalists.

But this has its difficulties. When we say that it is characteristic of humanity to think, we do not mean that every
individual man thinks. We know that not everyone does.
We are not even speaking of every individual man : we are
thinking of the class of men as a whole, and we say of this
class that it is characterised by the power of thinking. If
you work it out you will find that every valid argument makes
use of some universal term. It would seem, therefore, that
these general terms cannot be mere names, they must represent

something real, although it cannot be perceived by any of the five senses. People who believed that these universal terms had a real existence were called Realists. The fundamental philosophical arguments of the Scholastics were concerned with this controversy between the Nominalists and the Realists.

This may seem a trivial issue to divide philosophy, when there is so much to be done—and indeed it is. But it is nevertheless important, and is still a real issue to-day in its modern form. But to-day it does not hold the entire field : it has retired into a more modest position among the problems of philosophy.

THE BEGINNING OF MODERN PHILOSOPHY

IT is obvious to us, surveying philosophy from a distance, that no progress could be made along the lines of disputing over and patching up the Christianised Aristotelianism of the day. The more one struggled in it, the more one became entangled, like a fly in a spider's web. The only hope was for some strong man to come along and break the many fine threads that held philosophy down. These strong men came as a part of that general rebirth of the spirit which swept Europe as a whole in the fifteenth and early sixteenth centuries, and is known as the Renaissance. Francis Bacon, Queen Elizabeth's famous Lord Chancellor, was one of the leading men in this movement in England. But however much he deserves mention for his services in beginning to break the web, we must pass over him in favour of René Descartes, who so completely swept aside the toils of scholastic philosophy that they could never be repaired.

René Descartes was born of a noble family in Touraine in 1596. As a young child he seems to have been precocious and always asking why—a good training for a philosopher. From the time he was eight years old until he was sixteen Descartes studied at the Jesuit College of *La Flèche*, where he was a brilliant pupil and laid the foundations for his subsequent life of learning. After a few years in Paris, spent chiefly in the prosecution of his mathematical studies, he set out to see more of the world. In 1617 he joined the army of Prince Maurice of Nassau at his own expense, a practice which was common among young French nobles at the time; and later he served under other leaders. But it so happened

tribute to his independence of thought and wide reading. He had studied medicine, philosophy, science, and only in some branches of science had he found anything that could be regarded as certain knowledge. The other subjects were riddled with dispute and doubt, but no one doubted that $2 \times 2 = 4$. So he set himself to work on the methods of science and mathematics, which appeared to be the most fruitful methods if one may judge by results. He therefore propounded three rules to guide him in his thinking : first, to accept as true only that which is clearly known to be so on the basis of evidence ; secondly, to analyse a complicated problem into its simplest elements ; and thirdly to collect all the evidence possible before judging, and to arrange it in order of importance. He thus intended to put philosophy on its feet again by finding some fact which was undoubtedly true and arguing from it by unimpeachable reasoning, when, of course, his conclusions must be true. That was the method of geometry, and had proved very successful there, so why not in philosophy ?

It is, of course, difficult to find a statement that everyone would regard as indubitable. But Descartes had surely plumbed the depths of doubt before he finally selected *I think, therefore I am* (*cogito, ergo sum*) as the sure starting-point of his philosophy. It must be a really accomplished doubter who could doubt of that. It was obvious to Descartes that he thought ; he had inside information on that point ; even if he was mistaken and only thought that he thought, he still thought. It was also obvious that he could not think unless he was there to think, and therefore he must exist. His starting-point was therefore valid ; it satisfied the first of his rules of method, namely, that he would accept as true only that which is clearly known to be so.

STEPS OF REASONING THAT LEAD TO BELIEF

HE had now to take his second step, and proceed by infallible reasoning to the next conclusion. So Descartes first considers the self that thinks, and finds that he is finite and imperfect. But nevertheless he has the idea of a perfect Being. Now where can this have come from ? It cannot have come from himself, for he is finite and imperfect. It must have come from an infinite and perfect Being. But if so, such a Being must exist and have put the idea into his head. This Being, which is perfect in every respect, can of course be no other than God. Thus Descartes finds that his own imperfection and incompleteness imply the existence of God—a thought which, however abstract and artificial it may seem in his own words, cannot be overlooked even to-day.

Now of course, the battle is over. By God, Descartes means " substance infinite, eternal, immutable, independent, all-knowing, all powerful, and by which myself and all other things which exist . . . have been created and produced," and with this all-wise, all-powerful, and benevolent spirit nothing is beyond our power. God, being all-powerful, can make the world, and has made it. Further, being kind, He cannot wish to deceive men ; it cannot be true, as Plato held, that the world is a deceptive and unreal shadow-show. Neither is it consistent with the nature of God that He should act in a capricious and arbitrary manner ; He will set Himself fixed rules and abide by them. Thus we get a proof of the laws of nature. God becomes the guarantor of the existence of all nature, of all that we see and hear and experience. He is also the guarantor of our existence ; everything depends upon Him, and the more we think about things the more we see the necessity of God to explain them.

God also has another function in the Cartesian[1] universe. Descartes considers matter, following the scientific thought of the day, as inert, dead. Therefore no material thing can of its own accord affect another, or even change itself. If anything changes it must do so because something has acted upon it. But this agent cannot be material, for only spirit has initiative. This spirit is God. God becomes the cause of all motion and change—He becomes the *First Cause*. This doctrine is known as *Occasionalism*, because it holds that things need the intervention of some outside force on every occasion that they change or affect anything. They do not change by their own nature.

DESCARTES SETS THE PROBLEM FOR KANT

THE legacy that Descartes left to his successors was a problem over which philosophers can still wrangle. It is the old problem of mind and matter. It was Descartes

---

[1] Cartesian is the adjective derived from the Latin form of Descartes' name, which was Cartesius. Most scholars of Descartes time wrote in Latin.

who raised the issue in its modern form and set all succeeding philosophical brains buzzing to find a solution. This question did not particularly trouble the Greeks; they knew there were minds and there was matter in the world, but they did not feel an urge to examine the relationship of the one to the other. The advent of Christianity set the first stage in the problem. One of the essential features of this religion is its insistence on the spirit, or soul, and the life and affairs of the spirit. The spread of Christianity and the reasonings of the Christian Fathers and the Schoolmen served to lay still more emphasis upon the importance of spirit.

Then came the Renaissance and the great scientific discoveries of the time. Copernicus revolutionised men's ideas of the universe and reduced not merely man, but man's earth to the insignificance of a Euclidean point in the vastness of interstellar space. The balance of mind and matter, which Christianity had weighted in favour of mind, swung over to the other extreme, and thought made rapid advances in the world of matter, while in the exploration of the mind it stood still.

Descartes lived at a time when the vastness of the physical universe was being revealed. As a scientist he was impressed on the one hand by the immensity of nature, and as a philosopher he could not ignore the importance of spirit. As a result his philosophy is rent in twain by this division. The habit of thinking in terms of matter and spirit is so ingrained in our mental make-up that we do not often realise that it is a habit and has had to be formed. Descartes has had perhaps more influence in forming this way of looking at things than any other man.

When Descartes set out to explore these two fields—the fields of matter and of mind—he found that matter was the more fruitful for his purposes. Following his method, he first attempts to free his mind from all prejudices and to look at the subject on its merits; affirming connections between ideas where he clearly sees them to hold good, as, e.g. one does in geometry. Now, he says, he can clearly conceive of extension, figure, and motion, and various modes of these. From them he can think out a sort of mathematical physics. This method, it will be noticed, is a method of reasoning. By reasoning we discover fact. But also in the other parts of his work Descartes admits that we know things by our experience of them. Experience gives us a knowledge of fact too. The point of his famous " I think, therefore I am," is just that it unites both these approaches to knowledge. " I think," is fact, revealed to us by experience. From this fact Descartes argues to the existence of the world, not by actually experiencing it, but by reasoning from what is implied in the fact.

This seems simple enough, but it was just this point of his philosophy that divided philosophers for the next two hundred years. He had used two ways for discovering truth—truth is what is perceived to be rationally necessary, and also it is what is perceived to be objectively knowable. And he had never decided which criterion of truth he would rely upon. This breach widened as subsequent thinkers took up one side or the other until by the end of the eighteenth century it became unbridgeable. It was this situation which ultimately set in motion the massive machinery of the mind of Immanuel Kant.

REASON THE DISCOVERER OF TRUTH

DESCARTES had freed himself from the toils of strangling Scholasticism, but he had no energy left to separate the various suggestive lines of thought that his fertile mind had originated. It was the task of his followers to do this. Thinkers on the Continent generally developed the line of Rationalism which Descartes had inherited from Scholasticism, although he had changed it in the process. The first of the thinkers in this tradition is *Gottfried Wilhelm Leibniz*.

Leibniz was born in Leipzig in 1646. His father was an esteemed Professor of Moral Philosophy at the University, and also a practising lawyer. Though the father died when the young Gottfried was only six years of age, the atmosphere of the family was one of learning and acquaintance with the latest and best thought of the time. The young man continued in this way, and before his death he had distinguished himself in many fields. At the age of fifteen he entered the University of Leipzig, and five years later was refused his Doctor's degree on account of his youth. He thereupon applied to the University of Nuremberg, which not only recognised the value of his thesis by conferring the doctorate upon him, but also offered him the Chair as Professor of Law. His keen legal intellect was used in the service of several of the German princes. But he did not confine his energies solely to politics. He also found time to delve very deeply into mathematics, and discovered a new method of the differential calculus just about the same time as Newton also discovered it. He also wrote advocating the union of the Catholic and Protestant Churches—a very troublesome question in Germany at that time, when the whole country had been torn by religious wars.

Not content with learning all that he could, he also wished to spread abroad learning, and in 1700 induced Frederick I. of Prussia to found the Academy of Sciences at Berlin; and he had schemes for founding them in many places. He was already a Fellow of the Royal Society of London, a distinction conferred upon him for his invention of an intricate calculating machine. Clearly he was no "arm-chair philosopher," but instead he let his acute mind range over many problems. But he was too advanced for his time; his projects only came into their own, if at all, long after his death. This was the case with his plan for the foundation of Academies, for the Union of the Churches, for a universal scientific language, and for his faith in the power of geometry to solve many more problems than it could at the time. This busy life came to an end in 1716, a rather sad end, for Leibniz had not a friend near him in Hanover when he died.

The aspect of Cartesian philosophy that attracted Leibniz was the working out of a concept to lead to new truths. For example, if you know what a triangle is you can deduce a number of interesting facts about it without requiring to know anything else. You see that it has three sides; if you are clever enough you can deduce from this that the sum of its angles is 180°. Thus, from the mere idea of triangularity you can by reasoning arrive at a number of other facts that you previously did not know. This was Descartes' method with the idea of God. He formed a clear conception of God, and then drew out the implications of it. It does not affect the principle of the process that these implications were rather conservative; that, in fact, Descartes' God supplied him with just the sort of world he wanted.

THE MONADIC THEORY OF LEIBNIZ

LEIBNIZ was attracted by this doctrine, which we may call rationalistic. It is the attempt to understand the world by reasoning from a given fact. You take an idea and see what is implied in it. This method was so much used in Leibniz's philosophy that one of his commentators maintains that Leibniz started from propositions, *i.e.* statements, and not from facts. Some propositions are universally true : in fact all propositions which are not inherently self-contra-dictory are necessarily true.

But though they may be true, *i.e.* not self-contradictory, they may not be true of actual fact. For instance, it is true that a circle is a plane figure bounded by a line every point upon which is equidistant from the centre. This is true whether there are any circles in existence or not. That is what Leibniz meant by truth—a sort of rational consistency. He did not mean correspondence with fact—that gives only actuality. A statement is true if it is not self-contradictory ; it expresses actuality if it corresponds with fact.

Clearly on this scheme there are a number of possible judgments which are not actual ; the sphere of the possible is wider than that of the actual. In other words, very many events that are quite possible never happen. There is also another difference between the rational and the actual. Judgments of rational necessity are necessary : judgments of actuality are contingent. They must be possible but they need something more to make them actual. This something more is the power of God. In creating the world God could have created any one of a number of possible ones, but apparently not more than one. The reason why He should have created just this one must have been that it was the best. There must have been sufficient reason why God should have created this best of all possible worlds. This unexplained Principle of Sufficient Reason accounts in Leibniz's mind for the difference between the possible and the actual.

As to the nature of the world which God has created Leibniz agrees with the Greek Democritus that there are many elements or atoms in it. These ultimate constituents of the universe Leibniz calls Monads. No two of these monads can be the same : if they were they would be undistinguishable, and so not two but one. On the other hand, if we know there are two, they must be different in some respect in order for us to know it. It is not very clear what these monads are except that they are self-complete systems of something. They are not spatial. They are most probably systems of judgments, or possibly centres of activity and energy. There must be a number of them to account for the large diversity of things in the world.

The conclusion of the matter is, then, that Leibniz in trying to think out the nature of the Universe, *i.e.* in trying to bring Fact into accord with Reason, arrives at an even more rationalistic conclusion than had Descartes. There is no attempt to go to experience and see what the world is like. Instead he starts from judgments of reason, and by analysing them arrives at a system which might possibly be the world he is trying to understand. Whether it is world or not depends upon God, who has created and made actual one of the possible worlds. Leibniz thus brings Fact into accord with Reason, which was the problem bequeathed him by Descartes, by the *tour de force* of the power of God. However true this may be, it is not very explicit as an explanation.

THREE GREAT BRITISH PHILOSOPHERS

THE rationalism that is found in Descartes is developed by Leibniz until it has become quite extreme. We must now return to our starting-point in Descartes and trace the history of the other suggestive line of thought, namely, the appeal to experience, which is called *Empiricism*. It is interesting to note that this should have been developed chiefly in Britain—a country whose people are supposed (by themselves) to be noted for practical common sense and not so logical as the Latin races. In this sense John Locke (1632–1704) was a typical Englishman. He puts his faith more in experience than in system : if a fact will not fit into a system of reasoning so much the worse for the system.

John Locke was an English gentleman, born in Somerset, and educated at Westminster and Christ Church, Oxford. He was tutor in philosophy at Christ Church, but did not like the Scholasticism that was current there. He turned away from barren reasoning to experiment, and for a time practised as a physician. When he was thirty-four he left Oxford to become private secretary to Lord Ashley, afterwards Earl of Shaftesbury. Under him Locke held various political offices and suffered reverses when Shaftesbury fell from power. At this time he found it expedient to travel on the Continent. He thus had a varied experience, and from it his ever-active mind derived stimulus and help. He was of a very tolerant and broadminded nature, arguing vehemently in pamphlets, correspondence, and published works for liberty of thought in religion and politics. His chief work, the *Essay Concerning Human Understanding*, was in preparation for twenty years and finally published in 1690.

We can sympathise with Locke in his method when he says at the outset that he will avoid all metaphysical speculations and will be satisfied " if in this historical plain method he can give any account of the ways in which our understandings come to attain those notions of the things they have and can set down any measures to the certainty of knowledge."

Locke called his method " the new way of ideas." The first step in this doctrine is " that the mind knows not things immediately, but only by the intervention of the ideas it has of them " (*Essay concerning the Human Understanding*, IV. 4. 3). By " idea " Locke meant not only ideas in our sense of the word, *i.e.* thoughts, but sense data—" Whatsoever the mind perceives in itself, or is the immediate object of perception, thought or understanding " (I. I. 8). We think of physical objects by means of these ideas, and the idea is actually in the mind or present to it in a sense in which a material object never can be. I know the Queen's Hall, for instance, through the idea of it that is present to my mind. However large-minded I may be I cannot have the Queen's Hall in my mind.

In brief, Locke's theory of knowledge is this : All our knowledge of Reality is mediated by ideas, which are directly present to the mind. These ideas all come from experience —experience of objects in the world around us, and of our own mental life within. Sometimes Locke says they are caused by the material things (II. 8. 11), sometimes that they are copies of material things. " It is therefore the actual receiving of ideas from without that gives us notice of the existence of external things and makes us know that something doth exist at that time without us, which causes the idea in us " (IV. 11. 9).

That then is the view. It was put forward to meet the difficulties Locke and others felt in bridging the gap between the mental and the material. He could not think of a mind knowing material objects direct, so he interposed a third thing, the idea, to effect the connection. There is no difficulty in a mind knowing an idea and the idea resembles the object. All that we need to add to this account is his defini-

abandoned. When you come to think you will see that the colour of an orange is no more dependent upon its being seen than is its shape. If there were no one in the world it is true that there would be no knowledge of colour. But it is equally true that there would be no knowledge of primary qualities either. From the theory of knowledge point of view, both primary and secondary qualities are on the same footing.

The next point that attracted Berkeley's attention was Locke's retention of abstract ideas. How could he possibly believe that it was possible to have an abstract idea which was " a particular sensible image " ? Berkeley challenges him to imagine the abstract idea of a triangle—a triangle that is neither scalene, isosceles, equilateral, but all and none of these at once. Of course, if ideas are pictures or copies of external things as Locke held, there can be no general or abstract ideas. And in particular the idea of substance as an " unknown something " had to go. Can anyone picture to himself an unknown something ?

Finally, Berkeley cleared up another untidy patch in Locke's philosophical garden by getting rid of the rubbish of external objects. If Locke was to maintain that the only things we know are ideas, he was not entitled to say that we know external objects that cause ideas in us. Berkeley perceived this, and in the interests of consistency confined himself to ideas. " All the choir of heaven and furniture of the earth —in a word, all bodies which compose the mighty frame of the world—have not any subsistence without a mind ; their being is to be perceived or known." This follows neces- sarily from Locke's belief that an object is nothing but a " collection of ideas."

So far Berkeley has been clearing the rubbish from Locke's garden. He must now plant his own flowers. The chief contribution he makes is the development of the other side of the knowledge relation, *i.e.* the perceiving subject. If the essence of an object is to be known, then the essence of a subject is to know. The mind or spirit is not known as an object ; it is the subject which knows ; and in the last resort objects are dependent upon minds for their existence. If we left this here it would mean that things would pop in and out of existence as they were seen and forgotten, and this does not seem to be true. So Berkeley is led to posit the mind of God, who gives everything continuous existence, in that He always perceives everything.

That is the point of the limerick on Berkeley's philosophy :

> There was a young man who said, " God
> Must find it most frightfully odd
>   That this sycamore tree
>   Should continue to be
> When there's no one about in the Quad."

The answer to this is—

> Dear sir, your astonishment's odd,
> I am always about in the Quad,
>   And that's why this tree
>   Doth continue to be,
> Since observed by yours faithfully,
>   God.

A THOROUGHGOING SCEPTIC : DAVID HUME

BERKELEY had carried the empiricist method of understanding nature one step farther than Locke. Hume was to complete the process. He completed it in that no further progress was possible along those lines, for he arrived at the end of the road and discovered as his goal—nothing. Hume's philosophy is a most thoroughgoing scepticism. Hume himself was a Scottish man of letters, born in Edinburgh, and educated at the University. He travelled in France, but spent most of his time in writing, and was unusually naïve in his attempts to receive public notice of his works. His mind was perhaps too acute for him to achieve wide circulation, though his sceptical conclusions brought him notoriety.

His philosophy was in the same tradition as that of Locke and Berkeley, namely, in examining the nature of knowledge he decided to look into his own mind and see how it worked. Consequently, he followed them on the road of ideas, though he changed their terminology, and gave the name *impression* to the general object of experience, restoring *idea* to its more familiar use as a remembered impression. He followed Berkeley in his rejection of external things, but went one farther himself in rejecting minds or spirits, which, for Berkeley, had been the foundation of the universe. In this he was more consistent than his predecessors. If you define impressions as independent and unrelated units, you must ultimately find that you are left with them unrelated and individual as you found them. You cannot build anything out of them, and if you have nothing but them, you cannot relate them to each other by something else, say, a mind.

always clear and interesting. He settled down here to a
regular routine of life, enlivened by visits from friends and
travellers, but never disturbed from the even tenor of his
way. The following quotation from Heine gives an idea of
his life, exaggerated of course, but artistically true.

> " He lives an abstract, mechanical old-bachelor
> existence in a quiet, remote street of Königsberg, an
> old city on the north-eastern boundary of Germany.
> I do not believe that the great cathedral clock of that
> city accomplished its day's work in a less passionate
> and more regular way than its countryman, Immanuel
> Kant. Rising from bed, coffee drinking, writing,
> lecturing, eating, walking, everything had its fixed
> time, and the neighbourhood knew that it must be
> exactly half-past four when they saw Professor Kant
> in his grey coat with his cane in his hand step out of
> his house door and move towards the little lime-tree
> avenue which is called after him, *The Philosopher's
> Walk*. Eight times he walked up and down that walk
> at every season of the year. . . . The good citizens
> saw nothing in him but a professor of philosophy, and
> when he passed at the appointed hour they gave him
> friendly greetings and set their watches."

Physically, Kant was very weak. He was short—about
five feet tall—and rather deformed in the chest. He had
always to be careful about his health. But he had an impressive head—fresh in complexion, with a high forehead, and
clear piercing eyes. His nature was kindly and ready to
recognise merit in others. As we should expect, he was very
modest, almost shy.

THE RECONCILER OF TWO SCHOOLS OF THOUGHT

SUCH is the man who by his intellect and energy was able
to sort out the tangle into which philosophy had got
itself. He was bred in the continental Rationalism of
Descartes and Leibniz, and by his wide reading he came in
at the death of Empiricism through Hume. He says that
it was Hume who woke him from his dogmatic slumber.
The problem before him was how to put an end to the vain
conceits of reason and bring it once again into harmony with
the world. His analysis of perception showed that for the
apprehension of even the simplest fact there are needed both
the material given in experience and a principle of interpretation supplied by the mind. Kant shows, as against the

British Empiricists, that the mind is not passive in apprehension, but actively interprets what is presented to it by
the senses.

Take, for example, the hearing of a clock strike three.
This is not simply a matter of remaining passive while the
successive strokes force themselves upon your consciousness.
You have certainly to hear them all, and Kant would say
that this is the work of sense. But more is required. In
order to know that it is one clock that is striking three and
not three clocks striking one, you must recognise the second
and third strokes as of the same sort as the first. As Kant
says, there must be a synthesis of recognition, and this is
the work of the mind. Furthermore, not only must the
three strokes be heard and recognised, but they must be
apprehended together as three. This involves holding the
first stroke in mind when the second strikes (how else should
we know it was the second ?) and the first two when the
third strikes. This is the synthesis of reproduction in
imagination. All this is involved in merely hearing a clock
strike three. It is obvious that some such process is necessary
in coming to know anything at all ; thus both experience
and reason are necessary to all knowledge. In Kant's words,
" Thoughts without content are empty ; intuitions without
concepts are blind."

In this way Kant answers Hume's main contention that
ideas are independent and unrelated units. On the contrary, in order to know anything at all there must be some
sort of relation. Kant has less difficulty in showing from
the same argument that the very existence of knowledge
implies the unity and identity of a mind or self. If each of
the strokes of the clock appeared to three different men,
one stroke to each man, none of them would know that there
had been three strokes. But as we do know that there were
three strokes they must have appeared to one and the same
consciousness. Thus the existence of knowledge implies a
relatively permanent self, and so Hume's second sceptical
point is answered.

The third point, namely, in regard to causation, is the
most difficult, and here Kant attempts to show that the way
of looking at events as cause and effect is not merely a custom,
as Hume would have it, but is an ingrained necessity of the
mind, one of the ways in which our minds work.

Kant's reconcilation of the two schools, then, is something like this. He admits that if reason is allowed to soar unfettered it gets out of all relation to experience. He has therefore " to limit reason to make room for faith." On the other hand, the Empiricists were equally one-sided in excluding reason from knowledge, and Kant has to bring it back into its own. Reason provides principles in the light of which we interpret the facts of experience, and only in the union of reason and experience can we have knowledge. Beyond that is the sphere of faith.

The result of this limiting of reason is to confine our knowledge to those cases where there is present both a sense-content and an activity of mind. This, Kant argues, deals with the whole of the realm of nature, the world of what he calls *phenomena* or appearances. But behind this world is a world of things-in-themselves, *noumena*, real objects that we can never know as they are, but only as they appear. Our knowledge can never extend thus far. Knowledge stops where experience stops. Besides these things-in-themselves, there are three other concepts which we can never know, but can only believe in : *God*, *Freedom*, and *Immortality*. These are matters for faith, and can never be either proved or disproved by reasoning, because they are outside the realm where experience and understanding unite to give knowledge.

It should be remarked that Kant's thought is essentially systematic—his mind must have been like a wonderful filing-system—and in this short outline the architectonic or system-building has been ignored. This gives a somewhat different impression of his work, but in a notice of this size it cannot be avoided.

"THE RATIONAL IS THE REAL, AND THE REAL THE RATIONAL " : HEGEL

HEGEL is perhaps the greatest philosopher of Idealism that the world has ever known. His thought develops immediately from Kant, but it also draws upon the thought of many other philosophers, particularly Plato and Spinoza. It is encyclopædic in its range, Hegelianism being not so much a set of doctrines as a point of view which affects the whole of knowledge. Once you adopt Hegelianism everything is seen in a rather different light.

Hegel himself was admirably fitted to develop such a system. He showed philosophical aptitude at an early age. At school he excelled in all subjects, and began to make notes on the concept of history, æsthetics, literature. He also showed an interest in systematic arrangement and precise definition of his thoughts. From the age of fifteen his biography becomes the record of his philosophical development. It was only natural that Hegel should spend his life in academic circles. After leaving the university at Tübingen he was successively a private tutor, professor at Jena, editor of a small newspaper, rector of a college, professor at Heidelberg, and finally, from 1818 to his death, professor at Berlin.

It is impossible in a short space, and very difficult in any space at all, to give an insight into the Hegelian point of view, but it may be worth while to summarise Hegel's main contribution to the history of philosophy. Starting from Kant's philosophy, Hegel soon saw the impossibility of believing in the unknowable things-in-themselves. So, for the sake of consistency, he denies the existence of these *noumena* and boldly asserts that the real world we know is rather like what Kant called appearance. This is the real world, and it is a rational world. " The rational is the real and the real the rational." This is a clear statement of his idealism. Everywhere in life and knowledge we see in varying degrees of explicitness the Spirit which underlies nature. The world is spiritual, *implicitly* in the realm of nature studied by the scientist, *explicitly* in its highest expression in Art, Religion, and Philosophy.

Hegel's doctrine falls naturally into three sections : *Logic*, *Natural Philosophy*, and *Philosophy of the Spirit*. The Logic outlines the method of development of our thought. Thought in the real world does not develop in a straight line, deducing one thing from another. It has a systematic or organic development, which Hegel calls *dialectic*. The method is this : first of all, some statement or belief is held as true. This is the *thesis*. Then it is seen that it is not true, and the truth of the opposite position is seen. This is the *antithesis*. Finally, even this is seen to be inadequate, and the truth of each of the two opposing positions is included in a wider *synthesis*.

Take, for example, the notion of freedom. At first it appears that freedom means to be free from determination or control. This is the thesis. It is seen to be false, and freedom becomes the submission to a law imposed from outside. This is the antithesis. This also is not satisfactory, and finally freedom is seen to be determination from within—

self - determination : this is the synthesis. It includes the freedom from external determination (thesis) and also the submission to some form of determination (antithesis) in a wider synthesis of self-determination. This process of dialectic is seen throughout history. History for Hegel is he dialectical working out of an idea, and, in the last resort, of The Idea, *i.e.* the Absolute.

This is seen in the system of his work. First comes the Logic—Spirit examining its own functioning. It then passes over to Philosophy of Nature—concerned with not-Spirit. It is finally synthesised in the union of these two in the Philosophy of the Spirit. These three stages Hegel sometimes calls the *Subjective*, *Objective*, and the *Absolute Spirit*. This Absolute Spirit takes up in itself the valuable elements of the two earlier stages and unites them in the highest development of Spirit—Art, Religion, and Philosophy. It should be noticed that in each of these three moments of the dialectic method there are subordinate dialectical processes. It is dialectic within dialectic.

Within this comprehensive framework Hegel expresses his views on a very wide variety of subjects. As we have already remarked, his works formed an encylopædia written by one man. History, science, æsthetics, social studies, all come under his purview, as well as philosophy in its narrower sense. Hegel is here at one with Plato in regarding the philosopher as " the spectator of all time and all existence."

PHILOSOPHY AFTER HEGEL

WE are now coming to more recent philosophy, and it is becoming more difficult to get the historical perspective. The systems of nineteenth-century philosophers have not yet had time to settle down to their proper level among their contemporaries : we are in a region where loyalties to schools of thought become more personal and less rational. We are at the same time on ground that is more familiar to the general reader, and it is probably only necessary to see the new philosophies in their relation to the general development of philosophy and not so necessary to give a detailed account of them. We are now surveying the fourth field of our philosophical inheritance.

Hegel's systematic philosophy proved very attractive to certain thinkers in various parts of Europe, and mention should be made of them. There is, firstly, Karl Marx, the author of *Capital*, the bible of revolutionary Communism. Until recently the more striking political implications of Marx's works overshadowed the philosophical. It must be admitted that Marx was not primarily interested in the theoretical question, but rather in its practical application. Marx's contribution was to turn the Hegelian conception of history upside down and stand it on its head. Instead of history being the evolution of the Spirit, it is for Marx the account of how material conditions—the civilisation and economic conditions—determine man's life and thought. This is the *materialist conception of history*, a conception that still believes in the dialectic, but it is a dialectic of material forces. Marx works out his theory with a voluminous array of historical facts culled from original records which have been ignored by the historians. Marx's philosophical importance is slight, but in giving the best-known account of an inverted Hegelianism he states a position which may one day be developed more fully.

Another line of development of Hegel's thought is to be found in the works of T. H. Green, Bradley, and Bosanquet. Green, who died in 1882, was Professor of Moral Philosophy at Oxford. His main influence is on ethics, but he prefaced that with a metaphysic which argued to the necessity for a spiritual principle in nature somewhat along the lines of Hegel's thought. It was at least thoroughly idealist.

F. H. Bradley, 1846–1924, was a pupil of Green's, and is perhaps better known for his searching analysis of traditional British philosophy and his vigorous statement of an idealist position. Until Green and Bradley introduced the German influence into Britain, British philosophers were still muddling on with a patched-up Humean Empiricism. But after their writing no one even in England could afford to ignore Kant and Hegel. Bradley's main business was to show that the world as we think it is Appearance. It is riddled with contradiction—in fact, thought itself implies a relation of subject and predicate, whereas Reality cannot be thus relational. After a searching criticism of what we take to be Reality, Bradley rejects it as Appearance, and turns to consider where Reality really is to be found. He finds it in feeling; in the immediacy of sentient experience do we find that absence of relation, of otherness, which is Reality. Bradley is often referred to as a sceptic, but really he is more of a mystic. Reality, being relationless, must include everything that is;

not space and time, but one continuism—Space-Time, which has both spatial and temporal characteristics. *Space is temporal and time spatial.* The unit of this continuism Alexander calls a point-instant. A point-instant is just a momentary or " pure " event. It is the stuff the world is made of. The things we know—rocks and stones and trees—are just certain groupings of point-instants. Even the mind itself is made of the same stuff as other reality, namely, Space-Time. " My mind is within my body *in the same place* as the nervous system." But though mind is of the same stuff as mud, it is of higher order. It emerged later, and has a more highly organised nature.

Alexander explains even the supreme values of Truth, Goodness, and Beauty on these lines of emergent evolution. The primary stuff is Space-Time. A modification of this is the world of physical things, and, thirdly, there emerge these values which Alexander calls *tertiary qualities.* But they are nevertheless constituted of Space-Time. The last quality of Reality that has emerged so far is Deity. This is something higher than our mind, but it is still a modification of Space-Time. We do not know exactly what is the nature of this deity : we only know that it is more than spirit, although at the same time it is spirit.

It would be unfair to criticise a theory so briefly, and possibly unintelligently, summarised as this. But we may note its significance. In the first place, the old realist belief in matter, as something you could bump your head on, has given way to a new concept—Space-Time. Though it is not in the ordinary sense of the word material, it is nevertheless objective, and will serve as a basis for a realistic metaphysic. We might note, secondly, that many mathematical physicists are finding this way of regarding the world helpful. Modern philosophy is receiving many contributions from the higher mathematics at the present time. One wonders if we shall not soon have to borrow Plato's notice-board to hang outside our Philosophy departments — *Let no one ignorant of mathematics enter here.*

THE PRAGMATISTS JOIN WITH THE IDEALISTS

FOR an account of Pragmatism the reader must be referred to the section on *Philosophy's Problem.*[1] Here we need only remark that the main bone of contention between the

[1] See page 366.

Pragmatist and the Idealist is the question of the Absolute. A typical Idealist believes in a standard of truth independent of the individual mind, though not independent of mind as such. Metaphysically, he believes in an order of reality that is absolute ; it is the self-substantiating standard ; it is there as a fact. The Pragmatist, however, dispenses with the belief in the Absolute and relies on a very humanist standard—namely, what is good enough for the purpose is all the good there is. If a theory works it is true, and it is all the truth we can hope for. When it ceases to work, a new one must be found which will then be true as long as it satisfactorily solves the problem. Pragmatism in its essence is really as old as the Greek Sophist Protagoras— " Man is the measure of all things." America is the real home of modern Pragmatism, which has received its clearest expression in William James (1842–1910) and in John Dewey (born 1859). Dewey has deservedly a large following in America to-day. In this country Pragmatism is chiefly associated with the name of F. C. S. Schiller.

The reader who has got thus far has now surveyed the field of philosophy up to the present day. The survey is admittedly cursory and perhaps even superficial. But so it must be with every first approach. One cannot see everything until one has become familiar with the main features ; then the detail may be revealed at successive approaches. The reader who wishes to know more, is now advised to go to the texts themselves.

SUGGESTIONS FOR FURTHER READING

C. E. M. Joad's *Guide to Philosophy* (Gollanz) covers the whole field of philosophical thought from the Greeks to modern times. It is written in non-technical language, and is designed for those who have no previous acquaintance with the subject. G. Watts Cunningham's *Problems of Philosophy* may also be studied. Another good introductory book is J. Wolfenden's *Approach to Philosophy*. Bertrand Russell's *Problems of Philosophy* (Home University Library, Thornton Butterworth Limited) is a good introductory book, especially for those who find the theory of knowledge attractive.

Books on Ethics tend to be technical, and contemporary ones especially lose sight of the wood among the trees. But a good introductory book which has not this fault and is pleasant to read, is Herbert Samuel's *Practical Ethics* (Home

mathematician. This led easily to a geometrical view, which conceived the ultimate nature of the universe as consisting in relations between bodies in space.

The picture changed somewhat with the discoveries of Isaac Newton, and the concepts of cause and effect and of force played principal parts in a mechanical interpretation of the universe. God was now the engineer. Darwin carried on the idea into biology, and the German philosopher, Engels, found clockwork in history. To-day, with Albert Einstein, who asserts that his theory is built up exclusively on concrete experiment, the geometrical conception has returned, but it is a geometry of figures. The mechanist theory has not disappeared, however, for, in a modified form, it has found a home in Soviet Russia. The author's contention is that, throughout history, scientists have been directed in their researches by the theories of philosophers, just as much as philosophies have been built up on the findings of physicists.

Yet science to-day, he says, bangs the door on philosophy. It asserts that only those aspects of things which lend themselves to accurate measurement are suitable material for science. The author of this article believes that the results of science have been circumscribed, and fruitful developments checked by this limitation of its scope and neglect of philosophy. Strict adherence to this shutting-out obsession, he remarks, has led to the exclusion of the conception of force *from mechanics, of* purpose *from biology, and of* consciousness *from psychology—to have found a universe without purpose, force, or consciousness would be a disappointing end to Man's great adventure of intellectual discovery.*

It should be asserted once again that in this article dealing with the great modern problem of the relative positions of Philosophy and Science, the author definitely writes from one side— that of philosophy—as befits the scope of this book. But the recent advances of science have very strongly modified his views.

" How charming is divine Philosophy," said Milton—but he expressed a worthy sentiment which is unfortunately shared only by an enlightened minority ! To the ordinary man the word all too often implies either listening to dry and uninspiring lectures, or else contemplating a row of books whose contents are as forbidding as their covers. The word " Science," on the other hand, conveys to him a somewhat romantic idea of careful and accurate observations, intimately connected with real things-that-matter, which lead ultimately to marvellous applications—to wireless and cinemas, and to those mighty engineering feats which appear characteristic of a new age.

The two subjects thus seem to be almost complementary opposites : Philosophy, highly abstract and speculative, dealing with unreal and insecure beliefs ; Science, concrete and certain, dealing only with ascertained fact. It is the scientist who has appropriated the motto :

> . . . *To the solid ground*
> *Of nature trusts the mind that builds for aye.*

And this in spite of the fact that natural science seems to change its theories every few years, while the opinions of Socrates are still valuable after twenty-three centuries. There are even men of science who share in the fashionable prejudice, and who feel that the subject in which they delight is so firmly grounded on facts that it has only the most remote connection with abstract speculations on the nature of being or on the existence of God.

Of course one has to admit that these two branches of knowledge have for quite a long time evolved along different lines. One result of this unfortunate and unnatural divorce is that they have gradually developed very different technical vocabularies. Hence, anyone who wishes to be understood both by philosophers and by scientists, and, above all, who wishes to be understood by the non-specialist, has to write in a somewhat popular manner. Not only is he thus always perilously poised between the Scylla of obscurity and the Charybdis of triviality, but he is always vulnerable to Faraday's gibe that it is impossible to learn anything from popular books.

THE PUBLIC'S DEMAND FOR POPULAR SCIENCE

YET the consideration of the connection between science and philosophy is one of the crying needs of our day. The ordinary man, for instance, is not interested in the technique which alone makes scientific advance possible. He looks for interpretations, he wishes to know what science can tell him about the world in which he lives. The great demand for popular books (such as those recently published by distinguished men of science), which are full of dubious and naïve philosophical pronouncements, is an illustration of this insatiable curiosity.

Consider, for a moment, the *facts* observed by an astronomer. These consist simply of readings on clocks, observations of coincidence between dots on photographic plates, movements of needles in electrical measuring instruments, and so on. The astronomer is no more interested in such facts than is the man in the street, but on them his philosophical activity builds a magnificent edifice of speculation, more or less substantiated by further observations. Now he sallies forth boldly from his observatory and issues philosophical pronouncements on how the world was formed, or on how the stars are born, and why they die, and about whence came the nebulæ. Notice that only a careful philosophical analysis of the grounds which allow judgments on these issues to be advanced would permit a correct valuation of their validity.

Both to the scientist and to the philosopher an analysis of the relation of philosophy to science is of importance. It is essential to the former to understand the implications of the subject he studies, and it is equally essential to the latter to be kept in continuous contact with the concrete realities of nature.

RELATION OF PHILOSOPHY AND SCIENCE

PHILOSOPHY, says Ueberweg, is an advance upon and an outgrowth from the conception of mental development in general and of scientific culture in particular. In the many systems of philosophy, developed by the genius and the restless curiosity of man, this conception is modified according to the characteristics peculiar to each. Yet in all cases " philosophy " is included under the generic notion of *Scientia* and is as a rule distinguished from the particular sciences by the specific feature that it is not occupied, like them, with a limited province of things but with the nature, laws, and connection of whatever actually is; Philosophy is the science of principles.

Thus, in one sense, science and philosophy must be considered as being merely different aspects of one great enterprise of the human mind: the intellectual adventure of attempting to make intelligible to ourselves something of the structure of the Universe and of the relation of man to his surroundings. But, as we have already said, this conception is no longer universally admitted. For several centuries the differences and divergencies between the two aspects of *Scientia*—rational knowledge in its most general aspect— have been stressed at the expense of the unity of ideal which should have served to make them one. Nowadays there are many men of science who would be prepared to assert that science owes nothing whatever to the influence of philosophy, and that the history of scientific progress is also the history of the gradual emancipation of the human mind from the fetters and superstitions imposed on it by the philosophies of bygone ages.

Thus, quite recently, one of our most distinguished mathematicians stated that, in his opinion, philosophy had never exerted the slightest influence on the development of real science. When confronted by specific instances of the reality of this supposedly non-existent influence, he then altered his standpoint, but argued stoutly that this influence had been wholly for the bad. Evidently, if we found ourselves forced to agree to such views, the present essay would have to be concerned not with the relations between the two aspects of man's persistent and long-continued attempt to understand his universe, but merely with an historical description of the gradual removal from natural science of philosophical irrelevancies. To this might be added a few—probably philosophical—remarks showing that, unfortunately, traces of philosophy and of anthropomorphism (*i.e.* such statements as seem to allow human prejudices to intrude themselves into theories) were still left in modern science ; one might conclude by discussing how these might be removed. Incidentally, we should also have denied philosophy's right to existence.

Although it is almost certain that the idea that science and philosophy are necessarily antagonistic is due to a profound misunderstanding of the scope of each, it is yet both interesting and important to ask how this view has arisen. We all know, of course, that it did not exist either among the Greeks or among the Scholastics of the Middle Ages, to whose bold speculation and logical subtleties the structure and powers of the modern mind owe so much. In those days it appeared obvious that the goal was the pursuit of Truth, and that all roads which seemed promising and all conclusions which deepened our understanding of the processes of Nature were equally valid and would necessarily converge in the end.

Plato and Aristotle were investigators of Nature as well as builders of philosophical systems and, even at the beginning of the modern age, Galileo and Kepler were influenced almost as much by metaphysical considerations as by the results of their observations or experiments; while each of them used against his scholastic opponents the weapons of dialectic and logic familiar to the latter, weapons which nowadays appear typical of the philosopher.

A MIGHTY CAMPAIGN TO CONTROL NATURE

YET to-day natural science and philosophy certainly seem to be moving in different directions, and it is usual to assume that this separation is the result merely of the increasing specialisation which the enormous growth of detailed knowledge has rendered necessary. If the scientist has to wade through the mass of material accumulated by his predecessors before he can himself hope to add his brick to the scientific edifice, how can he be expected to acquire in addition the technical equipment of a professional philosopher ? And if the latter has to study the history of philosophy and to become acquainted with the ideas and speculations of a long line of metaphysicians stretching, say, from Thales [1] to A. N. Whitehead, how can he in turn find time to acquire the mathematical and experimental technique needed to appreciate the value and importance of modern physical theories ? Now, in a sense, there is probably some truth in this view, but it is certainly not the whole truth. To accept it would involve accepting also the opinion that we lack the capacity to produce the man of genius who combines in himself a profound understanding of both scientific and philosophical methods. As a matter of fact, such men are not as rare as some would have us believe and, happily, depth of understanding is not necessarily proportional to the amount of detailed knowledge at one's command.

Actually, it appears probable that the tendency to separate sharply metaphysical speculation from positive science is due, in some measure, to one of the deepest impulses of the Western mind : the Will to Power and the Lust of Conquest. Western Man wishes above all things to obtain control of the forces and of the materials which surround him. He wishes for a natural science which will provide him with the possibility of overcoming the limitations of space and of time, and with the power to obtain from the earth, the sea, and the sky the immense quantity of materials and of energy which typify for him his domination of the world. The question as to whether a science which gives him these things

[1] See page 394.

also gives him a profound and intimate *understanding* of things appears almost irrelevant. It would be interesting to have this as well, but it is not the essential need. To *control* Nature by understanding her ways is said to be the object of science : but *control* and not *understanding* is the aim.

Now, it must certainly be admitted that a profound understanding of the intimate nature of a phenomenon, or of its connections with other phenomena, is not essential to us if our aim is control or conquest ; ontological discussions, with their endless arguments on the real inner nature of things, may hamper rather than help the man of affairs or of action. There thus arises, not only a tendency to ignore arguments basing themselves on grounds other than those of positive science, but even a tendency to develop views which might help to place the latter outside the reach of any such criticisms.

PHILOSOPHIES THAT HAVE GLADDENED SCIENTISTS' HEARTS

FURTHERMORE, it must be admitted that natural science has achieved its most remarkable successes by implicit reliance on that combination of experimental method and speculation peculiar to it, and often by ignoring—almost systematically—arguments advanced against its conclusions from the standpoint of philosophy.

It is thus not difficult to understand the prestige which has gradually gathered round the present orthodox position, which may be spoken of as the *positivistic standpoint*. We shall have occasion to discuss the bearing and validity of this position. It has its roots like all other philosophies far back in the past ; but it received its first clear exposition with Auguste Comte and achieved almost perfect expression in the works of Ernst Mach, Avenarius, and other writers of the anti-metaphysical [1] school. It will be sufficient to mention here its principal articles of faith. It is supposed that it is possible to acquire true knowledge about things without presupposing any theory of their ultimate nature. It is asserted that, on the whole, those aspects of things which lend themselves to accurate measurement are really suitable

---

[1] The word metaphysics means literally " beyond physics." It is a name given to a portion of Aristotle's works which came after his *Physics*, and it means speculations on the nature of Being, Truth, and Knowledge.

material for science, and that it is thus only with regard to these aspects that we can learn anything about which we can be absolutely certain.

The essential task of the scientific philosopher is thus to remove from science all considerations and aspects which are merely metaphysical, and therefore obscure or uncertain. Hertz, for instance, wished to remove the notion of *force* from mechanics ; the behaviourist school refuse to consider *consciousness* in psychology, and many biologists attempt to ignore the notion of *purpose* when studying the behaviour of living things. The validity of the position outlined above is obviously open to doubt, but we do not wish to press the argument just yet : our object being at present merely to understand the grounds which have led to the divorce between science and philosophy. It will be obvious that it implies a definite view, which is not necessarily forced upon us by the nature of science itself, and that there are many reasons which would lead us to dissent from it.

In the first place, if we accepted the positivistic claim, it would be clear that the fundamental questions discussed by the philosopher would be of no real importance to the man of science. Yet, on opening Bertrand Russell's *Problems of Philosophy* we find, amongst others, the following chapter headings : *The Existence of Matter ; On our Knowledge of General Principles ; Truth and Falsehood ; Knowledge, Error, and Probable Opinion.* Now could anyone seriously maintain that our scientific opinions—or even our work in the laboratory—are entirely uninfluenced by our views on these subjects ? After all, the philosopher is merely trying to express logically and unambiguously what we know about these things, and his conclusions must ultimately affect the way in which everyone of us reasons and thinks. For mark this : there is no escape from metaphysics ; the choice before us lies merely between being bad philosophers, assuming unquestioningly and implicitly numerous doubtful propositions, and being good—or, at any rate, honest— philosophers, attempting to examine critically and to express in words the ground of our beliefs.

In the second place, we all know that both our metaphysical and scientific views are profoundly different from those of the Ancients or from those held in the Middle Ages. We can suppose, of course, that the scientific change has been in no way conditioned by the philosophic change, that the two are independent of each other, and that the curious parallelism they exhibit is quite accidental. But if, on the other hand, we refuse to be satisfied with such a naïve and facile solution, it will be obvious that the deeper connections between these changes in outlook can only be exhibited by a philosophical analysis of the positions involved, that is, by an examination of general principles.

In the third place, there has occurred during the last thirty years an alteration both in our scientific and in our philosophical views, of a nature so deep and far-reaching that it can only be called a revolution. One might characterise this change by saying that it consists largely of an attempt to replace the study of a universe of things by the study of a universe of events. In a way, the change might also be shortly described as being an attempt to dethrone " substance " and to set up " history " in its stead. Now it is not really a difficult task to show that the scientific change has been brought about largely by philosophical criticism, while the metaphysical change has been caused through the adoption of points of view forced on us by the new discoveries and theories of natural science.

SEXTANT AND COMPASS OF MAN'S INTELLECTUAL ADVENTURE

LET us assume that a certain reciprocal influence exists between philosophy and science, and that it is of such a nature that a real understanding of the intellectual adventure of man can only be obtained by a study of this twofold aspect of *Scientia*. Two questions then arise : What is the nature of this influence, and, further, how may it best be exhibited ? To answer these questions fully would require far more room than there is available here. But one might say, broadly, that the nature of the influence is threefold : it is fertilising, conservative, and critical. Its most important aspect is undoubtedly the first, but since, like most processes of fertilisation, it is exerted only for a short time, its real rôle is often overlooked. Yet there is no doubt whatever that the general philosophy of the seventeenth century affected most profoundly and directly the scientific views of Kepler, Galileo, and Newton, and that it acted definitely as a fructifying force. Of course, once these pioneers had laid the foundations of the scientific edifice, their followers found no difficulty in building on them, and once the methods had been worked out it was unnecessary to consider the philosophical implica-

15

tions. On the other hand, we have quite recently seen men like Bergson, B. Russell, and A. N. Whitehead, deeply versed in and influenced by the scientific technique and culture of our time, proposing systems of philosophy which carry most obviously the imprint of the scientific ideas to which they owe their birth.

Again, we have expressed the opinion that the influence might be conservative. By this we did not mean that it tended to prevent progress, but merely that philosophy, for instance, might preserve or enshrine an axiom or an opinion which *at a later period* might bear most excellent fruit. As an instance of this, we might mention the case of the *Principle of Least Action*, which has now assumed in theoretical mechanics a position of predominating importance. It is not difficult to understand its meaning, and it will clarify the subsequent discussion if we attempt to explain it here. We may attach to every particle of matter a certain numerical coefficient—called its *mass*—which summarises its mechanical behaviour. If this particle moves with any velocity from a point A to another point B very near A, then the action over this short distance will be found by multiplying together the mass, the velocity, and the distance :

$$\text{Action} = \text{Mass} \times \text{velocity} \times \text{distance}.$$

Suppose, now, that we throw a cricket ball through the air. Then its velocity will alter at every point of its path, but we can divide its trajectory into an enormous number of very small distances and calculate the action over each element of distance. The total action over the whole path can then be found merely by adding together all the little bits of action ; and the Principle of Least Action then assures us that the total action over the whole *actual* trajectory will be less than the action over any other path would have been. The *meaning* of this law is very strange : it is almost as if the cricket ball, before travelling through the air, was able to decide what the action along different paths would be, and then decided to take that path which would make the total action a minimum.

VOLTAIRE'S GIBE AT GOD'S "MEANNESS"

THERE are other principles which bear a certain resemblance to this. Hero of Alexandria had noticed that when a ray of light is reflected from any surface, it always travels in such a way as to make its total length of path a minimum ;

A GREAT WIT : VOLTAIRE

a mere specification of our own mental processes, telling us little or possibly nothing about nature, but certainly something about ourselves . . . at the farthest point that Science has so far reached, much, and possibly all that was not mental has disappeared, and nothing new has come in that is not mental. . . ."

Needless to say, the reader will at once notice the difficulty of reconciling an anti-anthropomorphic ideal with complete and confessed ignorance of an objective and real world. But let us pass over this point : the world we study is, then, a world of appearances. We know only phenomena lying outside Man, and the *noumena*—or things-in-themselves—lie for ever beyond our ken. The phenomena we observe possess certain features in common with one another, and these features may be abstracted to the exclusion of others. For instance, rays of light of different colour all possess the property of being bent when they pass through a glass prism. We may ignore the colour, concentrate on the bending and measure it. The different rays will be bent by different amounts, but they possess in common a certain mathematical aspect which we can express by one of the laws of physics : Snell's law of refraction. We can continue our investigation in this way, connecting phenomena by laws and gathering laws into theories. Now, most scientists consider that this uniform and graded progression from crude observation to the careful observation of numerical data, from the generalisations known as laws to the inductive generalisations known as theories, represents the proper method of science.

It will be obvious, of course, that a number of problems at once clamour for attention and discussion. How do we know that our laws or our theories are true ? If we accept their validity, what, exactly, will they tell us about the universe ? If this method of study is really valid, is it the only method which we can profitably adopt ? In any case, what do we mean by using the word " true " when speaking of a theory ?

Well, in answer to such questions, a number of facile answers are proposed. On the face of things they are perfectly satisfactory. Indeed, one is almost forced to admit that, having once granted the initial postulates of an external world uninfluenced by man and of a mind which knows only phenomena, it seems vain to attempt to struggle against the answers proposed.

WHAT IS TRUTH? THE PHYSICIST'S ECHO TO PONTIUS PILATE

WE must first agree as to the meaning we intend to attach to the word *true*. A law will be a true expression of the observations on which it founds itself if none of the latter falls outside its scope. Since all laws are only approximate expressions, and have only a regulative and never a constitutive validity (that is to say, since their reality is logical and mental, and does not correspond to anything in the nature of things) it is always possible to establish a valid law, though often it may be so complex as to be expressible only in the symbolism of mathematics. Again, a theory will be true if it allows us not only to arrange known laws into a logical and coherent framework, but, further, to prophesy the form of laws not yet discovered and to guide future research.

Many scientists would urge that there is no other criterion of *truth* ; we can never really ask anything beyond ; Does this theory work ? Does it produce results ? It seems that there is no more sense in asking whether the atomic theory is " true " than in asking whether it is blue, or in asking whether a hammer is true. The point is : Does it work ? Does it produce results ? Notice that, according to this view, theories need not even be consistent with one another : no one objects to using a hammer *and* a chisel, and so no one ought to object to using a particle-atomic theory on Tuesdays, Thursdays, and Saturdays, and a wave-atomic theory on Mondays, Wednesdays, and Fridays.

The philosophical theory of the nature of truth which we have just outlined represents the view usually spoken of as *pragmatism*, or the view that truth is that-which-works and produces results. We may then say that the modern scientist is not only a positivist but also a pragmatist. All too often, however, the man of science does not stop within the bounds of his pragmatic positivism, which should make him consider his views merely as working hypotheses necessary to him in the laboratory or in the study. Sometimes he abandons this doctrine and delivers pronouncements on the structure of the Universe, and of man's relation to it. Actually, his positivistic position should forbid him to do this and, above all, it should prevent him from extending it in such a way as to make it appear that his is the *only* method by which sure and certain knowledge may be obtained. In practice, therefore, the scientist is no pragmatic positivist ; whatever he may imagine himself to be.

THE WORLD AS THE MECHANICAL CONSTRUCTION OF A SUPER-ENGINEER

FOR our present purpose, the structure of laws and the relation of phenomena to reality may be passed over in silence. What is more interesting is the structure of the theories which the man of science proposes for our acceptance. Fifty years ago, theories tended to be mechanistic, and some of the great Victorian investigators often declared that they were unable to understand any theory which did not allow them to construct engineering models which were representations on the physical and material plane of the inner connections of the structure of Reality. The grounds on which these Victorian opinions were based were partly historical and partly anthropomorphic. It is well known that at the end of the seventeenth century Sir Isaac Newton developed, on simple and easily understood axioms, a vast structure of rational mechanics. He assumed only geometrical principles descriptive of motion—for instance, that bodies tend to move in a straight line. He added to these a method of measuring forces and a strict definition of mass. He supposed that all particles of matter attract one another and that the force they exert diminishes with the distance, so that if they are twice as far apart they only exert one quarter the pull. Using these ideas, he succeeded—thanks to his amazing mathematical genius—in explaining, strictly and quantitatively, the structure and movements of the Solar system. This extraordinary success led people to believe that all physical phenomena must be explainable in somewhat the same way. In other words they thought that the substructure of the Universe must be mechanical, and that God was a super-engineer.

Besides the historical aura which had gathered round the sanctified mechanistic explanations, the latter also owed much of their prestige to the fact that they are particularly pleasing to the human mind by virtue of early and continuous familiarity. Thus, we find it exceedingly difficult to realise how light, as such, may be thrown back from a mirror. But the difficulty is resolved when we remember that a ball may bounce off a wall, and when we think of both the light and the ball as being *reflected*. Thus we *explain* the reflection of light by means of a mechanical analogy. This particular reason for the prestige which attached itself to mechanistic views may be spoken of as the anthropomorphism which it necessarily carries within itself, but the existence of which it does not openly avow.

Now, unfortunately, as time went on it was found necessary to attribute to various elements of the substructure of the universe mechanical properties which were not only unlike those possessed by ordinary matter, but which were also directly contradictory to one another. The ether, for instance, which had been invented in order to account for the transmission of optical, electrical, and magnetic forces was considered to possess either an enormous or a very small —almost negligible—density ; to be infinitely rigid or infinitely pliable ; both to exist and not to exist, and so on.

THE WORLD AS A MIGHTY GEOMETRICAL THEOREM

THERE existed in science, however, another method of approach : the purely mathematical or geometrical. Its roots went back to Pythagoras, who said that number is the essence of all things ; through the influence of Plato and Descartes this method had never really passed into oblivion.

Towards the beginning of the present century this tendency suddenly blossomed forth, gained much prestige through the success of Einstein's theories of relativity, and may now be said to have ousted the older mechanism from its former position of predominance. The idea is this : a number of laws and of observations are known which apply severally to different fields of experience. We wish to unite these laws by means of a theory. But how do we know that the essential connections can be exhibited by *mechanical* models ? Are we certain that the continuous search for mechanical analogies will necessarily be successful ? It might well be that the connection which our theories should exhibit would turn out to be expressible only in mathematical symbolism. After all, mathematics is more fundamental, more abstract, more general than mechanics. And this represents the point of view of the triumphant geometers of to-day.

Perhaps " geometers " is not quite the right word to use. In modern times geometry itself has become so abstract that its ideas can no longer be adequately represented by lines and curves drawn on paper. The modern geometers, revelling in multi-dimensional spaces, function theories, and curious axioms, have developed a new symbolism which really resembles algebra far more than it resembles the old Greek geometry of Euclid and his successors. They now describe this work as being an *analysis* ; and thus they would prefer to describe their theories of the physical universe as being *mathematical* rather than geometrical, and they might sum up their ideal of scientific achievement by the formula that " God is a mathematician."

This changed viewpoint is considered as marking a great advance on the older mechanistic ideal. For, firstly, it is supposed that it means the abandonment of still other anthropomorphic features, since it is so much more abstract. Secondly, it is supposed that it also indicates a removal of certain metaphysical elements, such as forces and hidden motions ; and hence it tends to make Science more objective, general, and powerful. Lastly, it removes, at one fell swoop, numerous logical and philosophical difficulties—such as those which surrounded the older use of the words " cause and effect."

However this may be, the triumph has only been won at a heavy cost ; no less than giving up the idea that the universe is ultimately comprehensible ; that is, that its structure can be understood in terms of concepts gathered from our everyday experience. Until a few years ago it had always been assumed that the world of reality corresponded in some way with the world of appearance, and that the connections between them could be made comprehensible : that is, could be exhibited, perhaps visually, perhaps only æsthetically, but at any rate in some *common-sense* way. It now appears, to judge from the pronouncements of eminent mathematical physicists, that this bold idea has been abandoned. " New refinements of experimental technique brought new observational knowledge which showed that the workings of nature could not be explained in terms of the familiar concepts of everyday life. New and unfamiliar concepts were found to be necessary ; the age of common-sense science had passed. We are now finding that every effort to portray the external world brings us up immediately against concepts which we can neither picture, imagine, nor describe." [1]

These words help to explain the vain attempts which were made some ten years ago by non-mathematicians to understand the Einstein theory of Relativity, then at the heyday of

[1] Sir James Jeans, *The New Background of Science.*

its press popularity. Ultimately what these people wanted was an explanation of the structure of the theory in terms of the old and familiar mechanical analogies and concepts. Since, however, the essence of the theory was the abandonment of these and their replacement by pure mathematical symbolism, their efforts were doomed to disappointment. They asked for mechanics and they were given mathematical symbolism. They ought not to have been dissatisfied, since this is what the theory set out to give, and the mechanical analogies presented by the popularisers were really quite beside the point.

THEORIES THAT IGNORE THE BEAUTY AND PASSION OF LIFE

BUT it must not be supposed that the changed standpoint of natural science has succeeded in removing all difficulties. A number of problems of the greatest and most immediate importance face us, and they clamour for consideration. For example, we still have with us the old unsolved problem of matter and mind. If we separate man from nature, if these two are different in essence, how can they act and react one on the other ? Again, if we suppose that the nature of things can only be expressed mathematically, must we for ever abandon the attempt to deal systematically with the qualities themselves, with the colours, the sounds, the shapes which are for all of us the most real aspect of the world, and which transform the quantitative nothingness into that great plenum of passionate beauty and colourful experience, in which we live and have our being ?

On a narrower plane, are we condemned for ever to attempt the Sisyphus-like labour of constructing sciences of biology and of psychology with the very inadequate concepts and tools of the mathematical phyiscist ?

These, of course, are general philosophical problems. As such, the positive scientist will at once refuse to consider them. But he has no right to evade the issue in this way : these problems have reached their present acute form because science has progressed in a particular direction. As these problems have all been raised by science itself they should not be wholly unloaded on to the philosopher, whose only answer might have to be : Change your axioms and your fundamental postulates, and these urgent problems will not arise.

Within twentieth-century natural science, problems abound,

triviality beyond compare. At best, it was obvious that it only answered the question " how ? " and not " why ? " Yet it was the latter which was really important : Man had been given life and placed in the world to fulfil the highest of destinies. The universe had been made for him and to allow him to work out God's purpose.

"THE ONE REMAINS ; THE MANY FADE AND PASS "

IT is obvious that we have travelled far from such views. The mediæval philosophy, which was only a generalisation of such a teleology, has been largely overthrown in the popular mind by the advancement of natural science. (Is it not evident that this mere fact indicates clearly that modern natural science implies the acceptance of a metaphysics irreconcilable with that of the scholastics ?) But to return to the idea of change—in itself a fact puzzling to the philosopher concerned with the attempt to make the universe intelligible to the understanding. Why should things alter and take on fresh forms ? Is not, perhaps, the old idea first proposed by Parmenides, that the universe is a vast and unchanging stable sphere, the only rational and logically comprehensible philosophical representation of reality ? Is not all change a mere illusion caused by the incomplete and unsatisfactory nature of our senses ?

It is hardly necessary to add that such a theory is negatived by the first act of perception : things really do change and alter. The Scholastics—the monkish philosophers of the Middle Ages—therefore adopted the old Aristotelian notion of the Potential and the Actual. They expanded these notions and fitted them into a Christian philosophy. Their central idea was that there existed an Absolute Actuality which united in itself the two notions of the Unmoved Mover of Aristotle and the Personal Father and Creator of the early Christians. This was the Godhead who, by His perfect love and beauty, caused alteration and change in all that was potentially the bearer of a higher and nobler existence : He was the *alpha* and the *omega*, the beginning and the end.

Thus we have, on the one hand, the world of matter, of the Potential. On the other, we have an Absolute Actuality causing change, causing an actualisation of the Potential. Between these two stands man, an essential link, partaking of both. Now, follow out a few of the implications of these ideas. To begin with, we shall note that God is also eternal

Reason and Love, both the creator and the end of the Cosmic Scheme. If this be so, the whole of his creation must be rational and understandable by the mind of man. There is no room in such a scheme for principles of uncertainty or for confessions that the universe may be so complicated that the mind of man will not be able to comprehend the meaning of the natural laws which it discovers or codifies.

Again, if man is the centre of the universe, it appears most probable that his dwelling, the Earth, is also the centre of the physical universe. We may even go farther along this line of argument : if man embodies the divine purpose, then the senses which God has given him should be sufficient to reveal to him the essential structure of the Cosmos. There should be no talk of primary and secondary qualities or of a world of mathematical relationships as opposed to a world of colour, sound, and scent.

However, we are not concerned here with a general explanation or defence of the philosophic background of the Middle Ages. It will, of course, be evident immediately that such views have much to recommend them ; they are not only adventurous and satisfying, but they are also in very close empirical relationship with the actual world immediately revealed by our senses, which are after all our only gateway to knowledge of the external world. It is probable, indeed, that our most promising line of advance, either in philosophy or in modern science, is to attempt to bring back something of these older ideas into our present schemes. But, I repeat, it is not our purpose here to extend this discussion, but merely to use it as a background against which to exhibit as clearly as possible the philosophic foundations of the science of to-day. Our immediate object is to explain how it was possible to replace the old categories of Potentiality and Actuality, Matter and Form, and so on, by our mathematical concepts of Space and Time, Mass and Energy.

COPERNICUS, HERALD OF A NEW AGE

As we all know, this fundamental change took place at the time of, and shortly after, the Renaissance. It would be foolish, of course, to ascribe it purely to the influence of one man, or even to that of a small number of men. The correct view is probably that in those days there was given a new orientation to the Western mind. That long-drawn-out episode was one in which every European shared ; but still there is no doubt at all that it is possible to name a series of men in whom the new tendencies crystallised to a pre-eminent degree.

It is in this capacity for expressing with great force and clarity, in their lives and in their thought, the full tendencies and capabilities of an age that the genius of these men resides. Hence, it will simplify our task to consider their work ; but, since it is not our object here to write a history of science, we need only study the philosophical implications of their researches. If we were forced to give a date for the beginning of the new movement, we should probably be safe in choosing 1543, when the Pole, Nicolaus Copernicus, gave his consent (on his death-bed) to the publication of his great book, *De Revolutionibus Orbium Cœlestium*. He proposed, indeed, a tremendous revolution in human thought : no less than the abandonment of the view that the earth was the centre of all things. He proposed the replacement of this common-sense deduction from observed facts by the seemingly far-fetched theory that the Sun was the centre and the Earth but one of the wandering planets ! This idea seemed to be in flat contradiction, not only with the prevailing philosophy, but also with the facts of everyday experience. Let us examine a few of the objections which might be raised against it.

(1) As we have already pointed out, the scholastics believed implicitly in the reality of sense data. The Copernican view of a rotating earth and a stationary sun contradicts what we actually observe. On the other hand, the theory of Ptolemy (accepted in those days and fortified by the respect acquired by its thirteen centuries of existence) accepted these sense data : the earth was still and the celestial bodies rotated around it.

(2) The Ptolemaic theory was a link in the prevalent philosophy, the breaking of which would weaken the whole chain. And mark that, actually, there were no known phenomena which the older view could not explain.

(3) If the earth spins on its axis towards the West, then when a stone falls from a tower it should fall East of the latter, since the soil has moved westwards while the stone was in no way connected with it.

(4) If the earth rotates round the sun, then we should see the nearer " fixed stars " altering their position, just as fairly distant objects seem to move against the more distant background when we ourselves change our position.

And against these formidable arguments, what could Copernicus urge ? Only one thing : his theory was mathematically simpler. It threw the facts of astronomy into a simpler and more harmonious *mathematical* order : to " save the phenomena "—that is, to give a satisfactory theoretical explanation of them—he needed only 34 epicycles instead of 80.

Truly not a powerful argument, and no one would have

(1) MOVEMENT OF THE EARTH

While the stone drops to the ground, the earth moves, so that the point Y now finds itself underneath the stone. So the stone would apparently move westwards. In actual fact, of course, the stone continues to share in the movement of the earth (Newton's First Law of Motion), and therefore seems to fall vertically. The law referred to was not discovered until much after Copernicus' day.

considered it at all if the ground had not been well prepared for its acceptance. However, we should remember that astronomy was already considered largely as a branch of mathematics : the geometry of the heavens. Indeed, Ptolemy himself, in so many words, had rejected the attempt to interpret the idea of crystal spheres physically (*i.e.* in modern terms *meta*-physically). Again, at the beginning of the sixteenth century, the Platonic philosophy was in the ascendant, and in Platonism (especially in the books then known, *e.g.* the

Timæus), there exists a powerful Pythagorean influence. We should remember that it was Pythagoras who first expressed the Credo of the mathematical philosopher : Number is the essence of all things.

A DISCOVERY THAT SHOOK THE FOUNDATIONS OF CHRISTIAN PHILOSOPHY

ONE of the important features of this revived Platonic philosophy was the idea implicit in it that it was legitimate to attempt the construction of a universal mathematics of nature, though how this was to be achieved remained an unsolved problem. Already with Leonardo, however, we begin to notice the growth of an interest in the mathematical aspects of phenomena : in gates as " potential levers," in the mechanics of the movements of limbs and of birds. Evidently one of the most obvious fields in which to attempt the application of mathematical-geometrical methods was that of astronomy ; for this science, as we have said, was already considered as a branch of geometry. In time, the question would arise as to whether it was not legitimate to simplify astronomical problems by changing the ultimate point of reference from the earth to the sun, as would naturally be done in any geometrical problem (" true " in geometry= " true " in astronomy). Nor was tradition wholly against this. Indeed, Ptolemy himself had already asserted definitely that it is legitimate to interpret the facts of astronomy by the simplest geometrical scheme which will " save the phenomena," no matter whose metaphysics may be upset. In other words, astronomy is essentially to be considered as a branch of mathematics, and any attempt to interpret its findings by investing them with physical reality is open to misconstruction: a more modern " twentieth-century " position it is hard to conceive. Nor had there been universal agreement among the ancients as to the interpretation to be placed on these astronomical data : some had rejected the " earth-centric " system in favour of the mathematically simpler " sun-centric " scheme. And it was the discovery of this fact which finally set the feet of Copernicus on the road to his most fruitful speculations.

It is well known that it was only on his death-bed that he consented to the publication of his book : and, further, that a preface was included in which any attempt to attribute physical meaning to his mathematical theorems was explicitly rejected. This is usually presented either as hypocrisy or as cowardly pandering to the prejudices of the Roman Catholic clergy. But the considerations outlined above show that it was probably quite sincerely meant.

Nor did the Church show hostility to the scientific views themselves : they at once used the work of Copernicus in the construction of astronomical tables. The historic fight, which came to a head with the burning of Giordano Bruno and with the imprisonment of Galileo Galilei, was one between the Aristotelian metaphysics and that which grew from the scientific work of the pioneers of the modern age. It would be unfair to accuse the Catholic Church of those days of being opposed to enlightenment. Actually, all forms of organised religion were then united only by their hostility to the new philosophy. And this is easily understood when it is realised that the latter did indeed attack a system of metaphysics, which was not only eminently logical and closely in contact with immediate reality, but also gave to religion an essential place in the scheme of things. The slowing-up of scientific progress which occurred between the work of Copernicus and that of Galileo was largely due to the wars which devastated Europe at that time ; or it may be ascribed to the necessity for a period of germination. Merely to say that it is due to religious persecution is to exhibit unphilosophic prejudices and a belief in universal cowardice.

With the publication of *De Revolutionibus* the stage is set for the struggle. The fundamental questions are becoming clear : what meaning can we attach to the word " true " when we say that the " sun-centric " theory of Copernicus is true ? Is the universe as a whole, including our earth, fundamentally mathematical in its structure ? Are the stars bodies physically of the same kind as the earth and the sun ? An affirmative answer to these last two questions would overthrow the Aristotelian science of the Middle Ages, shake the metaphysic based on it, and clear the way for the development of our mechanical civilisation and for our present positivistic philosophy.

KEPLER'S VISION OF A VAST MATHEMATICAL HARMONY

IN spite of the clear formulation of these problems, over half a century elapsed before really new developments took place. It is true that, here and there, a few bold thinkers openly championed the new cosmology. They were usually men like

Giordano Bruno, who was interested mainly in the philosophical implications of the Copernican theories, and their work had little direct influence on the development of science. It would be interesting and fruitful to follow up the influence of Bruno on the subsequent development of metaphysics, but this is scarcely the place to do so.

It will be more profitable to consider shortly the work of that curiously interesting figure, John Kepler. It was he who discovered the mathematical laws which express, on the " suncentric " theory, the movements of the planets, *e.g.* in their motion they describe an ellipse and not a circle, as Copernicus had thought ; the line which joins a planet to the sun sweeps out equal areas in equal times (see Fig. 2). By these discoveries he exhibited the mathematical harmonies which the Pythagorean soul desired to find, and prepared the way for the giant systematisations of Isaac Newton. The questions, however, which face us here are :

(1) What influences led to the discoveries he made ?

(2) In what way did he generalise his ideas and thus influence his successors ?

In order to understand Kepler's work, the first thing we must clearly realise is the extraordinary mystical cast of his philosophy of life and nature. We might almost go so far as to say that anyone wishing to establish the curious claim that mysticism " pays " need go no further than to study his work. To him the universe appeared permanently pervaded by a geometrical deity : and this God was, so to say, expressed in the highest degree by the sun. The latter is obviously at the centre of the universe : " For who, in our most beautiful temple, could set this light in another or better place than that from which it can at once illuminate the whole ? Not to speak of the fact that not unfittingly do some call it the light of the world, others the soul, still others the governor—the all-seer. And so, in fact, does the sun, seated on his royal throne, guide his family of planets as they circle round him."

Kepler even applied the doctrine of the Trinity to his astronomical speculations : the sun is God the Father, the sphere of the fixed stars is God the Son, while the ethereal medium through which the power of the sun acts on the planets is the Holy Ghost. It is easy to understand why Kepler combined profitable astrological work with unremunerative astronomical speculations, probably quite sin-

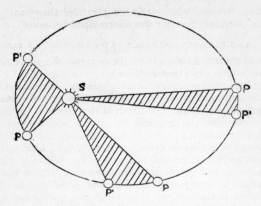

(2) KEPLER'S SECOND LAW

*If the areas SPP′ (which are shaded) are all made equal, then
the planet takes the same time to move from P to P′. Thus
the line SP sweeps out equal areas in equal times. This law
showed that the planets moved in a perfectly regular way.*

cerely. This peculiarly mystical cast of mind, in a way, unites
Kepler with many of the movements of thought typical of
the Middle Ages which, through him, have thus influenced
modern science. But he was too much of a scientist and too
much of a mathematician to be wholly satisfied with their
symbolic imagery, or to attempt their development in directions which would have appeared promising or worth while
to a Jakob Boehm.

A mathematician sees a mathematical world, and to John
Kepler, mystic *and* geometer, the world appeared as a vast
and intricate mathematical harmony. To him the underlying
mathematical harmony, which he discovered in the observed
facts, was actually the *cause* of the latter, the reason why
they are as they are. Thus, the "formal cause" of the
Aristotelians was to be interpreted mathematically. You
will notice how this is far from the teleological (or purposive)
explanations of the Mediævals.

According to the new philosophy it was not necessary to
show in what way the motion of the stars and planets, of the
sun and the moon, helped man to fulfil his eternal destiny.
It was only necessary to show that, by their motions, they

exemplified objectively certain geometrical theorems : if this could be done, no further questions need be asked.

THE PLANETS' ORDERLY PATH ROUND THE SUN

SINCE he believed strongly in these views, Kepler now threw himself, with unexampled fervour, into the task of exposing the hidden mathematical harmonies of Natural Creation which he felt convinced were revealed by the observation of astronomical geometry. He studied the ratios of the distances between the planets and the sun and connected these (incorrectly) with the existence of five regular solids. He showed that planets move in an orderly manner, and, finally, that the solar system can be considered as a unity. Multiply the distance between any planet and the sun by itself twice (*i.e.* obtain the cube of the distance) and divide the number thus obtained by the time it takes to go round the sun *multiplied by itself*, and you will get the same number for all the planets, which are thus, by a numerical bond, united into a system (see Fig. 3).

It is unnecessary, really, to go further than this : you will have exhibited the hidden mathematical harmony. Not that Kepler is satisfied with this work of his ; he still believes that yet finer and more beautiful harmonies are to be revealed ; for instance, it should be possible to gather all his laws together in the same way that he had already gathered together into a harmonious whole the observations made by the great Danish observer, Tycho Brahé. Nevertheless, this deeper and more subtle analysis would follow the lines that he had sketched out : he often says that his discoveries have shown the necessary and rational grounds of the structure of the world.

In addition to this thoroughly " modern " view of the fundamental nature of mathematics, Kepler also exhibits clearly yet another of the fundamental beliefs of the man of science of to-day : he is a thorough empiricist—that is, he believes in the primary importance of observed fact. He never thinks of ignoring observations which do not fit in with his views ; if his theories conflict with astronomical observations, the former must be abandoned or recast. The point must be strongly emphasised, for it is one of the most important contributions of Science to the realm of intellectual speculation. The world of thought must be modelled on the world of external reality : observed empirical fact must be accorded logical primacy.

KEPLER'S THIRD LAW

Planet.	Average Distance from the Sun.	Time of One Complete Revolution (in years).	D^3	T^2	T^2/D^3
	$= D$	$= T$	(approx.)	(approx.)	
Mercury	·3871	·2408	·058	·058	1
Venus .	·7233	·6152	·378	·378	1
Earth .	1·0000	1·0000	1·000	1·000	1
Mars .	1·5237	1·8808	3·54	3·54	1
Jupiter .	5·2028	11·862	140·8	140·8	1
Saturn .	9·5388	29·457	868	868	1

(3) *Since T^2/D^3 equals 1 in the case of the Earth, owing to
the units of time and distance chosen, this quotient also equals
1 for all the planets. For other systems* (e.g. *the satellites of
Jupiter*) *and other units the value of T^2/D^3 would change,
but remain the same for all the members of the family.*

GALILEO, FATHER OF MODERN SCIENCE

IF we now take stock of the position as it appeared at the
end of the sixteenth century, and as it is exhibited by the
work of Kepler, we see that the scientific world is becoming
more and more platonic and pythagorean ; the world of the
platonic ideas is suddenly found to be identical with the realm
of geometrical relationship. At the same time, the claims of
observation and empiricism as arbiters of philosophical truth
are being more and more widely admitted. The new metaphysics is beginning to appear : we hear talk of primary and
secondary qualities, efficient causation, quality and quantity
(with the stress on the latter). For the men of the Renaissance,
the causal harmony, which can be observed in the phenomena,
must there be verified with the greatest exactness and rigour,
and, above all, *quantitatively*. However, in spite of the
brilliant successes already obtained in the regions of
astronomy, the victory seemed far from won. No one would

have been able to prophesy how the new natural philosophy could be applied, for instance, to the study of optics or of mechanics ; it is evident that the fundamental axioms were not yet completely accepted or understood.

But great and immediate progress was to be made as a result of the work of that genius, Galileo Galilei, who, better than any other man, deserves the title of " the father of modern science." We need not enter into the details of his life, nor recount his scientific achievements : our primary concern is with his philosophical ideas. To begin with, Galileo is thoroughly in sympathy with the views of Kepler. To him, also, nature appears first and foremost as a theatre for the exhibition of a mathematical order and harmony. But he followed the tendencies further, and not only developed them, but gave explicit expression to them in his numerous philosophical writings.

He was attempting the reduction of the sensible world to a mathematical harmony. Now it is obvious that there are certain qualities of experience which lend themselves immediately to mathematical handling. You see a dish of apples on the table : you can think of their number, their geometric shape, their position on the table, and so on. All these characteristics lend themselves well to immediate representation by figures and by lines. These, says Galileo, are the characteristics which are suitable material for scientific handling, they are the primary qualities of the apples. On the other hand, the colour, smell, taste, or desirability of the apples may vary from individual to individual, and we cannot be sure of their reality. They are subjective and relative, secondary qualities of no interest to the scientist. Hence, if we wish to study any natural objects or phenomena we must begin by distinguishing carefully between the primary and the secondary qualities. The former are objective, immutable, mathematical, absolute, and a study of these leads to real (scientific) knowledge. The latter are subjective, relative, sensible, fluctuating, and a study of these leads only to opinion.

This distinction embodies a tremendously bold metaphysical assertion, which cannot really be justified on any grounds whatsoever—not even on pragmatic grounds, since other axioms *might* have led to equal success. The best that can be said about it is to repeat with Voltaire : " Croyez-moi, mon ami, l'erreur aussi a son mérite."

THE FATHER OF MODERN SCIENCE: GALILEO

THE QUESTION OF TIME : THE GREAT PUZZLE

HOWEVER, one is inclined to think that this restriction of the province of science to the study of number, figure, magnitude, position, and motion was indeed a step necessary to the erection of our present scientific edifice. It is, nevertheless, a fact that it entails an abdication : Galileo renounced the old adventurous wish to extend the power of man's reason over the whole realm of phenomena. It is probably due to this unfortunate distinction in the field of knowledge, between what is supposed to be suitable material for science and what is considered irrelevant, that a position has now arisen in philosophy which makes it impossible for us to refute the belief usually referred to as solipsism (*i.e.* that the only reality we can become aware of is that of the ideas in our own minds). In the scientific field it has probably forced psychology and biology to restrict their ambition to a study of trivialities or of side issues—it necessarily emasculated these budding sciences.

We repeat : the doctrines enunciated by Galileo may have been necessary, but it is in the highest degree probable that future progress will come largely through the fusion of what is worth while in these ideas with the essentials of the mediæval view. Not, of course, that Galileo was always so revolutionary. Very often we find him refuting his Aristotelian opponents by their own maxims : *Nature does not that by many things which may be done by few . . . nature is inexorable,* and so on. And in this way he fulfilled the useful function of ensuring that these important precepts should be incorporated and assimilated in the new scientific philosophy.

Galileo's study of the motion of celestial bodies led him easily and gradually to the study of the motion of bodies on the earth's surface. Bruno's idea that the stars were bodies built of the same substance as the earth facilitated this extension. But to do this successfully necessitated also a recasting of the meanings of the words space, time, force, and causality, in such a way as to make these concepts useful to the mathematical physicist and adapted to the quantitative standpoint of the latter.

Space had hitherto been considered as the boundary between objects ; it now becomes something underlying them or occupied by them ; indeed, it becomes identical with the realm of geometry.

As regards *time*, we have already said that to the scholastic philosophers it was, in a way, an abstraction from physical phenomena which was essentially irrepresentable by a dimension or a length. Of course their clocks gave them a measure of its passage, but not of its real rate of flow. It was to be thought of as something essentially qualitative. Now, even in his earliest observations, Galileo's mind is already turning to methods of time measurement. It was no accident that it was he who discovered the law of the pendulum and made the first clocks which had any pretence to accuracy. Before his day the functioning of clocks depended on flow of water or on the rate of burning of a candle : it was he who first thought of applying controllable *cyclic* processes. Implicit in his work is the idea of time as a continuum, stretching out backwards into the past and forwards into the future with the present merely as a moving boundary : an essentially quantitative concept. Thus, with Galileo, time first begins to assume the aspect of an irreversible fourth dimension, almost spatial in its attributes.

COMPARISON OF THE MEDIÆVAL AND SCIENTIFIC POINTS OF VIEW

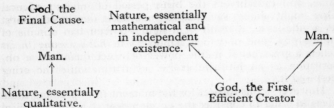

[From Burtt, "*Metaphysical Foundations of Modern Science.*"

The immediate practical gain brought about by the adoption of these views was immense. We glimpse the possibilities inherent in a philosophy which considers the world as a vast machine to be studied quantitatively. The cost, of course, was correspondingly high ; false and unanswerable problems arose, such as those of memory and of the relation between time lived and time measured on clocks, problems which the work of subsequent centuries has only sufficed to make more obscure. Using these allied concepts of time and space, together with the vulgar notion of force and of resistance, Galileo now laid the foundations of the science of dynamics.

To him, therefore, the problem of causality appeared in a somewhat different light from that in which it had appeared to Kepler. It was not so much a question of exhibiting the mathematical beauty and harmony discoverable in natural phenomena as of showing what forces were concerned in the production of the observed mechanical changes : perhaps the first clear statement of the modern metaphysic of *Power*.

A SOLDIER-PHILOSOPHER WHO BANISHED BEAUTY FROM HIS UNIVERSE

ONE notices here, then, the birth of the second great movement of modern science : the mechanical world view, the world machine. It is probable that this has now outlived its utility ; mechanical interpretations are certainly somewhat under a cloud nowadays, though for the wrong reasons. With Kepler we saw the laying of the foundation underlying the geometrical view, which flourishes to-day, and in the next paragraph we shall have to consider Descartes' development of this. Already, we can see how our discussion has clarified certain of the issues of which we spoke. It must be obvious, for instance, how powerful were the fertilising influences of purely philosophical ideas regarding the nature of space, time, and causality at the birth period of modern science. One might almost say that Science itself developed almost as a side-issue, a result of a fight between two schools of philosophy, one of which happened to hold as one of its tenets a great belief in the power of exact quantitative observation as an ultimate arbiter of truth, while the other despised it.

However, let us forbear for the moment from pressing these ideas in order to consider the development of the geometrical world view as expressed by that famous gentleman, soldier, and philosopher of Touraine, René Descartes.

Here again we are immediately struck by the tremendous power attributed to mathematics—it is no less than the key to all knowledge of nature. With Descartes, the problem of science is merely whether or not it is possible to extract from phenomena those aspects which are geometrical, and every other magnitude must be reduced to mathematical dimensions before it can be handled effectively. With him as with Kepler, the human mind appears as being fashioned not so as to understand *anything*, but so as to understand mainly mathematical relationships. In this field, nevertheless, there is one significant change from the position of Kepler : mathematics and geometry are bursting aside the bonds and limitations of spatial representation, geometry need not be the Greek representational science of Euclid, the figures of which are always ideally capable of being drawn in sand or on paper. It was Descartes who invented co-ordinate geometry, in which an attempt is made to unite algebra and geometry ; it was he who assumed that there exists a correspondence between the realm of number and the realm of space : Pythagoras and Euclid are to be united.

Descartes further attempted to apply, in detail, his geometrical theories to the world-machine by extending their application to regions which Kepler had not ventured to enter. His bold attempt failed, and in a way this was a great misfortune both for science and for philosophy. It failed when confronted by some of the most obvious and elementary facts of motion ; thus, two bodies identical geometrically (say a ball of brass and one of wood) do not behave in identical ways when placed in the same position (say when they are both placed in a vessel full of water). The key to the solution of this problem, of course, was given later—mainly by Isaac Newton—when the importance of mass was clearly understood ; but this notion itself is not really entirely reducible to geometry. Still, in spite of his relative failure, Descartes' work had an enormous influence on the later progress of science and laid the seeds of the fruitful developments of to-day.

Consider now his notion of the world machine, as the objectification of a geometrical theorem. What room is there in such a world for the miscalled secondary qualities, for the ideas of beauty, of colours, and of sounds, ideas which filled the world of the mediæval philosopher and which were for him—and for us in our everyday lives—the experiences which give to the world reality and to life value ? They are evidently not immediately reducible to geometry, hence they are not so real as the others, says Descartes. We must, for purposes of analysis, divide the universe into two principal aspects : the world of extension—*res extensa*—and the world of mind—*res cogitans*.

The first is the province of science, the second cannot be treated scientifically at all. But he adds, somewhat illogically, that this world of secondary qualities is not less real than the other. Needless to say, one question which must necessarily be faced by this type of philosophy is this : If nature is geometrical in essence, where shall we place the *Res Cogitans*, the world of unextended thinking spirits ? Put it in the pineal gland, says Descartes impatiently ; it is extended to just beyond the physical body, says Henry More, inconsistently.

DEBTS THE MEDIÆVAL SCIENTISTS OWED TO THE PHILOSOPHERS

HOWEVER, this problem did not really worry the new philosophers very greatly. The followers, more Cartesian than Descartes himself, had no hesitation in dumping the whole of the world of secondary qualities, all the joy and beauty, the fragrancy and the colour of human life, into the nervous and circulatory systems : with Hobbes, for instance, the mind is something located and wholly confined within the body.

It would be interesting to continue our inquiry into the genesis of the scientific notions of to-day, and to show, at each point, how their development was influenced by philosophical theories. But we have probably gone far enough in this direction to exhibit two things : firstly, that the claim of the positivists (that they are able to develop a science free from metaphysical assumptions) is worthless. The very words they use—space, time, causality, and so on—are metaphysical in essence ; the sense in which they are used is not even unambiguous, since, in fact, an alternative meaning was formerly attached to them. The aims and ideals which the man of science has in mind are purely metaphysical, and the methods he uses in his researches are largely the application of a philosophical theory, and are only acceptable after their philosophical implications have been discussed. Lastly, his criteria of truth and of proof cannot be justified merely by scientific considerations.

Secondly, it must not be assumed that the explanations given by the new philosophers were considered by them as being finally satisfactory. All of them used the idea of a Godhead to complete their work. Very often, God appears as a metaphysical notion or concept rather than as a living reality ; but this is not the point. The thing that matters is that, in their opinion, the scientific scheme needs extra-scientific ontological (*i.e.* that concern the abstract essence of things) elements to give it substance and human value. This is the case not only with Kepler and Galileo, but also with Descartes and even with Newton. Now, these men were all interested in explaining the real world, and an attempt merely to build up schemes of relationship possessing no explanatory value would not have interested them. Here metaphysics— as a study of the world of reality—appears in another light. It supplies the motive force for purely scientific researches ; it supplies the scheme of explanation which fills the skeletal structure of the scientific world with substance and with life. This necessary function of metaphysics is one aspect of what we called earlier its conservative function, as a preserver of well-established and universally accepted truths.

SCIENCE IGNORES MAN'S IDEAS

THE new scientific methods involved the idea of a universe of objects having no necessary connection with human existence or with the human mind. The Realm of Nature was now thought of as simply existing, quite apart from the accidental feature of our own perceptions. As Engels, the famous collaborator of Karl Marx, has well said : " To the scientist, nature is primary and spirit secondary ; and this is the position we speak of as being materialism."

But a little reflection will show that this position cannot be the correct expression of the whole truth. For in what sense do colours, sounds, harmonies, scents just *exist*, out there, away from our minds ? Hence the acceptance of the new ideas caused a concentration of philosophical attention on the problems left ignored by the scientists, and was directly responsible for the growth of idealistic philosophies, the polar complement of scientific materialism.

The history of thought from the seventeenth to the nine-teenth centuries illustrates this in excellent fashion. The new problems, raised by the materialism of science, bring questions also which philosophers face and which they can answer only by stressing those idealistic aspects of Reality neglected by the new school. A really satisfying answer eludes their efforts, partly, no doubt, because they accept as necessary categories of explanation the space, time, and causality of the physicists. As a result, their conclusions seem to be somewhat lacking in force and clarity. Indeed, it is only quite lately—during the present century—that an effort is definitely being made to get rid of these unsatisfying concepts and of this inadequate terminology.

These statements obviously need amplification and justi-fication. The reader should refer to the section, *Philo-*

sophy's Problem, and study the accounts of the work of Locke, Berkeley, Hume, and Kant[1]—a mighty succession of thinkers. He will find Locke separating sharply the primary qualities which are measurable and real from the colours and the sounds which he considers in some way to be illusions ; Berkeley demonstrating that there are no primary qualities at all, and that the reality of the Universe depends on the existence of an Ideal God ; Hume showing fairly satisfactorily that even cause and effect are mere convenient habits of mind. And lastly, Immanuel Kant [2] attempts a gigantic reconciliation between the mathematical materialism of science and the prevailing idealism of philosophy. His problem was to construct a scheme which would allow for the existence, not only of a world of phenomena (or things-as-they-appear) which the man of science could investigate, but also of a subjective world which would serve to interpret the former and to endow it with content and meaning. Partial success certainly crowned his efforts, and his work continues to influence us profoundly. Most amusing is his list of Antinomies (or contradictions) :

1. *Thesis :* The world had a beginning in time and has limits in space.
   Antithesis : The world is without beginning and without limits in space.
2. *Thesis :* Every composite substance in the world is made up of simple parts.
   Antithesis : There exists nothing simple.
3. *Thesis :* Freedom is a reality. There may be an absolute, uncaused series of effects.
   Antithesis : All things whatsoever take place in accordance with natural law.
4. *Thesis :* There belongs to the world an absolutely necessary being.
   Antithesis : Nothing is absolutely necessary.

THE FAR-REACHING REVERBERATIONS OF KANT'S THEORY

REALLY, one might almost be tempted to look upon Kant's list as an abstracted programme of future research in natural science. One has only to open any of the recent books in which an attempt is made to outline the progress of physics to be once again confronted with this list of antinomies, with

[1] See pages 422–434.   [2] See page 430.

thesis and antithesis neatly docketed, and all under such labels as *The newer problems of astronomy*, or *Unsolved problems of Quantum mechanics*, or *God and Science*, etc. etc. The only difference with Kant's list being that the theses and antitheses are removed to different parts of the books, and that no attempt is made to resolve the antinomies they express.

For instance, consider the first in connection with the enormous amount of controversy which has raged round the interpretation of the Theory of Relativity, with its " finite-but-unbounded " pseudo-spherical space-time, its notions of the volume of the universe, its expanding universes, and so on. And what of the second antinomy in connection with the modern atomic and electronic theories ? Or of the third in connection with the Heisenberg Uncertainty Relations, which seems to assert the existence of freedom of action among atoms, the behaviour of which is exactly expressed by mechanical and statistical laws ? However, we must firmly resist the temptation to follow further this fascinating topic.

It may well be asked why we have spent so much space in discussing the philosophical ideas of the eighteenth century, while paying only the most cursory attention to the development of pure science. Yet the reason is not really difficult to understand : when the age of scientific genius opened, the pioneers were greatly influenced by purely philosophical considerations, and the growing-point of both science and philosophy were identical ; such men as Descartes were equally great in both spheres. Now, once the scientific method had been hammered out, the rest was an obvious and natural development of principles, and a working out of details. Here the direct influence of philosophy is minimal and need not greatly concern us. On the other hand, the reaction of the practical successes of science on philosophy was tremendous, and the new results had to be, as it were, digested and assimilated. These labours have taken philosophical thought about 250 years, and it is only quite recently that it seems that it will again influence practical science.

Perhaps, however, to say that contemporary philosophy had no direct influence on science during all these years is going rather too far. Thus it would be hard to overestimate the influence of Kant, whose followers produced in Germany a certain highly intellectual atmosphere and milieu peculiarly favourable to the growth and free development of accurate scientific work of the highest quality. Besides this, of course,

16

philosophy continued to play a continuously critical rôle, and it did a great deal to keep within bounds the (dare we say it ?) romantic outbursts of the scientists.

THE ORIGINS OF MODERN CHEMISTRY

So far we have considered mainly the development of the science of physics, and we have said not a word about chemistry. Yet everyone knows that, as regards the material advancement of our civilisation, this science is at least as important as physics itself. It has given us, amongst a host of other things, such essential commodities as cheap and plentiful metals and alloys, coal and light oils, food substitutes and drugs. It affects our lives closely and intimately at every moment, and yet its philosophical influence has been very small. This is due largely to the fact that modern chemistry, in as far as it is not mere classification, consists almost entirely of an application of the principles and methods of physics to another range of phenomena.

In chemistry, the Aristotelian and scholastic elements took longer to eradicate : the application of the maxims and ideas of the Galileo-Newton school was considerably more difficult. The older chemists were much concerned with the qualities of bodies : such as their colour and their actual physical state. Similarly, their idea of an element was Aristotelian : it was wetness or coldness, metallicity or combustibility, and they could not abandon their idea that such qualities were really important. Now in this case, the idea of a conservation of elements could not make any appeal, since obviously there is no conservation of redness, for instance, or of combustibility. The older chemists were quite convinced that there could be true creation or destruction of matter, and yet, without belief in a law of conservation of mass, modern chemistry could not be born.

La science exige le concept de chose, says Meyerson. That is, modern science presupposes conservation of some kind. The concept of *energy* is useful to the physicist precisely because it is conserved, and the second law of Thermodynamics, which asserts that energy gets steadily less available, is felt to be an unsatisfactory intrusion into what would otherwise be a pleasingly formal scheme. Hence chemistry was forced to remain Aristotelian until criteria were discovered which allowed the man of science to define unambiguously what he meant by " chemical substance " and by " element."

The Hon. Robert Boyle, indeed, proposed our modern definition of an element—a substance which cannot be broken down into anything simpler—before the end of the seventeenth century. No one, however, paid any attention to his remarks, and soon the theory of combustion, put forward by Becher and Stahl, held the field triumphantly. Although it is probably untrue to say that this *Phlogiston Theory* blocked the way to useful research, it was undoubtedly Aristotelian in its conception. It postulated the possession by all combustible substances of a principle of combustibility (*phlogiston*) which escaped during burning and was dissolved by the air. Phlogiston was thus a sort of semi-material substance, a hybrid of the two kinds of elements—of sensation and of substance.

The theory was overthrown by Lavoisier, who quite typically started his career as a physicist of the Newtonian school. He showed how to use the concept of mass as a criterion for the discovery of elements, made people understand the importance of quantitative relationships, and established the primacy of the balance as the tool of the chemist, By thus applying the principles of physics, he set chemistry on to a very successful road, and fully deserves the famous remark of Wurtz : *La chimie est une science française. Elle fut fondée par Lavoisier, d'immortelle memoire* (Chemistry is a French science. It was founded by Lavoisier, of immortal memory).

"THE DEBATE CONTINUES": MODERN THEORIES

ALTHOUGH chemistry was greatly helped by the application of the new methodology to its province, it is probable that the scientific historian of the future will decide that the case is quite different with biology. After resisting the introduction of the Galilean method for quite a long time, it succumbed at last ; and in the nineteenth century it abjured its own fundamental principles and took over, *en masse*, the methodology of physics. Many competent judges consider that the indigestibility of this meal has stultified significant advance. Nevertheless it appears probable that this sudden conversion of biology to the quantitative philosophy will prove, in the end, to have been a blessing in disguise. Signs are not wanting, nowadays, of the long-expected reaction of biology on physics ; and if this occurs it is very probable that entirely new points of view will be introduced into the latter.

In order to understand something of the conflict which has raged in the biological world for the last hundred years, we must consider shortly the tenets of the two competing philosophies of vitalism and mechanism. In ancient and medieval times there was no sharp line of demarcation between the study of biology and that of physical science. Both were intimately concerned with the classification of natural phenomena, both accepted the primary importance of what are now termed secondary qualities; and it appeared obvious that discoveries in either branch would serve to throw light on the problems of the other.

But with the development of physics, brought about by the work of the Galileo-Newton school, this position changed. It appeared that the methods typical of physical science were incapable of throwing light on the problems which interested the biologist: growth, reproduction, and so on. It even seemed impossible to express in a useful manner the kind of question which scientific research might be expected to answer, at any rate as long as one used the vocabulary of the newer sciences. So it became customary to speak of a " vital force " which exhibited its potency in biological changes. Originally, this probably meant only that the complexity of the facts observed in the consideration of living things, rendered it impossible to abstract the primary qualities which were the concern of positive science; or rather, that the abstraction of these to the exclusion of others led to concentration on unimportant aspects and side issues.

Now, the work of Newton had endowed the word *force* with a perfectly definite meaning which it had not had before : forces tend to move matter. Hence, gradually, the words " vital force " came to mean merely that in living things, a mysterious something existed which tended to upset the generalisations of physical science, and which was even capable of acting like a catalyst (or that which produces change without itself undergoing change) in the production of chemical compounds which could not be produced outside the living body.

In reality, the adoption of this point of view meant that the whole of the biological position had been, as it were, outflanked. It meant that biologists had accepted the new terminology, and were asking questions about living things, which could quite well be answered by the newer sciences of chemistry and of physics. The older biologists, for instance, might ask the question : " Why is this rose red ? " and by this they would have meant " Why is the quality of redness bound up with that of greenness, etc., in such and such a floral pattern ? What use does it serve ? " and so on. The newer biologists would mean : " What chemical compounds produce this redness ? How did they arise ? What energy relations are involved ? " Being unable to answer these questions, they took refuge in the operation of the mysterious vital force, which, they thought, must have been able to synthesise the necessary compounds from the elements obtained from the earth and from the air.

The progress of chemistry dealt a deadly blow to these futile notions. About a hundred years ago the German chemist, Wöhler, synthesised, in his laboratory, the chemical substance *urea* " without the aid of a kidney, either a dog's or a man's." Until then this compound had only been obtained from living things, under the supposed action of the vital force. Now it had been built up without its aid, and this discovery was soon followed by others of a similar nature.

A new epoch seemed to have dawned. Triumphant mechanism was about to extend its victorious sway over yet another region of knowledge. " Give us test-tubes, chemicals, and the resources of a laboratory and we will soon demonstrate that our positive science can tell us all that is worth knowing about life ! " cried the jubilant biological mechanists.

PROGRESS OF THE EVOLUTIONARY THEORY

AT the same time, theories of evolution began to attract universal attention. The painstaking labours of the geologists and of the biological classifiers had shown clearly that there had existed on this earth numerous forms of life quite different from those which exist to-day, and that there was a carnal and genetic continuity between those forms and theories which we know. The process of development, which has produced the living organisms which now cover the earth from these past forms, was spoken of as an *Evolution* of life.

The problem to be solved consisted, therefore, of explaining this process of evolution. Erasmus Darwin and Lamarck had already proposed explanations, but these had been considered unsatisfactory : they were indeed very much out of sympathy with the prevailing scientific views of that day. But now came along something very much more consonant with materialistic mechanism : Charles Darwin, Erasmus Darwin's grandson, and a most excellent naturalist, proposed to account for the evolution of living forms by an automatic process which employed as its mechanism the Survival of the Fittest, Natural and Sexual selection. In spite of the anthropomorphic significance attached to the words " fittest " and to the lack of exact definition of the terms employed, the theory had an immediate and resounding success. This was no doubt partly due to the political and economic theories in vogue at that time : any scientific theory which seemed to sanction the régime of cut-throat competition and *laissez-faire les plus forts*, which seemed to show that this was all for the best and in accordance with the Will of God, was certain to make a tremendous impression on the Victorians.

A GREAT VICTORIAN'S ATTEMPT TO EXPLAIN THE WORLD

IT was not long before an attempt was made to extend the ideas of Darwin to the whole field of human experience. Herbert Spencer added to them the sociological and philosophical ideas of Auguste Comte, and built up a gigantic and comprehensive systematic philosophy. Spencer considered that the whole of the organic world was only a product, a continuation, a more complex manifestation of the inorganic. The former had evolved from the latter by progressive " integration and differentiation " : the two differed only in degree of complexity, and the organic was the effect of which the inorganic was the cause. Thus Spencer attempted to cover with a single generalisation the nebular hypothesis of Laplace—an expression of the evolution of the inorganic world—and Von Baer's Law of Development. And he thus thought to express the whole of reality in one vast and all-inclusive formula. This attempt completely belied the hopes and ambitions which it had aroused.

It is indeed obvious that we do see men becoming corpses, but we do not see corpses becoming men ; and that in regarding the inorganic (which is a corpse) as a *cause* of which the organic (which is a living body) is the *effect*, Spencer's whole system postulated precisely that phenomena of spontaneous generation whose possibilities there are ample reasons for doubting, and whose actuality innumerable experiments have failed to reveal.[1] Furthermore, in Spencer's system there is really no question of "becoming"; his usual method is to reconstruct the process of evolution with already evolved fragments. A child, in the same way, reproduces the design of a jigsaw puzzle; but does not by this create the artistic masterpiece which may apparently be produced by his efforts.

For reasons of this sort, Spencer's interesting attempt to generalise the Darwinian theory was considered as a failure, and the centre of interest shifted elsewhere. The alternative to this view is some kind of vitalism, or rather what would better be called organicism. But the vitalism of to-day has only the slenderest connection with that of a hundred years ago, with its vital forces and so on: it is really far more in contact with the scholastic ideas. Thus the neo-vitalists claim that the *vraie vérité* of biological speculation is Aristotelian rather than Newtonian, and that we shall never build up a worth-while science of biology by considering only the mechanical, physical, and chemical phenomena attendant upon the process of living. They believe that the continuous search for immediate and efficient (mechanical) causes in biology is a profound mistake. What we ought to look for, they say, are the *purposes* aimed at by living things; we must not be frightened of using teleology merely by the outcry raised by the mechanists. This newer position is summed up by saying that the living organism must always be considered as a " concrete sensual whole," and that it is to be studied as such. The whole of this position is being brilliantly supported by the recent philosophical work of Prof. A. N. Whitehead, and it might perhaps be pointed out that the continuous discovery of yet smaller and smaller organisms would in any case have led scientists to ask whether the ultimate structure of the universe was not indeed organic.

THE PHILOSOPHERS HIT BACK

WHILE all these developments were taking place in biology, the idealistic philosophy elaborated by Kant and his School was beginning to have its influence on science itself. We say " idealistic " advisedly, since it will be remembered

[1] That is, the idea that living things can be manufactured in the laboratory by a sufficiently skilled chemist. This opinion is a corollary to the belief that life is nothing more than a complex chemical phenomena. The fact that this spontaneous generation has never been observed and that its possibility seems ever more doubtful tends to throw discredit on mechanistic biology.

that Kant's position amounted to supposing that the man of science could only study *phenomena*, and that these were mental. The realistic aspects of Kant's position were connected with the noumenal grounds of experience, and these are outside the field of the study of science.

The limitations imposed on scientific knowledge by the acceptance of this position were the occasion for much acute discussion and argument. Ir deed one might go further and say that the whole of the modern philosophy of science resolves itself into an epistemological [1] discussion. For if science is concerned only with insubstantial appearances of things, if it is merely a creation of our imagination, how is it possible for it to tell us so much that is useful, and obviously true, about the external world ?

Among the forerunners of this epistemological movement must be numbered Ernst Mach, whose historical studies on the science of mechanics have had enormous influence. He accepted the position that we could only know the appearance of things—the phenomena—and that the only appearances we could agree about, and which we could thus consider as being truly objective, were relations between quantitative data. The rôle of science, according to Mach, is to co-ordinate and arrange these phenomena into an easily available scheme of mere relations. It is an " economy of thought," and therein lies its justification ; the things with which it deals, both its laws and its theories, are mere concepts whose function it is to economise time and thought. Obviously if this be science, we must then strive to keep it in its proper place and to purify it from all anthropomorphic elements and from all metaphysical taint. Mach's work thus consisted largely of a critique of physical science directed to this end. He examined, for instance, Newton's laws of motion, his concepts of force and of mass, his ideas on causality, etc., and showed how they might be re-expressed in such a way as to remove all possible objection. In this, Mach's work may be said to prepare the way for a union of idealistic philosophy and positivistic science. At the same time, it succeeds only by robbing science of any real explanatory value and makes it much too thin an affair. The followers of this anti-metaphysical school express a position to which no true scientific pioneer could ever give whole-hearted allegiance.

[1] Epistemology is the branch of philosophy which concerns itself with the theory of knowledge.

THE LAND WITHOUT PHILOSOPHY : SOVIET RUSSIA

NOR has this work been allowed to pass without provoking a powerful reaction. A movement of thought exists which, starting with Kant, and developed by Hegel and Engels, led to the founding of the School of Dialectic Materialism which is the official philosophy of the U.S.S.R. Communists would probably dislike hearing their beliefs spoken of as a philosophy. They would prefer to refer to them as the " Materialist Conception of History." " From this point of view," says Engels," the final causes of all social changes and political revolutions are to be sought, not in men's brains, not in man's better insight into eternal truth and justice, but in changes in the modes of production and exchange. They are to be sought, not in the *philosophy*, but in the *economics* of each particular epoch. . . . The conflicts of mankind are not primarily mental conflicts in the opinions and passions of human beings, but are the result of the conflict between productive forces and modes of production. . . . This conflict exists, in fact, objectively outside us, independently of the will and actions even of the men that have brought it on. . . ."

It will be noticed that it is here asserted that the real nature of things exists outside ourselves and is independent of our minds : it is thus materialistic. Since it is perceived as an eternal conflict it is said to be a *dialectic*—a struggle. This theory of reality is capable of the very widest extension, and nowadays it is even applied to such subjects as physics : an attempt is made to show that modern science has evolved in such a way as to meet the needs of industry.

It would be interesting to discuss the exact relations between the philosophy of Marx, Engels, Lenin, and Stalin. Broadly, it may be said that Marx was the most Hegelian and least materialistic of them, while Engels was little more than a mid-Victorian materialist. Lenin owes more to Engels than to Marx, but attempted to synthesise their view, while Stalin probably considers himself as the practical interpreter of Leninism. This movement, incidentally, provides a magnificent refutation of the opinion, so often advanced, that philosophy has, and can have, no influence on everyday affairs. Is it possible to think of the Russia of to-day without this philosophical system ? The Bolsheviks detest the views of Mach and of his followers, and their ablest representative,

V. I. Lenin, in a penetrating book on *Materialism and Empirio-Criticism*, attacks Mach in the most violent terms, comparing his work to a Judas' kiss which betrayed science to philosophy.

INSTRUMENTS : THE EYES AND EARS OF THE MODERN PHYSICIST

IN spite of arguments such as those advanced by Lenin, and in spite of the doubts which must inevitably assail us as soon as we begin to reflect on the implications of Mach's position, it must be admitted that his work has had enormous influence in moulding the mind of the modern physicist. His writings, by their combination of charm and lucidity of expression, together with the remarkable breadth of view exhibited by the author, possess much persuasive power. Their most immediate effect was probably the preparation of the soil in which flourishes the physical science of to-day with its extreme stressing of the geometrical aspects of reality.

This return to Cartesian views will always be closely associated with the name of Albert Einstein and the famous theory of Relativity. It is often asserted—indeed by Einstein himself—that this theory is free from any metaphysical taint, is based solely on immediate empirical data, and is firmly rooted in experimental observations. But this is only partly true : undoubtedly experiment and observation play their part, but so they do in any theory—whether philosophical or scientific. As a matter of fact, Einstein's whole mode of explanation is profoundly influenced by a definite metaphysical attitude and is the product of a perfectly explicit ideal of the rôle and function of science : the influence of the Machian school of thought is evident at every turn.

It will be remembered that the development of mechanistic views had led to a very coherent theory of an " ether of space." Mechanical actions—such as light-waves, electric and magnetic actions and thermal radiations—could be propagated across apparently empty space. Now, this " action-at-a-distance " is really quite irreconcilable with the existence of a world machine. Where are the invisible pulleys, rods, and levers ? If they are only metaphysical constructions they have no place in the scientific scheme. Still, it was quite possible that they might possess substantial existence, and yet that the insufficiency of our senses was such that it was not revealed to them.

Medievalists would, of course, at once exclaim, " Rubbish ! The human senses are all sufficient for the task of exploring the nature of the universe ! " But this attitude is not that of the modern man of science, who has much greater faith in his instruments than in his eyes or ears. Therefore, physicists started arranging definite experiments which would reveal the existence and properties of the ether. Unfortunately all such experiments failed, and it was the resounding failure of the one carried out by Michelson and Morley which was the occasion for Einstein's proposals.

EINSTEIN'S THEORY OF A MATHEMATICAL UNIVERSE

IN effect, these were that it might be more profitable to abandon the attempt to construct a model of the imaginary world-machine, and to content ourselves with the building up of systems of theorems which would give us pragmatically useful results. The argument would run as follows : if we decide to use ordinary Euclidean geometry we can list the physical properties common to all bodies at rest. We can even extend our investigations to bodies in motion, if they are separated from one another by great distance so that they only disturb one another very slightly. Descartes showed us that this kind of geometry is very closely connected with algebra, and his discovery greatly simplified subsequent investigations.

To every point in space, said Descartes, we can attach three numbers, which represent its distance from any point. The ordinary geometry of space then becomes merely the investigation of possible relations between the three numbers corresponding to any point moving about on the surface of any geometrical figure.

In mechanics, however, we are concerned also with *movement*, that is, change of position with time. The Cartesian method can be extended to such cases ; to our spatial numbers we add a fourth which represents *time* position. We thus have *four* numbers (co-ordinates), and mechanics becomes the investigation of relations between those numbers in all sorts of possible motions. It was the recognition of this which led the great Laplace, over a hundred years ago, to describe mechanics as a " four-dimensional geometry." One important point must be noted : the notion of *force* does not easily fit into this sort of scheme. For—perhaps because of its origin—this concept always appears to us as closely connected with the idea of *cause and effect* ; forces cause changes of motion.

It would therefore be desirable to get rid of it ; ideas of causality are anthropomorphic and unsuited to geometry. Who would dream of asking the *cause* of the fact that the angles of a triangle add up to two right angles ? The question has no meaning ; the fact is already included in the definition of the triangle itself. Furthermore, the notion of force itself seems to be brought in only to " explain " the breaking down of geometrical laws.

The first law of motion, for example, states that every body tends to continue in its state of rest or of uniform motion in a straight line. Now consider the motion of the moon ; does it move in a straight line ? No, it moves round the earth. Very well then, invent a force of gravity. Consider a piece of iron near a strong magnet ; does it stay at rest ? No, it moves towards the magnetic pole. Very well, invent a magnetic force.

But we might tackle the problem in another way. If we suppose that we have decided not to introduce the notion of force, we could alter our system of geometry so that bodies still moved in their ordinary, so to say " natural " path, but this path would no longer be the straight line. This is, more or less, the suggestion carried into effect by Einstein. He was fortunate in being able to utilise the mathematical labours of Riemann to help him in the construction of his theory of General Relativity, which is largely a geometrical restatement of the older mechanics.

This tremendous and epoch-making work will always stand out as amongst the greatest achievements of the human intellect. It is practically the consummation of one of the great currents of thought which have permeated our Western science. Yet, it is all too probable that its ultimate philosophic consequences will be of the slightest. The implications of Einstein's position are already to be found in the work of Descartes and the critique of recent years has added little of essential novelty.

For example, much discussion has centred on the union of space and time, or rather of spatial and temporal co-ordinates, proposed in 1908 by Minkowski. Yet what is this but a statement of the mathematical needs of any theory which proposes to embrace in its comprehensive sweep the phenomena of change and of motion, and to express the whole of the geometrical aspect of the universe ? After all, space and time are different for the human consciousness,

PROFESSOR ALBERT EINSTEIN

and no amount of mathematical subtlety will suffice to combine them, except on paper.

Again, we have heard, *ad nauseam*, discussion centering on closed universes and events marching backwards in time, of people getting younger as they travel, and so on. Yet what are these but the old antinomies discussed by Kant, or else a mere *reductio ad absurdum* of the idea of transmitting energy or matter from place to place at a speed greater than that of light ?

PUZZLES THAT CONFRONT THE MODERN PHYSICIST

BUT there is, so to say, a fly in the ointment. The geometrical theories swept all before them in their triumphant progress. Yet, beneath the surface, the quantum theory was steadily progressing ; and the facts it deals with are really irreconcilable with pure geometry. For geometrical theories are essentially continuous—a straight line, for example, is not merely a numbered array of points. Now, the universe exhibits for our confusion a double aspect : sometimes it seems to be continuous and fluid, at other times it seems to be made up of atoms, each one of which is unchangeable but can alter its position or its association with other atoms.

The quantum theory is concerned with the discontinuous aspect ; it deals with atoms, or rather little packets, of energy. Its fundamental assumption is that energy exchanges always take place in such little packets or *quanta* ; the handing over of an infinitely small amount of energy is not possible. Just in the same way, we cannot, in practice, pay over an amount of cash except in multiples of one farthing, or one *centime*, or one *pfennig* ; the quantum of cash varies, but an infinitely small amount cannot be paid over. Mechanics, of course, loves to deal with atoms ; but geometry cannot do so satisfactorily. And the annoying thing is that this complementary duality of continuity and of atoms runs right through modern science.

Thus we have not only our quantum theories of energy, but also our thermo-dynamics (which are continuity theories). Again, waves of light are essentially continuous, but the energy they carry from place to place is concentrated in little packets. Finally, to cap everything, physicists had become used to dealing with atoms of electricity and with atoms of matter. Yet lately it has been found that even these atoms sometimes behave like waves. On shooting a stream of atoms of electricity through thin metal foil on to a photographic plate, a pattern is obtained on the latter which very closely resembles that which would be developed if a beam of light waves passed through the foil.

What the full meaning of this duality will turn out to be is still obscure. At the moment, mathematicians are occupied in attempting to build an insubstantial bridge between the two regions. The idea seems to be that what they have in common can only be expressed in symbolical mathematics. They have put up on their door the highly metaphysical warning : " Metaphysicians please keep out. Work in progress." One hopes that this foolish notice will resolutely be ignored. The questions asked are obviously philosophical and there is no reason to obey the injunction, especially at a moment when mathematicians seem to have no fear of issuing from their closely barred studies in order to issue metaphysical pronunciamentos which are said to be derived from the contemplation of the mathematical harmony revealed only to the initiates.

THE UNIVERSE AS A SERIES OF EVENTS

IT is probable that the geometric-atomic duality is related to our views of space and of time. So-called " classical " modern science has always looked upon the universe as being composed of objects spatially determined and moving about in time. This view is insufficient ; the universe is not made up of things, but of things happening, a universe of events. And when this view has been more completely worked out— a task of critical and analytic creation which is now engaging the attention of our ablest minds—it will probably be seen that the duality of which we have spoken is a necessary consequence of the insufficient and unsatisfactory views of space and of time which have been assumed axiomatically by science for over three hundred years.

This increasing concentration of attention on the universe of *events* may be illustrated by considering almost any of the recent developments of the philosophy of nature. Consider for a moment the position of Bergson—one of the best-known of our modern philosophers—with his stress on *duration*, his negation of substance and of things, his comparison of the universe with a picture which is *being* painted rather than with one already painted, his famous phrases, such as :

un crystal, comme un individu, est une histoire (Literally :
" A crystal, like an individual, is a history.") And of course,
A. N. Whitehead's work also stresses the importance of
such ideas.

Even within physics itself, Einstein's work shows the
influence of these same tendencies. For instance, the mass
of a body varies with the speed : one cannot attach even to
this concept a purely statical significance ; time is intrinsic
to its nature. In the same way, energy is not really conserved,
since matter can be transformed into it ; there remain no
unchanging substances, only events are left ; the concept of
space-time itself expresses this essential dynamism.

In the biological philosophy of Le Dantec we find once
again this stress on *events*. He thinks of every organism as
a continuous series of creative functionings and as never
remaining identical to itself from one moment to another :
un individu c'est une histoire (" An individual is a history ").
We must not think, he says, of a man called " William "
but we must try to think of him as a functioning, a " William-
ing " ; one should say : " It is William " in the same way
that we say : " It is raining " or " It is freezing " ; and
if he dies, one should say : " It does not William any
more."

Whether these ideas are correct or not is not the point
here. It is obvious that they all have something in common,
that they all stress the new views : the importance of events,
the insufficiency of the old statical picture of the world, with
its insistence on the all-comprehensiveness of the concept
of substance.

Would it be too hopeful to suggest that the advent of these
ideas indicates the beginning of a new philosophic and
scientific renaissance, the ultimate effects of which may be
as great as those of the renaissance of the sixteenth century ?

There is just a possibility that this may be the case, but
it is equally possible that the germ of the new world-outlook
may be destroyed in a welter of blood and war resulting from
the madness of that economic and racial nationalism which
is running riot through the world of to-day. And yet ideas
are hard to kill ; our science survived the chaos of the
religious wars and of the bloody anarchy which marked the
emergence of modern nationalism. Who knows ? Perhaps
such struggles are the inevitable pangs which attend the
birth of really great ideas.

PHILOSOPHY AS A HELP-MEET FOR SCIENCE

WE have so far striven to exhibit the continuous reciprocal influence of philosophy on science by describing, all too shortly, the genesis and development of some of the great movements of thought the sum-total of which makes up the philosophical background of our time. We can now attempt to summarise a few of the conclusions which have emerged from this discussion.

To begin with, we have seen that it would be possible to separate *Scientia* into pure philosophy and pure science in such a way that these two regions of thought would seem to be quite independent of each other. But this would be an arbitrary and illogical separation, having no justification in fact and quite divorced from the historical development which has, in fact, occurred. Philosophical considerations have always played an all-important rôle in science, and this was never greater than at the time when modern science was being born. It might be urged that once this fertilising influence had played its part, philosophy ceased to affect the further development and working out of the scientific scheme. In this sense, science would be merely the application of a philosophic methodology. But even if we grant this, it becomes obvious that it would be hopeless to attempt to understand science without reference to its origin : science carries within itself no principle of explanation ; the latter is supplied by metaphysics. It is the refusal to recognise this fact which is the ground error of positivism.

In addition to this, however, philosophy has exerted a continuous influence on the actual development of science in two main directions, by playing—

> (*a*) a systematising rôle ;
> (*b*) a critical rôle.

In the first connection, it has set certain ideals to the man of science, and it has shown him how, by generalising his views and his opinions, he could rise to fresh heights and connect into a coherent and unified whole the region of knowledge which he surveys or cultivates.

In the second connection it has often served as a repository for well-substantiated ideas or opinions which could find no suitable place in contemporary scientific schemes. Further, by virtue of the continuous criticisms which it has directed

against metaphysically unsatisfactory theories, it has sometimes caused these to evolve in new directions. A case in
point is the long war which it has waged against mechanistic
interpretations in biology. As a result of this we find
vitalists or organicists starting researches and discovering
new facts which accord with their views. It may well be
that this clearing of the ground for the development of new
knowledge is one of the most essential functions of philosophy.

HOW SCIENCE SOWS THE SEED OF PHILOSOPHIC THOUGHT

RECIPROCALLY, we find that science has indeed exerted a
profound influence on philosophy. To begin with, it
is continuously setting metaphysicians all sorts of difficult
problems. The scientist is always reaching new conclusions and
opening up new vistas which make it necessary for the philosopher continually to restate his position in new terms. The old
conclusions usually stand, and only minor adjustments may
be necessary. But philosophy is alive and in close contact
with reality. This implies that it must continually be re-
adjusting itself into equilibrium with a changing environment.
In a civilisation which is altering in outlook and in mode
of life as rapidly as ours, this continuous restatement of old
positions in a new scientific terminology absorbs a great
deal of time and effort.

Again, broadly speaking, modern metaphysics is fundamentally idealistic. In a sense this is true even of the
philosophy of Bolshevism, since the dialectical materialism
of Engels and Lenin may almost be considered as a polar
opposite of our Western Idealism, the two standing in
somewhat the same relationship as the two opposite poles
of a magnet. Now, we have shown that this idealistic position
may be considered as the polar complement of the materialism
of science. In the same way that philosophy acted fructify-
ingly on it at the Renaissance, science by an inevitable reaction
set the lines on which philosophy has subsequently evolved.

Even in matters of detail this continuous influence is
noticed. For example, modern physics pays much attention
to cosmological speculations, and this no doubt accounts,
at least in part, for the concentration on these which is
noticeable in the work of most modern philosophers.

It is obvious also that the theory of primary and secondary
qualities raises fundamental issues with regard to the place
of æsthetics in general philosophy, and hence we find many

modern philosophers, such as Benedetto Croce, struggling with such problems. Indeed the whole question of the concrete relation between quality and quantity has been made ever more obscure by the natural development of science. Hegel's utterances on this point have given issue in diverse and even opposed contexts to powerful trends of thought. An appreciation of these elements in his philosophy is fundamental to the exposition of the system of dialectical materialism which, as we have mentioned already, affects the framework of orthodox science in Russia, whilst a definite Hegelian influence is apparent in the thesis of Nietzsche on *The Will to Power in Science*, a thesis which, particularly through the extended influence of the school of Vaihinger, has in turn exerted its influence upon the philosophical approach to scientific methodology. In that tradition of philosophy which has sought above all to effect a thorough-going rational continuity between the provinces of science and philosophy, there can be little doubt that the most acute and exhaustive treatment of this problem of quality and quantity is that set forth by Whitehead under the various headings of *The Theory of Vectoriality* and *The Theory of Vibratory Organic Deformation*. Unfortunately anything approximating to a proper exposition of these several points of view is here impossible, and we must be satisfied at having indicated the problems in question.

AN OLD PROBLEM RE-STATED : FREE-WILL AND DETERMINISM

WE cannot avoid reference to the problem of causality, which has been penetratingly discussed by E. Meyerson, the importance of whose work has not yet been fully realised. The position he develops is roughly as follows : The human mind seeks, above all, elements of permanence and unchange-ability beneath the flux of phenomena. The idea of cause and effect is one of the artifices we employ to exhibit real per-manence beneath the appearance of change. Now, the first philosopher to show this was Parmenides, who imagined the world as a vast sphere always identical to itself. This attempt merely to deny the occurrence of change is negatived by the first act of perception, and we are, therefore, forced to look for permanence elsewhere. For instance, we can suppose that very small portions of the world remain always the same. This leads to the atomic theory of Democritus, and gradually, by development and modification, to our modern ideas on the subject of atoms. Or, as an alternative, we may look for permanence in some kind of conceptual abstraction from the whole of the world of science. Thus we may develop ideas of Energy, or of Momentum, and these magnitudes will be of use to us if they remain constant in quantity, for this is always the essential point. In the atomic theory, for instance, the really important thing is that there is a conservation of atoms, or, as we might say, a conservation of matter.

Meyerson has developed such ideas in great detail. He has investigated carefully the whole structure of science, and has shown how the scientist has striven, everywhere and always, to find those principles of permanence which allow him to study the phenomena. Much of his analysis may be un-questioningly accepted, and from this it appears that the principle of causality forms an intrinsic part of the scientific scheme, or at any rate of that part of it which is concerned with mechanical or atomic actions to the exclusion of purely geometrical aspects. Yet, quite lately, it has been shown (by Heisenberg) that, in the study of actions between atoms, the causal principle cannot be directly applied. It would appear either that we must abandon our belief in the universal applicability of the principle or else recast fundamentally our notion of space and of time.

Somewhat fantastic speculations have been developed from this principle of Heisenberg's. Thus it has been said that recent progress in atomic physics has opened the door for belief in free will. But we should not be led astray by these speculations : belief in the freedom of man to work out his own destiny is ultimately a matter for metaphysical argument, and any physicist who delivers himself of pronouncements on it steps, *ipso facto,* outside his universe of discourse. All that the physicists are able to say is that it seems probable that it will be for ever impossible to abstract from phenomena those aspects which describe the behaviour of atoms *completely* in terms of cause and effect.

"TIMES BEHIND TIMES IN ENDLESS SERIES"

IT is evident from all this discussion that numerous tasks face the philosopher who is concerned with the problems arising out of the integration of metaphysical and of strictly scientific beliefs and opinions. Besides the problems arising out of the Principle of Heisenberg (indeterminacy) and the reaction of this on the Doctrine of Free Will, we have the much wider problem as to whether the universe is really—ultimately and completely—describable in terms of the classification of physics. As problems subsidiary to this, we might note all those questions concerning the relation of logic to mathematics, and of mathematics to science, so much discussed by people like Henri Poincaré and Bertrand Russell.

The position at the moment appears to be that the present foundation of science is too narrow : our views of Space and of Time, for instance, are obviously insufficient. We therefore find metaphysicians concerning themselves with space-time continuums, while on the more scientific side we find able writers like J. W. Dunne suggesting most revolutionary changes. The latter has proposed substituting for our ordinary scientific time-concept a theory of serial time, times behind times in endless series. He has shown how a concept of this kind would remove many contradictions from our present views, while being wide enough to include in its comprehensive sweep most of the facts and observations of psychology and of psychical research. The position would appear to be, either that we shall have to accept ideas such as Dunne's, or else go right back to the beginning, and start again with new space and time concepts which would unite the ideas of the scholastic philosophers and those of the modern man of science.

THE UNENDING QUEST

THESE, then, are a few of the tasks which are now being faced. It seems probable that within the next hundred years it will be generally admitted that to identify science and mathematics, as is now so often done, is a fundamental mistake, and that it is merely allowing the means employed to attain an end to preponderate over that end itself. Further, it will be recognised that science is essentially forced to be something more than a mere *catalogue raisonné*, even if the catalogue be a geometrical list of theorems : that it is in its essence explanatory and to a certain degree philosophical. The acceptance of such views will involve the abandonment of the positivistic position and will open the way for a vast development of the allied sciences of biology and of psychology.

At the beginning of this essay we listed four characteristics which we considered as typical of the modern scientific outlook, namely :

(1) Its stress on quantity as opposed to quality.
(2) Its unbounded faith in mathematics.
(3) Its positivistic character.
(4) Its belief in a pragmatic theory of truth.

It will now be obvious that these are all closely connected and that the origin of these ideas goes back to the work of the pioneers of the sixteenth century. Thus, if we have faith in the power of mathematical analysis and are impressed with its æsthetic charm, we shall wish to employ it in our examination of nature. Since some aspects of things lend themselves very easily to this kind of treatment, we shall wish to abstract them to the exclusion of others. Hence we shall be led to the separation of appearances into primary and secondary qualities ; and we shall have to attempt to justify our action by developing positivistic ideas. As a result of all this we obtain considerable command over that part of reality which is mechanical : we shall be able to construct very efficient locomotives, cranes, and guns. This need not surprise anyone, because it seems likely that it is the Will to Power which originally provided the motive force for the development not only of European action, but also of European thought.

Now, in what sense are our views of the reality of nature correct and our theories true ? The only reply we can make is that they lead to useful results : the machines function, the electric light goes on when we pull down the switch. And this is the kind of answer which leads to a pragmatic theory of truth.

The fundamentals of our world-view and of our science lie close together, and their connections can only be expressed in philosophical language. The success of our science has been great, and the shadow of our power covers the globe. The subtlety and understanding shown by our philosophers yields second place to that of no previous culture. But it would be a bold man who would dare to assert that our triumphs represent a final answer to all our inquiries about God, about nature, and about man himself ; or that the answers given by our science suffice to silence further questioning.

The task of intellectual investigation on which our race is engaged is as full of adventure as that of geographical exploration typical of the age which is now closing. The

dangers and the hardships may be less obvious, but the difficulties and the rewards are as great. Influencing and correct-
ing each other, the two branches of *Scientia* continue their
approach towards an ever more correct expression of the
true nature of things.

The goal — the perfect understanding of Truth itself —
can never be reached ; but does this matter ? It is this
noble striving towards an unattainable ideal which gives to
Man his dignity and adds to human experience that touch of
passion which makes our lives beautiful and worth while.

FOR FURTHER READING

IT is possible that some readers may wish to follow further
their study of the fascinating topics treated in an elementary
way in the present article. The University of London now
award a degree in the History, Method, and Principles of
Science, and there is a special department at University
College where the subject is studied. Courses of lectures
are given, and students have the advantage of discussing their
difficulties with specialist teachers of distinction and eminence.
In most towns where there is a university there are also
occasional public lectures, which are nearly always worth
attending. Some of the smaller institutions (*e.g.* the Ports-
mouth Municipal College) also run special courses in the
subject.

For the benefit of those who are unable to attend the
lectures, a short bibliography is appended, but it should be
remembered that the literature is enormous and that many
of the books that should be read by the serious student have
not yet been translated (*e.g.* some of those by Cassirer,
Meyerson, Husserl, and Duhem). Furthermore, a really
profitable course of reading should include books on metaphysics, logic, and on the history of science.

One of the simplest and most entertaining accounts of the
history of physical science, with a pronounced astronomical
and cosmological bias, is Oliver Lodge's *Pioneers of Science*
(Macmillan). Perhaps the best introduction to the subject
is N. Campbell's *What is Science?* published by Methuen.
It is a simply-written and well-balanced book, but the presentation is somewhat one-sided, for Campbell is influenced by
Poincaré's positivist theory. Facts, the author says, which
are universally verifiable, are proper material for the scientist.

Another good book is *An Introduction to Science* (Thornton Butterworth Limited, Home University Library). A. N. Whitehead, in his *Nature and Life* (Cambridge University Press), explains some of his valuable views in non-technical language. A book which created a great sensation in its day, and much of which is still valuable, is Karl Pearson's *The Grammar of Science*. Pearson's views tend towards the positivistic idealism of Mach. Sir James Jean's *The Background of Science* (Cambridge University Press) is worth reading, less for the philosophy it presents than for the really brilliant explanations of modern physics.

Rather more difficult books include two by Professor A. N. Whitehead, *Adventures of Ideas* and *Science and the Modern World* ; both are published by the Cambridge University Press, and both are exceedingly important books, which must be read in order to understand the present position. All H. Poincaré's books are worth reading. They are well written and replete with wise sayings and epigrams. A good one to begin with would be *Science and Hypothesis* (The Court Publishing Co.). A brilliant, critical, and philosophical analysis of the development of physical science up to the time of Newton is *The Metaphysical Foundations of Modern Science* (Kegan Paul and Co.), by Professor Burt.

Basil Willey's *The Seventeenth Century Background* (Chatto and Windus) is a very well written and acute study requiring little technical knowledge. Among histories of science, we should mention Singer's *History of Biology* (Oxford University Press), a very useful book, and especially Wolf's magnificent *History of Science, Technology, and Philosophy in the Sixteenth and Seventeenth Centuries* (Allen and Unwin). The latter is a unique and monumental work.

INDEX AND PRONOUNCING GLOSSARY

Compiled by L. M. MONT-CLAR.

How to use this index.—In order to facilitate immediate reference to the principal entry on a particular subject, the page number for this entry is set in italics, thus : *258.* Subsidiary references to the subject which occur elsewhere in the book are indicated by numerals in roman type, thus : 387. References to illustrations are indicated by numerals in roman type surrounded by square brackets, thus : [156]. Cross references given in the index refer only to the index pages.

The pronouncing glossary.—Where the pronunciation of proper names and technical terms is not immediately understood from the spelling, or where the spelling may be misleading, a separate pronunciation is given after the first index entry. In simple cases a hint may be considered sufficient ; in all doubtful cases a complete phonetic re-spelling is given. The word is broken into syllables as it is spoken, and an accent mark (´) follows the syllable on which the stress is placed. The notation used for the phonetic re-spelling is as follows :

ā	mate	a	*pat*	ė	there	th	*th*in
ē	mete	e	p*e*t	å	father	TH	*th*ine
ī	mite	i	p*i*t	ẹ	her	zh	leisure
ō	mote	o	p*o*t	aw	*aw*l	ch	*ch*urch
ū	mute	u	n*u*t	oi	*oi*l	g	*g*et
ōō	boot	oo	f*oo*t	ow	*ow*l	j	*j*am

The French nasalised *n* is denoted by italicising the vowel and the nasal concerned, thus : u*n*, bo*n*, vi*n*. The German modified ö and the similar French sounds are denoted by *oe*, the German soft ch and g by *ch*, and the guttural ch (as in Scots " loch ") by CH. The French *u* and the German modified ü are indicated by ü.

ABELARD (àb'lar), PETER, 42, 163.
Abilities, 58–79, 264.
Abnormal psychology, 23–24, *99–134.*
Accountancy, training for, 284.
Achievement, 136–137.
Action Française (àk'sē-*on* fra*n*-sāz), 329.
Actions, judgment of, 137, 147.
Activity Theory of Causality, 374.
Actor, psychological type, 73.
Adams, Sir John, 286.
Adler (àd'lér), Felix (fā'liks), 99, 122, *129–133.*
Adrian, Dr., 38.
Adult education, 189.
— Education Committee, 338.
— psychology, 16–18.
Advancement of Learning, The, 168.
Æsthetic (ēz-thet'ik) values, 358.
Affections, 79–84.
Afferent (af'er-ent) nerve, 30 [31].

Alexander, Samuel, 437–438.
American education, 195.
— election system, 325, 333–334.
Analytical psychology, 122.
Anaximander (an-aks-i-man'der), 395.
Anaximenes (an-aks-im'en-ēz), 398.
Animal psychology, 22–23.
Anthropomorphism (an-thrō-pō-mor'fism), 445.
Anti-Corn Law League, 327.
Appearance and Reality, 361–370.
Apperception, 180.
Appetites, 80.
Aquinas (ak-wīn'as), Thomas, St.,66,74,412.
Architect, psychological type, 73.
Aristocracy, 343.
Aristophanes (ar-i-stof'an-ēz), 157.
Aristotle (ar'ís-totle), 25, 144, 157, 167, 294, 342–344, 360, 379, *406–410.*
Army, education for, 283.